Encountering the Other(s)

Encountering the Other(s)

Studies in Literature, History, and Culture

Edited by
Gisela Brinker-Gabler

STATE UNIVERSITY OF NEW YORK PRESS

The editor gratefully acknowledges the permission of the journals and publishers to print essays and poetry that follows: *Chapter 5*: "The Construction of the Other and the Destruction of the Self: The Case of the Convention Hearings," appeared first in a different version in *Vice Versa*, Montreal (Canada) 1992. *Chapter 11*: "Andean Waltz" was published in a slightly longer version in *Holocaust Remembrance: The Shapes of Memory*, ed. Geoffrey Hartman (Oxford: Blackwell, 1993). *Chapter 14*: The three poems by Abena Busia are from her volume of poems *Testimonies of Exile*, published by African World Press, Trenton, NJ 1990.

Cover art adapted from an original drawing by MAF Räderscheidt, "Die Seele der Nacht," 1991.

Published by
State University of New York Press, Albany

© 1995 State University of New York

Printed in the United States of America

For information, address the State University of New York Press,
State University Plaza, Albany, NY 12246

Production by Bernadine Dawes • Marketing by Fran Keneston

Library of Congress Cataloging-in-Publication Data

Encountering the other(s) : studies in literature, history, and
  culture / edited by Gisela Brinker-Gabler
      p.   cm.
    Papers of a symposium held in the fall of 1991 at the State
University of New York at Binghamton.
    Includes index.
    ISBN 0-7914-2159-7 (hardcover)   — ISBN 0-7914-2610-0
(pbk.)
      1. Literature, Comparative—History and criticism.   2. Culture
conflict in literature.   3. Literature and history.   I. Brinker
-Gabler, Gisela.   II. Title: Encountering the others.
PN871.E53   1995
809—dc20   94-30706
                                                               CIP

2 3 4 5 6 7 8 9 10

Table of Contents

Preface

The essays in this volume were presented as papers at the symposium "The Question of the Other," held at Binghamton University, State University of New York, in fall 1991. They provide insight into the wide variety of critical paths through which one may approach the other as that alterity within oneself, as well as that which is other by race, gender, class, or ethnicity; other wo/men in other societies and cultures. Because of the complexity of this question of the other/s, the essays that follow are of cross-disciplinary nature. Contributors represent the fields of Comparative Literature, Philosophy, English, German, Spanish and Portuguese, Education, History, and Political Science, and very often their investigations transgress disciplinary boundaries in thought-provoking ways. The cross-national and cross-disciplinary exchanges during the conferences have been highly productive. It is hoped that the critical dialogue presented in this volume on one of the most pressing questions today will contribute to further intense discussions and re/visions during the years to come.

The symposium was made possible through a generous grant from the German Academic Exchange Service (DAAD), New York, for which I am genuinely grateful. Also, the DAAD provided a publication subsidy, which is gratefully acknowledged. Special thanks are due to Dr. Heidrun Suhr, Director of the DAAD, for her vital encouragement and helpful assistance in preparing this event. Additional funding for the symposium was given by the Max Kade Foundation, New York, for which I am especially grateful. Partial funding and support, which is gratefully acknowledged, was also provided by the Research Foundation of the State University of New York at Binghamton; the Dean of Harpur College, Sharon Brehm; and the following groups: Graduate History Society, Graduate Student Organization Comparative Literature, Lesbian Caucus, Women of Color Caucus, and the Women's Studies Program.

I would also like to to extend my thanks to my colleagues at Binghamton University for their support and suggestions, especially Carole Boyce Davies, Christopher Fynsk, Marilyn Gaddis Rose, Frederick Garber, Zoja Pavlovskis-Petit, Dennis Schmidt; to the student's committee and symposium's assistants for their engagement and help, Beatriz Aguirre, Siga Fatima Jagne, Gladys Jimenez-Munoz, Eileen Rizo Patron, Charles Talcott, Laura Tuley, Ingrid Gomboz, Pauline Hubbel, Anastasia Paraskevoulakou, Milo Sweedler; to Carol Less and Edie Ruhl for the administrative and writing assistance; and to Elizabeth Naylor Endres for her meticulous proofreading. And I want to convey my sincere appreciation to all participants of the symposium and contributors to this volume for their commitment and cooperation which made working with them a pleasure, indeed. A final thank-you note is dedicated to Kai and Udo Brinker, who have been supportive in many ways.

Introduction

GISELA BRINKER-GABLER

I

Any examination of the question of the other/s leads to the radical questioning of the foundations of Western thought. This question, which according to Wlad Godzich "figures as a leifmotif in many of the current discussions of knowledge,"[1] is related both to various critiques of the subject—a concept integral to Western humanism—and to the challenges to Western thought and politics created by the post-1950s liberation movements of diverse groups of others—those who are "other" by race, ethnicity, religion, gender, or sexual orientation, for example.

The following is a brief outline of hermeneutic, ethnographic, epistemological, and postcolonial perspectives on the question of the other/s. It does not claim to be a comprehensive account of the specific historical processes which for the past four decades have governed the complex developments of theories and methodologies that address this question, nor of the pattern of interactions between them.

One of the characteristics of Western metaphysics is to deny the otherness of the other/s—or if not to actually deny its/their otherness, then at least to appropriate it, subsuming the *other/s* dialectically within the *same* of the absolute subject. "From its very beginnings philosophy has been stricken with horror by anything that is other and remains other, as if it had an incurable allergy to it," the philosopher Emmanuel Levinas writes in his essay "Die Spur des Anderen" (The Trace of the Other).[2]

Levinas sees this appropriation of the other/s—which leads to its/their destruction—as a feature of Western civilization and of the Greek culture it is based on: "throughout all its adventures, consciousness finds its way back to itself *as* itself, comes home to itself like

1

Odysseus, who throughout all his journeys is heading only for the island of his birth."[3]

By contrast, Levinas conceives the other/s in terms of alterity, exteriority, distance: as something radically different—radical in terms of the illimitability of the other/s, which is something we cannot fully comprehend. Or to put it another way: the other/s is/are not other in a relative sense—other *than*, Levinas explains in *Totality and Infinity*.[4] The possibility of a differentiation by category or type would in itself demand a level of commonality that would destroy otherness. The other/s do/es not limit the same but call/s for and create/s response/ibility. For Levinas the face-to-face relationship with the other/s is always an ethical relationship.[5]

What would it mean to experience an encounter with the other/s *as* other? It would not mean the denial of the same, for the same is experiencing the encounter. But it would mean the acceptance of the other/s from the outset. In such an encounter otherness could be experienced, but without the violence of comprehension that would reduce the other/s to the self. It is neither a relationship of knowledge nor a question of coming within close proximity of the other/s: "If you try to approach the rainbow too closely, it will disappear," as Theodor Adorno explains in his theory of aesthetics.[6] This realization means, with respect to those who are of other cultures, that *their* culture should not be interpreted based on an orientation towards one's *own* culture, nor should it be experienced in terms such as "similar to" or "just like."

But how can this happen? Is not the encounter with the other/s an encounter in which I must observe the other/s in order to understand it/them: in other words, to separate the known, the familiar, from the unknown and unfamiliar as it relates to myself or my world?

Ethnology is the study of foreign cultures, of the experience of foreignness. It subsists on the difference between the same and the other/s, between one's own culture and the foreign culture. An ethnological model emphasizing writing as construction rather than representation was developed by author, ethnologist, and ethnopoet Michel Leiris. His alternative, surreal ethnography was a precursor to an ethnographic practice that is now called "postcolonial" (as represented by James Clifford).[7]

There is a connection between Leiris and Levinas. Leiris demonstrates how, when what you are trying to capture slips between your fingers, you are left with nothing but its shadow. What you are left with, from the ethnographer's viewpoint, has already become a trans/lation, something totally dependent on one's own language, one's own body, one's own resources of tradition and powers of articulation.[8] This realization allows Leiris to distinguish between "the exotic" and "exotism." "The exotic" is a distortion of the other or its degradation to an object of projection. In ethnographic "exotism," which always sets limits on the other's/others' space, the search for the "truth" in a foreign culture refers to the authentic experience of otherness. This is a combination of developing an awareness about otherness and coming to terms with oneself.[9] Whatever can be experienced about otherness— for we can never possess the original—is always dependent on one's own cultural background, one's own system of perception. This means that Leiris's ethnography is always an ethnography of one's own culture as well as of the foreign culture one is studying.

Now if the encounter between what is one's own and what is foreign is conceived as surpassing logic/reason, the validity of tradi- tional scientific methods is called into question. The next step is the opening up of ethnography into ethnopoetry. But there is a danger here: The opening up into (surrealist) literature, the insight that one is left holding nothing but a shadow, could lead to a problematic ethno- graphic practice that, in the avant-garde tradition, may give itself "artistic license" to undertake the encounter with the other/s. David Thomas mentions this when he quotes James Clifford: "But is not every ethnographer something of a surrealist, a reinventor and reshuffler of realities? Ethnography, the science of cultural jeopardy, presupposes a constant willingness to be surprised, to unmake interpretive syntheses, and to value—when it comes—the unclassified, unsought other."[10] As Thomas points out: "Why . . . reshuffle reality as opposed to contesting it in the name of other realities . . . What role is there in a surrealistic ethnography for the cultural methodologies of other peoples?"[11] And finally, "reshuffling realities" takes on a problematic aspect if one forgets that these realities are being *lived* by others.

Leiris's approach is different after all, then, for he sees his own concept of local ethnology as something that can prevail over *White* ethnology. As he writes in "Ethnologie und Kolonisation" (Ethnology and Colonization) in 1950, local ethnology's purpose is "to further the interests and endeavors of colonized peoples as they themselves understand them."[12]

The hermeneutic and ethnographic perspectives I have introduced have this in common: they grapple with the ongoing process of constituting a self through an encounter with the other/s. The other is other because it is focalized by an observer, by a self by whom, in turn, the others are used in the process of defining the self.

One of this century's most influential thinkers to address the question of the self/other is Michel Foucault. For Foucault, the role of the contemporary intellectual is not to invent a new episteme but rather to work toward facilitating a less hegemonic kind of discourse about what truth is. Like many philosophers in this century he re-examined and took issue with Hegel and his notion of a dialectical *Vermittlung* between self and other. In his project, called "archeology," Foucault focuses on certain discursive articulations of identity within rational humanism, which, unlike Hegel's *Aufhebung*, have resulted in socio-historical practices of exclusion. Any articulation of identity is understood in terms of exclusion and estrangement and otherness as always subjected to the same.

Foucault takes as his starting point several systems of categorization and various types of discourse—differing ways of constituting knowledge and power relations. For Derrida, however, as Corbey and Leerssen argue, "thought itself is a form of hegemony, totalitarian in its claims to understand, to comprehend, to force Otherness and Absence in terms of presence and understanding."[13] Derrida thus conceives difference as a primary condition: difference precedes all multiplicity (which has always been a multiplicity of single details).

The various critiques of the Western subject have had a tremendous effect on critical interventions in diverse representational discourses that have constructed others *within* Europe—women, the insane, homosexuals, Jews—as well as others *external* to Europe. However, those theories have also been questioned and are perceived to have only limited value with regard to various groups of others, such as women and the colonized. Teresa de Lauretis, for example, criticizes Foucault's notion of sexuality, which is understood "as a construct and a (self)-representation, but not as gendered, not as having a male form and a female form, but taken to be one and the same for all—and consequently male"[14]—"hom(m)osexuality," as Luce Irigaray puts it.[15] Gayatri Chakravorti Spivak, among others, writes of the textual figure of femininity in Derrida's deconstruction, criticizing his ahistorical usage of something that it is in fact "'determined' by that very political and social history that is inseparably co-extensive with phallocentric discourse, and in her case either unrecorded in accessible ways, or recorded in terms of man."[16] Spivak writes that, unlike Derrida's project, "the collective project of our feminist critic must always be to rewrite the *social* text so that the historical and sexual differentials are operated together."[17] By referring to the "feminist critic," Spivak addresses the question of position, the need to reflect one's privilege of language and space. The question of the other/s is indeed a question of position, whether one resists referring to an extratextual reality or establishing new meanings, or focuses on spaces both discursive and social that exist, since practices have (re)constructed them.[18]

Many studies have appeared within the last two decades that show how, in the course of Western expansion and hegemony, the non-Western worlds were represented as Western scenarios. To mention only a few of these influential studies, each dealing with a specific group of "others," constituted as such by the discursive practices and colonizing missions of a dominant European/Western group: Edward Said's *Orientalism* (1978), Peter Hulme's *Colonial Encounters: Europe and the Native Caribbean, 1492–1979* (1986), Tzvetan Todorov's *The Conquest of America* (1988), Peter Mason's *Deconstruction of America: Representation of the Other* (1990), and V. Y. Mudimbe, *The Invention of Africa: Gnosis, Philosophy and the Order of Knowledge* (1988). Said, for example, applies Foucault's discourse analysis to orientalism; Mudimbe combines African perspectives with Foucault's analyses of the connection among knowledge, discourse, and power; Levinas's use of alterity inspired Todorov's study of the conquest of America; Mason employs a deconstructive interpretation of ethnographic representations of the "New World"; and Spivak uses deconstruction in her readings of representations of women and the "Third World." Spivak, like other scholars of colonialism, is suspicious of her own role as an investigator of non-Western origin, viewed, as she says, by indigenous theorists investigating "the matter of the colonies" as too committed to Western theories.[19]

Decolonization is a multifaceted process that deals with economic, social, political, psychological, linguistic, and epistemological phenomena. Decolonization as a critical practice developed in connection with the independence movements in colonies since the 1950s. Decolonization both as a process and as a critical practice is based on the conceptual set of opposites: center/margin, which describes the relationship of colonial or otherwise dominant powers to former colonies or developing nations. At the discursive level, it can be described as a combination of liberal and Marxist discourse. The various critiques of the subject and the poststructuralists' questioning of the *fixed* nature of the relationship between center and margin led to the development of "postcolonial criticism." But in contrast to poststructuralism (or to what has been called "antihumanism"), the postcolonial project has *always* set itself a political agenda, a politics of location in order to develop a perspective for change.

Spivak, in her reading of the Subaltern Studies project, a postcolonial historical reconstruction of the Indian colonial "experience," credits the participating historians with revealing the "limits of the critique of humanism as produced in the West," that is, the Western neglect of how important it is for those who have been colonized to reconstruct their own subjectivity, experience, and identity.[20] But with regard to the very specific methodology of the Subaltern Studies group, she underlines the fact that even here there is a danger of objectifying the colonized/the subalterns, of allowing them to be taken hold of/brought under control—even if, as is the case here, the point is to reconstruct their self-determination. The task of rediscovering a subaltern consciousness is impossible if it is carried out as a project seeking "authenticity." However, just because there is a question as to whether there can be an "authentic" voice does not mean that one must give up looking for one. To keep on looking for authenticity is legitimate, according to Spivak, so long as the restoration or reconstruction of a subject is carried on as a process of change that has a strategic purpose—*not* as something that makes a statement about the essence (of the subject). Denying the necessity of the "strategic use of essentialism" would mean acquiescing into complete non-representation such as that produced by poststructural discourse. Spivak suggests in her essay "Can the Subaltern Speak?"[21] that the subaltern analyst or intellectual uses another form of communication—a "speaking to" in which the intellectuals/the elite would neither deny their discursive role nor presume the "authenticity" of the other/s and so would allow for the possibility of a reply from the other/s: the voice of the individual other would be understood not as an authentic statement (and thus a statement about the essence of his/her culture), but as something defined by a specific ideological position.

In his essay "Ethnic Identity and Poststructuralist Difference," R. Radhakrishnan addresses what he calls the "postmodern paradox": the privileging of the marginal while ignoring the need to empower marginal groups.[22] The practice of privileging the marginal—a plurality of marginal positions—also produces the effect of undermining real difference, creating in-difference toward the specific marginal positions. Radhakrishnan proposes a theory that "divest[s] itself from economics of mastery and yet empower[s] the 'ethnic', contingently and historically" (202).

Localization and empowerment do not necessarily mean a call for the rediscovery of the "original" culture, the "true" self. In *Wretched of the Earth* (1963), Franz Fanon already was emphasizing not the return to "pure" or "precontact" culture but the dynamic nature of all cultural formations.[23] This calls for a project of *developing* culture, which Fanon considered to be the task of the national liberation struggles against colonialism. The shift in opposition movements in the 1970s and 1980s toward the differentiation of marginalized groups—which allows for a multiplicity of voices and experiences—has been crucial in the development of a new notion of cultural identity and of the emphasis on a politics of location. Stuart Hall, among others, has pointed out that cultural identification need produce not an essence but rather a point in transition, a site, which is "subject to the continuous 'play' of history, culture and power."[24] Instead of being thought of as a historical *fait accompli*, identity is understood as a process that is never complete—something that falls within the scope of representation, not outside it.

Representations of otherness have participated in and continue to be a part of the production and reproduction of inequality and injustice. For those who are still struggling for better material conditions, a new model of politics that allows for heterogeneity and new alliances seems appropriate. To paraphrase Norma Alarcon (who also addresses the structural difference created by women's specific locations, especially with reference to Chicanas): it is a model that not only accepts the continuous production of differences that destabilize collective identities but also takes into account the need for cultural identification and group solidarities. This model could overcome oppression through an understanding of the mechanisms at work in the practice of "othering" in the past and present.[25] This strategy responds to the double bind of those who have been marginalized (in this case the Chicanas): resisting de/color/ization, de/class/ification and de/gender/ing, as well as paternalistic "communal modes of power." Exploring one's location by examining the ways one has been positioned and by creating ways to re-position oneself allows for resistance and transformation. It also opens up the possibility of making *chosen* alliances within specific cultural and historical contexts and their power mechanisms.

The development of culture and identity as an ongoing process by which cultural identification as well as particularity/specificity are taken *provisionally*, as I suggest calling it, seems to be a project that would empower those who have been oppressed and marginalized by various practices. To create, however, the potential for Western hegemony's history of exclusion and subjugation to come to an end, this process must be two sided, originating from colonial subjects and old Western subjects as well.

Those who in Western discourse have been constituted as other/s are no longer external or distant. They are im/migrating not only into the traditional immigration countries such as the United States and Canada but also into the colonizers' nations and into those countries in the process of building a "New Europe." I would like to imagine, for a moment, a "New Europe" that is a *developing* culture: an association not of *given* cultures but of *constructed* cultures, constructed in specific and diverse historical responses to specific social and political configurations, and one open to the reconstruction and development of a new open community that can draw on the multiplicity of cultural experiences as well as countercurrent voices that have been marginalized. In order for this to take place, "Old Europe" and its subjects must continue their process of decolonization based upon specific historical, political, and socio critical analyses of their inheritances. Only when this happens can languages of ex/change emerge, in a "listening to" and "speaking to" each other that invites response/ibility without reducing differences between others, and from which new conceptions of communal and political spaces can develop.

II

The following essays reconsider different theories and practices with respect to their implicit culture contact/otherness model and political implications. They focus on the ability of literature to perceive and acknowledge otherness and explore aesthetic experiences of the other/self, of otherness and cultural contact. They also investigate the conditions of and for the identification of individual and collective selves and of individual and collective "others" that are becoming more and more complex. They study the consequences of the homogenizing force of cultural domination and colonization and explore possibilities for transformation, and for articulation of alternative values and devising strategies for alternative practices.

Stephen David Ross, in "What of the Others? Whose Subjection?" investigates through a wide variety of discourses the dynamics of self/other as relations of subjectivity and subjection. These relations, where subjectivity is inseparable from subjection, mark our monstrosity, the otherness of truth, which raises important questions. What of our subjection to the other, marked by its others? What are the others of the other? What are the limits of our responsibilities toward the others? And what if our responsibilities toward the others represented the limits of our world, perhaps as Western, perhaps as rational?

In "Response to the Other," Bernhard Waldenfels begins with the philosophy of Husserl and Merleau-Ponty as well as the ethnology of Levi-Strauss to discuss the preconditions for an encounter with the other without minimizing or even destroying it. A work of alienness (*Fremdheitsarbeit*), as he suggests, requires a change of attitudes toward the other/s, taking the other/s as a request or stimulus *to which* we respond and must respond in whatever we are saying or doing.

In "Xenophobia, Xenophilia, and No Place to Rest" Angelika Bammer addresses the conflicts of love and fear of the other as they are played out in academic cultural studies contexts. Paradigms of multi-culturalism and diversity, she argues, do not necessarily preclude a complicity in the appropriation and degradation of Third World people. To engage in the problems of the encounter with others she concentrates on two opposing positions, one by Tzvetan Todorov, the other by Homi Bhabha. Todorov argues for certain "absolute principles" that allow for condemning or lauding certain *forms* of cultural behavior on the condition that we understand (our own) culture to be formed, and continually re-formed, by its relation of contiguity and contingency with others. In contrast to this position, Bhabha rejects any universalist framework. He argues for a concept of 'radical particularism' and a politics of difference, that is, a politics based on recognition of conflict and even incommensurability.

How do literary texts offer possibilities to uncover the dynamics of self/other, to encounter the other by resisting "othering"? But also, how may literature be an accomplice in reducing or excluding the other? Frederick Garber in his contribution, "Maelzel and Me," presents a reading of Poe's hardly known text "Maelzel's Chess Player" and E. T. A. Hoffmann's story "Die Automate." In his discussion he takes up the problems of self-constitution and fuses them with questions of alterity, the numinous and the human. He argues that the encounter with the anthropomorphic mechanized chess player and the automaton "Talking Turk" allows for a subversion of the binary self/other in favor of an insistence on *both/and*. Making use of Emerson's phrase NOT ME, Garber unfolds the dynamics of the pairing ME/NOT ME that always establishes ME, but also simultaneously oneself as NOT ME and the NOT ME as ME. The acts of self-constitution emerge as manifold practices based on humans in relations.

In "It Has, Like You, No Name: Paul Celan and the Address of the Other," Jason M. Wirth addresses the possibilities of poetry with special focus on Paul Celan in the context of the Kabbalah, Walter Benjamin, and Emmanuel Levinas. Celan continuously invokes in his poems an unspecified "you." As dialogical language his poetry is a movement toward "something standing open, inhabitable." It addresses the other but cannot name the other. Embracing the failure of the naming of the other, this address becomes the rehabilitation of speaking after language had to go "through the thousand darknesses of murderous speech."

In "*Blutschande*: From the Incest Taboo to the Nuremberg Racial Laws" Christina von Braun investigates the change of the meaning of *Blutschande*. Where it originally designated the sin of intercourse with one's own blood relatives, with siblings, father, mother, it comes to designate the sin of intercourse with alien blood lines, alien races in the texts of racist anti-Semitism. The author places this change in meaning into the context of a mythologizing brother-sister love in the literature since romanticism, in which this love appears as the "purest" form of the relationship between the sexes. The attraction to one's own self-image, own's own blood, is linked to the exclusion of everything that represents "otherness." This indicates a complex change in the concept of the 'self' and also exhibits a secularization of the Christian image of salvation. The image of the "impure Jew" is constructed as a counter to one's own image of purity. The "impure Jew" corrupts the Aryan race with his blood and leads it to ruin.

One aspect of Christina von Braun's discussion of the sacrificial death of the other (real woman) that is inherent in the utopian ideal of love is further elucidated in Michael Strysick's reading of Gilman's *Yellow Wallpaper* and Duras's *The Malady of Death*. In the context of the problem of Western thought's totalizing structure—which fails to recognize the other in terms of itself and its infinity—developed in the works of Levinas, Blanchot, and Derrida, Strysick finds in the texts by Gilman and Duras a critique of the economy of the same and the optics of totality that results in blindness and/or violent neutralization of the other (woman).

Colonial discourse is the space in which fantasies of "otherness" abound. Susanne Zantop concentrates in her contribution, "Domestication of the Other: European Colonial Fantasies 1770–1830," on a crucial moment in European colonial history and a particular colonial relationship, that between Europe and its rebelling colonies in the Americas. She traces a series of shifts in the colonial paradigm that translate into changes in representation: from stories of unrequited love and guilt to stories of marital bliss; from tales of desire and abandonment to tales of permanent commitment. As Zantop argues, these shifts towards "love" and successful domesticity, seemingly an improvement over previous colonial models, in fact mask the violence of colonial appropriation only more effectively, while providing "legitimate" channels for pent-up colonial desire.

Literary representations of the other in colonialist writing are more often than not characterized by means of attributing restricted and deficient capability of language to the colonized. Konstanze Streese, in "Writing the Other's Language," focuses on this stylistically recurrent and conceptually symptomatic reduction of the culturally other/s to a status of social inferiority within the colonial paradigm and sets them against contemporary narratives critical of colonialism and the various strategies of representing the language of the other employed in order to discontinue the tradition of the "manichean aesthetics" (JanMohamed). She argues that a paradigm of internarrative dialogue suggests itself as a possible means for the literary emergence of the self from its fantasies about the other.

Sander Gilman's "The Jewish Nose: Are Jews White? Or, The History of the Nose Job" focuses on the body and how fantasies about race inscribe themselves upon it. Beginning with an analysis of the question "Are Jews white?"—which preoccupied much of the science of race in nineteenth-century Europe—he shows how fantasies about skin color, closely related to the representation of physiognomy, patterned European Jews to doubt the validity of their very bodies. The result is the generation of specific forms of aesthetic surgery, such as rhinoplasty.

Just as fantasies about race inscribe themselves upon the body, they also inscribe themselves upon texts and the canon, as Aaron Perkus argues in "The Instincts of 'Race' and 'Text'." Referring to an article by Henry W. Grady (1885), in which he defends the segregation of races in the New South by referring to the naturalness for races to stay apart ("race instinct"), Perkus parallels Grady's argumentation with the arguments put forward by the National Association of Scholars in their defense of the Western canon. Perkus argues that their concept of texts and the canon is based on an understanding of a text as a given, independent from social and academic practices naming it as such.

Therefore, their defense of the traditional core curriculum based on "proven standards" can be read as a continuation of segregational politics based on "text instinct."

There are an estimated fifteen million refugees worldwide, fifteen million persons who, if their story were to be told, would be eligible for refugee status in another country. Robert F. Barsky's "The Construction of the Other and the Destruction of the Self: The Case of the Convention Hearings" analyzes the practice of the refugee hearing using Canada's Convention Refugee Hearing as an example. By making use of the realm of discourse analysis and the works of Mikhail Bakhtin, he argues that refugee "hearings" are constructed in such a way as to virtually preclude by a process of othering and authoring any possibility that the subject's true testimony can be "heard."

Leaving one's world and culture behind—voluntarily or involuntarily—means engaging oneself in a complex process of compromising one's identity and otherness. Velma Pollard, in her essay on Olive Senior's story "The Arrival of the Snake Woman," discusses one of the rare examples that gives historical and literary reference to the East Indian in Jamaican society. Senior describes the integration of an East Indian woman into an early twentieth-century hill village in Jamaica populated largely by people of African descent. Historical fact as interpreted by the folk forms the background against which the plot is played out. The importance of the story lies in its identification and exposure of stereotypes associated with the other race of which Miss Coolie is a member.

Expressions of self-identity and "otherness" are central to the emergence and development of minority discourses. Eliana Rivero's "The 'Other's Others': Chicana Identity and Its Textual Expressions" focuses on texts by Mexican American women that emerged during the historical period of Chicano "Renaissance" in the sixties and that remain invalidated by the dominant critical discourse in Chicano literature. These texts bespeak an acute awareness of cultural otherness, of personal experiences of hybridism in the production of language and identity. This otherness responds to the experience of being part of an ethnic minority, and just as much to the consciousness of femaleness within their own particular cultural group.

The experience of exile informs the work of the scholar and poet Abena Busia from Ghana. Three of her poems are included here: "Migrations," "Petitions," "Achimota: From The Story My Mother Taught Me."

Personal history, memoirs, photographs, family albums, and interviews are interwoven in Leo Spitzer's documentation of Jewish refugee experience in Bolivia in the 1930s and early years of World War II. Coming to the New World as persons who had been "othered" by anti-Semites in Nazi-dominated Central Europe, the refugees nonetheless carried cultural baggage with them that profoundly colored their own impressions of the people and physical environment they encountered in Bolivia. Reflecting on Central European popular and literary representations of "America," "Indians," and alien "others," as well as on popular and elite Bolivian notions about Jews and foreigners, Spitzer probes the role of images, stereotypes, and cultural memory as influences in the formation of cultural identity and as factors shaping cross-cultural communication and acceptance.

In "Isabelle Eberhardt Traveling 'Other'/Wise: The 'European' Subject in 'Oriental' Identity," Sidonie Smith explores the embodied positionalities of Isabelle Eberhardt, a European woman who decided to live in the desert of North Africa while adopting a male nomad identity. As Smith argues, the nomads of the desert offered Eberhardt a metaphor for her essential "self," that "otherness" she felt within her. As much as her life marks a transgression of a conventional European, specific woman's life, and as intensely as she embraces the "other," "nomad" self, even subjugating herself to the other in her marriage with her "native" lover, she also carries with her "cultural baggage," her European identity. Her journal shows the complex interplay of resistance toward European (women's) life and her identification and internalization, respectively, of Western individualism, concepts of 'romantic artist' and 'love', and preconceived images of Africa and the primitive past that involve her in the domestication of the other.

Ineke Phaf's contribution, "Nation as the Concept of 'Democratic Otherness'," concentrates on Carlos Fuentes' novel *Cristobal Nonato* (Christopher Unborn) in which a birth is announced as possible "Otherness from a New Body." This unborn project incorporates the reconstruction of a mutilated Mexico in 1992 as well as a series of critical questions on cultural politics in its history. Fuentes argues that its efforts of innovation have to be related to the democratic dynamics of "social selves" in an overall process of international modernization. The fetus named Cristobal finally succeeds in overcoming colonialism by symbolizing these future possibilities of unlimited transformational capacities already located in his genes. He functions as a memory-play in order to prognosticate a "peripheral modernity" as the critical concept for nations and its languages on the American continent, with the history of Mexico—the New Spain—as an example.

The final contribution, "The 'Other' as the 'Self' under Cultural Dependency: The Impact of the Postcolonial University" by Ali Mazrui, explores the possibilities of overcoming cultural dependency in Africa by concentrating on the institution of the university. Virtually all universities in sub-Saharan Africa are based on Western models by structure, language, and curriculum. This produces not only academic dependency but a dependency that has an impact on the society as a whole; Mazuri explicates this in his discussion of the functions of culture and types of dependency. As he argues, in order to decolonize modernity African societies must be allowed to influence fundamentally the educational systems (domestication) that are to re-examine and reform students' admission requirements, curricula, faculty recruitment criteria, and the general structure of the educational system in order to relate universities to both the economic and cultural needs of the society as a whole. Furthermore, to overcome cultural dependency on the West, strategies of diversification of the cultural content of modernity and of counter-penetration of Western culture by African culture are to be employed.

Notes

Translated by Elizabeth Naylor Endres

1. Wlad Godzich, "The Further Possibility of Knowledge," foreword to *Heterologies: Discourse on the Other*, by Michel de Certeau (Minneapolis: University of Minnesota Press, 1986), viii.

2. Emanuel Levinas, *Die Spur des Anderen: Untersuchungen zur Phänomenologie und Sozialphilosophie* (Freiburg and Munich: Verlag Karl Alber, 1987), 211; "Von ihrem Beginn an ist die Philosophie vom Entsetzen vor dem Anderen, das Anderes bleibt, ergriffen, von einer unüberwindbaren Allergie" (trans. into English by Elizabeth Naylor Endres).

3. Levinas, *Spur*, 211; "durch alle Abenteuer hindurch findet sich das Bewußtsein als es selbst wieder, es kehrt zu sich zurück wie Odysseus, der bei allen seinen Fahrten nur auf seine Geburtsinsel zugeht" (trans. into English by Elizabeth Naylor Endres).

4. Emmanuel Levinas, *Totality and Infinity: An Essay on Exteriority*, trans. Alphonso Lingis (Pittsburgh: Duquesne University Press, 1969), 35–40.

5. Levinas, *Spur*, 225.

6. Theodor W. Adorno, *Aesthetic Theory* (London and Boston: Routledge, 1984), 185.

7. James Clifford, "On Ethnographic Surrealism," in *The Predicament of Culture: Twentieth-Century Ethnography, Literature, and Art* (Cambridge, Mass.: Harvard University Press, 1988), 117–51.

8. Hans-Jürgen Heinrichs, "Einleitung" (introduction), Michel Leiris, *Die eigene und die fremde Kultur: Ethnologische Schriften*, trans. Rolf Wintermeyer, ed. Hans Jürgen Heinrichs (Frankfurt am Main: Syndikat, 1979), 38.

9. Heinrichs, "Einleitung," 38.

10. Clifford, "On Ethnographic Surrealism," 147.

11. David Thomas, "From Gesture to Activity: Dislocating the Anthropological Scriptorium," *Cultural Studies* 6, no. 1 (January 1992): –26; 16f.

12. Leiris, *Eigene*, 70; "den Interessen und Strebungen der kolonialisierten Völker, so wie diese selbst sie verstehen, zu dienen" (trans. into English by Elizabeth Naylor Endres).

13. Raymond Corbey and Joep Leerssen, "Studying Alterity: Background and Perspectives," in *Alterity, Identity, Image: Selves and Others in Society and Scholarship*, ed. R. Corbey and J. T. Leerssen (Amsterdam and Atlanta: Rodopi, 1991), xii.

14. Teresa de Lauretis, *Technologies of Gender: Essays on Theory, Film, and Fiction* (Bloomington: Indiana University Press, 1987), 14.

15. De Lauretis, *Technologies*, 17.

16. Gayatri Chakravorty Spivak, "Displacement and the Discourse of Woman," in *Derrida and After*, ed. Mark Krupnick (Bloomington: Indiana University Press, 1983), 185.

17. Spivak, "Displacement," 185.

18. De Lauretis, *Technologies*, 26.

19. Gayatri Chakravorty Spivak, *The Postcolonial Critic: Interviews, Strategies, Dialogues*, ed. Sarah Harasym (New York and London: Routledge, 1990), 69f.

20. Gayatri Chakravorty Spivak, "Subaltern Studies: Deconstructing Historiography," in *Other Worlds: Essays in Cultural Politics* (New York and London: Methuen, 1987), 209.

21. Gayatri Chakravorty Spivak, "Can the Subaltern Speak?" in *Marxism and the Interpretation of Culture*, ed. Cary Nelson and Lawrence Grossberg (Urbana: University of Illinois Press, 1989), 271–313.

22. R. Radhakrishnan, "Ethnic Identity and Post-Structuralist Difference," in the special issue *The Nature and Context of Minority Discourse*, ed. Abdul R. JanMohamed and David Lloyd, *Cultural Critique* 6 (spring 1987), 202.

23. Franz Fanon, *The Wretched of the Earth* (New York: Grove Press, 1963).

24. Stuart Hall, "The Local and the Global," paper read at Binghamton University, 1989.

25. Norma Alarcon, "Chicana Feminism: in the Tracks of 'the' Native Woman," *Cultural Studies* 4, no. 3 (October 1990): 248–56; 252.

PART I

The Challenge of the Other/s

CHAPTER 1

What of the Others? Whose Subjection?

STEPHEN DAVID ROSS

Derrida speaks of the other as philosophy's limit, surprising us obliquely with the question of danger:

> Philosophy has always insisted upon this: thinking its other. Its other: that which limits it, and from which it derives its essence, its definition, its production. . . . [D]oes the limit, obliquely, by surprise, always reserve one more blow for philo-sophical knowledge?[1]

I hope to defer, at least for the moment, the privilege of philosophy, our philosophy, of Western reason and philosophy. For the moment. To set aside the special intimacy of philosophy with the limit, its limit, the other, its other. If we accept such an intimacy. As if we were not always touched intimately by others, intimate with others, however painful and dangerous that intimacy may be. As if we did not always confront our limits, however blind to those limits we might be. As if we were not many others. As if they were not us.

Derrida challenges us to imagine a relation to our limits as a relation to an other, *our* other, placing us in danger. Can we measure the other at the limits of who we are except as danger, a threat to our otherness? Why emphasize our surprise, as if that did not repeat a production of the other, this time as unanticipated threat, however indirect? This obliqueness, with which we gaze with fascination at the other: with what authority?

> We know that the membrane of the tympanum, a thin and transparent partition separating the auditory canal from the middle ear . . . , is stretched obliquely. . . . The tympanum squints [*louche*]. (Tympan, xv)

19

Perhaps we hear the authority of the subject, recalling Irigaray's response: "But what if the 'object' started to speak?"[2] where

> any theory of the "subject" has always been appropriated by the masculine. (*Speculum*, 133)

> The 'subject' sidles up to the truth, squints at it, obliquely, in an attempt to gain possession of what truth can no longer say. (*Speculum*, 136)

I squint, obliquely, at the object of my fascination, my desire, the other subject, bringing her under my gaze, drawing her limits. Do you doubt that she, a black (or tan or white or yellow) woman (perhaps a man, a child, an animal; even money or power), tests, exceeds, my limits as I mark hers (or its)? What blow, what danger, does she (or he or it) threaten? How can civilized (do I mean Western?) people represent a danger to each other? We need have no fear of the other. We belong together. We find ourselves intimately in proximity.

And the others? What of the others?

Still within philosophy—do we hope to leave it?—we find the reemergence of the subject as every subject collectively disperses. Can we ask the color of the subject, what race or gender, what nationality? Can the other possess a body, a gender, this other beyond being? Can the other escape its subjectivity even as it falls upon ours? In Levinas,

> It will . . . be necessary to show that the exception of the "other than being," beyond not-being, signifies subjectivity or humanity, the *oneself* which repels the annexations by essence.[3]

Do we save the primacy of the other for me within the intimacy of our subjectivity, even the subjectivity of the other? Does my subjectivity, my desire and freedom, of this *oneself*, find its limits only in the limits of another subject?

> The freedom of another could never begin in my freedom, that is, abide in the same present, be contemporary. (*Otherwise*, 10)

Perhaps the freedom of another cannot belong to me, cannot be given by the essence of my subjectivity, cannot belong to any essence, even that of subjectivity, its or mine. May I refuse the symmetry of subjectivity in my utter responsibility before the other, even as it may not be reciprocated, placing me in terrible danger? And what kind of danger? What height of danger?

> The unlimited responsibility in which I find myself comes from the higher side of my freedom, from a "prior to every memory," an "ulterior to every accomplishment," from the non-present par excellence, the non-original, the anarchical, prior to or beyond essence. The responsibility for the other is the locus in which is situated the null-site of subjectivity, where the privilege of the question "Where?" no longer holds. (*Otherwise*, 10)

Where "Where?" and also "Who?" no longer hold. I find my responsibility toward the other at the null-site of subjectivity, perhaps the other's and my subjectivity, where the other does not, cannot, reciprocate my unlimited responsibility, in a memory prior to every memory, immemorial, a responsibility, a relation, prior to every measure, yet still the highest.

We remember Anaximander, where things

> make reparation to one another for their injustice according to the ordinance of time.[4]

Things in time, under law and measure, make endless restitution to each other for their injustices. We find unlimited immemorial injustice in close proximity, perhaps, to unlimited responsibility, tempered by the terrible danger that every act of reparation endlessly repeats injustice, that even justice repeats injustice: every law; every measure. Above all, the injustice of the highest.

And the others? What of the others? Do they appear in this space of immemorial injustice at the null-site of subjectivity, where neither a where nor what nor who of subjectivity holds even as my subjectivity is demanded as the price of my unmeasurable responsibility? Certainly the other means unforgettable pain.

> The one is exposed to the other as a skin is exposed to what wounds it, as a cheek is offered to the smiter. On the higher side of the ambiguity of being and entities, prior to the said, saying uncovers the one that speaks, not as an object disclosed

by theory, but in the sense that one discloses oneself by neglecting one's defenses, leaving a shelter, exposing oneself to outrage, to insults and wounding. (*Otherwise*, 49)

Does the pain, my suffering, the danger and reality of my pain and suffering, save me from seizing the other as my other, or do I lose the other in the wounds of the others? Do I enslave the other in the height of my utter responsibility? Do I enslave the other as I enslave myself in even greater intimacy? And what of the lower?

Do I forget thee, my others, in your silences, in my injustices, because I can never hold the null-site of subjectivity, where power and desire impose themselves, because even as I acknowledge the asymmetry of my relation to you, I acknowledge you always as *my* others, where I am high, however ambiguously?

Perhaps we hope to remember the victims, new and old, even as we have no idea, no dream, whatever of what might constitute compensation for their victimization. Perhaps another restitution is required for the injustice of this remembrance, of which Lyotard speaks in relation to Levinas:

> By turning the I into its you [*toi*], the other makes him or herself master, and turns the I into his or her hostage.[5]

If this sounds like Hegel's slave mastering the master, it becomes Levinasian (if such a state of mastery were possible) at the point where the other dissolves:

> Levinas comments upon the destituteness of the other: the other arises in my field of perception with the trappings of absolute poverty, without attributes, the other has no place, no time, no essence, the other is nothing but his or her request and my obligation. (*Differend*, 111)

What could I owe to such a hollow other except what I might owe to a god without a name, to the highest being? What restitution to an absolute poverty, rather than to disease and famine? What of the living others? What of the silent victims of our injustices?

How can a woman testify publicly, on national television, before fourteen men, of private injuries? Were they unproved, or were they unheard? How could they be heard in such a hearing? Paraphrasing

Catherine MacKinnon: are sexual injuries defined as crimes by men in public but experienced as injuries by women in private, effectively silencing them as victims?[6] What restitution can we dream of for their injustices? What public standing can be granted private wounds? What hope do our institutions offer of granting private victims public standing? What institution represents the bankruptcy of male, white, Western institutions in drawing public lines around and through intimate relations, sexuality and desire, memory and history, lines that do not hold, that endlessly ensnare countless victims? If no institutional lines can divide sexual intercourse and rape, as MacKinnon suggests, what does that say about our institutions? What does that say about our proximities?

Lyotard reminds us of other victims:

38. . . . [a]n . . . animal is deprived of the possibility of bearing witness according to the human rules for establishing damages, and as a consequence, every damage is like a wrong and turns it into a victim *ipso facto*. . . . That is why the animal is a paradigm of the victim. (*Differend*, 28)

Derrida presses the monstrous truth upon us that we require such victims for our subjectivity, that subjectivity is inseparable from subjection, from victimization.

carnivorous sacrifice is essential to the structure of subjectivity, which is also to say to the founding of the intentional subject and to the founding, if not of the law, at least of droit, the difference between *la loi* and *droit*, justice and droit, justice and law remaining open over an abyss.[7]

We find ourselves trapped by our subjectivity, "like a dog."[8]

Derrida calls "dogmatic" the side of Heidegger that preserves the opposition of humanity and its other within the repudiation of every such opposition. Man still exercises privilege over animals and machines under the sign of *Geschlecht*.

Here in effect occurs a sentence that at bottom seems to me Heidegger's most significant, symptomatic, and seriously dogmatic.

This sentence in sum comes down to distinguishing the human

Geschlecht, our *Geschlecht*, and the animal *Geschlecht*, called "animal."[9]

Apes, too, have organs that can grasp, but they do not have hands. The hand is infinitely different from all the grasping organs—paws, claws, or fangs—different by an abyss of essence. Only a being who can speak, that is, think, can have hands and can handily achieve works of handicraft.[10]

The key word is *our*: *Our Geschlecht*. This is a humanism if "certainly" not metaphysical:

In its very content, this proposition marks the text's essential scene, marks it with a humanism that wanted certainly to be nonmetaphysical—Heidegger underscores this in the following paragraph—but with a humanism . . . that inscribes not some differences but an absolute oppositional limit. (*Geschlecht II*, 173–74)

What makes it humanistic is its inscription in the hand, marking an infinite difference: the gift.

the name of man, his *Geschlecht*, becomes problematic itself. For it names what has the hand, and so thinking, speech or language, and openness to the gift.

Man's hand then will be a thing apart not as separable organ but because it is different, dissimilar from all prehensive organs (paws, claws, talons); man's hand is far from these in an infinite way through the abyss of its being. This abyss is speech and thought. (*Geschlecht II*, 174)

Others speak of the phallus. By and within man's gift Heidegger reinscribes *Geschlecht* upon desire.

Geschlecht becomes the root of many words for the things males and females have and do for the sake of the first two meanings: *Geschlechts-glied* or *-teil*, the genitals; *-trieb*, the sex drive; *-verkehr*, sexual intercourse; and so on. (*Geschlecht II*, 191–92)

The gift—of language, speech, or thinking—is given not to animals or machines but only to "us." Similarly, *Geschlecht* is always "ours." The abyss belongs to neither animals nor machines, never to Them. For Heidegger, language, the gift, representation, in a movement that opposes dogmatism, reinscribes it dogmatically both within *Geschlecht* and against those who do not think like Us. The difference between humans who do not think and other creatures is infinite, marking the absolute limit of "Man."

We hear in Derrida something largely unheard in the Western tradition, certainly unheard on its humanistic side, the human—nearly always Human, a point of privilege and authority—founded on the subjugation of, violence toward, animals, all turning around the law of sexual difference.

> there was a time, not long ago and not yet over, in which "we, men" meant "we adult white male Europeans, carnivorous and capable of sacrifice." (*Force of Law*, 954)

Martha Nussbaum paraphrases Walter Burkert on animal sacrifice, repeating human supremacy.

> By expressing their ambivalence and remorse concerning even an animal killing, by humanizing the animal and showing a regard for its "will," the sacrificers put away from themselves the worst possibility: that they will kill human beings, and kill without pity, becoming themselves bestial.[11]

These words come close, if not close enough, to Derrida's extreme suggestion that subjectivity requires subjection, traditionally the subjection of animals, animals instead of humans, leading to the subjection of not quite high enough humans, the suggestion that

> carnivorous sacrifice is essential to the structure of subjectivity (*Force of Law*, 953)

When we ask about this "essential"—Jewish, Greek, or Christian, even German—as *Geschlecht*, we find ourselves in that uncanny space of injustice in which European humanity repeats the fetish of The Human.

> There is no animal *Dasein*, since *Dasein* is characterized by
> access to the "as such" of the entity and to the correlative
> possibility of questioning. It is clear that the animal can be after
> a prey, it can calculate, hesitate, follow or try out a track, but it
> cannot properly question.[12]

The "*Dasein*" and "as such" belong to Heidegger. The "it is clear"
appears to belong to Derrida, however unclearly, followed by a dogmatic quotation from Michel Haar:

> The leap from the animal that lives to man that speaks is as
> great, if not greater, than that from the lifeless stone to the
> living being.[13]

Is the measure clear? To us? That animals have no world, or, as Derrida
says, in spite of Haar, that "the animal *has* and *does not have* a world"?
(*Of Spirit*, 50). Does violence, does spirit's flame, compel us to sacrifice
animals? To God? To Us? To our consumption, our instrumentality? To
the high side of our freedom, our subjectivity? Are our gifts still the
measure of citizenship in the highest realm? And the others?

Elizabeth Marshall Thomas tells stories of lions in the Kalahari
desert, summarizing their relationship to the Juwasi Bushmen as one of
mutual respect:

> All of us assumed that the people, not the lions, determined the
> events.
> But the lions also had a share in shaping the relationship.
> A truce if ever there was one, the people-lion relationship
> wouldn't have worked unless both sides had participated.[14]

The Juwasi and the lions could easily have killed each other; leopards
killed Bushmen and were killed by them, shown no respect. Yet,

> [t]he truce was quite remarkable. While we were in the Kala-
> hari, we knew of only one person who had been injured by a
> lion . . . among fifteen hundred deaths recalled by the hundreds
> of people whose testimonies I was able to examine, only one
> death was said to have been caused by a lion. . . . We knew of
> no lion killed by a Bushman. (*Lions*, 83)

This relationship no longer holds, as lions no longer live side by side with Bushmen.

Are these not others, even our others, Juwasi and lions? Do we, as Derrida says, define our subjectivity by subjection. And whose subjection?

According to Public Broadcasting, September 28, 1991, ten thousand square miles of the Amazon rain forest in Brazil disappear every year.

According to *Time*, September 23, 1991,

> Since 1900, 90 of Brazil's 270 Indian tribes have completely disappeared, while scores more have lost their lands or abandoned their ways. More than two-thirds of the remaining tribes have populations of fewer than 1,000. Some might disappear before anyone notices. (48)

Time reports that there are estimated to be 15,000 cultures remaining on earth, while of the earth's 6,000 languages, 3,000 have no children who speak them. *Time* reports that the earth has 265,000 species of plants—fewer each year—of which only 1,100 have been intensely studied by Western science, while 40,000 or more may have undiscovered medicinal or nutritional value for human beings. For human beings. And what of this disclosure in *Time*, what does *Time* represent for Us and the others? What gifts?

"Man" appears, in the narrative of *The Order of Things*, at a certain point in the "analytic of finitude," defining "our modernity," unmistakably Western:

> Man, in the analytic of finitude, is a strange empiricotranscendental doublet, since he is a being such that knowledge will be attained in him of what renders all knowledge possible.[15]

This irruption of Man constitutes a certain Subject, grounded in finitude, at the same time—its doubling—constituting and completing the ground of knowledge. The subject here—clearly The Subject—comes to possess knowledge in Himself of what makes knowledge possible, closing the circle of objective truth within the sphere of sovereign subjectivity.

What spheres comprise the orbit of the authority of The Subject? Shall we suppose, with many others, that the narrative of "our" postmodernity irrupts in Heidegger's words in *The Origin of the Work of Art*, speaking of "the thingness of the thing" and "the basic Greek experience of the Being of beings as presence"?[16]

The process begins with the appropriation of Greek words by
Roman-Latin thought. *Hupokeimenon* becomes *subiectum*;
hupostasis becomes *substantia*; *sumbebekos* becomes *accidens*.[17]

We have noted the privilege granted this basic Greek experience,
vanishing into "our" Latin-Roman oblivion to Being—an absolute
privilege rescinded by Heidegger even while granting another privilege
to German, in the highest *Geistlichkeit* of *Geist*.

> *Roman thought takes over the Greek words without a corres-*
> *ponding, equally authentic experience of what they say,*
> *without the Greek word.*[18]

I am speaking of the special relationship, inside the German
language, with the language of the Greeks and their thought. It
is something which the French are always confirming for me
today. When they begin to think they speak German: they say
definitely that they would not manage it in their language.[19]

Derrida returns us to Spirit:

> Twenty years later, Heidegger will have to suggest, in short,
> that the Greek language has no word to say—nor therefore, to
> translate—*Geist*: at least a certain *Geistlichkeit*, if not the
> *Geistigkeit* of *Geist*....The *Geist* of this *Geistlichkeit* could be
> thought only in *our language*. (*Of Spirit*, 70–71)

German even more than Greek and English. Not Latin or French. Not
Hebrew. Not Egyptian.

Yet within the Latin word something appears, marking what has
always appeared, that seems to vanish obscurely into *hypokeimenon's*
thingliness: that even before The Subject is placed under things as their
foundation, supporting their weight, their *subjectum*, the subject as
subjectus is thrown under the dominion of others' authority, weighed
down by injustice. If Man is thrown down—projected—as the ground
of whatever knowledge we may have of things in virtue of the em-
pirico-transcendental possibility of knowledge residing in Himself,
Subject and Object of all knowledge, it is in virtue of masking, ob-
scuring, in the closure of the circle of power, the authority vested in
Him as a subject thrown under the dominion of others. Masked in

Heidegger, present only obliquely in Foucault's representation of "Man,"[20] more apparent, perhaps, in Derrida, is the thought that the constitution of the subject—especially The European Subject—constitutes Our Subjection. The story of the "We" here is the subjugated narrative of subjection whose insurrections we strive to promote.

The Subject, even as the ground of knowledge, of things in their thingliness, upon whom all beings, objects, rest unfolds through history repeatedly as a site of subjection. That is what perhaps makes Hobbes in a certain way inevitable in our political discourses, in relation to the authority that constitutes authority's truth. From the state of nature to absolute sovereignty, subjects find themselves already subjected to unknown, enigmatic authority. Certain representations of this truth appear in Foucault, strange perhaps in the context of the suggestion that this immemoriality of power constitutes a new truth, emergent within the development of a new subject, Man, in relation to power:

> The "man" that the reformers set up against the despotism of the scaffold has also become a "man-measure": not of things but of power.[21]

Foucault describes this emergence of a measure of power in terms of the unfolding of rules:

> Through this technique of punitive signs, which tends to reverse the whole temporal field of penal action, the reformers thought they were giving to the power to punish an economic, effective instrument that could be made general throughout the entire social body, capable of coding all its behaviour and consequently of reducing the whole diffuse domain of illegalities.[22]

The economic instrumentality, the generality and coding of illegalities, appear in Foucault as irruptions, discontinuities and breaks, while I am thinking of them here as present from the beginning, even before the beginning, within the relations between subject and technē. Among the rules, in particular, is what Foucault calls *the rule of lateral effects*, a reworking of Hegel's celebration of the slave's mastership, as if slavery were not always degrading, as if subjectivity were not always abject under authority:

> The penalty must have its most intense effects on those who have not committed the crime; to carry the argument to its limit, if one could be sure that the criminal could not repeat the crime, it would be enough to make others believe that he had been punished.[23]

The most intense effects of punishment and domination fall on others, not on those degraded. That must be one of the most intolerable abjections of our memory of slavery.

The rule of lateral effects tells yet another story, close to Anaximander. For within the restrictive economy of punishment as example and deterrent, there unfolds the unyielding truth that to be human is to belong to systems of authority and regulation, that human beings materialize as human subjects, not as *hypokeimata* but as sites of subjection, thrown down under others' authority. Here discipline and punishment define a certain epoch's dynamic of subjection where, within the very idea of a Subject as a citizen within a realm of Ends there are already presupposed the authorities of Reason, Truth, and Law to which every citizen is to be subjected, even voluntarily, the authority of technē. Older than any kingdom of Law and Ends rule the injustices of authority and reason, any authority and any reason, dominions of power to which "we" find ourselves subjected.

Dostoevsky's Underground Man speaks famously to this point of subjection from within the depths of our abjection:

> Oh, tell me, who first declared, who first proclaimed, that man only does nasty things because he does not know his own real interests; and that if he were enlightened, if his eyes were opened to his real normal interest, man would at once cease to do nasty things, would at once become good and noble because, being enlightened and understanding his real advantage, he would see his own advantage in the good and nothing else, and we all know that not a single man can knowingly act to his own disadvantage. . . . Oh, the pure innocent child! Why, in the first place, when in all these thousands of years has there ever been a time when man has acted only for his own advantage?[24]

This critique of Socrates' repeated claim in the dialogues that no one knowingly acts against what he takes to be the good has two parts. In the first place, that of the advantage of the good, the two competing claims fall within instrumentality, address its force, again the authority of technē. The second speaks to the "within" of technē, granting the force of its authority.

> Why, one may choose what is contrary to one's own interests, and sometimes one *positively ought* (that is my own idea). . . . And, after all, that is not all: even if man really were nothing but a piano key, even if this were proved to him by natural science and mathematics, even then he would not become reasonable, but would purposely do something perverse out of sheer ingratitude, simply to have his own way.[25]

Reason, instrumentality, and law, whether or not we can or ought to defy them perversely, work by imposition, authority, and power, and we are thoroughly subjected to them whether at their best and worst, in their very nature, in our abject nature, in our intimacies. The inescapable truth about the Underground Man is that his perversity is monstrous and ineffective, abject, and his conviction that human beings might choose perversely to oppose reason unfolds without historical confirmation. Human beings abjectly choose reason—perhaps another monstrosity. The truth the Underground Man represents is that this choice and this rationality belong to authority and impose themselves upon us as subjects, subjecting us to their rule. The truth he emphasizes shows that authority is inescapable in the joint proximity of abjection and subjection.

> And, indeed, I will at this point ask an idle question on my own account: which is better—cheap happiness or exalted sufferings? Well, which is better?[26]

We ask, instead, which is more abject? And what more abject than unlimited responsibility before the others we have subjected?

Shall we so quickly give up the dream of a praxis free from subjection? Can we continue to dream of life without subjugation, domination? Nietzsche and Foucault did not think so, returning us to danger. In the latter's words,

> Humanity does not gradually progress from combat to combat until it arrives at universal reciprocity, where the rule of law finally replaces warfare; humanity installs each of its violences

in a system of rules and thus proceeds from domination to domination.[27]

This play of domination upon domination manifests the injustice of history's praxis, caught up in the dream, but not the possibility, of resolution and universality, in the "always more" that unfolds within the injustices of violence and domination. Here the injustices of violence and domination give rise to justice, to violence and domination but also violence against violence and the domination of domination.

The nature of these rules allows violence to be inflicted on violence and the resurgence of new forces that are sufficiently strong to dominate those in power.[28]

How does the other resist domination? How can we, in our subjection, compensate for our injustices, our abjection? Is it possible that we can do no other before the danger of the other? And what of the others? Always others, always injustices. In Trinh Minh-ha's words:

The Master is bound to recognize that His Culture is not as homogeneous, as monolithic as He believed it to be. He discovers, with much reluctance, He is just an other among others.[29]

With much reluctance and danger, just an other. And the others, do they discover, with reluctance, that their heterogeneity belongs intimately to the West? Always their subjection; our abjection. Unending injustices; endless restitutions.

Notes

1. Jacques Derrida, "Tympan," *Margins of Philosophy*, trans. A. Bass (Chicago: University of Chicago Press, 1982), x–xi.

2. Luce Irigaray, *Speculum of the Other Woman*, trans. G. Gill (Ithaca: Cornell University Press, 1985), 135.

3. Emmanuel Levinas, *Otherwise than Being; or, Beyond Essence*, trans. A. Lingis (The Hague: Martinus Nijhoff, 1981), 8.

4. Anaximander frag. 2.34, from John Mansley Robinson, *An Introduction to Early Greek Thinking* (Boston: Houghton Mifflin, 1968), 34. Also, the Anaximander fragment, quoted from Martin Heidegger, "The Anaximander Fragment," in *Early Greek Thinking* (San Francisco: Harper and Row, 1984), 29: ". . . kata to chreōn didonai gar auta dikēn kai tisin allēlois tēs adikias."

5. Jean-Francois Lyotard, *The Differend*, trans. G. Van Den Abbeele (Minneapolis: University of Minnesota Press, 1988), 111.

6. MacKinnon's own words are: "Rape is only an injury from women's point of view. It is only a crime from the male point of view, explicitly including that of the accused." (Catharine A. MacKinnon, *Toward a Feminist Theory of the State* (Cambridge: Harvard University Press, 1989), 180.

7. Jacques Derrida, "Force of Law: The "Mystical Foundation of Authority," trans. M. Quaintance, *Cardozo Law Review*, 11 (July/August 1990): 953.

8. That is the way K. dies, at the end of The Trial (Franz Kafka, *The Trial*, trans. W. and E. Muir, revised by E. M. Butler [New York: Modern Library, 1937], p. 286). See also Polymestor's curse upon Hecuba, "Thou wilt become a dog with bloodshot eyes" (Euripides, *Hecuba*, in *The Complete Greek Drama*, vol. 1, ed. W. J. Oates and E. O'Neill, Jr. [New York: Random House, 1938], 838).

9. Jacques Derrida, "*Geschlecht II*: Heidegger's Hand," in *Deconstruction and Philosophy*, ed. J. Sallis (Chicago: University of Chicago Press, 1987), 173.

10. Martin Heidegger, "What Calls for Thinking," in *Basic Writings*, ed. D. Krell (New York: Harper and Row, 1977), 357.

11. Martha C. Nussbaum, *The Fragility of Goodness* (Cambridge: Cambridge University Press, 1986), 37. She is paraphrasing Walter Burkert. See Walter Burkert, *Greek Religion: Archaic and Classical*, trans. John Raffan (Oxford: Basil Blackwell, 1985). As close as she comes, however, she does not see what Derrida sees, that this animal sacrifice is another injustice.

12. Jacques Derrida, *Of Spirit*, trans. G. Bennington and R. Bowlby (Chicago: University of Chicago Press, 1987), 51.

13. Michel Haar, "Le Chant de la terre," *Cahiers de L'Herne*, 1987, 70; quoted in *Of Spirit*, 53.

14. Elizabeth Marshall Thompson, "Lions," *New Yorker*, October 15, 1990, 82.

15. Michel Foucault, *The Order of Things* (New York: Vintage, 1973), 318.

16. Martin Heidegger, "The Origin of the Work of Art," *Poetry, Language, Thought*, trans. Albert Hofstadter (New York: Harper and Row, 1971), 22–23.

17. Ibid., 23.

18. Ibid.

19. *Of Spirit*, 69; W. J. Richardson, "'Only a God Can Save Us': The *Spiegel* Interview," in *Heidegger, the Man and the Thinker*, ed. T. Sheehan (Chicago: Precedent Publishing, 1981), 62.

20. But emphasized elsewhere, especially where Foucault speaks of genealogy as the "insurrection of subjugated discourses." ("Two Lectures," in *Power/Knowledge: Selected Interviews and Other Writings 1972–77*, ed. and trans. Colin Gordon [Brighton, Sussex: Harvester Press, 1980]). Even here, as the subjugation and insurrection testify to injustice, we wonder at the subordination of pain and suffering within the positivities of discourse.

21. Michel Foucault, *Discipline and Punish*, trans. A. Sheridan (New York: Random House, 1979), 74.

22. Ibid., 94.

23. Ibid., 95.

24. Fyodor Dostoevsky, *Notes from Underground and The Grand Inquisitor*, trans. R. E. Matlaw (New York: Dutton, 1960), 18.

25. Ibid., 23, 28.

26. Ibid., 114.

27. Michel Foucault, "Nietzsche, Genealogy, History," *Language, Counter-memory, Practice* (Ithaca: Cornell University Press, 1977), 150–51.

28. Ibid., 151.

29. Trinh T. Minh-ha, *Woman, Native, Other: Writing Postcoloniality and Feminism* (Bloomington: Indiana University Press, 1989), 98–99.

CHAPTER 2

Response to the Other

BERNHARD WALDENFELS

My reflections on the response to the other should be taken as reflections on the meta-question: How to question the other without falsifying the phenomenon of the other by the manner in which we question it? We can pose questions such as: What is the other? How do we acquire or experience knowledge of the other? How do we speak of the other? And finally: How do we speak to the other? We thus pass from a mode of being through a mode of experience, and a mode of speaking to a mode of allocution. Finally, what does it mean to direct our questions to the other? Is it an it-other or a s/he-other, or something beyond both? So many questions, so many pitfalls. What I want to offer may be understood as part of a *Fremdheitsarbeit*, "work in alienness," used in a sense similar to that described by Freud as "work in grieving."

Experience of the Other

In order to avoid any preconception of the other that has not been drawn from experience itself, phenomenology goes back to the situation where the other appears as such and where its otherness becomes questionable. I propose to take this first step by following Husserl, for his approach to the other seems to me more radical than those theories of communication and language that already move in the field of common goals and rules, as they take for granted what has to be questioned in its own sense.

First a few words about the terms with which we are going to formulate the question. In German I would not hesitate to speak of somebody or something that is *fremd* and use the word *Fremderfahrung* in a similar sense as the word *Fremdsprache*. Nevertheless, the word *Fremdheit* remains highly ambiguous. In English we may choose between at least three expressions. There is the "alien" that belongs to the other; there is the "foreign" that comes from the outside; and there is the "strange," which looks or sounds curious. Finally, we may simply speak of the "other." Each expression bears some inconvenient features. The mere "other" (ἕτερου, *aliud*) can be taken as a pure contrast to what is the same (ταὐτοῦ, *idem*), whereas what I want to stress is much more a kind of otherness that is opposed to the self (αὐτόζ, *ipse*) and its own.[1] In addition to this I do not want to thematize phenomena as belonging to the other, coming from the outside, or being unfamiliar as special phenomena, but rather to show that there is a dimension of otherness, or *Fremdheit*, that pervades all that is taken as our own inner and familiar world. Otherness presents itself as a central feature of all our experience and not as something special. The otherness of foreign people, foreign languages, or foreign cultures is thus symptomatic of what belongs to any experience. The "alien" begins at home. Considering the fact that there is no English expression that covers the multiple sense of what is *fremd*, I shall change the expression from context to context, giving a certain preference to the term *alien* or *alienness* as coming closest to the issue of appropriation.

Now, Husserl circumscribes the experience of the other in a paradoxical way, characterizing it as a "verifiable accessibility of what is originally inaccessible."[2] This kind of direct definition contains several different noteworthy aspects:

1. The alien is not defined by what it *is*. This ontological kind of question presupposes that the alien is embedded in some essential structure that can be known in advance. Neither is the question of the other reduced to the question of knowledge of it. To ask how we gain knowledge of the other would still presuppose too much, namely a pure fact we know or do not know. On the contrary, to define the alien by its accessibility means that the way of approach belongs to its own being. It is what it is while appearing in this or that way. In other words, we are confronted with a phenomenology of the other whose logos is taken from the phenomenon itself.

2. The alienness exists not in something not yet known, as a sort of deficit, but in something that becomes known only in this paradoxical mixture of presence and absence, of proximity and remoteness. In this sense the alien resembles the past to which we gain access only by recollection. Merleau-Ponty thus speaks of an "original of the elsewhere,"[3] and Levinas writes: "The absence of the other is his presence as of the other."[4]

3. The alienness is not restricted to the experience of the other but also colors the experience of myself. I will never be one with myself in terms of complete self-presence; I have only restricted access to myself. I am related to myself in a special way. I can appropriate my being to some extent, but I shall never be the owner of my life. Being born means that we owe our place in the world to an event that we can never transform into an act of our own; there is a form of past that has never been present to us. Being born by the symbolic birth of name-giving means, as Lacan puts it, that we are spoken by the others before we speak to them. This temporal and intersubjective otherness has its effects on the phenomenon of mirroring, which provides us an image of ourselves, but an image marked by cracks and fissures. The "broken Coriolanus" will never find its integrity, except an imaginary one that may end in death, as in the case of Narcissus.

4. The alienness is not a merely transitory and fugitive phenomenon, coming and going; rather it consolidates itself into a world of alienness. According to Husserl, life world as a whole is divided into home world (*Heimwelt*) and alien world (*Fremdwelt*). While being in the world we are never completely at home.

5. Finally, the paradoxical definition, claiming a certain accessibility of the alien, excludes the possibility that otherness could ever be total and complete. Take the example of foreign language. If a foreign language were totally incomprehensible, it would not even be incomprehensible *as language*, it would be reduced to mere noise. But that is not all. The alien becomes all the more seductive and threatening the closer we come to it. As Freud writes in his essay *Das Unheimliche*, the "uncanny" is "in reality nothing new or alien but something which is familiar and old-established in the mind and which has become alienated from it only through the process of repression."[5] Thus, alienness penetrates what seems more than anything else to be our own: our body, our language, our person, our friends. The *horror alieni* that may originate from this uncomfortable condition has not been invented by philosophers, but neither has it been banned by them.

Appropriation of the Other

It has often been claimed that Western thought and practice have to be characterized as a process of appropriation and domination of the world. Descartes thus proclaims at the beginning of modern times that human beings should become "masters and owners of nature," and this includes the mastering of others and of ourselves. In a similar way, according to Locke, it is labor that gives a "right of property," extending from one's own person to the work of our hands and changing nature from a "common mother" into a furnisher of "the almost worthless materials."[6]

The process of appropriation is based on what C. B. Macpherson has called "possessive individualism." This includes the atomization of the world into individuals, and from the struggle of each of them for self-preservation arises a strong barrier between the spheres of ownness and alienness. Now, appropriation is realized by different forms of centrism. First there is a kind of *egocentrism* that reduces the alien to the own. The other appears as my double (*alter ego*), as a variation or extension of the own. The well-known method of empathy presupposes that I have something of my own that I can put into the other's soul or mind. This sort of egocentrism, centered on the ego and its own sphere, is completed by an egocentrism centered on the logos as a set of common goals or rules reducing the alien to the common. The own and the alien are nothing more than parts of a whole or cases of a rule. Subjectivity is overcome by transsubjectivity, which leaves no real place for intersubjectivity. *Ethnocentrism*, centered on the "we" of one's own group, tribe, nation or culture, can be taken as a collective form of egocentrism, but in its specific forms, especially in the form of *Eurocentrism*, it should sooner be interpreted as a mixture of ego- and logocentrism. When we refer to Europe, we often do so in a certain way, for we do consider and defend it not as one culture among others, which would be completely legitimate, but as the incarnation or vanguard of mankind. What does not fit into the scheme of great Reason, true Faith, or real Progress becomes marginalized or, finally, eliminated. Thus, the figures of the wild, the child, the fool, or the animal are heterogeneous figures, populating the borderlines of an all-encompassing or all-regulating reason. The history of the Crusades, of colonialization, and mission could not have been what it was, namely a mixture of ignorance, curiosity, arrogance, and good will, without such a fixed idea propagating the appropriation of the world.

At present, there are many signs indicating that this process of appropriation so typical of our Western civilization has come to a dead-end. Egocentrism has been increasingly undermined by a *decentration* of the individual and the collective ego. Rimbaud's famous words "je est un autre," that is, "I is another," demonstrate in their agrammatical form that speaking and spoken ego do not coincide with one another. Never shall I be able to say in a complete way what or who I am. There are always voices behind me of which I cannot take possession. The place from which I speak is always displaced; I am here and elsewhere, and that means there is no center of speech. Similar things could be said about any attempt to feel oneself completely at home in one's own tribe or nation. Recent forms of nationalism or tribalism are, at best, to be interpreted as filling up a vacuum of sense or as an inappropriate reaction against different forms of over-universalism. As regards the process of logocentrism, according to Foucault and others we are confronted with a *dispersion* of reason. Reason is dissipated into rationalities, into forms and worlds of life not subject to one and the same standards and paradigms. There are heterogeneous and incompossible orders that cannot be realized simultaneously.

Does this mean that we are left with only differences and pluralities? In this way we would stagger from one extreme into the other. If we reflect on the fact that the own is what it is only in contrast to the alien, we see that both originate from a common process of *differentiation*, and this process, opening a social field, takes different forms and achieves different degrees. Following Merleau-Ponty or Norbert Elias, we can speak of an intertwining of the own and the alien that leaves behind any form of ontological or sociological atomism. Atomism may be the result of social processes of over-individualization, but it is not a starting point. But instead of going into the details of a theory of social order,[7] I prefer to take a look at the field of people whose task it is to come to terms with the alien: I mean the ethnologists.

The Paradox of a Science of the Alien

Let us go back to the beginning of our reflections. If it is true that experience of the other means "accessibility of what is originally inaccessible," how can we make it accessible without diminishing and abolishing its alienness? To claim that every appropriation is limited because of the open horizons of experience and understanding will not suffice to break or stop the process of appropriation. Even in this case the alien would be only relatively alien, as something that has not yet been given or understood, but waits for it. Gadamer thus declares that "alienness and its overcoming"[8] is a central problem of hermeneutics. Phenomenological experience and hermeneutic understanding of the other remain ambiguous as long as they cling to a logos encompassing us both—the own and the alien.

Ethnology as an empirical science is confronted with this problem in an even sharper sense. If every science consisted in determining what is undetermined, in explaining and understanding what cannot be explained or understood, then ethnology as the science of the alien would be a science that tended toward its own abolition. The more it succeeded, the more it would cancel itself, losing itself by losing its object. This is so because a determined, explained or understood alien would cease to be alien. The alien would vanish. This is what I call the paradox of a science of the alien.

The dilemma of science working against its own project may be the reason why, since Rousseau's times, ethnology has been accompanied by a certain uneasiness or even by a sort of guilty conscience. The dilemma is part of every kind of ethnology that preserves its philosophical impulse, questioning the other or the alien and not only collecting strange and exotic things. It is not so amazing to see that a certain shift has taken place recently within the field of ethnology. This can be clearly shown by considering a certain tension within the work of Lévi-Strauss, the most important ethnologist of our time.

In Lévi-Strauss's work we find two contrasting trends. On the one hand ethnology is practiced as a *science of the universal* in terms of *transcultural* structures and codes, reducing the alien to a preliminary form of alienness that, in the long run, will turn out to be a pure variant of invariant rules and structures. But on the other hand, ethnology retains the paradoxical form of a *science of the alien* based on the experience of the other and on an understanding of the alien as an *intercultural* phenomenon that changes from epoch to epoch, from region to region. In this context, Lévi-Strauss characterizes ethnology by a movement of *détachement* and *dépaysement*, which comes close to the phenomenological *epoché*, inhibiting the presumptions of one's own culture. Lévi-Strauss quotes from Rousseau's *Essay on the Origin of Languages*, in which the author writes: "Quand on vent étudier les hommes, il faut regarder près de soi; mais pour étudier l'homme il faut apprendre à porter sa vue au loin; il faut d'abord observer les différences pour découvrir les propriétés."[9] The ethnological view allows us to see ourselves from a distance, from outside.

This has as its consequence a *doubling* and *multiplication* of ethnology. First, ethnology is split into an ethnology of the other (allo-ethnology) and an ethnology of ourselves (auto-ethnology). But the latter can once more be multiplied into an ethnology exercized *by ourselves* or *by the other*.[10] As Husserl remarks, "for myself I am also a stranger for those who are strangers for me."[11] There may thus be ethnological research of Western culture practiced by the Japanese or Africans, penetrating the Western monopoly. There is more than one science of the other, because the concrete forms of alienness differ from each other like the foreignness of foreign languages differs from one language to the other. The different forms of ethnology are something like the prolongation of two gazes that cross each other but do not converge. As Lacan confirms, you will never catch sight of me where I see you and vice versa; I will never catch sight of you where you see me.[12] In a related sense, science of the alien is an occasional science with regard to the standpoint of the investigator in the same way that the so-called occasional expressions such as "I," "thou," "here," and "now" refer to the speaker's situation.

But if it is true that the different ways of looking at the other and the different investigations of the other do not converge and do not lead to a universal consent, how is it possible that we nevertheless have intercourse with each other, living in a common world? How is it possible to understand the other "without sacrificing him to our own logic or our own logic to him"? It is Merleau-Ponty who puts forth this question in his article "From Mauss to Lévi-Strauss."[13] He answers this question by going back to a specific form of ethnological experience that is capable of testing the self through the others and the others through ourselves. The ethnologist is able to make this experience because there is a "wild region of himself which is not invested in its own culture and by which he communicates with the others."[14] If we were completely at home in our own culture, the other would remain completely outside of it; there would not be any threshold between our own world and that of the other. A threshold, that is, a place of passage or transition we cross but do not surpass in a definitive way.

The same problem has been articulated by Lévi-Strauss in one of his latest publications. In a speech on the topic of "The place of Japanese culture in the world," delivered in Kyoto in 1988,[15] Lévi-Strauss starts out from a certain incommensurability of cultures. This leads him to the dilemma that we have no common criteria for judging foreign cultures because either we take them from our own culture, breaching the rules of objectivity, or we take them from the foreign culture, giving up our own standards. Faced with this dilemma, Lévi-Strauss invokes the attraction (and, we should add, repulsion) of the other culture: the invitation, incitation, or appeal to which the ethnologist's look responds and that initiates his research without being integrated into its results. This kind of attraction is the intercultural and also the ethnological phenomenon par excellence. Renouncing this phenomenon means renouncing the ethnological experience from which every science of the alien has to start. This science escapes from its self-dissolution only if the alien is more than something not yet known or understood. But what does this "more" mean, that attracts or repulses us? What kind of logos is capable of doing justice to it?

Response to the Other

In order to avoid the dilemma of either dissolving the alien by appropriation or dissolving the own by expropriation, I offer not a better definition of the alien but rather a certain change of attitude. Instead of asking *what* the alien is or *how* it functions, I take the alien as *what* we respond *to* and what we must respond to, whatever we say or do. That means that we can speak of the alien only in an indirect way, understanding it as something other and more than our familiar conceptions and projects suggest.

What we respond to is a kind of invitation, provocation, stimulus, incentive, or call, a kind of *Anspruch* to be characterized as a combination of appeal and claim. These are different shades of something belonging to the same dimension of challenge and response. The alien should be understood not as something at which our saying and doing aims but as something from which it starts. It resembles surprising or frightening noises like a cry in the night, or *Einfällen*, that is, ideas that come to us not when *we* want them but when *they* will. These are events that precede our intentions: they strike or overcome us, deviating from and exceeding our intentions. This inexhaustibility of the alien could be illustrated by examples from different fields of experience. Why does Sophocles' *Oedipus the King* continue to move us, although we already know what will happen? Why does a pianist play again and again Beethoven's last sonatas, although he knows them by heart and by finger? What is the force of attraction by which the eros surpasses the pure satisfaction of sexual needs and resists the trend of pure habitualization? What is the sense of the Jewish prohibition of images that also makes sense beyond the region of religion, as in Levinas's emphasis on the human face that cannot be described as something or somebody we represent and get to know?

What has been said in a very sketchy way has far reaching consequences. If all our saying and doing and also our looking at and listening to is a sort of responsive at-tention, then we are forced to revise the famous theories of intentional acts or rule-guided behavior, and replace them with a theory of responsiveness. Of course, the response cannot be reduced to the pure causal effect of a stimulus as behaviorists formerly assumed; instead we must free these key concepts from their behavioristic framework.[16]

But that means that our behavior is not only related to sense and rules, but first of all it is related to an appeal that stimulates it. Without such an appeal nothing will happen at all. Insofar as this appeal is not yet normalized and will never be completely normalized, that is, reduced to an ordinary event, it does not have sense and does not follow rules but rather provokes sense and exceeds rules. There we find a barrier against every sort of appropriation that either derives the alien from the own or bridges the gap between the two. What the alien is or means is determined during and by the event of response, and it will thus never be determined in a complete and univocal sense. The different attempts to appropriate the alien are based on a certain oblivion. They forget the difference between *what we respond to and the answers we give* while responding to a certain appeal. I call this difference responsive difference.

But there remains a last objection. One might argue that at least the answer I give belongs to me as my own answer. So, in a certain sense, responding would still remain centered on myself as a speaker. To this objection I would reply as follows: There are different kinds of answers, more reproductive and more productive ones. If an answer is given that not only reproduces and transports an existing sense but, on the contrary, produces and invents sense, then in giving such a creative answer, the respondent *gives what he did not have before.* Modifying a famous dictum by Kleist, we could speak of fabricating thoughts by responding to the other. These thoughts belong neither to me nor to the other. They are something between us, and such a "between" is the root of every form of inter-subjectivity and inter-culturality.

Notes

1. I thank Mike Mulcahy for his linguistic assistance. As to this difference, see Ricoeur's last work: *Soi-même comme un autre* (Paris: Editions du Seuil, 1990).

2. See Edmund Husserl, *Cartesianische Meditationen*, Husserliana I (The Hague, 1950), 144; English trans. 1960, 114, and in addition, my paper "Experience of the Alien in Husserl's Phenomenology," *Research in Phenomenology* 20 (1990): 19–33.

3. Maurice Merleau-Ponty, *Le Visible et l'invisible* (Paris: Gallimard, 1964), 308; trans. Alphonso Lingis, *The Visible and the Invisible* (Evanston: Northwestern University Press, 1968), 254.

4. Emmanuel Levinas, *Le temps et l'autre* (Montpellier: Fata Morgana, 1979), 196; trans. Richard Cohen, *Time and the Other* (Pittsburgh: Duquesne University Press, 1987).

5. *Standard Edition of the Complete Psychological Works of Sigmund Freud*, ed. and trans. J. Strachey, A. Freud, A. Strachey, and A. Tyson (London: Hogarth, 1955–74), 17:241.

6. John Locke, The Second Treatise of Government, V.

7. For more on the concept of order I use, see *Ordnung im Zwielicht* (Frankfurt am Main: Suhrkamp, 1987).

8. Hans-Georg Gadamer, *Wahrheit und Methode*, 2nd ed. (Tübingen: Siebeck, 1965), 365.

9. See Claude Lévi-Strauss, *Anthropologie structurale II* (Paris: Gallimard, 1973), chap. 2.

10. See Marc Augé's contribution to *L'autre et le semblable*, ed. M. Segalen (Paris, 1989).

11. Edmund Husserl, *Zur Phänomenologie der Intersubjektivität*, 3. Teil, Husserliana XV (The Hague, 1973), 635.

12. See *Le Séminaire de Jacques Lacan*, bk. 9, Les Quatre concepts fondamentaux de la psychoanalyse (Paris 1973), 95.

13. Maurice Merleau-Ponty, *Signes* (Paris: Gallimard, 1960), 144.

14. Ibid., 151.

15. French version: "La place de la culture japonaise dans le monde," *Revue d'esthétique* 18 (1990).

16. It is Kurt Goldstein who in his medical studies speaks of a deficient responsiveness (*Responsivität*) of the organism in order to explain the behavior of the patient (*Der Aufbau des Organismus* [The Hague: Martinus Nijhoff, 1934], 270). Concerning this issue see also my books: *Ordnung im Zwielicht* and *Der Stachel des Fremden* (Frankfurt am Main: Suhrkamp, 1990), which are part of a larger project dealing with the problem of responsiveness.

CHAPTER 3

Xenophobia, Xenophilia, and No Place to Rest

ANGELIKA BAMMER

In 1981 Gayatri Spivak's English translation of a short story by the Bengali writer Mahasveta Devi was published in *Critical Inquiry*. This story, "Draupadi," and the translator's foreword that accompanied it, has, along with a later essay by Spivak, "Can the Subaltern Speak?,"[1] been a frequent touchstone of debate within the developing field of cultural studies in general and post-colonial studies in particular. Its contribution (as indeed that of all of Spivak's work) has been to identify and begin to investigate some of the most urgent questions in the analysis of the global politics of culture: Who speaks for whom and with what authority? What is the relationship between "our" (Western-based) critical theories and interpretive practices and "their" ("Third World" situated) knowledge, struggles, and experience?

"Draupadi" takes place in West Bengal (the northern Naxalbari region) in 1971. Having just entered the by then armed struggle between East and West Pakistan with its own military forces, the Indian government has seized the opportunity to crack down on the local rebellion by a coalition of peasants and intellectuals against the fraudulent collaboration between landholders and government. This rebellion, in operation since the late 1960s, has now begun to spawn a series of similar rebellions throughout the subcontinent and has thus become a real threat to the existing hegemony. It is at this point in the conflict that the story's action unfolds.

The narrative paradigm of "Draupadi" is a villain/hero plot. The hero, Draupadi, is a tribal woman wanted by the authorities for her participation in the rebellion; the story recounts the events leading to her eventual apprehension, torture, and rape. The villain is Senanayak, an Indian army officer, "specialist in combat and extreme-Left politics." It is he who has Draupadi taken prisoner and orders her subjugation

45

with the words, "Make her. *Do the needful*" (281). "Draupadi," together with Spivak's presentation of the text, problematizes the very categories (categories that have been subjected to intense critical scrutiny in academic cultural studies in recent years)—"First World"/"Third World," for example, or "primitive"/"civilized"—in the name of which the violence of the plot unfolds. Using the narrative paradigm of Mahasveta's story as a model, the translator's foreword begins by positioning us ("First-World scholar[s] in search of the Third World" [261]) in the villain role: Senanayak, Spivak suggests, is essentially us, at least he is the "closest approximation" (261). The translated text, published and circulated within the context of Western academic circles dedicated to critical theory and progressive politics (feminist, deconstructive, and Marxist work in the fields of minority discourse, postcolonial and marginalized cultures), is thus presented as a mirror in which "we" are enjoined to behold ourselves.

Yet where and in whom? The issue is immediately complicated by the fact that Senanayak (and thus, to the extent that he is us, we, too) sees the very others he is pitted against within himself. Through a process of projective identification, he has become them, as it were. He has come to know them so well (in some ways, "better than they [know] themselves" [273]), that he has come to think and even feel like them in a way; he has come to understand "them by (*theoretically*) becoming one of them" (274). The emphasis, however, (albeit a parenthetical one) is on the word *theoretically*. "Theoretically," Senanayak has become like "them," these tribals whose insurrection challenges not only his authority but the grounds on which that authority is based. In Senanayak's case these grounds are represented both by the Army Handbook he consults and the classical texts of Western culture ("He is Prospero as well" [274]) that constitute his legitimating frame of reference.

"In theory Senanayak can identify with the enemy," even as "in practice, he must destroy [them]" (261). For in practice, of course, he is not like "them" at all: their languages, their methods, their aims—their frames of reference, in short—are different. And it is this latter—sameness and difference in practice—that "Draupadi" focuses on. In so doing, the "First World"/"Third World" categories that it and the introduction invoke are immediately de-essentialized. Spivak pointedly eschews a nativist stance in favor of a situationalist politics: what matters she maintains, is not who we see ourselves as (the well- or ill-intentioned projective identification), but who we *functionally* are. It is in this sense that Spivak includes herself in the "we" for whom Senanayak stands: "as I look in the glass . . .," she writes, "it is Senanayak . . . that I behold" (262).

The approximation between us and Senanayak, Spivak explains, lies less in the arguable fact that the tools we use ("instruments of First World life and investigation" [261]) are complicit in the appropriation or degradation of Third World peoples. Rather, it lies in the degree to which we are "pluralist aesthete(s)" (261) or, at least, function as such: someone for whom the other is a source of curiosity and exoticized interest; an object of study. For a pluralist aesthete (even one imbued with multicultural p.c.) the other is not a subject with whom to engage in an attempt to understand what "difference" really means—what it has meant historically and what it feels like—but an object to be taken up in the self-serving quest for stimulation, entertainment, or new markets. The problem, as Spivak here and elsewhere insistently points out, lies, not in our intentions, but in the systemic violences of which we are a part and from which we, willy-nilly, profit.

Senanayak carries an "*anti-Fascist paperback* copy of [Hochhuth's] *The Deputy*" with him even on search-and-destroy missions; he writes articles in which he demonstrates his support for the rebellion "from the point of view of the field hands" (280) even as he orders and carries out orders that this rebellion—and the "field hands" engaged in it—be put down. As he is portrayed in this text, Senanayak is less evil than ill, a man suffering from the peculiar illness that Renato Rosaldo has diagnosed as "imperialist nostalgia": the desire to have back that (or those) one has participated in destroying.[2] As he destroys his enemy and in so doing successfully carries out the mission with which he has been charged, he is thus "at once triumphant and despondent" (280). For he at once hates and loves this other whom he, in his obsession, both has become and can never be. He suffers from xenophobia *and* xenophilia.

When an other is perceived as threatening, it is precisely, I would argue, for the degree to which this other seems not just "different" but—uncannily—strangely familiar, even, one might say "same." The resulting dilemma is how to respond to this threat in a way that removes this other(ness) without undoing one's self in the process. The primal horde of Freud's "Totem and Taboo" resolves this dilemma in the most compellingly logical of ways: it destroys the threatening other in its midst by literally incorporating him into itself. This is the extreme gesture of xenophilia: the devouring embrace that takes the other in until there is nothing left of "them" but us. The alternative—the non-appropriative approach "that leaves the other alive in her/its place"[3]—is infinitely more difficult and risky.

The purpose of this essay is to raise questions about some of the ways in which this conflict between fear of and desire for the other— between the impulse to destroy and the counterimpulse to embrace— plays itself out in academic cultural studies contexts. I will accept as an operating assumption Spivak's contention that we ("pluralist aesthetes of the First World") are, effectively, Senanayak, wielding "instruments of First-World life and investigation" that can be seen as, and indeed often are ("willy-nilly," as Spivak drily adds), complicit with the appropriation, degradation, and, in the extreme, destruction of those others for whom Draupadi—the tortured and laughing dark-bodied tribal woman—stands in. Obviously, the violence enacted upon the protagonist of Mahasveta's story—upon the body of a woman, an "illiterate" tribal, a "native" from the "Third World"—is not the same as the act of reading or studying (about) her from the remove of our "First World" privilege. Yet in this very remove, in the distance between her and us, lies the danger that we might lose sight of the fact that the "objects" of our study are also and, above all, agential subjects: subjects to whom we are connected ("willy-nilly," again) across our respective differences.[4]

Like Senanayak, we (progressive-minded, cultural studies intellectuals), presuming ourselves, like him, to be globally informed, know that, as he puts it, "turn by turn the world will change" (274). And, like Senanayak, our aim, in light of this fact, is to "have the credentials to survive with honor...in every world" (274). For Senanayak this means that "if he can change color from world to world," he can remain in charge and continue to "represent the particular world in question" (274). The question to be negotiated is the price, exacted and paid on all sides, for this process of changing color. For the stakes are not just, as Senanayak puts it, "survival with honor"; they are also (and this he judiciously keeps to himself) the renegotiation of power in a changing world. Senanayak is willing to "change color," to "go native," as it were, so that his power—his ability "to represent the particular world in question" in both senses of the word *represent*[5]—can remain in place and unchallenged. What this means—whether honor and power can go together and make common cause, whether they can work together toward emancipatory ends or are effectively locked in a struggle of conflicting interests, whether and how "changing color" as a strategem of resistance on the part of the marginalized and oppressed is different from the "same" tactic on the part of those in power to keep these very "others" under surveillance and in check—are questions we must consider in the process. In order to map out the conceptual and political terrain that these questions traverse, I will engage two opposing positions, one by Tzvetan Todorov, the other by Homi Bhabha: the former arguing for the relativizing discrimination of universalism, the latter cautioning against its totalizing erasure of difference.

Ethics and Universalism

Tzvetan Todorov's *Les Morales de l'histoire* (The Morals of History) is divided into two parts: "Face aux autres" (Facing the Other) and "Entre nous" (Among Ourselves). The first section, "Facing the Other," concludes with an essay entitled "Remarques sur le croisement des cultures" (Notes on the Crossing [*croisement*] of Cultures). It begins with an observation that is no less provocative for being so indisputable:

> In undertaking to reflect on intercultural relations we come up against a peculiar difficulty, which is that the whole world already seems to have reached agreement on their ideal state. It is really quite astonishing: even as racist acts proliferate, no one lays claim to a racist ideology. Everyone is for peace, for coexistence in a state of mutual understanding, for fair and equitable exchanges; this is proclaimed at international conferences, affirmed at special meetings, repeated by the media; and yet we continue to live in a state of incomprehension and conflict.[6]

Already implicit in Todorov's assessment of the state of things is the position that xenophobia (which in practice often takes the form of what he rather obliquely refers to as "racist acts" (*comportements racistes*) and xenophilia are two sides of the same coin. What passes as progressive multiculturalism, Todorov proposes—the refusal to judge other cultures, cultures different from one's own—is often less a recognition of difference based on an interactive *engagement* with the other than a *failure to engage*, a fear of unintentionally exposing one's own culturally learned ignorance and biases. "Behind the fear of judging," Todorov writes, "is the spectre of racism" (115). In this light, some of what passes as tolerance is less an enlightened ideal than a form of moral weakness. Instead of an affirmation of values one holds to be true, it signals a suspension of values.

Xenophilia, as Todorov describes it, is an act of disconnection from our cultural moorings. By this he does not mean that to be of a culture is to be grounded, or rooted, in that culture ("humans are not trees," he remarks, ". . . that is precisely our privilege" [119–20]). Rather, he insists, to be of a culture is to be an involved participant in the constant process of negotiation (or "translation," as he prefers) among and between its many internal cultures. For culture, he insists, is never singular, much less homogeneous; it is always heterogeneous and plural, a hybrid amalgam of the many different cultures of which it is constituted. He thus rejects not only the reactionary model that defines culture only in terms of a single, national(ist) tradition but also the model traditionally favored by the Left that opposes (emancipatory, but oppressed) "minority" cultures to a (powerful, but oppressive) "hegemonic" culture. To be of a culture conceived in national terms (to be "French," say, or "Bulgarian") is, as Todorov explains, both to invoke a structural artifice and to signify one's involvement in this intracultural translating process. Xenophilia is a step outside that process, an act of imaginative projection into the culture of an other rather than the mutually challenging process of intra- and intercultural engagement.

Whether it takes the form of what he calls "cultural malinchismo" ("the blind adulation of Western values" [112]) or the reverse gaze through Western eyes toward the "noble savage," such xenophilia is an attempt to disown the culture-in-process of which we are a part; it is a call, not for change, but for substitution. Effectively, then, and this is the focus of Todorov's concern, such an act of self-displacement puts in jeopardy our ability to make moral judgments, as we are no longer part of the process of negotiating values, means, and ends that is intrinsic to being of a culture. The result of such disconnectedness is an ultimately amoral relativism. And, as Todorov suggests, such relativism could not inconceivably lead to "tolerance" of such things as gas chambers or human sacrifice on the basis of the argument that they are the domain of another culture before which we liberal-mindedly suspend judgment.[7] Against such relativism Todorov argues for certain "absolute principles" (113). In acts of judgment, therefore—acts not to be confused with acts of knowing (the epistemological) or acts of advocacy/ intervention (the political)—he proposes a kind of universalism: "I must be able to say not that a certain culture as a whole is superior or inferior to another...but that a certain aspect of a culture, whether it be our own or another, a certain form of cultural behavior, should be condemned or lauded" (116). This does not, he hastens to add, means transcendence (rising above our particularity) nor insularity (limiting the world to our own boundaries). Rather, it means evolving our principles of judgment out of our commitment and responsibility to the culture—our own—in which we are participating agents. At the same time—and this is the critical nexus on which his argument turns—we must understand that culture to be in a continual process of (trans)-formation through its relations of contiguity and contingency with others.

It is in their denial of these relations that xenophobia and xenophilia not only resemble one another but are harmful in similar ways. Xenophobia calls for a politics of repression; xenophilia tries to deny this repression. In practice, this denial of repression means that the xenophiliac takes the xenophobe's stance and turns it upside down; the one professes to love what the other claims to hate. The process of othering, however, by which the subjectivity of the other person or group was initially eclipsed—they remain "they"—remains unchanged and unchallenged.

This was precisely the problem that Rainer Werner Fassbinder wanted to address with his play *Garbage, the City and Death.* Scheduled to be staged in Frankfurt during the 1974–75 theater season, it was instead cancelled in the wake of massive protests against its perceived anti-Semitism. As Daniel Cohn-Bendit noted,[8] defending Fassbinder and the legitimacy of his play, what has typically taken place in German contexts around questions of Jewishness and anti-Semitism is "shadow boxing with history rather than an attempt to deal with the current situation."[9] The controversy generated by Fassbinder's depiction of a "Rich Jew"[10] who was neither noble nor (in any obvious way, at least) a victim, dragged the debate over German anti-Semitism out of the shadows of the past and resituated it in an emotionally charged encounter between Germans and Jews in contemporary West Germany. As such it was, as Cohn-Bendit maintained, both "important and good."[11] The point, as Fassbinder saw it, was to counter the repression and displacement of anti-Semitism into a cloying philo-Semitism by "show[ing] opportunistic philo-Semitism to be merely an introverted form of anti-Semitism."[12] This "opportunistic" link between philo-Semitism and anti-Semitism[13] ("now that antifascism and active solidarity with Jews are available for free, they're crawling out of the woodwork, the hypocrites,"[14] Fassbinder commented cynically) was dramatically demonstrated in the controversy over *Garbage, the City and Death* in the alliance that was formed between the German Jewish Community (Jüdische Gemeinde) and the ruling conservative Christian Democratic Party (CDU) under the leadership of the Frankfurt Mayor Walter Wallmann.[15] More recently, in the United States, we witnessed a particularly American version of such an alliance, this time turning on the issues of gender and race, in the spectacle of white, male senators (including such notable racists as Strom Thurmond) rushing to embrace the cause of antiracism in the name of an African American man: Supreme Court nominee Clarence Thomas. In each case, a culturally and historically specific variant of xenophilia was employed in a struggle for power in which the self-interest of those in power at stake was only dimly concealed. In the case of Clarence Thomas, the rhetoric of race was used to deflect attention from the conservative and male interests Judge Thomas's election would presumably serve. In the Frankfurt case, the accusation of anti-Semitism was used to detract attention from the interest of real-estate speculators in keeping capital-poor immigrant and migrant workers out of lucrative neighborhoods.

Needless to say, the Left is not immune to such machinations. One need only think of the particular twist given the German philo-/anti-Semitism turn by the New Left in the sixties and seventies when it embraced the cause of the Palestinians as a displaced expression of anti-Israel sentiment. Wearing a *kafiyya* (a Palestinian headscarf) was, for the duration, almost a necessary part of a radical student's uniform; by contrast, Judaica (the Star of David, for example) were noticeably absent icons. What was (once again) repressed, in the process, was the history of German anti-Semitism and its genocidal past, a history that rendered a critically differentiated discussion of Israel in the present difficult and intensely uncomfortable.

Such a turn (from anti- to philo-, from -phobia to -philia) is obviously easier to effect than the laborious deconstruction of a hardened stance from the inside. In an illuminating article on the "'New' South Africa," Rob Nixon details the difficulties entailed in any process of deconstruction and, using his own country of South Africa as an example, illustrates some of the reasons why such a process is necessary.[16] In so doing he also shows how and why the hero/villain paradigm is problematic.[17] The problem is most evident in the rhetorical slippage in public debate from the political to the ethical. The equation of power with oppression—an equation that renders power "bad" while equating powerlessness with goodness—is often the beginning of this slide. A good other, in these terms, is a victimized other; powerlessness is recast as the moral high ground. The danger of this position becomes evident in the backlash reaction when these "poor, but good" folk—whether they be Native Americans, Black South Africans, or Turkish migrant workers in Germany—begin to speak out, not as victims, but as subjects in their own right who know and watch out for their own interests.[18]

Drawing a complex sketch of a South Africa in the throes of transition, Nixon warns of accepting as fact the "end of apartheid" proclaimed by De Klerk in February 1990. His warning is addressed in particular to well-meaning progressives—liberals and the Left—for whom the anti-apartheid cause had long played the role of a kind of holy war. The hero/villain scenario had been staged as if history were a medieval morality play: Mandela, the Black African liberator, had taken on messianic proportions, while De Klerk's White South African predecessors (Hendrik Verwoerd, John Vorster, and P. W. Botha) had easily filled the diabolic counter-role. The success of the anti-apartheid cause as a world movement, Nixon proposes, "was in large part proportionate to the Manichean clarity of the issues at stake, as a showdown between good and evil, victims and villains, Black and White, oppressed and oppressors, the people and a racist minority" (18). This "Manichean clarity" blurred in the comparatively more benign, good-will atmosphere of the De Klerk regime, an atmosphere clouded, at the same time, by events such as the trial (and subsequent conviction) of Winnie Mandela and the bloody Inkatha/ANC feuding that tarnished the noble victim image traditionally conferred on South African Blacks. When the "stark binaries" no longer fit, Nixon notes, "confusion and disillusion" (18, 20) set in.[19]

In a telling example Nixon illustrates both how these binaries had for such a long time been maintained as matters of fact and why this "fact" had seemed so necessary. In his recreation of the Soweto uprising of June 1976 for *Cry Freedom*, he recounts, the film director Richard Attenborough had deliberately "decided to omit the presence of black policemen on these grounds: 'To have had blacks firing at blacks, would have been too confusing'" (19). The story of history was thus rearranged to fit a hero/villain plot that could be converted more easily into political mobilizing currency. The price paid by all in the process was the inability to follow the story as it went on past the point where the familiar plot had become functional. In concrete terms, as Nixon documents, this meant that media coverage declined and international attention shifted elsewhere; the South African players, meanwhile, were left to their own—unequal and often desperate—devices.

Difference and Diversity

In his opening presentation at the 1985 Conference on Bilingualism in Rabat, Todorov described the way "multiculturalism" was being orchestrated and played out at the time within French avant-garde intellectual circles: "There is currently a kind of multiple identity craze [*euphorie du dédoublement*] in those circles that think of themselves as avant-garde, at least in France; works that glorify cosmopolitanism, that go on about the beauty of the mestizo, and that speak with passion of multilingualism have multiplied of late."[20] Against this "doubling euphoria" he sets the actual, not metaphorical, experience of exile. Specifically, he describes his recent experience (in 1981) of returning to his native Bulgaria for the first time since his emigration in the early sixties and finding himself reunited for a brief, ten-day visit with family and old friends in his "home town," Sofia. However, instead of the fashionable "euphoria of disharmony" his Bakhtin-quoting, identity-deconstructing colleagues in Paris might have expected him to feel, his return home is more "an experience of malaise and psychic oppression" (20). What others extol as the cosmopolitan rush of multiculturalism represents for him a state closer to schizophrenia: he feels divided within himself, or, as Adrienne Rich puts it, "split at the root."[21]

The atmosphere described by Todorov in which it is "in" to be multicultural—to, if not "be," then "go," ethnic or native—is one that is not unfamiliar to us in American cultural studies circles. Indeed, it is a stance enacted as well as analyzed of late in an increasing number of disciplines.[22] "Going native" is a way of accommodating a state of flux in which cultural identities (individually and in the relationships within and between groups) are continually being destabilized: "going (as opposed to being) native" acknowledges at one and the same time both the constructedness, hence provisional status, of any identity and the need to be grounded, even if provisionally, in a locatable place ("going native" as a cosmopolitan gesture). The situation that gave rise to this stance is evocatively sketched in James Clifford's introduction to *The Predicament of Culture*. Clifford begins by describing the state in which we find ourselves ("ethnographic modernity") as one in which being "off center among scattered traditions . . . is an increasingly common fate" (3). Rather than lament this state as one of "lost authenticity," however, he reconfigures it as one in which "a truly global space of cultural connections and dissolutions has become imaginable," a trans- or pluricultural space in which "local authenticities meet and merge in transient settings" (4). While the achievement of this state undeniably entails destruction and loss (the negative pole of the "predicament" of his title), Clifford nevertheless emerges with a positive outlook on emergent "cultural futures."[23] In this uncertain, but nevertheless utopian, light, "[t]he 'filth' that an expansive West . . . has thrown in the face of the world's societies" still undeniably remains filth, but it also becomes "compost for new orders of difference" (15).

What does this have to do with the topic at hand: the relationship between xenophobia and xenophilia? In a way, it simply does away with it, problematizing the assumptions of otherness on which these categories rest to such a point that they ultimately—deconstructed— disappear. If, as Clifford puts it, "identity considered ethnographically, must always be mixed, relational, and inventive" (10), the boundaries between "self" and "other" are effectively undone. Yet only theoretically (or textually, perhaps) is the crossing, much less dissolution, of boundaries, thus uncomplicated. In practice—even in historically minded theoretical or textual practices—the case is generally quite different. The difference is the difference that power makes. Xenophilia, for example, is not the same in its "cultural *malinchismo*" form as in its "noble savage" projection. The envious, admiring, or desirous gaze projected from the West onto its other (Mr. Kurtz's gaze, say) is not the same as the gaze with which a Malintzin Tenepal[24] might have beheld the *conquistadores*. The "noble savage" (or "authentic native") myth represents an act of appropriation: the other is brought in (physically, as was the practice in the eighteenth and nineteenth centuries when "natives" or "savages" were put on display in European capitals, or discursively/symbolically, as is now the custom) to entertain, revitalize, or in some other way assist a perhaps ailing, but still hegemonic, culture. Cultural *malinchismo*, on the other hand, is an act of *disap*-propriation: the native culture is shed for the price of access to an other—dominant and dominating—culture whose hegemony is thus acknowledged and affirmed.[25] Individually, then, the tales a Kurtz or a Malinche, say, tell are very different, particularly if one reads them in light of the historical impact of the tellers' actions on their respective cultures. Each culture is transformed in and through the encounter with the other; but the one (Kurtz's colonial empire) is empowered while the other (La Malinche's native culture) is brought down. It is when they are read together that these two stories eventually converge to become two variants of one story: the (hi)story of the hegemony of the West in relation to its "other"—colonialism and racism inflected by gender and class—and the (hi)story of resistance to this domination.

And thus I return to the place where I began, namely Spivak's contention that "we" are Senanayak, in effect, if not intent. While Spivak begins by saying that she "will not go so far as to suggest that, in practice, the instruments of First-World life and investigation are complicit with" the construction and maintenance of "First World" hegemony, she, in so saying, suggests it. Todorov would probably submit that the difference lies in the ends to which these "instruments" are put. Do they circulate as objects of use and exchange in a constantly renegotiated (multi)cultural economy or are they wielded as the sole power currency in a global economy that is increasingly monocultural? Homi Bhabha, who like Spivak speaks from the position of a "post-colonial critic,"[26] leaves the question open. The complicity that Spivak is inclined to deny is, according to Bhabha, a matter for investigation. A critical cultural studies, he notes, should not foreclose on, but vigorously investigate, such questions as

> whether the "new" languages of theoretical critique (semiotic, post-structuralist, deconstructionist etc.) simply reflect those ["Third World"/"West"] geopolitical divisions and spheres of influence? Are the interests of "Western" theory necessarily collusive with the hegemonic role of the West as a power bloc? Is the specialized, "textualized", often academic language of theory merely another power ploy of the culturally privileged Western élite to produce a discourse of the Other that sutures its own power-knowledge equation?[27]

Such an investigation could, no doubt, begin by considering the relative weight of the string of qualifiers ("simply," "necessarily," "merely") in Bhabha's questions. It could also begin by probing the significance of these questions to the current debates over "multiculturalism" in academia.

Bhabha begins by positing that "cultural diversity" is the conceptual framework for the operative paradigm of multiculturalism. Yet diversity, its rhetoric to the contrary, he argues, ultimately constitutes a homogenizing grasp. As he puts it, the "creation of cultural diversity [entails] . . . a containment of cultural difference."[28] This is precisely why, he (like Todorov) points out, racism and multiculturalism can— and do—so easily co-exist. But where Todorov had argued for an enlightened form of universalism, Bhabha counters with the concept of a radical particularism. For "the universalism that . . . permits diversity," he insists, "masks ethnocentric norms, values and interests."[29]

Instead of diversity, what Bhabha calls for is a politics of *difference*: "the notion of a politics which is based on unequal, multiple and *potentially antagonistic*, political identities."[30] In the end, therefore, the politics of culture envisioned by Bhabha—a politics based on the recognition of conflict and even incommensurability—stands in marked contrast to the cultural agenda proposed by Todorov. Todorov insists not only that differences can be accommodated in a social community but that they are constitutive of it. For, as he sees it, it is the constant work of intra- and intercultural contact and translation that allows a culture to function. Moreover, it is this process of translation that effectively constitutes a "trans"cultural realm beyond the particularity of each contributing culture. For this reason, he concludes, "[t]here is no reason whatsoever to renounce the idea of a human [or cultural] universality;"[31] we can have universality without giving up particularity. Indeed, he insists, we must work *through* the particular (*il faut la creuser*) "until we discover the universal within it."[32] Bhabha's counter is blunt and uncompromising: "The difference of cultures cannot . . . be accommodated," he concludes, "within a universalist framework."[33] The space of difference, as he sees it, begins at the limits of (Western) liberal relativism; it is there that differences meet, but without reconciling translation. What happens, in this model, to concepts like 'human rights'—a concept based on the assumption of transcultural, if not universal, values—remains a haunting and perplexing open question.[34]

The Todorov model tries to avoid conflict by appealing to something shared (a common humanity, common interests, similar conditions of desire or fear); in the process, it tries to uphold the Enlightenment ideal of civil (civilized?) society. Nowhere is this agenda more evident than in a remarkable, recent short text by Julia Kristeva: an open letter to Harlem Désir, the co-founder and one of the principal organizers of the French anti-racist coalition group, SOS Racisme.[35] In this letter, dated February 1990, Kristeva calls for a return to the "revolutionary universalism" contained in the spirit of the French (not the German, she hastens to clarify) Enlightenment. The perfect (and again, she adds, particularly *French*) exemplar of this spirit is Montesquieu's *De l'esprit des lois*. For, as Kristeva sees it, Montesquieu offers a model of civil society within the framework of national culture based on "integration without homogenization" (*intégration sans nivellement*). Moreover, she goes on, in such a society in which the "spirit of concord" has elevated the nation to a communitarian plane beyond struggles for power and internecine strife, the relationship between "us" and "them" could be commensurately civilized: "we" could show respect for "them" (those "others" that "we" have generously let in), while "they" could show "us" their gratitude (31). Kristeva thus takes Todorov's emphasis on active participation in a cultural community a decisive (and, to my mind, deeply problematic) step further by suggesting that in the interests of civil society we need to live by the standards and basic codes of the national community ("France," say) with which we, by choosing to live there, have signalled affiliation.[36]

Countering this integrationist, let's-all-be-civilized model is the one put forth by Bhabha, a model that assumes that conflict cannot be avoided because it is endemic to the situation we are in: not a people united (unité nationale) by common outlook (esprit général), to use Kristeva's/Montesquieu's terms, but rather a fluctuating, contestable mix of groups of people with "different sorts of interests, different kinds of cultural histories, different post colonial lineages, different sexual orientations."[37] In short, as Bhabha sees it, the "place of difference and otherness" is "the space of the adversarial."[38]

One obvious problem with the "spirit of concord" model is that it assumes a historically altogether unwarranted state of mutual good will. In reality, as we know, this good will dissipates quickly when the expected response ("respect" or "gratitude," say) is not forthcoming. In that case, "-philia" all too quickly reverts to its inverse to become phobic. When the "natives" become restless, they all too often—even to the most xenophilic gaze—tend to appear more "savage" and less "noble." Disappointment over the fact that the other is not who we thought (or wanted or needed) them to be can easily turn into vengeful resentment. On the other hand, to posit the "place of difference and otherness . . . [as] the space of the adversarial" also leaves a self/other model too much in place. For difference is not only the oppositional line separating "hegemonic" and "marginal" it is also the sometimes uneven, sometimes almost invisible line that runs through and between diverse and historically different groups of "others," such as Jews and Turks in Germany, African Americans and Asian Americans, or Xhosas and Zulus in South Africa.

One of the challenges we all (particularly to the extent that we are Senanayak) face is understanding the ways in which epistemological/ analytic, moral, and political categories are separate and at the same time inseparable. (For this reason, it seems to me that any recourse to the Enlightenment would more profitably take us to Kant than to Montesquieu.) "Right" in the epistemological/analytical sense is not necessarily "right" in the moral or political sense; indeed, they might be altogether different or even at odds. By the same token, things that appear separate or even opposite (xenophobia/xenophilia, say) are often just variants of the same base impulse: the anxiety over difference, the uneasy encounter with the racially, ethnically, or culturally defined other. This is why, as the second half of my title suggests, between xenophobia and xenophilia there is "no place to rest": both constitute the place of fear and denial from which we must, for all our sakes, move on.

Notes

1. Spivak's translation of "Draupadi" was first published in *Writing and Sexual Difference*, ed. Elizabeth Abel (Chicago: University of Chicago Press, 1982); it was reprinted in Spivak's *In Other Worlds: Essays in Cultural Politics* (New York and London: Methuen, 1987). References, given by page number in the main text, will be to the initial publication. "Can the Subaltern Speak?" appeared in *Marxism and the Interpretation of Culture*, ed. Cary Nelson and Lawrence Grossberg (Urbana: University of Illinois Press, 1987).

2. Renato Rosaldo, "Imperialist Nostalgia," in *Culture & Truth: The Remaking of Social Analysis* (Boston: Beacon Press, 1989).

3. Hélène Cixous, "Poetry is/and (the) Political" (paper presented at "The Second Sex: Twenty Years Later," a conference on Simone de Beauvoir, New York, 1979), 2.

4. In *Simians, Cyborgs, and Women: The Reinvention of Nature* (London: Routledge, 1991), Donna Haraway examines the disastrous consequences of Western scientific practices that ignore (or deny) the subjective agency of the objects it studies.

5. For a critical and in-depth discussion of the doubled meaning of *representation*, particularly as it has been deployed within the framework of Marxist analyses and taken up by French "post-Marxist" theorists like Foucault and Deleuze, see Spivak's "Can the Subaltern Speak?" 276–79.

6. Tzvetan Todorov, *Les Morales de l'histoire* (Paris: Grasset, 1991), 109. My translations; additional citations are given in the text by page number.

7. This question of (multi)cultural relativism, particularly in light of the imbalance of power between the "West" and the "Third World," is at the heart of Alice Walker's novel *Possessing the Secret of Joy* (New York: Harcourt Brace Jovanovich, 1992). Walker acknowledges the historical complexity of the issue and the legitimacy of the argument for cultural autonomy. At the same time, her text is an impassioned demonstration of her belief that certain acts, such as the mutilation of others' (in this case, women's) bodies, spirits, and selves, are violations that cannot be "tolerantly" relativized.

8. Cohn-Bendit is well known as an activist from both the West German and French student movements of the late sixties and early seventies. Since 1989 he has been in charge of a special Office of Multicultural Affairs (Amt für Multikulturelle Angelegenheiten) in the West German city of Frankfurt. In the Fassbinder controversy, he was speaking, and

was called upon to speak, not just as a leftist activist, but also from his personal perspective as a German Jew. It is worth noting in this context that Frankfurt is a city that has not only traditionally been a center of German-Jewish culture and wealth, but that, more recently, became the German city with the highest percentage (20 percent) of so-called foreigners. (*Ausländerdichte*, "foreigner density," is an actual statistical category in Germany.) About two-thirds of these "foreigners" are migrant workers (*Gastarbeiter*) of whom the largest and most "othered" group have been the predominantly Muslim Turks. For a description and discussion of the class and ethnic dimensions (including the relationship between racism and anti-Semitism) of "multiculturalism" in present-day Frankfurt, see "Das Amt für multikulturelle Angelegenheiten—ein persuasives Programm" and the interview with Cohn-Bendit in Claus Leggewie, *Multi Kulti: Spielregeln für die Vielvölkerrepublik* (Berlin: Rotbuch Verlag, 1990), 46–68.

9. Elisabeth Kinderlen and Dany Cohn-Bendit, "Ein Vor-Gespräch anstelle eines Vorworts," in *Deutsch-jüdische Normalität . . . Fassbinders Sprengsätze*, ed. Elisabeth Kinderlen (Frankfurt am Main: Pflasterstrand 1985), 10.

10. The characters in the play are not personalized but, as their "names" make evident, deliberately stereotyped.

11. Elisabeth Kinderlen and Dany Cohn-Bendit, "Ein Vor-Gespräch," 8.

12. Daniel Cohn-Bendit, "Zeugen der Zeit: Gespräche zweier Betroffener," in *Deutsch-jüdische Normalität*, 33.

13. While certainly not limited to the German context, anti-Semitism and philo-Semitism are certainly (or, at least, have historically been) a particularly typical German form of xenophobia and xenophilia.

14. Ibid., 33.

15. In a later (1984) election campaign this same Wallmann, again running for office on the CDU ticket in Frankfurt, used racism, in particular xenophobic sentiment against Turks, as a central campaign strategy.

16. Rob Nixon, "'An Everybody Claim Dem Democratic': Notes on the 'New' South Africa," *Transition* 54 (Sept. 1991): 20–35.

17. Nixon's critique of the hero/villain model as a basis for historical judgment and political action is developed in "Mandela, Messianism, and the Media," *Transition* 51 (Jan. 1991): 42–55.

18. A related phenomenon is the ambivalence, criticism, and often downright hostility encountered by members of minority groups who attain status, power, and wealth as our colleagues in academia.

19. This state of confusion was nowhere more evident than in the state of the Left (beginning with the confusion over who "Left" referred to) in relation to the Gulf War in early 1991. The problem was how to rethink oppositional politics when the comfortable, old "Manichean clarities" of the 1960s—"poor, but noble" victims struggling against "evil and powerful" oppressors: Salvador Allende and the CIA, North Vietnamese peasants and General Electric—did not fit the current picture.

20. Tzvetan Todorov, "Bilinguisme, dialogisme et schizophrénie," in *Du bilinguisme*, ed. Abdelkebir Khatibi (Paris: Denoel, 1985).

21. I borrow the term from Adrienne Rich's essay "Split at the Root" in *Nice Jewish Girls: A Lesbian Anthology*, ed. Evelyn Torton Beck, rev. and exp. ed. (Boston: Beacon Press, 1989).

22. Most notably in cultural studies, broadly defined, and cultural anthropology, the phenomenon of "going native" has become an object of critical attention. It is an issue that is addressed in and informs, among others, James Clifford, *The Predicament of Culture: Twentieth-Century Ethnography, Literature, and Art* (Cambridge: Harvard University Press, 1988); Trinh T. Minh-ha, *Woman, Native, Other: Writing Postcoloniality and Feminism* (Bloomington: Indiana University Press, 1989), as well as a number of the contributions in *Writing Culture: The Poetics and Politics of Ethnography*, ed. James Clifford and George Marcus (Berkeley and Los Angeles: University of California Press, 1986). It is a central focus in Marianna Torgovnick, *Gone Primitive: Savage Intellects, Modern Lives* (Chicago: University of Chicago Press, 1990) and Rey Chow, "Where Have All the Natives Gone?" in *Displacements: Cultural Identities in Question*, ed. Angelika Bammer (Bloomington: Indiana University Press, forthcoming).

23. This sense of new possibilities emerging is reflected and will presumably be explored in a new journal, *Emergences*, founded in 1989–90 by The Group for the Study of Composite Cultures at UCLA.

24. A Mexican slave woman, Malintzin Tenepal is more commonly known by the name (La) Malinche, given her by her compatriots during the time of the Spanish conquest. Malintzin Tenepal served as a translator for Hernan Cortés and his army; she also became his mistress and bore his children. It is to these latter facts that the term *malinchismo* commonly refers. For a richly textured feminist analysis of the complex and ambiguous (hi)story of this Mexican/Chicana woman, see Norma Alarcón, "Traddutora, Traditora: A Paradigmatic Figure of Chicana Feminism," *Cultural Critique* 13 (fall 1989): 57–87.

25. In "Remarques sur le croisement des cultures," Todorov describes "cultural *malinchismo*" alternately as the "blind adulation of Western values" (112) and the "blind adoption of the values, the issues, and even the language of the metropolis" (121). However, he has elsewhere (notably in *The Conquest of America: The Conquest of the Other*, trans. Richard Howard [New York: Harper and Row, 1985]) presented a much more differentiated picture of this same gesture and the person, La Malinche, who gave it its name. As Alarcón points out, in *The Conquest of America* Malintzin Tenepal/La Malinche represents the "cross-breeding of cultures" and thus heralds not only "the modern state of Mexico" but "the present state of us all." Alarcón is quoting from Tzvetan Todorov, *The Conquest of America*, p. 101. As one who "glorifies mixture to the detriment of purity" (Todorov, *Conquest of America*, 101; quoted in Alarcón, "Traddutora, Traditora," 85), La Malinche, as Alarcón—and here, Todorov, too—sees her, is thus the paradigmatic figure of postmodern, hybrid identity.

26. See Gayatri Chakravorty Spivak, *The Post-Colonial Critic: Interviews, Strategies, Dialogues*, ed. Sarah Harasym (New York and London: Routledge, 1990).

27. Homi K. Bhabha, "The Commitment to Theory," New Formations 5 (fall 1987): 7.

28. Homi K. Bhabha and Jonathan Rutherford, "The Third Space" in *Identity: Community, Culture, Difference*, ed. J. Rutherford (London: Lawrence and Wishart, 1990), 208.

29. Ibid., 208.

30. Ibid., 208.

31. Todorov, "Remarques," 116.

32. Ibid., 122.

33. Bhabha and Rutherford, "Third Space," 209.

34. I am indebted to Leslie Adelson for reminding me of this particularly urgent question.

35. Julia Kristeva, "Lettre ouverte à Harlem Désir," in *Lettre ouverte à Harlem Désir* (Paris: Rivages, 1990), 15–37.

36. This is, of course, based on the assumption that this national community of our "choice" is a "free" and "democratic" society.

37. Bhabha, "Third Space," 208.

38. Homi K. Bhabha, "Signs Taken for Wonders: Questions of Ambivalence and Authority under a Tree Outside Delhi, May 1817," in *"Race," Writing and Difference*, ed. H. L. Gates, Jr. (Chicago: University of Chicago Press, 1986), 171.

CHAPTER 4

The Instincts of "Race" and "Text"

AARON PERKUS

It would be wonderful if there didn't have to be a debate over the curriculum and whether it is or isn't biased. It would be utterly fantastic if every text had an inherent essence, a transcendent quality that made the poetics of classification as easy as following a law of nature. This quality could then serve as an instinct—a text *instinct*. People would not have to huff and puff about the aesthetic and intellectual merit contained within the covers of these newly liberated textual citizens. Rather, the texts themselves would be instinctively attracted to their own kind. The role of the academic, therefore, would be miniscule (assuming that these texts are heterosexual). We would only need to facilitate this instinct by setting up a canon, an ample breeding ground for superior texts. The texts would be happy, we would be happy. But most of all, the National Association of Scholars[1] (NAS) would be happy—they could segregate the curriculum based on each text's manifest natural instinct.

One need only substitute the segregationalist term *race instinct* for the imagined term *text instinct*, and we are suddenly describing the activities of the New South during the period of post–Civil War Reconstruction. I believe that the fundamental similarities articulated by the process through which both the NAS and the New South commence nation building justifies reading these two communities against each other. My primary sources of comparison will be an article published in 1885 by the self-proclaimed "spokesman of the New South" Henry W. Grady entitled "In Plain Black and White"[2] and a two-page statement published by the NAS entitled *Is the Curriculum Biased?*.

I

Grady, aware that the New South's hegemony was being criticized by northerners, as well as liberal southerners, felt retaliation was in order:

63

The South cannot afford to be misunderstood . . . She cannot let pass unchallenged a single utterance that, spoken in her name, misstates her case or her intention. It is to protect against just such an injustice that this article is written.[3]

In a similar fashion, the NAS doesn't want its intentions misstated and thus responds to the proponents of multiculturalism:

We reject the allegations of "racism" and "sexism" that are frequently leveled against honest critics of the new proposals, and which only have the effect of stifling much-needed debate.[4]

By setting up a metonymous link between themselves and the position they are arguing from, both voices secure the authority and dignity of a gendered and racialized body being attacked—which masks the hegemony of their domination and discrimination. Michael Kimmel, in his article "The Cult of Masculinity," argues that this type of posturing is synonymous with the "American" stereotype. "The American acts aggressively, not like a bully, seeking a confrontation, but rather in response to provocation. . . . American aggression is usually, in this mythic representation, retaliatory, a response to an apparent injury."[5]

Henry Grady, as described in Ronald Takaki's *Iron Cages*, "called for reconciliation based on southern independence and industrial development—[He represented] the South and its postbellum commitment to progress."[6] These three terms: "southern independence," "industrial development," and "progress," when viewed against the backdrop of Enlightenment and social Darwinism, reveal the South's double agenda: (1) to gain independence from the North through industrialization and (2) to exercise self-rule apropos of "the new race of citizens."

In his essay "In Plain Black and White: A Reply to Mr. Cable," Grady agrees that the problem under debate is tremendous and that "it is important that this reply shall be plain and straightforward." Simply, he claims that "the South will never adopt Mr. Cable's suggestion of the social intermingling of the races. . . . Neither race wants it."[7] What the South does want, it would follow, is to continue adhering to its institutionally enforced "race instinct," which, when transgressed, surfaces as: "an antagonism . . . bred between the races when they are forced into mixed assemblages."[8] It is natural for races to remain apart, and to force people against their will, will produce "an internecine war."[9] Hence, by enforcing what is already seen as a natural instinct, the South is acting not only in the best interests of the White-supremacists who have always benefited from the status quo but in everybody's best interest. Segregation merely allows culture to proceed along its "great chain of being" uninterrupted.

Perhaps the New South never imagined "race" to be a scientific classification designed to discriminate and isolate any human whose "blood" was different then their own "Anglo-Saxon." To speak of "race" is to already have implied the problem through its canonical solution. This conception of a pure essence of race has never been mutually defined by "culture," "class," "gender," "language," "sexual orientation," and so on. All of these categories, like "race," made sense only when segregated from healthy normality. For Grady, it was simply a matter of superior and inferior blood. One hundred years later the NAS, whose slogan is: "For Reasoned Scholarship in a Free Society," has become alarmed by the "growing politicization" of the curriculum; it responds to the unnamed antagonists who wish to "reorient" the curriculum under the banner of "cultural diversity."

It is the primary chore of this essay to unpack the dirty laundry that has hitherto been hermetically sealed within the term *text*. I hope to place my reading close to the work of Lucius Outlaw's "Towards a Critical Theory of 'Race,'" which strives "to question 'race' as an obvious, biologically or metaphysically given, thereby self-evident reality."[10] Equally important has been Denise Riley's *Am I That Name?* in which she argues that "'women' is historically, discursively constructed, and always relative to other categories which themselves change."[11]

My argument holds that the category "text," far from representing a fixed object in the "real world," should be historicized in terms of the rhetorical hermeneutics that create the hegemony of "textuality" within social and academic practices. In other words, "texts" are constructed along the shifting and intersecting lines of "race," "gender," "class," "culture," and so forth; hence, one should not talk about a text apart from the historical conventions that named it as such.

The NAS, by choosing to include the word *reasoned* in their slogan, "For Reasoned Scholarship in a Free Society," has endorsed a word that, rather than transcending cultural differences, evokes what Foucault has called "hazardous plays of dominations."

As Henry Louis Gates asserts:

So, while the Enlightenment is characterized by its foundation
on man's ability to reason [only men can reason/ only Whites
are men/ only Western is White], it simultaneously used the
absence and presence of reason to delimit and circumscribe the
very humanity of the cultures and people of color which
Europeans had been "discovering" since the Renaissance.[12]

"The ability to reason" exists within a historically gendered and
racialized playing field that occludes alterity until it is discovered by
"society." Implicitly, to be "for reasoned scholarship" is to be for a
curriculum that is not "free" to everyone, only to those who possess
reason.   Enacting a circular logic, the NAS evokes concepts in their
credo ("scholarship" and "society") that they have already appropriated in their act of naming themselves (National = Society/ Scholars =
Scholarship). Hence they exist, as do the texts they judge, within a
hermetically sealed predication that simply refers back upon itself to
justify its own existence and standards.   From this safe space, they
argue for the maintenance of courses that "transcend cultural differences." I beg to question what they mean by "culture"—whose
culture counts as one that should be transcended? Where can these
Archimedes stand so that the world, as such, may be addressed? How
can one hold a "cultural conversation?"
     By "cultural conversation," I am referring to a popular evocation
of "culture" as a monolithic Western-male phenomenon. The phrase
comes from the greatly influential/canonical *The Philosophy of Literary
Form* by Kenneth Burke:

> Imagine that you enter a parlor. You come in late. When you
> arrive, others have long preceded you, and they are engaged in
> a heated discussion, a discussion too heated for them to pause
> and tell you exactly what it is about. . . . You listen for a while,
> until you decide that you have caught the tenor of the argu-
> ment; then you put in your oar. Someone answers; you answer
> him; another comes to your defense; another aligns himself
> against you, to either the embarrassment of gratification of
> your opponent, depending on the quality of your ally's assis-
> tance. However, the discussion is interminable. The hours grow
> late, you must depart. And you do depart, with the discussion
> still vigorously in progress.[13]

The allusion to a social gathering is defined in terms not only of gender but certainly of race and class as well. What remains undeflated, in fact elevated, is the fact that a parlor, and not some other location, signifies the type of atmosphere in which this is imagined to take place. This imagined community of "American" culture links up with middle-class respectability—middle-class culture. A culture that is always already defined as White, male, English-speaking, educated participants.[14] To gloss "American culture" in such terms, in fact to pit this type of socially respectable argumentation as the continuous dialogue/argument that represents all of us living in the United States not only is dangerous in its traditional conservative ramifications but betrays that fact that Burke sees the locus of conversation as serving the unchanging (read: silent) mores of the privileged guests.

The examples I have chosen are intended to painfully coalesce with this White, European, Middle-Class Male Habit of speaking for everyone. It is this narrow interpretation of "culture" that allows those privileged spokes*men* to create a discourse that delineates what is normal, standard, respectable, with the uncanny authority of an imagined community.

As Edward Said explains, "The power of culture by virtue of its elevated or superior position to authorize, to dominate, to legitimate, demote, interdict, and validate: in short, the power of culture to be an agent of, and perhaps the main agency for, powerful differentiation within its domain and beyond it too."[15] This project, then, would interrogate that agency that allows culture to speak its own name, on its own behalf, and toward its own ends. To create the text of its own intention. What I have in mind would follow the Foucaultian method of genealogy, which seeks to analyze "the various systems of subjection: not the anticipatory power of meaning, but the hazardous play of dominations."[16]

II

The remainder of this contribution follows the first four (of six) arguments raised by the NAS in defense of the traditional core curriculum. The NAS's opening argument reads:

First, any work, whether formerly neglected or widely known, should be added, retained, or removed from the curriculum on the basis of its conformance to generally applicable intellectual and aesthetic standards. A sound curriculum cannot be built by replacing those standards with the principle of proportional representation of authors, classified ethnically, biologically, or geographically.

The search for standards, especially along the lines of such obviously subjective grounds as aesthetics and intellect, far from being transcendent, rests on ideological criteria; Mudimbe argues, in *The Invention of Africa*, that "it is difficult to imagine these standards can emerge from outside the 'power-knowledge' field of a given culture, a field which, at a historical period, establishes its artistic bible."[17]

I see no reason to believe that the power-knowledge that has informed the construction of the curriculum is different than the power-knowledge that has constructed the nation. Althusser makes this point emphatically: "To my knowledge *no class can hold State power over a long period without at the same time exercising its hegemony over and in the State Ideological Apparatuses* . . . an ideology which represents the School as a neutral environment purged of ideology . . . [has become] *the dominant Ideological State Apparatus.*[18] By claiming that these standards are opposed to "proportional representation of authors, classified ethnically, biologically, or geographically," the NAS must maintain that the texts that are "added, retained, or removed" are themselves unrelated to ethnic/biological/geographical principals. They are without ideology. It follows that only superior texts should be allowed within academia. Hence, the "text" has an essence. The grounds of their academy relies on the NAS's ability to judge what superior texts are through the reified racism of science and Enlightenment and the free society of postbellum, post-Reconstruction, post-equality "America."

In imagining their community, as well as imagining itself as the voice of that community, the NAS justifies its role as custodian of the sovereign and limited boundaries of academia in lieu of establishing what is acceptable and what is abnormal. Again, one need only to replace the term *text* with the term *race* to see where Grady's ideology of "race instinct" unravels the NAS's denouncement of "proportional representation." To quote the spokesman of the South: "the white race will continue to dominate the colored . . . [even if] . . . the present race majority be reversed."[19] It would appear that a little superior blood goes a long way.

Grady attests that desegregation would make the schools of the New South "a hot-bed of false and pernicious ideas, or the scene of unwise associations."[20] The races/texts must not mix. "The South must be allowed to settle the social relations of the races according to her own view of what is right and best. . . . As a matter of course, this implies the clear and unmistakable domination of the white race in the South . . . simply the right of character, intelligence, and property of rule."[21]

Grady cites the president of the National Educational Association, Gustavus J. Orr, to ground his claims. "But I am so sure of the evils that would come from mixed schools that, even if they were possible, I would see the whole educational system swept away before I would see them established."[22]

The ideology that runs through the race and text instincts is diametrically opposed to mixing essences. Races, and texts, must remain pure of any inferior blood. What are the New South and the NAS so afraid of? Why is the notion of a mixed curriculum so dangerous? Perhaps they are afraid of what the offspring of such "intermingling" might look like; if they mix, the offspring will (like Caliban's curse) be revolutionary—hated by both sides, yet informed by each "essence." Only by segregating the "races" and "texts" can a single voice for "culture" claim its autonomy. Without segregation, the 'other' might penetrate the 'self,' thus engendering a mixed progeny. The pure voice of civilization would become the many tongues of anarchy.

III

Second, the idea that students will be discouraged by not encountering more works by members of their own race, sex, or ethnic group, even were it substantiated, would not justify adding inferior works. Such paternalism conveys a message opposite to the one desired.[23]

Grady, through evoking his perception of "the negro," concurrently evokes the antebellum practice of paternalism. "It is hard to think of the negro with exactness. His helplessness, his generations of enslavement, his unique position among the peoples of the earth, his distinctive color, his simple, lovable traits."[24] Rather than act paternally toward "inferior" texts, the NAS would have us read "studies that transcend cultural differences: the truths of mathematics, the sciences; history, and so on."

Read in reverse, any inclusion of texts based on "race," "sex," and "ethnic origins" would merely be an act of paternalism, and we know that paternalism is bad. I would like to know, however, what are "race," "sex," and "ethnicity" anyway? How are they defined? Can they be defined? Moreover, what is a text, except, consistent with the other categories, what one believes a text should be. According to Stanley Fish: "prejudicial or perspectival perception is all there is, and the question is from which of a number of equally interested perspectives will the text be constituted."[25] Hence, the ones looking for a "text" shall surely find one. Intellect and aesthetics, like paternalism, have always belonged to those who benefit from the power-knowledge in the first place. Rather than allow difference, "transcendent truths" imply that difference has no bearing on how a text is received by an imaginary unraced, unsexed, unethnic community. This community, nevertheless, happens to own the only microscope which is also unraced, unsexed, and unethnic, so their judgments are purely objective and not based on some paternal residue from antebellum practices.

To be paternal toward works that are different from (inferior to) the norm (superior) model would imply that those who, even condescendingly, patronize these texts must consider them as members of their own constituency. Why is the curriculum biased? Why is there segregation? One of Grady's nemeses, George G. Cable, remarked: "Even to lead would not compensate us; for the fundamental profession of American politics is that the leader is a servant to his followers. It was too much."[26] A segregated curriculum replaces the need for paternalism.

IV

Third, other cultures, minority subcultures, and social problems have long been studied in the liberal arts curriculum in such established disciplines as history, literature, comparative religion, economics, political science, anthropology, and sociology. But more important, mere acquaintance with differences does not guarantee tolerance, an ideal Western in origin and fostered by knowledge of what is common to us all.[27]

The NAS group together categories which they believe, or want us to believe, are analogical. "Other cultures, minority subcultures, and social problems" all are outside the walls of this imagined community, which has the privilege of self-fashioned normality. Perhaps they learned to use analogies from Western science. Nancy Leys Stepan, in "Race and Gender: The Role of Analogy in Science" argues that in the 1860s and 1870s, [t]he scientists' contribution was to elevate hitherto unconsciously held analogies into self-conscious theory, to extend the meanings attached to the analogies, to expand their range through new observations and comparisons, and to give them precision through specialized vocabularies and new technologies.[28]

Hence, binary oppositions such as White/Black, culture/nature, civilized/savage, male/female, inside/outside, same/other, which claim to be objectively studying differences, are informed by the very way these differences are originally posited before the investigations ever begin. Far from being arbitrary, these words, when used with all the authority science produces, become associated with the "truth" of Enlightenment. Not only has race been gendered and gender racialized but gender has meant White women and race has meant Black men within an interpretative system designed to make the researcher an invisible presence among the "other cultures." In the analogies of science this difference has meant being an "inferior race" or "gender," in the fantasies of industrial and technological progress this has meant to be barbarous, primitive, superstitious, emasculate, feeble, and savage.

That "other cultures" means "minority subcultures"—which in turn means "social problems" which evoke abnormality—assumes that there is a "culture" that is not being informed by differences, one that has no minority subculture nor social problems. Culture, like aesthetics, intellect, race, gender, and ethnicity, is never located within the tainted language of colonial discourse by the NAS.

Again, the NAS never states what it is that is common to us all, but such nineteenth- and twentieth-century established disciplines as history, literature, comparative religion, economics, political science, anthropology, and sociology have all historically argued that what we all have in common, and had I the time I would develop this further, is what Grady calls "race instinct." It would not take much imagination to enlarge this to encompass to notions of heterosexual instinct, sex instinct, class instinct, national instinct, and so forth.

> The difference is an essential one. Deplore or defend it as we may, an antagonism is bred between the races when they are forced into mixed assemblages. This sinks out of sight, if not out of existence, when each race moves in its own sphere. . . .

In my opinion it is instinctive—deeper than prejudice or pride, and bred in the bone and blood. . . . Without it, there might be a breaking down of all lines of division and a thorough intermingling of whites and blacks. . . . [T]he process of amalgamation would have begun. . . . The whites, at any cost and at any hazard, would maintain the clear integrity and dominance of the Anglo-Saxon blood.[29]

If we were not to respect these instincts, the "races" would wage an endless war that would naturally destroy the weaker, less vigorous race. Who benefits from such an instinctual drive? Who would really feel uncomfortable when such mixed assemblages occur? The NAS, while calling for a "much-needed debate" on an abstract level, actually felt "terrified," "intimidated," and "anxious" when a group of students and faculty, "mostly colored," "jammed into" a lecture that was sponsored by the Binghamton chapter of the NAS.[30] Whether the atmosphere was hostile and dangerous, or a "vigorous and unfettered debate of ideas" differs according to whom you ask. Who decides what behavior is an inappropriate cultural conversation?

V

Fourth, . . . From their beginnings, Western art and science have drawn upon the achievements of non-Western societies and since have been absorbed and further enriched by peoples around the globe.[31]

In *Black Athena*, Martin Bernal concurs that Western art and science have always drawn upon the achievements of non-Western societies; unfortunately, they have buried these sources in lieu of what he calls the Aryan model of Western Culture. According to Bernal, Ancient Greece was originally seen through the *Ancient Model*: "Greek culture had arisen as the result of colonization, around 1500 B.C., by Egyptians and Phoenicians who had civilized the native inhabitants." Then, due to a rise in racism and anti-Semitism in the first half of the nineteenth century, the *Ancient Model* was replaced by the *Broad and Extreme Aryan Models*, according to which "Greek civilization is seen as the result of the mixture of the Indo-European-speaking Hellenese and their indigenous subjects."[32]

Bernal begins to cash-out this debate with the axiom that "the 19th and 20th centuries have been dominated by the paradigms of progress and science."[33] This interpolation of the "great-chain-of-being" argument explains why those within the academy felt the *Ancient Model* violated "racial science as monstrously as the legends of sirens and centaurs broke the canons of natural science."[34] In other words, since science had proved its racial theories on intersubjectively objective grounds, and the humanities had modeled themselves after such positivistic "scientific inquiry," only the integration of the *Aryan Model* could bridge this embarrassing semantic gap between the reified status of science and the emerging humanities.

Bernal (whose work is suspiciously similar to George G. M. James's earlier text *Stolen Legacy*)[35] argues convincingly and thoroughly that the *Ancient Model* should be restored; what Bernal doesn't argue, historicize, or confront is the way the very academy from which he speaks has been defined along the same lines as the *Aryan Model* all along. In fact, this model that he attacks is the same apparatus which allows him (as a White European male Cornell professor) to speak.

I feel that Bernal is misleading in his portrayal of the movement from the *Ancient* to the *Aryan Model*; it would seem that his vision links racism to the theories of science and progress in a correlative fashion, whereas I would argue that without racism, sexism, and nationalism, there would be neither science nor progress as we know it. "The Black man serving as the necessary foil, the essential opposition, giving substance to the superiority of the white man."[36] The paradigms of both science and progress feed off of the illusion of hermeneutic idealism; explicitly, a real world exists that can be studied objectively.

In *Iron Cages* Ronald Takaki describes the relation between the nation and the newly emerging technology of the post–Civil War period: "Technology, both as ideology and as economic development, had an enormous impact on culture and race in America: It served as metaphor and materialist basis for domination of mind over body, capitol over labor, and whites over Indians, blacks, Mexicans, and Asians. "[37] As metaphor, technology served as a further justification of the "great-chain-of-being" model. Technology was seen as a racial progression across time. In this offshoot of social Darwinism, the possession and exploitation of technology guaranteed superiority along a evolutionary continuum. But whereas it was the English language that indicated civilization, the steam engine was now metonymous with the United States racist self-fashioned notion of expansionism, progress, and commerce. The human body, or more correctly the White male body, could now become mind, since the steam powered machine had become the body. "[T]he creation of the steam engine . . . brings the progress of the arts and enterprise and sweeps away the traces of savage life."[38]

Along the academia continuum, Bernal claims that "[v]ictors were seen as more advanced, hence better, than the vanquished, history— now seen as the biographies of races—consisted of triumphs of strong and vital peoples over weak and feeble ones."[39] Grady also uses health as an analogy of race: "Even if the vigor and volume of the Anglo-Saxon blood would enable it to absorb the African current."[40]

Technology, which was seen as the domination of the mind over nature, served as another metaphor for race instinct. Whites were seen as the only race to have technology, and thus must be the more advanced. Ad infinitum. While progress racialized, nationalized, and genderized the difference between technology and nature, the liberal arts were generated by the identical premises. Any type of liberal humanist comparison found its "truths" about differences—be they anthropological, sociological, comparative religion, and so forth—from within the stock of "cultural" metaphors readily accessible, in fact inseparable, from the language of that culture.

VI

In the two "cultural problem" debates I have been analyzing, all sides of this privileged conversation have implicitly identical ideologies that appear only to be debating difference. While Cable—the antiracism side of "Negro Problem debate"—denies the role of science in determining the race instincts of like for like, he leaves room for the race and gendered "social equity" that will take care of itself without the necessary policing of the borders. In a revealing earlier essay, he claimed:

> Our children will do as we did when we went to school. They will select and confer free companionship upon certain playmates, according to their own and their parents' ideas of mental caliber, moral worth, and social position, and the rest of the school may go its own way. This fact, then, is rather an argument against our hostility. The schoolroom neither requires nor induces social equality. Social equality is a matter of personal preference.[41]

For Cable, the instinct is social rather than racial; yet he agrees that "Negroes" are an "inferior race," a "lower class." Cable's fear, much like Grady's, is that the "races" will mix. While Grady believes this can be avoided by segregation, Cable believes that such regulations will only tempt both sides to transgress. In "The Silent South," published shortly after "Freedman's," Cable makes his ideological position clear: "Nationalism by fusion of bloods is the maxim of barbarous times and peoples."[42] Likewise, "[t]he National Association of Scholars is in favor of ethnic studies, the study of non-Western cultures, and the study of the special problems of women and minorities in our society."[43] As long as these disciplines don't interfere with the "humanities," why shouldn't they exist?

Martin Bernal's position in *Black Athena* appears to be attacking "racist" scholarship in the "West," but the way he frames the choices leaves no room for other influences. As James Donelan writes about Bernal: "[e]ither there was a racist conspiracy or there wasn't; either there was Afro-asiatic roots or there wasn't; either Bernal is right or he is wrong. Classical scholarship is a complex and subtle body of work, created by people with more diverse motives than pure nationalism or racial hatred."[44] Bernal's silencing and understating the voices of Black scholars like James and ben-Jochannan, who have already performed the research in this field, need to be challenged, as does his statement "I find it easier to place myself and my promotion of the Revised Ancient Model in the spectrum of black scholarship than within the academy orthodoxy."[45] Ultimately, who is selling thousands of books, being canonized, giving worldwide tours? To what extent has Bernal's "going native" allowed him to commodify that "experience" to the very academy he attacks?

The NAS celebrates the truths of science, reason, intelligence, and beauty, thus justifying their textual canon. The New South used the same truths to segregate along racial lines. Whereas harmony might be achieved through extracting, analyzing, and classifying the blood from a text—that blood would still only be seen with eyes informed by race, gender, class, nationality, sexual orientation, language, and so on; until objectivity bleeds Anglo-Saxon red, I will neither embrace this text instinct nor mend the walls that prevent the intermingling of pernicious ideas.

Notes

1. This article was written in solidarity with all who where interpellated by the infamous March 14, 1991 meeting of the Binghamton NAS. Within the hermeneutics of this public meeting, various complaints and allegations were made by SUNY Binghamton

NAS members against specific members of the audience. "The mere attendance of students of color at the NAS forum has been seen as an act of 'barbarism,' 'thuggery,' 'savagery,' 'mobocracy' and 'terrorism' (Statement from the Coalition of Concerned Faculty and Students). Compare with an NAS member's claim that "[t]hey [the crowd] may have been misinformed by their leaders who of course knew the National Association of Scholars to be an altogether peaceable organization but nevertheless mustered the crowd by arguing or insinuating that we are in some fashion tied to the Klan" (George Basler, "Event Shocks SUNY-B Campus" *Press and Sun Bulletin*, April 14, 1991).

2. Henry W. Grady, "In Plain Black and White: A Response to Mr. Cable," Century Magazine 29 (April 1885): 909–17.

3. Ibid., 909.

4. National Association of Scholars statement, *Is the Curriculum Biased?* available upon request by writing to the National Association of Scholars, Suite 250 East, Twenty Nassau Street, Princeton, N.J. 08542.

5. Michael S. Kimmel, "The Cult of Masculinity: American Social Character and the Legacy of the Cowboy," in *Beyond Patriarchy: Essays by Men on Pleasure, Power, and Change*, ed. Michael Kaufman (Toronto: Oxford University Press, 1987), 237.

6. Ronald Takaki, *Iron Cages: Race and Culture in 19th-Century America* (New York: Oxford University Press, 1990), 199.

7. Grady, "In Plain Black and White," 910.

8. Ibid.

9. Ibid., 911.

10. Lucius Outlaw, "Towards a Critical Theory of 'Race,'" in *Anatomy of Racism*, ed. David Theo Goldberg (Minneapolis: University of Minnesota Press, 1990), 59.

11. Denise Riley, *Am I That Name? Feminism and the Category of "Women" in History* (Minneapolis: University of Minnesota Press, 1988), 1–2.

12. Henry Louis Gates, Jr., "Writing 'Race' and the Difference it Makes," in *"Race," Writing, and Difference*, ed. Henry Louis Gates, Jr. (Chicago: University of Chicago Press, 1985), 8.

13. Kenneth Burke, The Philosophy of Literary Form (Baton Rouge: 1941), 110–11.

14. My reading of the cultural conversation model was heavily influenced by Bennedict Anderson's *Imagined Communities: Reflections on the Origin and Spread of Nationalism* (London: Verso, 1991) and George L. Mosse's *Nationalism and Sexuality* (Madison: University of Wisconsin Press, 1985). Anderson defines a nation as "an imagined political community—and imagined as both inherently limited and sovereign. It is *imagined* because the members of even the smallest nation will never know most of their fellow-members . . . yet in their minds of each lives the image of their communion" (15). Mosse takes a different yet complimentary perspective: "The national stereotype and the middle-class stereotype were identical" (16).

15. Said quoted in Patrick Brantlinger, "Victorians and Africans: The Genealogy of the Myth of the Dark Continent," in *"Race," Writing, and Difference*, ed. Henry Louis Gates, Jr. (Chicago: University of Chicago Press, 1985), 186.

16. Foucault, quoted in Brantlinger, "Victorians and Africans," 186.

17. V. Y. Mudimbe, *The Invention of Africa: Gnosis, Philosophy, and the Order of Knowledge* (Bloomington: Indiana University Press, 1988),10–11.

18. Louis Althusser, "Ideology and the Ideological State Apparatus," in Louis Althusser, *Lenin and Philosophy and other Essays*, trans. Ben Brewster (New York: Monthly Review Press, 1981), 75–83.

19. Grady, "In Plain Black and White," 917.

20. Ibid., 912.

21. Ibid., 917.

22. Ibid., 915.

23. National Association of Scholars, "Is the Curriculum Biased?"

24. Grady, "In Plain Black and White," 910.

25. Stanley Fish, "Demonstration vs. Persuasion: Two Models of Critical Activity," in *Is There a Text in This Class? The Authority of Interpretative Communities* (Cambridge: Harvard University Press, 1980), 467.

26. George W. Cable, "The Freedman's Case in Equity," *Century Magazine* 29 (January 1885): 412.

27. National Association of Scholars, "Is the Curriculum Biased?"

28. Nancy Leys Stepen, "Race and Gender: The Role of Analogy in Science," in *Anatomy of Racism*, ed. David Theo Goldberg (Minneapolis: University of Minnesota Press, 1988), 42.

29. Grady, "In Plain Black and White," 911.

30. Excerpts taken from Basler, "Event shocks SUNY-B campus."

31. National Association of Scholars, "Is the Curriculum Biased?"

32. Martin Bernal, *Black Athena: The Afroasiatic Roots of Classical Civilization*, vol. 1, *The Fabrication of Ancient Greece, 1785–1985* (New Brunswick: Rutgers University Press, 1987), 2.

33. Ibid., 7.

34. Ibid., 8.

35. For a lengthy discussion of the argument that "Greek" philosophy has its roots in Egypt/Africa, I recommend, besides the Bernal book, George G. M. James, *Stolen Legacy: The Greeks Were Not the Authors of Greek Philosophy, but the People of North Africa, Commonly Called Egyptians* (New York: Philosophical Library, 1954); Yosef A. A. ben-Jochannan, *Africa: Mother of Western Civilization* (Baltimore: Black Classic Press, 1988).

36. Lynn Segal, *Slow Motion: Changing Masculinities, Changing Men* (London: Virago, 1990), 172.

37. Takaki, *Iron Cages*,148.

38. Ibid., 151.

39. Bernal, *Black Athena*, 31–32.

40. Grady, "In Plain Black and White," 911.

41. Cable quoted in Takaki, *Iron Cages*, 208.

42. Ibid., 209.

43. National Association of Scholars, "Is the Curriculum Biased?"

44. James Donelan, "The Argument from Noise," in *Critical Texts* 6, no. 3 (1989): 104.

45. Bernal, *Black Athena*, 437.

CHAPTER 5

The Construction of the Other
and the Destruction of the Self:
The Case of the Convention Hearings

ROBERT F. BARSKY

This obsession of mine is beginning to disgust me; I can't tear my eyes away
from what I see day after day; I talk about it, I rave; this eternal recurrence is
unhealthy, malignant. . . . Other people's sufferings have been affecting me this
way lately; my head is full of their stories, my dreams are live with them, and
though no two are the same, they are all of the same kind: I strongly suspect
that those of my acquaintances who manage to live day after day with
equanimity are sleight-of-hand artists. Occupational bias leads the psychiatrist
to find insanity in the sane, the detective to perceive guilt in the innocent, and
the gravedigger to look upon the healthiest of men as a promising prospect.
—George Konrád, *The Case Worker*

In his 1969 novel *The Case Worker*, the Hungarian novelist and
essayist George Konrád recounts the history of a bureaucrat who works
in a government department in charge of removing children from their
homes if the hearth is deemed to be unsuitable for child rearing. Case
workers in the department rely upon hearsay, reports, letters, tips, and
so forth from neighbours or passers-by for their information, and the
narrator's job is to investigate the cases and to take appropriate action.
Each case is carefully documented and stored in a filing cabinet that,
"with its doors wide open . . . makes me think of an old man holding
open his dressing gown so the doctor can examine his abdomen."[1] The
narrator as *case worker* must face the unnerving task of tapping into
this record of human sorrow and misery in order to render a decision.
"Every morning," he recounts, "I reach with sickening pity into this
ancient object, where three rows of case histories, filed according to

date and category, await decisions" (11). Of course, the process of investigating each claim and taking action on particular cases takes a long time, sometimes many years, and meanwhile the files are transferred from one desk to another in a Kafkaesque fashion, and the suffering, the *raison d'être* of the files, continues unabated: "Now and then they are removed, stapled to sheets of background information, refiled under new reference numbers, sent for consideration to other offices, and returned dog-eared and covered with endless scribblings. And here they lie" (11). For its depiction of human suffering and its description of the bureaucratic process that the Hungarian government followed in order to deal therewith, *The Case Worker* is, sadly enough, probably unerring; and for its portrayal of the inadequacy of confessions and reports to account for the indignity of human suffering, it is decidedly insightful:

> I sometimes wonder what would happen if suddenly they [the files] were to start talking. What sounds would issue from that cabinet! Children's cries, women's moans, resounding blows, quarrels, obscenities, recriminations, interrogations, hasty decisions, false testimony, administrative platitudes, jovial police slang, judges' verdicts, the vapid chatter of female supervisors, the incantations of psychologists, my colleagues' embittered humour, my own solitary invective, and so on. . . . It would be as if a powerful radio had picked up all the stations in the world at once; all these sounds, en masse, would become as neutral and indifferent as the yellowing documents in my drawers. (11)

The administrative procedure described in *The Case Worker* in many ways mirrors that of the Convention Refugee determination process. Konrád's description of the trajectory followed by the case, with its "rarefied atmosphere that sparkles with procedural subtleties" (11–12) resembles the Convention Refugee claim's long trajectory from the initial interview to the decision; and, as in *The Case Worker*, the persons involved are often transformed in the process from living, breathing, suffering human beings into *reduced others*. The "seething human life that gave rise" to the files goes through the "showy acrobatics of official procedure," only to "crash land in [the case worker's] filing cabinet" (12), as though human suffering could only be engulfed by bureaucracy and decisions thereabout only rendered through trickery and deceit:

With a stroke of the surgical knife it might be possible to cut short the propagation of human weaknesses; but, just as a living body rejects alien matter, so everyday life evacuates all peremptory regulations, cosily dogmatic verdicts,—in a word, everything that is strictly logical and consistent—and then proceeds to solve its problems by quiet trickery and always in the most unexpected way. Which accounts for the fate of my pitiful, cruel, and sometimes rather ridiculous documents. (12)

There are many similarities between the fictionalized world of *The Case Worker* and the sorely accurate and nonfictional nature of the Convention Refugee Hearing; but this is not the only reason to begin an illumination of contemporary legal texts with the light of Konrád's novel. The fictionalized account of a similar procedure provides the discourse analyst with a condensed and dramatized, but nonetheless accurate and insightful, example of how confessional, rhetorical, administrative, and legal discourse work upon a broader compendium of discursive practices. The fictional account of the bureaucratic process offers a glimpse into the *whole process* and its effects upon specific characters, a description difficult to secure in the realm of actual legal process.[2] Furthermore, the texts used for the analysis of this productive discursive construction, in particular the texts by Mikhail Mikhailovich Bakhtin, are sometimes dependent upon (as in the case of studies of the relationship between discursive realms), or even indistinguishable from (as in the case of Dostoevsky's influence on Bakhtin), certain literary texts, suggesting that the process of creating (dialogue-ing with) characters in fiction bears an important resemblance to the process of presenting oneself through dialogue (an idea described in Bakhtin's "Author and Hero in Aesthetic Activity"[3]). Finally, as Bakhtin suggests in the 1919 article "Art and Answerability,"[4] "art and life are not one, but they must become united in myself—in the unity of my answerability" (2). This may explain why Bakhtin's work, no matter how useful or topical it is for other kinds of discursive practice, is most often written to illuminate literary texts and why literary texts can, in very short descriptions, describe in greater detail a process that through other means would require long discussions containing elaborate details.

The Refugee Claim Process: Othering

The bureaucratic process of making a Convention Refugee claim begins when a person requests refugee status at a point of entry into a country of which (s)he is not a citizen or landed immigrant. The claiming procedure is similar in most countries of the world by virtue of the existence of the 1951 Convention Relating to the Status of Refugees, to which ninety-five countries in the First World and developing world are signatories; therefore although the specific examples provided in this paper emerge from a Canadian context, there would (technically) only be slight variation if the claims mentioned had been made in receiving countries such as France, Switzerland, or Australia, or even in Bolivia, Djibouti, or Mozambique.

Most persons who wish to claim refugee status in Canada enter the country through an airport or an automobile checkpoint, and surrender themselves to officials at Immigration Canada. At that moment, they become claimants who are seeking Convention Refugee status and, ultimately, the right to settle in Canada. From the outset the problematic of such a claim is best construed with reference to some notion of otherness, an otherness that must be constructed according to prevailing discursive and normative rules active at the time when the refugee enters the country. I will begin by exploring otherness with reference to the work of the Russian philosopher of language Mikhail Mikhailovich Bakhtin because Bakhtin's theories concerning the production of self and other are particularly appropriate for cross-cultural research in otherness, and because they are well suited to a description and discussion of a related process that is of particular interest for the study of legal hearings: authoring. I shall then turn to the works of Erving Goffman and Pierre Bourdieu to take up the issue of auto-representation before returning once again to Bakhtin and notions of answerability, authoring and evaluation of one's own dialogic construction.

Any Canadian who returns home from another country must undergo routine immigration formalities; for example, if I were to summarily describe in Bakhtinian terms the procedure of my own return from an overseas journey, let us say England, I would have to begin at the moment when I am asked to present my passport and explain my presence to an immigration official at the point of entry. By subjecting myself to this process, I am being asked by a representative from Immigration Canada to construct myself as a straight-faced other—an honest, law-abiding Canadian citizen who had traveled to England for the reasons stated and had purchased goods not exceeding the amount I had written upon the immigration form. By speaking to the immigration official and constructing myself as this (hopefully) adequate other, I further legitimize the uniformed official as immigration officer, because I confirm his or her authority to act in a way appropriate to the office of immigration official. As soon as this formality is over, I would then be allowed to continue my journey; I would leave the liminal, indeterminate, marginal space that lies between the tarmac and the baggage claim area and return home in the form of a reconfirmed honest upstanding Canadian citizen.

The process would not be quite so simple for those passengers of the plane who had arrived in Canada with the intention of claiming political refugee status. After elucidating their desire to claim status, they would be taken aside by Immigration Canada officials who would prepare them for the more complex procedure of presenting another other; the other as political refugee, or, as they are called in Canada, the other as *Convention Refugee*. The procedure for claiming status in 1987, the period during which my research began, is described in two pamphlets published by the Immigration and Refugee Board and available at immigration offices and border crossings: *Refugee Determination: What it is and How it Works* and *Backlog Process: How the System Works.*[5] These are small and colorful publications, adorned with photos of immigrants and refugee claimants, and filled with details useful to persons who are seeking be admitted into Canada as refugees; and for the purposes of this study, they can be read as handbooks, instruction manuals on how to construct a suitable other for a Canadian Refugee Determination Hearing.[6]

A Bakhtinian reading of the process described in these pamphlets is revealing; because he pondered the relationship between *self and other, author and hero, space and time* and *inside and outside*, in various realms including the novel, the carnival, the legal hearing, and everyday conversation, Bakhtin has become a valuable reference whenever issues of *dialogue* or *self-representation* are raised. And because his work demands that these apparently binary categories be examined simultaneously, Bakhtin forces us to account for the "architectonics governing relations between them,"[7] a strategy that I will outline in this essay with respect to the notions of continuous *monitoring* and *evaluation* of discursive constructions in process. It is therefore valuable to think about Bakhtin when traveling from one country to the next; whenever issues involving ongoing intercultural exchange, the interaction of various national languages, the space within which certain kinds of interaction occurs, or the boundaries that separate linguistic or cultural activities are raised, Bakhtin's work could be called upon for new insights.

Bakhtin would undoubtedly have agreed that refugee claimants face an ominous process and that to describe oneself as a particular entity for the purpose of entrance into a country is a tricky matter that poses some of the same difficulties related to otherness as those faced by authors who seek to create heroes who will be able to assume a distinct identity in a novel ("authoring"). Holquist suggests that there is a kind of *consummation* that occurs in the latter process, because "I give shape *both* to others and to my self as an author gives shape to his heroes" ("Introduction" *A&A*, xxx). My previously-described task of creating an other for the purposes of reentry into Canada is a relatively simple example of this authoring process because I speak the language of the immigration officials, I was born and raised into the system into which I am requesting passage, and I am therefore likely to know the boundaries of what is permissible and admirable in Canadian society. By contrast, the refugee claimant who arrives in Canada has to worry about a whole series of culturally-contingent issues concerning otherness, first in the initial request for refugee status and later in the formal Refugee Determination Hearing, two authoring procedures that are far more urgent in terms of their survival than my own process of self-representation.

The refugee's primary concern is that his or her other be *productive* in the same sense that the persona that I created in my imaginary journey from England was *productive* in the fulfillment of my goal to return home; that is, the refugee's other must be able to portray a persecuted person who has acted, and will continue to act, in a manner that is consistent with the definition of the Convention Refugee so that the goal of obtaining status will be achieved. The kind of authoring that takes place during a Convention Refugee Hearing is no different from many other kinds of confessional or representational strategies that are formulated for interaction with officialdom (the passages from *The Case Worker* already cited announce the problems that being involved in such a strategy imply); in fact, one's ability to offer the right *face* is to some degree a measure of one's ability to survive within, or integrate into, our sociopolitical system.

Before turning to details concerning the auto-construction through discourse from a Bakhtinian perspective, it is worth elaborating issues relating to the refugee's facial strategy, for it is here that the initial questions concerning posturing, the relationship between inner and outer man, the assessment of one's own capacity to evaluate one's performance (through reference to a projected vision of one's own "face") during dialogue, and so forth are posed. The notion of "face" is elaborated in numerous works by Erving Goffman, in particular *Interaction Ritual: Essays in Face-to-Face Behaviour*,[8] wherein he describes the natural defenses, masks, and maneuvers presented during the process of oral interaction. Goffman's overall project of studying these rituals in some ways underwrites the kind of analysis I am now proposing with reference to the Convention Refugee Hearing:

> One objective in dealing with these data is to describe the natural units of interaction built up from them, beginning with the littlest—for example, the fleeting facial movement an individual can make in the game of expressing his alignment to what is happening—and ending with affairs such as week-long conferences. . . . A second objective is to uncover the normative order prevailing within and between these units, that is, the behavioral order found in all peopled places, whether public, semi-public, or private, and whether under the auspices of an organized social occasion or the flatter constraints of merely a routinized social setting. (*Interaction*, 1–2)

The beginnings of a study concerning the construction of a productive other could be viewed in terms of the (facial) relationship between the inner (wo)man and the postures and faces (s)he shows to the world; thus, in Goffman's words, "the term face may be defined as the positive social value a person effectively claims for himself by the line others assume he has during a particular contact" (*Interaction*, 5). This face, while produced by the individual, is created in continuous response to social context; as such when the social context is unfamiliar, the face is likely to be an uncomfortable one, confirming Goffman's view that "in general, a person's attachment to a particular face, coupled with the ease with which disconfirming information can be conveyed by himself and others, provides one reason why he finds that participation in any contact with others is a commitment" (*Interaction*, 6).

Goffman also suggests that the "face" is one of our personal resources, foreshadowing discussions of speech genres (Bakhtin) and discourse as commodity (Bourdieu), and also pointing in the direction of Bakhtin's views on answerability, with its correlate suggestion that speakers must take responsibility for their utterances because they in some ways shape the nature of the other. The interviewer in a Convention Refugee Hearing must recognize that the claimant, coming as (s)he does from another culture, may have a limited number of institutionalized "lines" and a choice of "faces" that does not include a properly Canadian bureaucratic face:

> The line maintained by and for a person with others tends to be of a legitimate institutionalized kind. During a contact of a particular type, an interactant of known or visible attributes can expect to be sustained in a particular face and can feel that it is morally proper that this should be so. Given his attributes and the conventionalized nature of the encounter, he will find a small choice of lines will be open to him and a small choice of faces will be waiting for him. Further, on the basis of a few known attributes, he is given the responsibility of possessing a vast number of others. (*Interaction*, 7)

There are other dangers suggested by Goffman; even if the claimant brings an appropriate face to the hearing, (s)he may shed it eventually as a defense against an antagonistic response; this breakdown of the unified face, at a time when verbal and textual consistency is essential, could endanger the claimant and leave him *out of face* or *in the wrong face* for the situation at hand:

> A person may be said to *be in wrong face* when information is brought forth in some way about his social worth which cannot be integrated, even with effort, into the line that is being sustained for him. A person may be said to *be out of face* when he participates in a contact with others without having ready a line of the kind participants in such situations are expected to take. (*Interaction*, 8)

It is in such a situation that the person concerned will lose his or her *poise*, which is employed by Goffman "to refer to the capacity to suppress and conceal any tendency to become shamefaced during encounters with others" (*Interaction*, 9).

    This kind of research dramatizes the degree to which the institutional face is (in most cases) a "face on loan," an unfamiliar face that is probably not in accord with other faces that the interviewee wears during a given day; it is a construction, socially contingent, continuously reviewed and renewed, and therefore always in danger of being confiscated; the very nature of our social organization is such that the social face can be "withdrawn unless he conducts himself in a way that is worthy of it" (*Interaction*, 10). Goffman goes on to suggest, in a passage that seems particularly pertinent to the material at hand, that the existence of so-called "approved attributes and their relation to face make of every man his own jailer; this is a fundamental social constraint even though each man may like his cell" (*Interaction*, 10). Even with reference to a small number of examples, it is clear that Goffman's ideas lay the foundation for later work on narrative self-construction, the ways in which we fashion ourselves through discourse. However, although such areas of Goffman's work as those I have cited would be suited to a study of the ideal live interview, there are shortcomings to his approach with regard to an understanding of the construction of a productive other in an inter-cultural setting, shortcomings that bring the analyst into the commodified speech world described by Pierre Bourdieu and, ultimately, back to "answerability" as described by Bakhtin. First, Goffman's work is largely intuitive and lacking in methodology; the same could be said for the works of both Bakhtin and Bourdieu of course, but in Goffman's hard-nosed descriptions there lacks the philosophical insights that compensate for problems of application. Second, it is too "occidentocentric," containing sparse and generally unusable discussions of cross-cultural face-saving situations and the complex ethnic and sociopolitical bases thereof. And third, Goffman's use of immutable categories are inadequate descriptions of how legal hearings, in particular Convention Refugee Hearings, unfold. He suggests, for example, that "the interchange seems to be a basic concrete unit of social activity and provides one natural empirical way to study interaction of all kinds" (*Interaction*, 20). When a stand-off or a snag develops during this interchange, it will, according to Goffman, be reconciled according to the following formula: there is a challenge, an attempt to reconcile, an offer of compensation, a punishment, and a gratitude. This may be an adequate description for informal social interaction, but to follow this apparently invariable formula for analyses of refugee hearings could be overly reductive. A snag in a refugee hearing often results in a complete breakdown, apparently inexplicable for those who are forced to adjudicate the case, wherein the refugee stops elaborating his answers, or stops telling the truth because (s)he feels that the Senior Immigration Officer (S.I.O.) or lawyer cannot be trusted with the details of the case. This event is not an effort of "face-saving" (as Goffman would call it) but rather it is linked to a series of culturally contingent norms concerning secrecy and trust. In short, where Goffman's work would be useful is as a sort of handbook which would be distributed to each refugee upon arrival in Canada, so that (s)he could avoid the pitfalls of Canadian social interaction rituals.

To move beyond notions of strategy and ritual and into the realm of productive construction through dialogue there are a number of strategies worthy of consideration. Certainly some reference to the work of Bourdieu, in particular that which has been assembled and translated as *Language and Symbolic Power*,[9] could offer some powerful analytic tools particularly for theoreticians sympathetic with the work of Bakhtin since there is, in my opinion, significant overlap. His studies of how discourse both *reflects* and *effects* the interests of the speaker through reference to notions and terminology from the marketplace ("exchange," "profits," "price formation," "value," "commodity," and so forth) helps clarify the degree to which, "quite apart from the literary (and especially poetic) uses of language, it is rare in everyday life for language to function as a pure instrument of communication" (66). Bourdieu provides an invaluable analysis of the conditions for success in the discourse marketplace by naming the obstacles inscribed into a system where each speaker has to compete to make him or herself *heard* and, as such, draws valuable comparisons between the authority and competence of the speaker, on the one hand, and the relative success of his or her utterance in specific speech situations on the other. The analysis of particular utterances also sheds light upon the operative official language (i.e., the hegemonic and not the national language), referred to by Bourdieu as the *linguistic law*, against which particular linguistic practices are measured; "this linguistic law has its body of jurists—the grammarians—and its agents of regulation and imposition—the teachers—who are empowered universally to subject the linguistic performance of speaking subjects to examination and to the legal sanction of academic qualification" (45). To understand why, even in light of his or her uttering the appropriate statements (on the level of content), certain refugees fail to succeed in the hearing it is crucial to account for this kind of power structure.

In reading Bourdieu alongside of Bakhtin, one feels a sense of continuous complementarity, suggesting that a full-length study of these thinkers would yield valuable fruits. Bakhtin's work is, however, somewhat less pragmatic and cynical, as interested in creativity and productive loving relations as in purely pragmatic interaction. And for complex study of the construction of a situated self and an understanding of how the self perceives (and therefore continuously regulates) auto-representation, it is essential to delve into essays such as "Art and Answerability" and "Author and Hero in Aesthetic Activity," both published in the collection *Art and Answerability,* because they explain difficulties inherent in establishing and monitoring a fruitful rapport with a constructed other, and in determining which other would be appropriate given the descriptions supplied in the two little information pamphlets.

Which Other Author? Bakhtin Reading Refugee Pamphlets

The pamphlets from Immigration Canada state explicitly that claimants are not expected to recount their complete life story; the members of the Immigration Review Board's Refugee Division, who are present during the Refugee Determination Hearing, are allegedly interested only in elements of the claimant's life that illuminate the claimant's experience as persecuted individual. According to the *Refugee Determination* pamphlet, members of the board are interested in the "eligibility" of the claimant and the "credible basis" of the claim (6). The claimant is not necessarily interested in exhaustive self-representation either; his or her own interest is limited to the final decision of the board—yes you are admitted as a Convention Refugee under the terms of the Immigration Act, or no, you have been refused refugee status into Canada and you must return to your country of origin. This partial vision of the human being characterizes our relations in everyday life, according to Bakhtin: "In life, we are interested not in the whole of a human being, but only in those particular actions on his part with which we are compelled to deal in living our life and which are . . . of special interest to us. And . . . least of all are we ourselves able or competent to perceive in ourselves the given whole of our own personality" (*A&H*, 5).

But in light of this limited vision and imperfect judgment, how can the refugee evaluate the success of his particular face? In the essay "Author and Hero in Aesthetic Activity," Bakhtin specifically addresses the issue of how "we experience outward appearance in the other" in the hope of understanding the nature of that "plane of lived experience" upon which lies "the aesthetic value of outward appearance" (*A&H*, 27). By doing so he offers particularly fortuitous observation concerning our ability to visualize ourselves as other and to continuously monitor the representation that we offer (in the face of the regard of the other): "[W]e are constantly and intently on the watch for reflections of our own life on the plane of other people's consciousness, and, moreover, not just reflections of particular moments of our life, but even reflections of the whole of it. And while seeking to catch these reflections, we also take into account that perfectly distinctive value-coefficient with which our life presents itself to the other—a coefficient which is completely different from the coefficient with which we experience our own life in ourselves" (*A&H*, 16). This kind of monitoring is crucial; however, as previously noted, it could lead to a breakdown during the hearing process if the refugee perceives that a particular question or response from someone present at the hearing is antagonistic; for no reason apparent to the adjudicators, the refugee at this point may heretofore refuse to answer questions or will act evasively in an effort to, in Bakhtin's sense, protect the image that the refugee claimant has of him- or herself.

Bakhtin also discusses our ability to assess this auto-representation in light of the unfinalized nature of dialogue, an element of extreme importance for persons who are being evaluated (i.e., for a refugee claim). The person, and I would suggest the refugee especially, comes into being during the process of speech and seeks consummation from the other as interlocutor: "If I am consummated and my life is consummated, I am no longer capable of living and acting. For in order to live and act, I need to be unconsummated, I need to be open for myself —at least in all the essential moments constituting my life; I have to be, for myself, someone who is axiologically yet-to-be, someone who does not coincide with his already existing makeup" (*A&H*, 13). It is in this context that one must understand Bakhtin's discussions concerning the "productive, constructive" (*A&H*, 5) nature of the author-hero relationship, as well as elements of a person's representation of the "outward image" (*A&H*, 28), in order to understand the nature of auto-"representation" (*A&H*, 28) and the "productive projection into the other and cognition of the other" (*A&H*, 26). Bakhtin suggests that representation of the self to the self cannot occur without the active intervention (through dialogue) with the other; although "my thought can place my body wholly into the outside world as an object among other objects, my actual seeing cannot do the same thing" (*A&H*, 28) because "I experience myself on a plane that is fundamentally different from the one on which I experience all other active participants in my life and in my imagining" (*A&H*, 32).

The *Refugee Determination* pamphlet notes that there are two possible scenarios for a refugee who makes the initial claim for refugee status: if the refugee is deemed "not admissible into Canada," or if the refugee "is inside Canada but has contravened the Immigration Act, then that person will be referred to an immigration inquiry" (6); if the refugee makes it beyond the initial request for status, (s)he will take up (temporary) residence in Canada pending the outcome of a Refugee Determination Hearing, the mechanics of which are described in the pamphlets. During this hearing, the Convention Refugee claimant must convince one of the two parties present—either the member from the Refugee Board or the independent adjudicator—that there is a credible basis for a refugee claim. The claimant must, in other words, convince one of these two persons that the events of his or her life coincides with, or could be an imprint emanating from, the template that is set out in the Immigration Act in the form of five definitions of Convention Refugee. The Immigration Act establishes these definitions in accord with the tenets of the *1951 Convention Relating to the Status of Refugees*[10] and to the *1967 Protocol Relating to the Status of Refugees*[11] (upon which the Canadian Immigration Act is based); and on page 5 of *Refugee Determination*, there is an abbreviated version of this definition:

> Convention Refugees are people who, because of a well-founded fear of persecution due to their race, religion, nationality, membership in a particular social group, or political opinion are unwilling or unable to return to their country of nationality or former habitual residence.

That the definition serves as a virtual template for refugee determination is clearly stated further on in the same pamphlet: "the panel applies the definition for refugees which was agreed to in the 1951 United Nations Convention Relating to the Status of Refugees to the evidence presented" (8). In other words, the rather limited narrative that the claimant is asked to recount determines his or her fate; according to the pamphlets, the only aspect of the decision process that stands outside of this oral testimony is Immigration Canada's overt intention to consider "the human rights record of the claimant's country of origin as well as previous Refugee Division decisions on nationals of the same country" (7). This is a small point, however, since, as the *Backlog Process* pamphlet states, "each case is treated individually and decisions are made solely on the basis of the definition of a Convention Refugee" (7). In order to describe the process of discursive construction, we shall for the time being leave aside any doubts as to the veracity of this statement, for it is clear from statistical evidence that factors such as employment levels in the host countries, the refugee's level of education, the country of origin, the various sociopolitical pressures active during a given historical moment, can all play roles in the acceptance or rejection of the claimant.[12]

Testifying as Authoring

The first step for an analysis of refugee testimony is to render an account of the stakes, and therefore the complexity, of the claiming process by describing the inherent difficulties of *authoring*.[13] The refugee gets *one chance* to make the case; although each claimant has the right to appeal according to current law, "the Federal Court will only consider questions of law or 'capricious' findings of fact; the appeal does not reconsider the merits of the claim for refugee status" (*Backlog* 8). The claimant, therefore, cannot afford to make any mistakes; the story must be consistent, clearly recounted, and in accord with the definition provided. Furthermore, because most claims cannot be substantiated through reference to written texts, the claimant must overcome whatever psychological, moral, or religious barriers might impede upon his or her ability to say everything that needs to be said. Persecution against individuals is generally clandestine, occurring in prisons or isolated areas, and is often conducted by official organizations such as the army or the police, who can ensure that no proof ever escapes the country (this is of course one reason why refugee testimony poses a threat to countries practicing human rights violations; such persons who choose to flee often become persecuted refugees simply through the act of fleeing). Barring the existence of a witness (who could be called to testify) or recorded material made of the persecution, the refugee cannot correlate his or her narrative. And persecution carried out on a daily basis against all persons who are members of a particular group, race, religion, or sex, for example, is difficult to document because it is deemed to be legitimate either on the basis of state law or religious practice (e.g., the treatment of women in Islamic countries). Walter Kälin, a Swiss refugee lawyer, notes the effect that this has upon refugee claimants during the hearing:

> Since few asylum seekers are able to prove their claims through written evidence such as decisions of courts, warrants of arrest or press reports of their arrest, many countries rely primarily

upon an in-person interrogation or a hearing to establish the facts and to examine the credibility of the applicant. In the absence of written evidence, the interrogation or hearing, and thus the communication between asylum-seeker and official, becomes crucial to the decision on political asylum applications.[14]

This "communication" process can become a productive construction only if the refugee as author is able to "take possession" of the refugee as hero. The hero as constructed other must become "so authoritative for the author [the claimant] that he cannot see the world of objects through any other eyes but those of the hero [constructed other], and cannot experience in any other way except from within the event that is the hero's [constructed other's] life" (*A&H*, 17). This would indeed be desirable; but what if the refugee hesitates, or misunderstands the question, or is distracted in his or her attempt to construct this productive other? The task is monumental, especially in light of the emphasis that immigration departments place on the notion of stability. Any factual or narrative inconsistency in the hearing is grounds for rejection since it suggests that the story might be untrue; and in his description of how the author proceeds to create the hero, Bakhtin offers a few of the reasons why such inconsistency may be part and parcel of any attempt of the process of self-description or creation of an other. Understanding that the author's ability to envision the hero is a long and complex procedure whereby "his reaction to the hero does not immediately become a productive reaction founded on a necessary principle," Bakhtin observes that "[b]efore the countenance of the hero finally takes shape as a stable and necessary whole, the hero is going to exhibit a great many grimaces, random masks, wrong gestures, and unexpected actions, depending on all those emotional-volitional reactions and personal whims of the author, through the chaos of which he is compelled to work his way in order to reach an authentic valuational attitude" (*A&H*, 6). If the countenance of the hero in the novel exhibits this kind of tentativeness, then the author will have to re-work the text or, at worst, the novel will be inconsistent, uneven or undialogic. But in the case of somebody who may have been tortured in their country of origin, can similar hesitations or false starts be re-written? What if one such error becomes grounds for rejection from Canada?

That the refugee should experience difficulties in recounting, in a linear fashion, the details of his or her own life is not surprising; in fact, virtually any self-representation contains potentially contradictory information that could be used to undermine the verity of the rest of the narrative. What is surprising is that someone who has undergone the trauma of persecution in another country should find him or herself in Canada attempting to relate an accurate, chronologically ordered, and systematically organized narrative to a couple of very important strangers. The refugee, with the help of a lawyer, must figure out what parts of his or her life should be recounted in order to ensure (or at least to encourage) the immigration officials' approbation. What is clear is that the refugee's (as hero's) vital interest in the events of his or her own life are mediated and permeated, or even diverted or suppressed, by the refugee's (as author's) interest in the hero as acceptable refugee. The refugee, faced with a system of legal authority that is fundamentally different from his or her own—in terms of criteria, validity of evidence presented, grounds for evaluation, and so forth—must somehow structure a stable credible "other" who will stand in his or her stead on judgement day.

Refugee claimants who arrive at a port of entry into Canada are expected to take into account all of these facts in order to adequately assess the many factors that are relevant to their claims. One of the implications of this is that the claimant must form a kind of empathy with the customs officials (the adjudicator and the immigration officer) who are doing the interrogating lest (s)he provides an image that is not in accord with the principles established and the interests at hand. The refugee claimant must experience him or herself from the position of the interrogator, a position that is not only foreign (as it would be foreign to anybody who is for the first time party to an immigration hearing) but foreign in the same sense that all Canadian customs are foreign to visitors. The refugee is being asked to utilize his or her particular perspective as an outsider to the court to evaluate the position of the "other" that he or she has been encouraged to create. Furthermore, the refugee must take this distance from him or herself while simultaneously sending back appropriate images of the immigration officers and the other parties to the hearing (the lawyer and the interpreter), just as I tried to do when I *faced* (i.e., put on a straight face for) the inquisitive immigration official at Mirabel Airport. The urgency of presenting the proper face is all the more evident when one considers that in rendering their judgement on the case, the Canadian officials are looking for a validation of their positions as respectable arbitrators and civil servants representing Canadian values and beliefs in exactly the same way that the refugee is looking for a validation to his or her claim for status as Convention Refugee. The officials, in other words, must be able to justify the decision within the logic of the system of which they are part.

Clearly then, the refugee faces the danger of misinterpreting the situation, misreading the questions or the replies of the immigration officer, de-emphasizing important elements or playing up unimportant ones, or offering an inappropriate face to the immigration officer, and that (s)he therefore risks offering inappropriate answers to the questions posed during the hearing; a nomad who has been persecuted in the country of origin, for example, could hardly be expected to be sufficiently well-versed in our culture to offer an accurate ongoing evaluation of his or her testimony in light of what is expected. The refugee continuously runs the risk of misreading the culturally contingent signs provided by the parties to the hearing, just as (s)he may, because of a sense of defiance or fear, refuse to give the information that would have otherwise validated the claim. To avoid this, the most obvious route for the claimant to follow is to heed the advice of his or her counsel, and to that degree the success of the claimant is largely dependent upon the advice of a lawyer; yet here too the claimant faces formidable obstacles. First the refugee needs a good legal and cultural counsellor; the immigration lawyer must bear the responsibility of giving solid advice to persons who are unaccustomed to Canadian legal proceedings and who are potentially unaware of the cultural and sociological framework within which their testimony will be evaluated. Second, no matter how good the lawyer might be, the refugee may choose to refuse legal advice because (s)he may be reluctant to put his or her faith in state officials or institutions; refugee claimants have often been subjected to persecution from a state apparatus similar to that one that is now conducting this potentially life-saving, potentially life-endangering hearing (persons whose claims are refused could be forced to return to their country of origin, where officials, fearing for the image of the country and the information disclosed by the claimant, may seek revenge by even greater levels of persecution). Finally the refugee may, overtly or not, follow the advice of some unnamed mediator—an uncle, a friend, a go-between— who helped ensure his or her flight from the country of origin, or the refugee may rely upon information received in one of the many organizations that attempt to assist refugees when they arrive in Canada. In most big cities black market "travel agents," international help organizations (such as the Red Cross or Amnesty International, church groups), and other local organizations all offer assistance and

advice to refugee claimants; if this advice is inappropriate or misunderstood by the claimant, the Board might rule against a refugee who
otherwise would have had a credible claim.

Authoring within the Realm of Intrinsic Structural Bias

Even a summary reading of these pamphlets, therefore, leads one to
understand that the drawbacks to an adjudication system so construed
are seldom the fault of one particular party to the claim—the lawyers,
the translators, Refugee Board, or the Federal Court judges. The problems are with a system that has been put into place to replicate and
legitimize itself. Rather than admitting persons according to the tenets
and the spirit of the convention, or as though it were a national obligation, Canada (and indeed most countries that accept refugees) admits
them in the spirit of maligned charity, as though Canadians were doing
the suffering persons of the world who are able to complete this
gigantesque process a great favor by offering them asylum and the
chance to lead a life without persecution. In fact, if we were to base our
analysis of the national objectives as regards refugees on the number of
people accepted into Canada each year, it becomes clear that Immigration Canada has no interest in addressing the international refugee
problem per se (there are, according to the conservative estimates of the
United Nations high commissioner for refugees, roughly fifteen million
refugees worldwide[15]) but rather is offering refuge to a minute proportion of persons, for reasons of the national collective conscience, in
order to fulfill international obligations (treaties, conventions, and so
forth), to ensure the maintenance of trade status (and other benefits of
international agreements), or in order to fulfill our own employment
needs. Given what we know about First World interventionalist practices from the works of Noam Chomsky (to whom I owe an important
debt for my analysis of these cases) and others, it is clear that some of
those persons who show up at our airports suffer due to the results of
our own government policies abroad. Every time Canada (or any other
country) exports nuclear or arms technology abroad, participates in a
military intervention, encourages the use of chemical-based fertilization
projects (the so-called green revolution for example), or places barriers
or restrictions upon trade with foreign countries, it is acting in ways
that can (negatively) affect domestic populations abroad. In government
rhetoric, the question of fulfilling a national *obligation* in light of
overseas policies is seldom, if ever, an issue and, if we inquire as to the

reasons in the spirit of Bourdieu's work, there is no reason why it should be. As long as the present power structures remain in place, there are no reasons, other than humanitarian, to offer aid to persecuted refugees. And humanitarianism, in the logic of capitalist profiteering and imperialist-style intervention and domination, is not a reasonable motivation.

Despite the problems outlined thus far, it is true that refugees do get admitted into the First World, and in relatively large proportions in some countries—notably Canada; but these percentages are a function of the number of persons who actually enter the system. Any refugee who wants to escape persecution, whether it be the (indirect or direct) fault of First World powers or not, must first be able to put him or herself in a position to be heard in Canada. That the First World immigration departments "hear" only a small percentage of the comparatively few claims filed in the world in a given year, and that countries in the First World take but an (ever-smaller) proportion of that percentage,[16] is testament to the fact that the international refugee system has built-in regulators that appear in the form of airport security systems, passport control stations, high-priced nonsubsidized airline tickets, off-shore border patrols, penalties for persons who assist refugees, laws permitting coast guard the permission to board vessels in international or domestic waters to "verify" and turn back "human cargo," and so forth. And that only a fraction of those persons who make it through this first line of defense actually receive status is testament to the fact that the legal system is itself a significant barrier for persons seeking freedom from persecution. I would suggest this system sets up an internal bias for "hearing" claims in the First World that come from persons who are already desirable for the First World, and that there is an intrinsic bias evident in the discourse of the hearing that demonstrates that the hearing is construed in such a manner as to favor persons who are appropriate to the employment requirements of this country.

It is true that the two pamphlets in question set out in relatively clear terms the basis for an acceptable claim and that all the refugee has to do is construct through discourse a representation of him or herself as "other" that would allow for a favorable ruling; but in order to successfully undertake this project the claimant needs excellent counsel, or else access to information concerning our society (a Western-style education, for example). Hence the immigration process favors the upper strata of Third World society, or the more privileged persons from societies that in some ways resemble our own. Therefore, the system is construed in such a fashion as to evaluate the refugee's ability to *integrate* or *assimilate* (into our workplaces, into our schools, into our political system), even though this is in no way stated in the pamphlets that are handed out in airports, or even in the laws that supposedly underwrite the refugee process. The only hint that the refugee has of this point is the not-so-subtle fact that the minister in charge of immigration in Canada was (at the time that this research was originally conducted) called the "minister of employment and immigration" (it is now linked to a minister of national security!), or the even less subtle fact that immigration policy until the First World War was designed and administered in part by major corporations, notably the railway industry.

Conclusion

As I conclude my reading of these pamphlets, I realize that there is very little encouragement that Bakhtin could offer refugees in light of the present system, a system that first generates refugees by conscious destabilization of Third World communities or pillaging of Third World resources and then shops around for labor bargains in the camps and migrations of persecuted refugees. Bakhtin's work, along with other tools of discourse analysis, can only offer us the instruments necessary to unravel the hierarchy of interests so clearly established in the legal hearing or the refugee hearing, and the motivation for imagining the creation of a system that contains the radical differences necessary to concede a place for the other as "the whole of a human being" (*A&H*, 5). Beyond that we need to rely upon soft and ephemeral notions that have little value in a discourse marketplace so construed, notions such as fair play, compassion, humanitarianism, responsibility. Perhaps the presence thereof is the only reasonable measure for the adequacy of systems of social organization, at least until the time when displacement of persons is no longer considered an undesirable aberration—or an issue for a minister of national security.

Notes

An earlier and different version of this essay appeared in *Vice Versa* 1992 (Montreal, Canada).

I would like to thank the Social Sciences and Humanities Research Council for Fellowships that have permitted me to further my research in this area of studies. Gisela Brinker-Gabler, through her generous invitation to participate in the conference that preceded this publication, has been an inspiration and an impetus for this manuscript as well as for my doctoral dissertation. I would also like to thank the Institut québécois de recherche sur la culture, in particular Denise Helly, and members of McGill University's now-defunct program in Comparative Literature, in particular Marc Angenot, Marike Finlay, Darko Suvin, and George Szanto. I deeply appreciate as well the input of Clive Thomson, Nicolas Van Schendel, Sam Abramovitch and Yzabelle Martineau.

1. George Konrád, *The Case Worker*, trans. Paul Aston (New York: Harcourt Brace Jovanovich, 1974), 63.

2. I have discussed issues concerning what literature *knows* in Clive Thomson, "Literary Knowledge: Noam Chomsky and Marc Angenot," *Intercultural Dialogue* (Amsterdam: Rodopi, forthcoming).

3. Mikhail Mikhailovich Bakhtin, "Author and Hero in Aesthetic Activity" (ca. 1920–23), trans. and notes Vadim Liapunov, in *Art and Answerability: Early Philosophical Essays by M. M. Bakhtin* (Austin: University of Texas Press, 1990). Henceforth cited as *A&H*.

4. Mikhail Mikhailovich Bakhtin, "Art and Answerability" (1919), trans. and notes Vadim Liapunov, *Art and Answerability: Early Philosophical Essays by M. M. Bakhtin* (Austin: University of Texas Press, 1990). Henceforth cited as *A&A*.

5. Immigration and Refugee Board, *Backlog Process: How the System Works*, catalogue number MQ21-16/1989E (Ottawa, 1989); and Immigration and Refugee Board, *Refugee Determination: What it Is and How it Works*, catalogue number MQ21-15/1988E (Ottawa, 1989). The process has been modified somewhat since the publication of these pamphlets; however the substance of the claiming procedure remains the same.

6. Office of the United Nations High Commissioner for Refugees has in fact published an actual handbook for this purpose, the *Handbook on Procedures and Criteria for Determining Refugee Status: Under the 1951 Convention and the 1967 Protocol Relating to the Status of Refugees* (Geneva, 1979), however it serves as a reference point more for adjudicators and legislators than refugee claimants.

7. Michael Holquist, "Introduction: The Architectonics of Answerability," in Mikhail Mikhailovich Bakhtin, *Art and Answerability: Early Philosophical Essays by M. M. Bakhtin* (Austin: University of Texas Press, 1990), xxiii. Henceforth cited as "Introduction" *A&A*.

8. Erving Goffman, *Interaction Ritual: Essays in Face-to-Face Behavior* (Garden City, N.Y.: Anchor, 1967). Hereafter referred to as *Interaction*.

9. Pierre Bourdieu, *Language and Symbolic Power*, ed. and Introd. John B. Thompson, trans. Gino Raymond and Matthew Adamson (Cambridge: Harvard University Press, 1991).

10. United Nations *Treaty Series*, vol. 189, 137.

11. United Nations, *Treaty Series*, vol. 606, 267.

12. See for example part 1, chap. 8, "The Appeal Process: Judge Mahoney Rules," in Robert F. Barsky, "The Construction Through Discourse of the Productive Other: The Case of the Canadian Convention Refugee Hearing" (Ph.D. diss., McGill, 1992, to be

published in a revised form by John Benjamins in 1994) in which a federal appeal court decision is cited as evidence that certain individuals can be rejected on the grounds that they are members of groups, or citizens of countries, that have been deemed undesirable for reasons that could only be described as racist.

13. I am making reference to Michael Holquist's pioneering article "Answering as Authoring: Mikhail Bakhtin's Trans-Linguistics," *Bakhtin: Essays and Dialogues on His Work*, ed. Gary Saul Morson (Chicago: University of Chicago Press, 1981), which brought to light for the first time many of the issues herein explored.

14. "Troubled Communication: Cross-Cultural Misunderstandings in the Asylum-Hearing," *International Migration Review* 20, no. 2, 230–41, 230–31. I have re-examined issues raised in Kalin's work in a recent article called "The Interpreter and the Canadian Convention Refugee Hearing: Crossing the potentially life-threatening boundaries between 'coccode-e-eh,' 'cluck-cluck,' and 'cot-cot-cot,'" *Traduction, Terminologie, Rédaction* 6, no. 2 (2e semester 1993): 131–156.

15. I say "conservative" because if the United Nations were to broaden the criteria of acceptance to include economic refugees and persons persecuted on account of their sex, which are in my opinion reasonable modifications even within the spirit of the present convention, there would be literally hundreds of millions of persons in need of safe passage and resettlement.

16. Consider, for example, recent German legislation concerning passage through third countries, French legislation concerning immigration eligibility, Canadian legislation concerning passage through third countries and counterfeit documentation, and so forth.

Interrogating Identity and Otherness

CHAPTER 6

Maelzel and Me

FREDERICK GARBER

Bekanntlich soll es einen Automaten gegeben haben, der so konstruiert gewesen sei, dass er jeden Zug eines Schachspielers mit einem Gegenzuge erwidert habe, der ihm den Gewinn der Partie sicherte. Eine Puppe in türkischer Tracht, eine Wasserpfeife im Munde, sass vor dem Brett, das auf einem geräumigen Tisch aufruhte. Durch ein System von Spiegeln wurde die Illusion erweckt, dieser Tisch sei von allen Seiten durchsichtig. In Wahrheit sass ein buckliger Zwerg darin, der ein Meister im Schachspiel war und die Hand der Puppe an Schnüren lenkte. Zu dieser Apparatur kann man sich ein Gegenstück in der Philosophie vorstellen. Gewinnen soll immer die Puppe, die man "historischen Materialismus" nennt. Sie kann es ohne weiteres mit jedem aufnehmen, wenn sie die Theologie in ihren Dienst nimmt, die heute bekanntlich klein und hässlich ist und sich ohnehin nicht darf blicken lassen.[1]

[The story is told of an automaton constructed in such a way that it could play a winning game of chess, answering each move of an opponent with a countermove. A puppet in Turkish attire and with a hookah in its mouth sat before a chessboard placed on a large table. A system of mirrors created the illusion that this table was transparent from all sides. Actually, a little hunchback who was an expert chess player sat inside and guided the puppet's hand by means of strings. One can imagine a philosophical counterpart to this device. The puppet called "historical materialism" is to win all the time. It can easily be a match for anyone if it enlists the services of theology, which today, as we know, is wizened and has to keep out of sight.][2]

Thus does Walter Benjamin begin his essay "Über den Begriff der Geschichte" (On the Concept of History). A hunchbacked dwarf (*buckliger Zwerg*) who stands for theology squats inside a mechanical

103

Turk. He guides the figure with strings, stringing along the public and any of its members who seek to beat the automaton at chess. Benjamin's mastery of overtones leaves no element in the scene free from the taste of irony. Theology is currently a small and ugly dwarf that has to keep out of sight, presumably because of its hideousness. Yet its potency can operate from secret internal places to foster the business of what seems its arch enemy, the Turk of historical materialism. The Turk, too, takes on ironies. He emerges from modes of eighteenth century exoticism, the charms and frissons of the vaguely Oriental put into the sardonic form of a mechanical puppet. But those are the charms of a device that needs a mover within itself to make its matches work, a ghost in the machine, a human at the center.

Like all prefatory texts this passage holds instructions for reading, a guide that, given the ironies rampant in the passage, ought to be taken with considerable care. Benjamin goes on to use theological analogies to make his case for the differences between a materialist reading of history and one that reads it only in terms of inevitable progress. At the beginning he speaks of the present's redemption of the past through "a *weak* Messianic power" (254) [*eine* schwache *messianische Kraft* (694)]. At the end he speaks of a redemptive mode of time (*Jetztzeit*). Filled with the presence of the now that mode ought to be called "messianic," for it is a moment in which the Messiah, as Torah readers argue, might choose to enter our lives. History is no more empty than the mechanical Turk. As the Turk appears to be hollow but is filled with potency so too is history filled with the potent immediacies of *Jetztzeit*, messianic time.[3]

Other vitalities are implicit in the passage on the Turk. Its multiplicities take in not only a set of analogies but analogy as such, what it is, how it works. Benjamin suggests the testing of an overt allegory. He wants to fashion for philosophy a workable analogy to the mechanical device, one that images the relations of theology and historical materialism in the complicated interplay of Turk and dwarf. Just as the automaton can answer each move of its opponent with a countermove, an opposing response (*Gegenzuge*), so can one set up a counterpart (*Gegenstück*) that responds to the odd pairing that makes the automaton happen. In his preface Benjamin suggests not only that his essay will build on analogies but that questions of analogy, its properties as an "answer," are built into the context of false Turk and genuine dwarf. These issues involve the immersion of the figures in illusion, their relations not only to the object of their duplicity but to duplicity as

such. Benjamin's mastery of overtones matches his masterful understanding of the questions of canniness and craft, pretense and potency,
implicit in the nature of this game-playing machine. In fact precisely
those questions had been implicit in earlier readings of the remarkable
device.

The automaton to which Benjamin refers was known as "Maelzel's
Chess Player." It was widely displayed in Europe at the end of the
eighteenth century and exhibited in America in the early part of the
nineteenth. Built by Baron Wolfgang von Kempelen in 1769, it was later
taken over by a technician named Maelzel, whose tours in America,
begun in 1827, made the machine so popular that it came to be known
under his name. At this distance it seems pointless to call Maelzel's
machine a fraud. "Illusion" makes the better term, since the question
always concerned how the Turk was used as a device *through which* to
play chess. Indeed, the matter of duplicity was so openly on the surface
that it became, for some observers (Hoffmann and Poe among them),
part of the meaning of the machine, part of its fields for speculation.
(Those fields include the question whether the "openness" of duplicity
was itself duplicitous.)

Whatever the intent of von Kempelen and Maelzel their primary
effect was to get the spectator going on puzzles of procedure, how the
operator worked the figure or caused it to be worked. The ultimate
exposure of Maelzel's machinations (two boys in Baltimore saw a
person emerging from the machine) did not end the lessons the machine
seemed always to foster. The chess player spawned a subsidiary industry
of its own, a substantial set of writings that sought to undo the
mockup's mystery, most of them attempts at quasi-scientific treatises.[4]
Most took the Turk as inanimate and illusory, worked upon and deceptive, a tool for the business of Mind that was patently not what it
seemed. The passivity of its status entwined with the way it was
perceived to produce a spectrum of solutions. Most were based on the
surmise that there was a person in the machine, the active and genuine
foil to the submissive, fictive Turk. That is, however single the Turk may
have appeared, he was most often taken as half of a binary setup, what
seemed a tidy passage of binary play. Yet this too could have been read
as part of the illusion the Turk fostered, and at least a couple of
commentators, Hoffmann and Poe, implied precisely that point. Taking
into the context a different sort of games-playing, they worked the
matter of illusion through its multiple implications until it got to the
point that Benjamin reached, the relations of duplicity to matters of

figuration, the relations of each of those to the shapes of personality. Putting the point another way: the machine could be taken as more than a toy for speculation (in several senses of the term) for it also could be taken as a model of the workings of Mind, even of Mind on minds as well as on the mindless. (That we are therefore put in the same status as machines could not have escaped some readers.)

Yet that does not exhaust the ironies that dogged the mechanical Turk. Maelzel died in 1838, and the machine was stored in the Chinese Museum in Philadelphia. That placement says a great deal about the pop Orientalism that skirts about the Turk but was never analyzed by Maelzel's commentators. In fact the machine took part in a myriad of discourses, ranging in tonality from an Orientalism so pop that it would put a phony Turk into a Chinese museum to ponderings of the relation of machines to their controllers, that is, of machines to us. For writers like Hoffmann and Poe, Maelzel's machine was a clustering site for all sorts of readings, including readings of reading itself. Benjamin's introduction to his discourse on history responds to a range of readings that had been broached a century before, responds by suggesting that range through a spectrum of implications.

The texts by Hoffmann and Poe display the image's flexibility, its capacity to absorb discourses and disclose their interrelations. Hoffmann wrote "Die Automate" in January 1814 and later took it into the collection *Die Serapions-Brüder.*[5] The central narrative of the tale involves the love of Ferdinand, young and impressively rich, for a woman he heard singing in the next room of an inn. That ground tone of desire takes the unhappy Ferdinand into unresolvable longing, into the making of a portrait that he secretes in a locket, into, finally, an encounter with the woman in a church where she is about to be married. Hoffmann offers no tight conclusion to the tale but only a hearsay remark that Ferdinand, evidently mad, was ultimately cured.

This tale of ambiguous appeasement is actually, however, a text within a text, the stratum that begins the tale having to do with a Talking Turk, a puzzling automaton given to cryptic utterance. The spectator would whisper a question into the Turk's right ear, at which it would turn its eyes and head, then whisper a low reply, the spectator sensing a movement of breath-like air that was gentle but manifest. The Turk's speech was oracular, its lips motionless, the figure itself a quirky composite of opposites that Hoffmann talks of as at once alive and dead (*lebendigtoten*).

Part of that life came from the figure's extraordinary lifelikeness: "eine wahrhaft orientalisch geistreiche Physiognomie gab dem Ganzen ein Leben, wie man es selten bei Wachsbildern . . . findet" [a truly Oriental cleverness in the physiognomy gave to the whole a life one rarely finds in wax images] (320). The automaton was about the height of a human being, an unexceptionable point. More striking in terms of lifelikeness was the touch of the breath of air that emerged from the automaton as it whispered its sententious replies. That act, in particular, seemed to unnerve the observers. But the exhibitor had other ironies with which to undo the audience, other sorts of sardonic play with the idea of *lebendigtoten*. That the Turk was in no more than a figurative sense alive, whatever that breath of air, that it had somehow to be connected to "die Rückwirkung eines denkenden Wesens" [the agency of a thinking being] (321) seemed obvious and unarguable; so obvious that the exhibitor played further on that question, disconcerting the curious at precisely the point where they expected confirmation. While the Turk was making its gestures and answering to queries, the exhibitor joked with spectators in another corner of the room, severing any suggestions of direct manipulation, leaving the audience aware that what had to be true was being openly denied. The acts of Turk and impresario seemed to argue for the impossible, that the automaton was "ein ganz für sich bestehendes Wesen, das irgendeiner Verbindung mit ihm nicht bedürfe" [a wholly independent being that needed no tie with (its owner)] (321). Yet the performance could as easily go in quite the other direction, toward an argument that stresses the Turk as a machine, confirming the need for those human ties that nowhere could be seen. After the figure gave several answers "setzte der Künstler einen Schlüssel in die linke Seite der Figur ein und zog mit vielem Geräusch ein Uhrwerk auf" [the artist put a key into the left side of the figure and, with a great deal of clamor, wound some clockwork up] (320). Further, he would, if requested, open a lid "und man erblickte im innern der Figur ein künstliches Getriebe von vielen Rädern" [and one saw inside the figure an elaborate mechanism made of many wheels] (320). This gesture not only showed that there was no room inside the figure for a person to hide; it confirmed the Turk's duplicity, its way of playing on perceptions and making the exhibit focus as much on the capacities of the audience as on those of the Turk. What the audience *knew* to be so, what could *only* be so, was in no apparent sense so; sometimes, at least. The impresario would never let the audience rest, never offer the comforting luxury of a conclusion.

The Turk, thus, was involved in two substantial modes of play, that of *lebendigtoten*, that of connection/disconnection, each stressing its own mode of irreconcilability. Together they affirmed the Turk's brazen stance in the world, its refusal of either/or and, it seems, any binary structure, its ultimate rejection of any resolution. Yet it refused such patterns and ends, such twonesses and conclusions, within a condition grounded in elemental twoness (*Zweiheit, Doppelheit*); that is, in absolute duplicity. That contradiction undoes the Turk's occasional claims for autonomy, its insistence that it is not a purely binary package. *Zweiheit*, and *Doppelheit*, like the English *duplicity*, echo the Latin *duplex*, "double," "twofold." If duplicity is twoness/doubleness, how could the Turk refuse twoness yet do so within a condition whose very name defines it as elementally double? The arguments of the language that fingers duplicity suggest that the Turk could not escape his doubled condition, whatever the figure may contend. At the end one had to deduce that the refusal of twoness must be the figment of a refusal, must be one more duplicity in those that surrounded the Turk. The automaton could, seriously, in no sense be alive. There had to be some connection with a living, active will, some other to the Turk that in effect ran the Turk, an other that could only be human. At the end the obvious won out, but only after gyrations and with no clear indication of how it had won out. That this pattern of deduction was a parody, a mockery, of the spectators' capacities, what they thought they knew or could ultimately know, emerges in their discomfort, their eventual itchiness. Part of the target of the scam was surely their radical vanities. That the target also could be our exhausted acceptance of twoness, that we might be driven by exhaustion to accept what we should not accept, could be ultimate ironies that will take some doing to unfold.

Whatever (for the moment) the case, that target took in questions of language and representation. If there is a sense in which the Turk seems trapped in language there is a corollary sense in which the words that stand for things seem very hard to resolve into the clarity of conclusions. If Benjamin was later to suggest that the Turk had much to do with questions of representation, so too did Hoffmann in his variant of Maelzel's machine, and so was Poe to do. One begins to sense that such matters may be endemic to the workings of the Turk, that they may be much of what the Turk is all about.

But the Turk's refusal of unified conclusions has more than parodies in mind. The questions the Turk fosters take in not only language but the relations of question and response, what the stranger knows of the lives of the audience. Ferdinand, already in love with the mysterious singer, whispers a question in the Turk's ear, gets only a rebuff, persists and then gets an answer that shakes him into uneasiness. Not only does the Turk know of the portrait in the secret locket but he advises Ferdinand that when he next sees his beloved she will be lost to him forever. Such unveiling of secrets turns out to be a regular pattern in the whisperings of the Turk. Whatever the tones of the Turk's replies, dry or roughly facetious [bald trocken, bald ziemlich grob-spasshaft], they were wonderfully relevant to that questioner. "Oft überraschte ein mystischer Blick in die Zukunft, der aber nur von dem Standpunkt möglich war, wie ihn sich der Fragende selbst tief im Gemüt gestellt hatte" [often (the questioner) was surprised by a mystical glance into the future, possible only from a standpoint deep in the questioner's soul] (321). Some technical genius who could work acoustical and optical contrivances had, as well, an extraordinary gift of insight (*Sehergeist*). That gift was scary precisely because it implied a connection (*Verbindung*) that the spectator could not know of and had no way to control. As Ferdinand puts the nervousness: "dem unsichtbaren Wesen, das sich uns durch den Türken auf eine geheimnisvolle Weise mitteilt, Kräfte zu Gebote stehen, die mit magischer Gewalt unsre geheimsten Gedanken beherrschen" [the invisible being who, in a secret manner, communicates with us through the Turk, has powers at his disposal that rule our most secret thoughts with magic force] (325). Those cryptic connections return in a later argument that probes the concept of spiritual or psychic rapport. They probe modes of sympathy that act more like empathy because the Turk seems able to rummage through subjective interstices, invading the questioner's soul. Ludwig puts that point in terms of player, instrument and harmony, suggesting that, after all, we are as much an instrument as is the talking automaton. The powers of the Turk strike our inner strings "welche sonst nur durcheinander rauschten . . . dass sie vibrieren und ertönen und wir den reinen Akkord deutlich vernehmen" [which otherwise only rustle among themselves . . . so that they vibrate and sound and we clearly perceive the pure chord] (334). Some mysterious power at the disposal of the Turk compels us to use him as a kind of mirror. His voice echoes our own but in an echo that needs his power to be brought into play, to turn subliminal mutterings into self-reflecting sounds. As Ludwig puts the point, "so sind wir aber es selbst, die wir uns die Antworten erteilen" [it is we who impart the answers to ourselves] (334). That the play of Narcissus and

Echo seems part of the Maelzel myth is one of Hoffmann's main contributions to the image's ramifications.

Another has to do with the way Hoffmann brings out a strain of subliminal uneasiness in our relations to Maelzel's device. Ludwig opens that uneasiness when he first enters the tale as part of a group discussing the Talking Turk. Such devices, he argues, do not so much counterfeit life as travesty it. From the time of a childhood terror over a waxworks exhibition he could not enter such places without being seized by an eery feeling ("grauenhafte Gefühl" [322]). The unstaring eyes of the figures seemed to unnerve him most, and a quotation from *Macbeth* seems most appropriate, most revealing: "Thou hast no speculation in those eyes / Which thou dost glare with." Hoffmann picks up Shakespeare's play on speculation/speculum to suggest that what terrifies us most is the absence of that which gives us back to ourselves, that which speculates, mirrors. That absence appears in the dummy's refusal to echo us back to ourselves. We do not see self in the other but only the blank and wholly other that holds no part of ourselves, that has no power to help us figure ourselves through reflection. What terrifies, then, has to do with that mirroring in which we see ourselves in others, see ourselves *as* other. Our capacity to project ourselves onto/into the world, those capacities through which we seek to be at home in the world, find only vacant frustration within those unspeculating eyes, those eyes that will not give back what we so intently put forth in pure intentionality. No wonder that Ludwig points out how, in waxwork museums, visitors tend to talk only in a whisper. We whisper into the face of the absolutely other, our voices subdued not only because what we see seems uncanny and ghastly but because it refuses to return us to ourselves (return us as a mirror does, as a photograph was to do; we are seeing one of the reasons why the daguerreotype would fascinate Poe). The rejection of "speculation" ("unreflecting" continues most of the contours of the pun) threatens those basic acts through which we put ourselves into the world, those acts that give us, effectually, our being in the world.

That such acts have much to do with questions of power in the world (something more than worldly power) emerges later in the text, where Ludwig returns to the relations of machines and humans, this time in terms of automata that play music. Outraged and indignant, Ludwig finds such activities abominable, unnatural. It is only the touch of the human that can give life to instruments, only the human touch and breath that "die unbekannten unaussprechlichen Gefühle erregen,

welche, mit nichts Irdischem hienieden verwandt, die Ahndungen eines
fernen Geisterreichs und unsers höhern Seins in demselben hervorrufen"
[arouse the unknown, inexpressible feelings that, related to nothing
earthly, evoke the intuitions of a distant spiritual realm and our higher
being within it] (338). It is now a question of our place not only in this
nether world but within the greater realm that enfolds our higher life,
that realm that is the home of our utmost capacities, the fullest possible
reach of our acts of self-constitution. Ludwig argues that even the most
unfeeling player has more of an inner impulse than any machine can
offer. *Any* person does more for the instrument and for us than does no
person at all.

Yet Hoffmann's uneasy humanism is in large part uneasy because it
carries within itself the seeds of its own undoing. "Isn't it the spirit,"
Ludwig argues, "that uses those bodily organs to bring into active life
that which sounded in its deepest depths?" [Ist es nicht vielmehr das
Gemüt, welches sich nur jener physischen Organe bedient, um das, was
in seiner tiefsten Tiefe erklungen, in das rege Leben zu bringen] (338).
Given the terms of Hoffmann's romantic humanism it is indeed as
Ludwig says; but those terms also include several strata of irony that
turn this humanist impulse back upon itself in precisely the same
gesture seen in other readings of romantic humanism, in those of, say,
Lord Byron and Edgar Poe.[6] The voice that speaks from within, that
speaks to our outer life about the higher realms available, speaks from
precisely the point where the voice of the Turk had spoken. That point,
as it turns out, is also the site of the whisper within the Turk that
Ludwig has concluded is our own voice speaking out, speaking answers
to ourselves ("it is we who answer our own question"). Hoffmann
never openly states that these contrary voices (the one that speaks a
transcendent future, the one that speaks an all-too-immanent present)
are precisely the same; yet he certainly makes clear that they speak from
the same place. It seems, Hoffmann argues, that we are incessant
whiners: we complain about automata that will not give us back to ourselves, yet we complain when their voices give us more than we want.

Ludwig later argues that the music we hear within us is none other
than the music that we hear within nature, those natural sounds that
echo the tones of primeval days. The multiple interrelations of all those
internal sounds never get spelled out in "Die Automate." They stay as
open, as unresolved, as any other conclusion, the human linked to the
natural through ties that always comfort, but also linked to itself
through ties that disconcert.

The Turkish automaton suggests fundamental ways in which we represent ourselves, our figurings of ourselves not only individually but as generic human figures. The responses of the Turk are modes through which the questioners constitute themselves both privately and generally. They are modes of self-making, self-elaborating, compelled by powers the spectators cannot understand. That Ferdinand's self-making nearly led to self-destruction—he approaches madness toward the ending of the tale—comes as a cogent statement on the dangers of self-constituting and the linkage of those dangers to modes of figuration, our compulsive fashioning of metaphors of ourselves.

How then to define oneself under such slippery circumstances? How can the text define itself, its contours and its context, when it refuses resolution, sardonically offering no more than a conclusion without conclusiveness? At the end we are never told how to work out the patterns of the anomalous *lebendigtoten*, if there are any patterns at all. Nor are we ever told how Ferdinand escaped madness, though he suggests at the end that the text could be a spoof, part of his passion for incompleteness. The content does not resolve nor is there any resolution in the text's own self-definition, its reading of what it is. Jean-François Ricci speaks of "Die Automate" as a hybrid attempt, "tentative hybride . . . récit, Märchen et dissertation" (314), all of these at once, all inseparable. Hoffmann's text takes in generic uncertainty in precisely the same way that it takes in existential uncertainty and the uncertainty of conclusions.

We ought by now to suspect that there is something in Maelzel's automaton that fosters misgivings about definition. Our suspicions are furthered by Poe's own reading of the image, his early text called "Maelzel's Chess-Player." When the piece appears at all it usually appears among collections of Poe's essays, for example in the second volume of the Library of America edition, from which I take my quotations.[7] It is routinely called an "essay" in the few studies of the work, in, for example, the early reading by W. K. Wimsatt, though in one of his footnotes Wimsatt puts "Essay" within quotation marks, as though he suspected something more (141 n. 11). The bibliographers at *PMLA* seem to have sensed something as well, since their category for its genre puts Poe's piece as a short story. In these scenes of categorical puzzle one suspects a subtext at work to which those categories respond, working, perhaps, in the automaton as such, certainly in the pieces by Hoffmann and Poe.[8]

Poe's text is itself a scene of such categorical puzzles. It prefigures the generic dilemmas in the essays about itself and the decrees of *PMLA* by thematizing such dilemmas near the beginning of the text. In fact the text not only suggests the quandaries it will cause but worries a version of those quandaries in the person of the Turk. Given that the question of genre is finally a question of kinds (the literature on theory of genre uses those terms interchangeably), Poe finds reason to worry the issues through a reading of the kind of Maelzel's automaton, its mode of being as well as its mode of being in the world. Automata, Poe implies near the beginning of his piece, should be spoken of as a kind, for their being is of a species peculiar to itself, different from anything else that seems to behave like them. At once device and figment, automata play with those properties in ways whose degrees of overtness fascinate Poe. Yet since overtness implies its requisite opposite the automaton also suggests a set of covert intentions, designs of the machine upon its audience. The question of its kind concerns not only the purity of its being, its autonomy, self-subsistence; the question also includes the purity of its intention, the purport of its design.

"There have been," Poe says "many and wonderful automata" (1253), and he goes on to describe a set. Drawing his account from sources such as Brewster's *Letters on Natural Magic*, he speaks of a tiny coach and horse with attendant coachman and page as well as a tiny lady who presented a petition to the child Louis XIV. He speaks also of an automaton in the shape of a magician who answered a limited number of questions already prepared on oval medallions, the magician responding with the relevant written answer. Poe posits no particular puzzles about either of these automata. One looks at the coachman or the magician and sees, at once, the claims and counterclaims, the openness of the pretense, the charms of a fiction that reveals itself as such while playing at what it is not. Poe finds far more remarkable the duck of Jacques de Vaucanson, exceptional not only for the nature of its activities but the quality of its representation: "The duck of Vaucanson . . . was of the size of life, and so perfect an imitation of the living animal that all the spectators were deceived" (1255).[9] But the duck that squawks and walks like a duck, eats and digests like a duck, is not in fact a duck, whatever the popular logic. The duck maker's handling of that logic fascinates Poe. The play around the duck works differently than the play around the coach or the magician because it takes representation to the point of intended deception. Poe begins his classifications with a remarkable example of the defiance of classification, the claims of a figment to be other than what it is, its refusal of the exclusions included in the question of kinds. He begins his classifications with an announcement of criteria that start to be undermined as soon as they are announced. One enters the question of kinds with the suggestion that the question cannot be pursued until its own grounds are queried, its own kind established.

Much of that querying focuses on fundamental issues in classification as such, especially the question of how it happens at all. Take, again, the duck of Vaucanson, which carries into the problem of the status of the automaton a flagrant presentation of what the automaton is not. It looks as a genuine duck would look ("Every bone in the real duck had its representative in the automaton. . . . Every cavity, apophysis and curvature was imitated" [1255]). It acts as a genuine duck would act, producing "the sound of quacking in the most natural manner" (1255). The Turk, on the other hand, pays little attention to the imitation of life; in fact it flaunts its unnaturalness. Its eyes "roll unnaturally in the head," while the figure as a whole is "artificial and unnatural," differing in that way from other of Maelzel's automata that are entirely "free from the semblance of artificiality" (1270). That is also how it differs from the duck of Vaucanson, which is publicly defined in terms of what it professes to be but actually is not, defined in terms of its *veritable* other. Underlying the duck's definition is an implicit pairing of contraries, lifelike/unlifelike, a pairing that seeks to clarify the being of the duck in terms of its acts and appearance before a curious audience. Underlying the Turk's definition is precisely the same pairing, this time, however, used to distinguish the Turk from other automata that look very different but are mechanically the same. Here there is no question of the object presenting itself as other than it is. As Poe's language repeatedly insists, the Turk is blatantly "unnatural," a term Poe uses for several reasons, not least because it suggests an additional tool for defining, another useful twosome, the pairing of natural/unnatural. Of course that additional pairing can also be used for the duck, its look as well as its action, though the relation of the duck to either of the pairings has to be very different from that of the Turk. Indeed the relation of duck and Turk is as much a play of contraries as any of the pairings Poe uses to define both.

Poe understands that terms like *lifelike* and *natural* have to be taken not only in terms of themselves but in terms of their opposites. He seeks to categorize, then, through radical oxymora that give the impression of pure binarity. He uses pairings such as lifelike/unlifelike and natural/unnatural as epistemological tools. He suggests through those tools that we cannot know and define what we think something is without also knowing and defining what we think it is not. Using that which we oppose and stands opposed to us, we draw upon the other in order to define ourselves, that other which shares the context in which we seek self-definition. Definition takes place in relation. It is a metonymical practice, taking into its activities other elements within a context. In their status as metonyms those elements offer a play of self and other, making the act of defining an elemental business of likening and unlikening. The business of figuration suggested in Hoffmann and Benjamin turns up in early Poe, in this anomalous text that ties questions of likening to questions of being, questions of context to existential status. With his passion for metonymy Poe would have understood Wallace Stevens's point that "one is not duchess / A hundred yards from a carriage."

We need not, however, go as far ahead as Stevens to find such points suggested, to worry questions of being in terms of questions of context. We gain a completer perspective on Poe's interest in these issues by recognizing that he was working with a kind of self-defining that had a crucial place among his contemporaries. We can gain that perspective by drawing on an instance useful not only for its prominence but, strikingly, for its timing. Poe's essay on Maelzel's Chess-Player was published in the *Southern Literary Messenger* for April 1836. Emerson's small book *Nature* was published anonymously the following September, and he puts into his introduction a way of reading these issues that is as illuminating for Poe as for Emerson's early attitude toward our status in the world.[10] Practicing a version of the binarity Poe had just put forth Emerson argues that

> philosophically considered, the universe is composed of Nature and the Soul. Strictly speaking, therefore, all that is separate from us, all which Philosophy distinguishes as the NOT ME, that is, both nature and art, all other men and my own body, must be ranked under this name, NATURE. In enumerating the values of nature and casting up their sum, I shall use the word in both senses;—in its common and in its philosophical import. In inquiries so general as our present one, the inaccuracy is not material; no confusion of though will occur. *Nature,* in the common sense, refers to essences unchanged by man; space, the air, the river, the leaf.[11]

One has, then, not only a pairing of Soul and Nature, Emerson's version of self and other, but a partly implicit duo ("duet" seems most accurate) of ME/NOT ME, each defining itself through relation in much the same way we saw suggested in Poe. Yet Emerson openly recognizes the ambiguity in his use of the word *Nature*. It is at once the inclusive term for all that is NOT ME but also, simultaneously, for what we usually mean by Nature, Nature "in the common sense [as] space, the air, the river, the leaf." His Nature is not only an element within itself but *also* the whole of itself, not only part of an encompassing context but *also* the entire context. That shifty definition ought to make us uneasy with the subject of his introduction, the apparently neater pairing of the implicit ME and the explicit NOT ME (a pairing we shall be drawing on for the rest of this book). Emerson can stand as touchstone not only for the mellifluous meeting of ME and NOT ME but also for the acknowledgement that such categories generate problems. He claims that "in inquiries so general as our present one, the inaccuracy [in the use of the term *Nature*] is not material; no confusion of thought will occur." Yet he also makes clear that the act of demarcation has endemic difficulties, that the way we use words like *Nature* creates slippery conditions that, at the least, ought to alert us to the presence of uncertainty.

Emerson seems to be seeking a way out of these dilemmas by his manner of printing the term. "NATURE" in all caps and "Nature" with an initial cap seem to mean the same, while "nature" all lower case and "*Nature*" italicized but with an initial cap appear, together, to have their own separate meaning. Yet though these categories seem to cohere, they may not really do so, for there is another use of the term ("in enumerating the values of nature") that, though all lower case, cannot be persuasively defined as belonging in either category. If it means the same as "NATURE," the use to which it seems closest, then it goes typographically askew, making the package inconsistent, indeterminate. Further, the question of typography brings in the question of written language, which the passage appears to privilege because of what it does with typographical maneuvers. But if the passage does so privilege, how are we to take its typographical skewing, its puzzling inconsistencies? And, given that all such passages build on oppositions, how can we handle what it does to the spoken language, what happens to the words when the passage is read aloud? In an ordinary oral voicing the term *Nature*, whatever its printing, sounds exactly the same whenever we speak the word, collapsing any distinctions the written had sought to make, fostering homogeneity. If there is an imperfect consistency in the written version of the text there is a disconcerting consistency when the text is read aloud. All distinctions break down into a general indistinction, Genesis run backward. Such results suggest the reasons for the privileging of written language, which seeks to offset the deceptive similitudes in the oral; but the passage as a whole suggests that the written can never quite cohere, make all its distinctions work out. Emerson argues that these slight inconsistencies should not bother us. Yet his comments are, simultaneously, a covering and uncovering that, whatever else they do, trouble the peace of binary conditions. Emerson's pairing of ME/NOT ME defines the problems of a condition as well as the contours on which the condition is built. He shares something more with Poe, than contemporaneity. His prefatory passage is an exercise in naming that, like all good exercises, shows the problems to which it is prey. If the pairing of ME/NOT ME helps us to understand something of Poe's own practices, that understanding includes the enigmas as well as the shapes.

Which means, that, however comforting the systems Poe proffers throughout his piece on Maelzel we ought to be uneasy when we find them so comforting. (That flagrant combination of openness and mystery was to appear eight years later in "The Purloined Letter," not a convincing model of a comforting text.) If, as we came to suspect, the openness of duplicity in Hoffmann's version of Maelzel was itself part of his tale's radical duplicity (the Turk trapped in the twoness he claims to disclaim) then such entrapment could be true of Poe's reading of the chess player. We ought to suspect such handiness as the pairings seem to purport, given that Poe never hands anything over so easily, given the suspiciously appealing neatness (when was Poe ever so appealing?) of the pairings we have uncovered (pairings that, perhaps, we have been appealingly *led* to uncover).

Consider what Poe does with Babbage's calculating machine, his linking example between the survey of automata and Maelzel's chess-playing machine. Babbage's "engine of wood and metal . . . not only compute[s] astronomical and navigation tables to any given extent, but render[s] the exactitude of its operations mathematically certain through its power of correcting its possible errors" (1255). It will even "print off its elaborate results, when obtained, without the slightest intervention of the intellect of man" (1255). Yet that, Poe argues, is not so wonderful after all, given the nature of mathematical solutions, given what a machine can do with them. Mathematical calculations, he argues, are "fixed and determinate. Certain *data* being given, certain

results necessarily and inevitably follow" (1255). This mode of calcula-
tion, self-contained, autonomous, depends on nothing except the
structure through which it functions. As Poe reads the science the
procedures of mathematics have no room for deviation, no place for
modification. This means that, however complex the problems mathematics poses, one can build a machine that can solve those problems.
Put another way, Babbage's calculating machine is an instance of pure
machine, as pristine in its mechanism as it is in its autonomy, pristine in
the one because it is so in the other.[12]

Whatever the level of purity to which Maelzel's machine aspires, it
has to be very different because it plays a different game. In chess, Poe
says, there is "no determinate progression. . . . No one move in chess
necessarily follows from any other . . . from the first move in the game
of chess no especial second move follows of necessity" (1256). Alge-
braic solutions depend on the certainty of operations, but the playing of
chess is always defined by uncertainty because one can never be sure of
the moves of one's antagonist. The antagonist, Poe says, has an "indeterminate will." It is because of that indeterminacy that Maelzel's machine is not "pure" in the way we can speak of "purity" in Babbage's
machine.

It looks as though we have uncovered another binary condition.
There is a certainty of "narrative" in mathematical modes that stands as
wholly other to the uncertainty of progression in any game of chess.
Poe's oxymoronic pairings continue with this play of determinacy and
indeterminacy, it too so neatly binary; yet we have already been alerted
by the fiercely defiant duck to be uneasy with such claims, to suspect in
these modes what we saw in the duck, at least the possibility of a
categorical breakdown.

Consider the question of my antagonist in chess, that person whose
will is so difficult to predict, who *by his very being* creates indeterminacy. Definition is again a practice relation, a metonymical act, the
antagonist what he is because he takes a particular stance in relation to
me. He is that which stands over against me (*anti*) in a condition of
struggle (*agon*), that which, in several senses, is my opposition. Yet
what I say of him he can say of me as well, the opposite holding true
from his side of the board. He is to me what I am to him. My
antagonist looks to me from my side of the board just as I look to him
from his side of the board (compare Irwin on mirroring). I stand as
antagonist to the one who stands over against me in precisely the same
way he stands as antagonist to me. It is beginning to look as though I

need him there in order to define myself, need to comprehend that which I am not in order to understand that which I am. In Emersonian terms I need a NOT ME in order to define a ME. But here too our relationship rests on parity. If what I say on these issues is true for myself it is true for him as well, on the opposite side of the board. He needs me as antagonist in order to be himself, needs me as a NOT ME in order to be his own ME. How obliging we are, how convenient the arrangement; yet how difficult it is to say we are any single thing. Each of us is at once a ME and a NOT ME, *at once* ourselves and our other's opposite. All those tidy demarcations between ME and NOT ME begin rapidly to collapse when we see what is involved in playing an ordinary game of chess. What seemed like pigeonholes come finally to be the home of a very different species, our image now that of a web of relations.

What then of the chess playing Turk and whoever/whatever it is that manipulates its moves? What then of the Turk's relation to the matter of ME/NOT ME? Poe claims throughout his study that the Turk cannot stand alone, that it is in no way autonomous, that human agency shapes its acts. He spends much of his study in showing how a man can be inserted into the table of the device so that he is invisible to the crowd and able to work the Turk to counter the antagonist's moves. Poe suggests that a system of mirrors within Maelzel's contrivance conceals the man inside. That system, he says, dupes the observer into believing that no one is within, that somehow, incredibly, the Turk is working alone. Yet of course the Turk is not, and that denial shows Turk and man to be in precisely the same conditions as those that drive the antagonists in chess. The Turk cannot do a thing without the man to maneuver it but the man's internal maneuvers would have no meaning, no function, without the figure of the Turk through which to make duplicitous moves. Insofar as the man within acts as an agent he cannot be more autonomous than the figure of the Turk. Neither agent nor Turk can be wholly agent or Turk without the presence of the other, without the other acting as Other. In the workings of the machine and the workings of the game of chess the same principles hold.[13]

Yet the players are not the same whatever the likenesses of condition, and those differences lead into grander readings of the text. The man can know himself to be NOT ME to the Turk but the Turk cannot know itself to be NOT ME to the man. Taken purely as object (however uncertain that taking) the Turk is all machine and needs the warm life within in order to be more. Distinctions like these are crucial not only because they differentiate us from machines but because they take Poe's text into sublimer figurations. Given those needs and distinctions, given those spatial relations, given the man within as an image of thinking direction, Poe takes us inevitably toward a reading of Maelzel's machine as a lucid, articulate allegory of a classical humanist stance. *Machine* is an old term for the human body, instances appearing as early as *Hamlet* in 1602 and in work closer to Poe such as Wordsworth's poem of 1804 "She was a Phantom of Delight." In this poem on his wife, Wordsworth speaks of seeing in her "the very pulse of the machine." That play of "pulse" and "machine" (each word has to take in several meanings at once) sounds from an old understanding of the relations between the machine and the life residing within, a life classically rendered as the ghost (the *spiritus*) in the machine. That old representation of the relation of spirit and body works subtextually through Wordsworth's poem and more openly in Hoffmann. A version of the old relation appears in Poe's reading of the question of Maelzel's Turk. When he argues for the existence of a ghost in the machine, Poe taps an ancient claim about the nature of the human, his piece at one of its levels a patent figuration of the way we work our lives. His reading of the allegory shows a refusal of categories that is as pointed in the Blake of *The Marriage of Heaven and Hell* as it is in the Wordsworth of "Phantom of Delight." This suggests that some current readings of terms like *machine* had gotten to be problematic. Those problems were, intensely, about the meaning of ME.

Or, continuing the allegory of the meaning of the human, the problems were intensely about ME as human figure, as figure for the human. Hoffmann had shown us as incessant whiners, complaining when the other seemed wholly, only, itself, complaining again when the other acknowledged our protest and took the part of ourselves, took part in ourselves. Poe, on the other hand, never grants the chance that the machine is pure machine, only a set of blank eyes that will not speculate on us. Poe's belaboring of the point that no machine can judge in the way a human can sends essentially the same message that Hoffmann's Ludwig had sent in arguing for the necessity of the touch of the human. The figure within the workings of Maelzel's Chess-Player is central in several ways, his literal positioning part of the allegorical framework that stresses human centrality. We are not only central *in* but also central *to* that mode of romantic humanism that makes us microcosmic, makes us that without which all things would be blank and inert. Emerson puts that centrality pointedly in the small book *Nature*:

> man is an analogist and studies relation in all objects. He is placed in the centre of beings, and a ray of relation passes from every other being to him. And neither can man be understood without these objects, nor these objects without man. All the facts in natural history taken by themselves, have no value, but are barren, like a single sex. But marry it to human history, and it is full of life. (Emerson 21)

Poe knows that positioning and its attendant fecundity; Hoffmann does too. It is part of what they responded to in the makeup of Maelzel's figure. Emerson stresses what was implicit in Hoffmann and Poe, the central significance of the human as maker of relation.

It is precisely that question of ourselves as makers of relation that helps us understand some of the nervousness we have seen. As Emerson makes clear we need to recognize not only human centrality but the human *in relation*. We need relation, as Emerson puts it, in order to be understood. Poe puts the point in terms of elaborate mechanism, reading Maelzel's machine as a requisite extension of the ghost within its contours, as inseparable from us as we are from it. Each needs the other in order to put itself into the world and do its work in the world. *Spiritus* needs *corpus* in the humanist allegory; Turk and *corpus* are inert without the inner life that thinks out their needs. That Emerson stresses not only centrality but the mutual dependence of man and "all objects" (neither can be understood without the context of the other) confirms what we have seen put emphatically in Poe, the metonymical basis of self-definition. It also goes, in Emerson's case, to explain the patent uneasiness in his introductory comments, their inadequate attempts at asserting demarcation.

What then of the uneasiness that emerges in Poe, emerges in great part because of his fervent insistence on, his demand that we recognize, the centrality of the human? What does this mean for Poe's reading of the problem of relation? Several facets of the problem emerge when we put our questions another way: how does Poe handle the difficulties implicit in our last quotation from Emerson's *Nature*, that paradox in which we are central but dependent? Poe's reading of Maelzel suggests a potential for ambivalence through precisely that paradox. Given that we define ourselves in and through relation it is always possible, indeed likely, that some element of the other will affect our reading of our-selves, affect that reading while helping to effect it. Relation establishes conditions in which the other may seek its voice. The endemic NOT ME, because it is NOT ME, will likely demand to be heard, demand the right to live within its own conditions of being, just as it does in Hoffmann. Of course we insist on dehumanizing the other as Poe does in *Maelzel*, insist on its lack of humanity; yet what Hoffmann had shown, what Poe was to show in as passionate a pointing as any of his time, is that the other can reverse our turn upon itself, in its turn turning on us. It will reveal itself to be (like every other Other) ME as well as NOT ME, part of what we confess to be radical humanity. Poe will speak of it as the Imp of the Perverse, stressing its relations to Origin, its Urhumanity. It will work through precisely the structure we have seen in Maelzel's device and its literary echoes, that effective centrality which steers us from within. It will turn romantic humanism militantly ironic, precisely as it is in Byron and Hoffmann. It will do so not only because it undoes some basic humanist claims but because it undoes them by confirming that the whisper sounding within us is as elementally human as anything else about us. That, it turns out, makes for one of the eloquent twists of Poe's ironic humanism: we who had desired an echo of ourselves in order to establish ourselves, we who, in Hoffmann's scene, had been uneasy in the face of the blank stare of the android because it has nothing within itself to cause speculation—we finally get our wish and hear a voice coming back to ourselves. That voice does the same as the whispering of Hoffmann's Turk, and does it to precisely the same tune and effect. Relation, it seems, can be a trap as well as a joy, a maker of discomfort as well as interconnection, a maker of discomfort *because* of interconnection.

One of the reasons we seek to assert a tidily binary pairing of self and its other is the comfort of that structure, the nice things the pairing says about us. The feel of such comfort comes through in Poe's study of Maelzel, comes through in order to collapse as it did in Hoffmann, as it would do in Benjamin. Take the relations of the figures in Hoffmann's "Automate." First there is the interplay of impresario and Turk, figured in the way the master disclaims all continuity, chatting loudly with the crowd while the Turk goes about his whispers. Second there is the play between us, the whisperees, and the hidden voice that whispers. Then there is the relation of the element within us addressed by that voice to the element that acts something like a superego, shocked by the contents of the whisper, suspecting it comes from within. Any of these pairings, taken alone, can lay claim, however uneasily, to a comforting sort of neatness, continuous within itself, discontinuous with the others; but, taken as a group of conditions within the content of Hoffmann's tale, the individual pairings seem less and less neatly demarcated, more and more invasive of each other's territories. The element within us to which the Turk ultimately speaks is also the element that speaks to our superego, to the voice of community that meets and speaks to the world. The relations of Turk and impresario get mixed up messily with our relations to ourselves, with our relations to the world, with our relations to the voice that whispers our disconcertion. Demarcations can only collapse before such mutual, multiple invasions.

Looking back to our earlier comments on Walter Benjamin's version of Maelzel, one can see the same patterns that appeared in Hoffmann and Poe. The crooked dwarf who squats within the Turk and manipulates its moves has the same spatial relation to the surfaces of the device as the voice within us has to Hoffmann's version of the superego. And if Hoffmann leaves us puzzled about the specific point from which our inner voice raises itself, we ought, perhaps, to be equally puzzled about the location of Benjamin's dwarf, which is, as Benjamin puts it, the point from which Theology speaks in our lives. That question about the locale of Theology is Benjamin's version of one of the questions we have seen, the matter of the dwarf's importance within the whole and his relation to that which he has been placed to maneuver. Here too the figure within needs that which is without in order fully to be an agent, so that telling the precise point at which each becomes wholly itself (if there is such a point) can get to be very difficult. Further (and in just the way we have seen in Hoffmann and Poe) the elements that make Benjamin's dwarf and Turk indispensable to each other are also the elements that make the acts of the dwarf crucial to the meaning of the whole. The voice of the dwarf Theology is fundamental to the comments on the workings of history that Benjamin makes in his text. The questions Benjamin raises about messianic time bring in precisely what he needs, an insistence that history can be broken into, its defenses perforated, in a way that changes it forever. Benjamin's version of Maelzel takes on political tangents but, like the versions in Hoffmann and Poe, it brings into modern view the ancient ghost in the machine and suggests the modern puzzlings about the relations of ME/NOT ME.

Those puzzlings put tidiness into the profoundest suspicion, suggesting that we should be uneasy whenever we seem to find it (or have it found for us). Tidiness may be one more figment in a collective of ideas that, whatever it is about, is always about figments, always addresses fictionality and may exemplify it. Binarity itself seems one more duplicity in this package of duplicities that, as far as we can tell, offers no open exit; but we must always be prepared to suspect that such assertions of no exit may themselves be duplicitous. "As far as we can tell" could turn out to be no more than a statement about entrapment.

Such dupery could extend to that question of kinds with which Maelzel is so obsessed, the question related so closely to the problematic of figments that we wonder whether "kinds" is itself an instance of those figments. Whatever else the commentators saw in Maelzel's device they always saw within it a parable of naming, how we decide to call a thing this instead of that, how, therefore, we seek to distinguish one thing from another. I know of no evidence that shows that Adam had the problems with naming that Hoffmann and Poe bring out, that Benjamin suggests in his reading of history. This time it is not a case of Genesis run backward but of Genesis updated, perhaps because the Deus who walked in the garden is now Absconditus, and "kinds" have started to slip along with everything else. The Talking or Chess Playing Turk coded in the name of Maelzel has a good deal to say about the greater meaning of ME. The Turk's whispers and games are designed to probe and ponder how we come to that meaning, to speculate about the fullness that Adam seemed to assume. Adam, of course, did all his naming at once, one beast after another, so he had many opportunities to test the look of one in relation to the look of another. Such comparisons and linkings, Maelzel's machine suggests, may be built into the bones of the matter of naming. Hoffmann's querying of the location of an all-too-knowing voice, Poe's querying of the possibilities for hiding a man in a machine, Benjamin's querying of the function of certain modes of time, come eventually to argue that naming, like all defining, is an act of figuration, profoundly metonymical; that naming is therefore an act of relation. Of course these questions extend to more than mechanical Turks and whispering persons. They also extend to essays that read like short stories, essays that might well be figments of the kind and are "really" (whatever that means) short stories in disguise. Whatever Poe's text ponders at any particular moment it is always pondering itself, the faces it puts to the world. Poe was to probe such questions of guise and disguise throughout his writing life, from this early point on. He was also to probe questions of the contexts of naming along with those questions of guise and disguise, figment and figuration, showing as he does in "Maelzel" that these issues are inseparable, that all have finally to do with questions of relation. Baudelaire seems to have inferred the fuller meaning of tales like "The Man of the Crowd," all that such tales suggest about being and relation, being in relation. Poe's study of Maelzel led to more than what he calls his "tales of ratiocination." It led to his understanding of the centrality of relation in our fundamental acts of being in the world.

Notes

1. Walter Benjamin, *Gesammelte Schriften*, vols. 1, 2, ed. Rolf Tiedemann and Hermann Schweppenhäuser (Frankfurt: Suhrkamp, 1974), 693.

2. Walter Benjamin, *Illuminations*, trans. Harry Zohn (New York: Schocken Books, 1969), 253.

3. For an elaborate reading of Benjamin's essay, with appropriate emphasis on the Messianic issues, see Rolf Tiedemann, "Historical Materialism or Political Messianism? an Interpretation of the Theses 'On the Concept of History,'" in *Benjamin: Philosophy, Aesthetics, History*, ed. Gary Smith (Chicago: University of Chicago Press, 1989), 175–209.

4. For a brief description of the literature, see W. K. Wimsatt, Jr., "Poe and the Chess Automaton," *American Literature* 11 (1939): 138–51. For a more detailed version, see Henry Ridgely Evans, *Edgar Allan Poe and Baron Von Kempelen's Chess-Playing Automaton* (Kenton, Ohio: International Brotherhood of Magicians, 1939).

5. I quote from Hoffmann's *Sämtliche Poetische Werke*, vol. 2, ed. Hannsludwig Geiger (Wiesbaden: Emil Vollmer Verlag, 1972). Material relevant to Hoffmann and automata can be found in the following: Bernhild Boie, "Die Sprache der Automaten: Zur Autonomie der Kunst," *German Quarterly* 54 (1981): 284–97; Bernhild Boie, "Der zärtliche Haubenstock und die schöne Automate: Zur weiblichen Kunstfigur der Romantik," *Seminar: Journal of German Studies* 20 (1984): 246–61; Rudolf Drux, "Retorten- und Maschinenmenschen in der Literatur der Vormärzzeit," *Deutschunterricht* 41 (1989): 9–19; Helmut Merkl, "Der Paralysierte Engel: Zur Erkundung der Automatenliebe in E. T. A. Hoffmanns Erzählung 'Der Sandmann,'" *Wirkendes Wort* 38 (1988): 187–99; and Gerhard Weinholz, *E. T. A. Hoffmanns Erzählung "Die Automate": Eine Kritik an Einseitiger Naturwissenschaftlich-technischer Weltsicht vor Zweihundert Jahren*, in *Literaturwissenschaft in der Blauen Eule* (Essen: Die Blaue Eule, 1991).

6. See my *Self, Text and Romantic Irony: The Example of Byron* (Princeton: Princeton University Press, 1988).

7. Edgar Allan Poe, *Essays and Reviews*, ed. G. R. Thompson (New York: Library of America, 1984).

8. Aside from Evans's study of the published reactions to the chess player (his book is largely a collection of those reactions), there is almost nothing written on Poe's seminal piece. Wimsatt comments on the unoriginality of Poe's arguments, whatever Poe's widespread reputation as a student of the problem. William Panek adds a brief comment to that issue: see "'Maelzel's Chess-Player,' Poe's First Detective Mistake," *American Literature* 48 (1976): 370–72. The only reading to develop some of the basic issues of the

text appears in John T. Irwin's analysis of the relation of Poe's inquiry to the nature of the game of chess: see "Handedness and the Self: Poe's Chess Player," *Arizona Quarterly* 45 (1989): 1–27. Irwin is especially useful on the mutually constitutive opposition of the players in chess and how that relates to the issues in Poe's study. For comments on the piece in terms of Maelzel's device and other "Maschinenmenschen" see Drux, "Retorten- und Maschinenmenschen." Michael Williams (in *A World of Words: Language and Displacement in the Fiction of Edgar Allan Poe* [Durham: Duke University Press, 1988]) does not develop his interesting suggestion that the idea of the pure machine made Poe uneasy because it "suggests a clear analogy to the image of the text displaced from its author" (301). In *From Poe to Valéry* (New York: Harcourt Brace, 1948) T. S. Eliot speaks of how Poe's "pre-adolescent mentality" delights in "wonders of nature and of mechanics" such as "mechanical chess-players" (19). In *The Counterfeiters* (Garden City, N.Y.: Anchor, 1973) Hugh Kenner speaks in passing of "von Kempelen's automaton, which was not only a counterfeit man but a counterfeit counterfeit, since it concealed a man" (22). Kenner has much to say about Babbage's calculating machines.

9. The duck of Vaucanson had also been referred to in *Die Automate*.

10. Ralph Waldo Emerson, *Essays and Lectures*, ed. Joel Porte (New York: Library of America, 1983).

11. Ibid., 8.

12. In "The Thousand-and-Second Tale of Scheherezade" Poe refers to the automata of Babbage and Maelzel among a list of miracles the young wife spouts to the doubting king (Edgar Allan Poe, *Poetry and Tales*, ed. Patrick F. Quinn [New York: The Library of America, 1984], 801).

13. "Wholly" becomes a difficult word in this context, perhaps an impossible one. In this context, it is clear, nothing can be wholly anything.

CHAPTER 7

Blutschande: From the Incest Taboo to the Nuremberg Racial Laws

CHRISTINA VON BRAUN

On December 2, 1603, Julien and Marguerite de Ravalet were executed on the Place de Grève in Paris. Their crime was incest: they had committed "a sin against their blood." Julien was twenty-one, Marguerite seventeen years old. They were the children of Jean de Ravalet, a landowner from Normandy. At thirteen, Marguerite's parents married her off to a tax-collector three times her own age. After a year's time, with her brother's help, she ran away from her husband. The husband launched a search for the brother and sister, pursuing them throughout France. In the end, they were captured in Paris. By this time, Marguerite had become pregnant by her brother. The punishment for incest was death. The father threw himself at the king's feet, and others sent petitions for mercy. But with the pressure he was under because of the Reformation and Counter Reformation, Henri IV could not afford to contradict the sexual code prescribed by the Church. The two youngsters, who were to go down in history as "les amants maudits" [the accursed lovers][1] were given a gravestone with this inscription:

Here rest a brother and his sister.
Traveller, ask not
Why they died.
Pass by here and pray to God
For their souls.[2]

About three hundred years later, in 1917, a book was published in Leipzig, written by Artur Dinter and called *Die Sünde wider das Blut* (The Sin against One's Blood). This work represented the very first

Rassenroman (racial novel), as the author himself noted.[3] Within ten years the book had a circulation of a quarter-million copies in Germany alone, reaching at least two million readers. Excerpts from the novel were distributed to girls' high schools, where romance stories were not usually allowed. The novel portrays the disastrous consequences of a love affair between an Aryan man and a half-Jewish woman. Every possible anti-Semitic cliché can be found in it: the Jews are evil, money grabbing, and ugly. But the sexual clichés are even more pronounced. The wife torments her Aryan husband with her insatiable desire for sex, while her father, a wealthy Jew, has child prostitutes working in the brothels he operates. His daughter, who has apparently inherited a modicum of decency from her Aryan mother, dies of heart failure when she learns of her father's brothels. But the child she and Hermann had together is ugly and a liar, and he also practices usury at school. Luckily he drowns before very long. Hermann then marries once more, this time an Aryan woman. But amazingly enough, the child of this marriage also bears the "mark of Cain" belonging to the Jewish race. It turns out that the mother's body was "poisoned" because she had been seduced by a Jew when she was younger. She kills herself and her child. At the end, only Hermann is left.

The novel provides many pseudoscientific annotations that refer again and again to the consequences of miscegenation with the "other culture" or the "foreign race" with its "alien blood." It is well known that the Nuremberg Laws of 1935 made reference to these kinds of "scientific" theories when they prohibited both marriage and extra-marital intercourse between Jews and "Aryans," "in order to protect German blood and German honor." Dinter also calls for the extermination of the Jews in this novel,[4] and in the postscript he anticipates the ideology that was to underlie the racial laws enacted at Nuremberg. He demands that "we must put a stop to the racial contamination of the German people by the Jews" by punishing by imprisonment "any Jewish male who dares to defile a German girl," and by "publicly branding the woman who so shames the blood of her people by having her hair cut off."[5]

The story of Julien and Marguerite de Ravalet, as well as the racial laws, are examples of the complete change in the meaning of the term *Blutschande*, literally "blood shame." This change in meaning came about in less than three hundred years. While the "sin against one's blood" had at first consisted of entering into sexual relationships with one's own family (one's own blood), it now refers to relationships with those of another race, those to whom one is not related by blood. But the term *another race* does not refer to just any other race, such as African or Chinese, for example. Whenever the term *Blutschande* occurs, it is used exclusively to refer to Jews and sexual relations with Jews.

The recognition that there is a close connection between anti-Semitism and the relations between the sexes is nothing new. The term *anti-Semitism* was coined in the second half of the nineteenth century by German anti-Semitic authors who thereby tried to transform the image of religious otherness of the Jew into biological otherness,[6] and, like other forms of racism, anti-Semitism was pervaded by sexual imagery from the very beginning. But in contrast to the kinds of sexual imagery found in other forms of racism, it is quite clear that anti-Semitism is associated with, among other things, the traditional clichés about women. In other words, Jews were endowed with all the bad qualities that, among Christians, were considered to be feminine characteristics: telling lies, being physically weak, and possessing an overwhelming sexual appetite that would bring disastrous consequences upon anyone involved. Some of these concepts appear to have been taken almost literally from the *Malleus Maleficarum* (the Dominican treatise on witches), which explains that women are more apt to be possessed by Satan because of their "insatiable carnal desires." It is also no coincidence that the great misogynists of nineteenth-century Germany were for the most part anti-Semites as well, and vice-versa. One of the most prominent of these was Otto Weininger, and it is no coincidence that he was an assimilated Jew; that is, he was baptized. He developed a correlation between Jewish and feminine characteristics in his book entitled *Sex and Character*, which caused a tremendous sensation when it came out. Also, the fact that the same term is used for the "emancipation of the Jews" and the "emancipation of women" shows that the prevailing *Zeitgeist* did indeed see a parallel between these two great social changes that took place within the same historic period from the beginning of the nineteenth century until the First World War.

The new connotations of the term *Blutschande* were reflected both on a metaphorical level and also in terms of changes taking place in society. Regarding the social changes, in the industrialized nations the ban on incest became somewhat less strict during the course of the nineteenth century. And yet we must keep in mind the fact that according to ethnologists, the incest prohibition is something basic to all

cultures. Toward the end of the nineteenth century the easing of the
incest prohibition can be seen very clearly in Freud's theory of the
Oedipus complex, which pronounced the mother-son relationship to be
the prototype of every other sexual relationship. One could argue as to
whether Freud was attempting to legitimize the *Zeitgeist*, giving
credence, so to speak, to the new social myth, or whether he was in fact
criticizing it. After all, his Oedipus theory implies that an effort must be
made to overcome one's incestuous desires, and for Freud, the success
of this effort is the precondition for culture. But on the other hand,
perhaps the fact that he was Jewish and that psychoanalysis was
considered by the anti-Semites to be a "Jewish science" actually helped
to legitimize incest and make the subject "fit for polite company."

There had been a transformation in the ideal of love, and not only
was this reflected in psychoanalytic theory, it also manifested itself in
real-life relationships between men and women. Following the Age of
Enlightenment there arose a new ideal of love and marriage that was
determined by concepts such as 'symbiosis'[7] and 'harmony,'[8] and along
with this ideal came the demand for marriage to be based on love—
pure passionate love and nothing else. One of the fundamental requirements of the new ideal was the couple's complete correspondence in
mind and soul and even in body,[9] which after all was something quite
new, because for centuries, going back even to pre-Christian times,
marriage had been considered an institution based on common sense, or
even asceticism.[10] In other words, the ideal of two people being together
(or if you like, "two-gether") changed into an ideal of two people being
just like one another, of them being as one; in short, it was an ideal of
brotherly and sisterly affection. It was primarily the rising middle class
that aspired to this ideal, the inspiration for which came both from anti-
feudal feelings and also Christian tradition, particularly the Lutheran
tradition.

One can hardly stress sufficiently the significance of this development, which took place throughout Europe, but above all in Germany.
It is even possible that the new ideal of harmony and close family ties
had a special attraction for Jewish families in particular. For the Jews,
staying together as a family had become a matter of survival throughout
the diaspora. In other words, one of the factors that made an interdependent German-Jewish society a conceivable and perhaps even an
attractive proposition may have been the amount of importance
attached to the closely interdependent family unit in Germany. That this
family "symbiosis" was in itself fostered by the desire to exclude

anything "foreign," anything to do with "another race," did not become apparent until later. This is undoubtedly one of the fatal misunderstandings marking German-Jewish history.

There were many factors that contributed to the development of this kind of "symbiosis of the sexes." To mention just one of them, I would like to point out that music was a characteristic part of this development, and I mention music because it has been such an outstanding part of German culture. During the nineteenth century both music and making music contributed to a process in which individual self-consciousness was absorbed into a spiritual merging with others. Richard Wagner stated repeatedly that the very aim of his music was to bring the listener to lose himself and his consciousness of self. He writes in a letter to a friend: "Now think of my music, with its tenuous, mysteriously-fluent juices, that soak through the subtilest pores of sensation to the very marrow of life; there to overwhelm all that bears itself the least like prudence or timorous self-preservation; to flood away all savour of the feint of Personality, and leave but a sublime wistful sigh of avowal of impotence."[11] It is this new role of music that Tolstoy criticized in *The Kreutzer Sonata*, which I will be discussing again later. Tolstoy writes, "Music makes me forget myself, my true condition, it carries me off into another state of being, one that isn't my own: under the influence of music I have the illusion of feeling things I don't really feel, of understanding things I don't understand, being able to do things I'm not able to do."[12]

In the course of the nineteenth century music increasingly became a means of spiritual and sensual communion; it offered a way for people to be together without engaging in dialogue. Incidentally, this is in contrast to the literary culture of the same period, which had an isolating tendency, a tendency to cut people off from one another.[13] Music, however, dissolved the boundaries existing between one person and another. In fact, I propose that this property of music gave a special significance to the German tradition of playing music within the family circle. Every member of the family was called upon to play in a "symphonic" orchestra, a duty nobody could escape without jeopardizing the *Gesamtkunstwerk*. This musical tradition, which demanded living-room "harmony," was a major factor in making families and couples so closely united that in the end individual personalities were no longer discernable. In many families, this musical tradition is still carried on and seems to provide an alternative to sexual and family conflict in a form of sensuality that confirms "oneness" and absence of conflict rather than "otherness" and dialogue.

It is in literature, however, that we see the clearest indication that the severity of the prohibition against incest has decreased. Perhaps this is because as religion became less important with the increasing secularization of society, it was art and literature that now offered the promise of immortality. A new kind of artist emerged in the nineteenth century: the genius who, as Novalis claimed, was both a poet and a priest. Because incest also held the promise of immortality, it was to become an important literary theme.

The story of the Ravalet brother and sister fired the imagination of writers and chroniclers from the early seventeenth century onwards. After 1800 this fascination with the story of the incestuous couple takes a new turn: it is now considered to be one of the great love affairs of all time. Jules Barbey d'Aurevilly, who dedicated his novella, *Une page d'histoire*,[14] to Julien and Marguerite, called the lovers "diabolical." For him, this word meant something both disreputable and fascinating; it meant pulsating life on the verge of death, horror combined with desire—it held all the connotations that in the nineteenth century were to be associated with the Devil, death, and blood, from Michelet's *La Sorcière* (The Witch) to Huysmans's *Là-bas* and Ernst Jünger's war diaries.

In other words, the concept of *Blutschande* as a diabolical sin gradually gave way to the notion that this sin is the embodiment of the "perfect" love affair—one in which the willingness to transgress all moral and ethical bounds still means wickedness but also a relentless loyalty to truth and thereby actually represents 'purity'. On another level, this notion of 'purity' was to correspond with the concepts of 'pure' race or 'pure' Christianity—a concept developed by Richard Wagner and other anti-Semites. Just how closely this idea of "purity" was associated with Christianity, on the one hand, and with an ideal of incestuous love, on the other, can be seen very clearly in the work of the poet Georg Trakl. His incestuous attachment to his sister Grete took place not only in his imagination but in real life. In his poem "To My Sister" he calls her "Good Friday's Child,"[15] and in the dramatic fragment "Revelation and Decline," he describes his sister in metaphors that derive directly from Christian imagery: "Oh, the sister singing in the thorn-bush, and the blood runs from her silver fingers. Sweat from her waxen brow. Who will drink her blood?"[16]

From about the year 1800, the love affair between a brother and sister was used increasingly as a motif in European literature. It became one of the great themes of novels and novellas found throughout literature from the Age of Enlightenment to the twentieth century. To name only a few examples: Schiller's *The Bride of Messina*, Goethe's *Wilhelm Meister's Apprenticeship*, Tieck's *Peter Leberecht*, and from France, Chateaubriand's *René* and *Attala*. I should also mention Byron and Wordsworth, who were both affected in real life by situations involving incest. The motif of incest reemerges in the work of Grillparzer, and, of course, it is used later as a prominent theme by Robert Musil and Thomas Mann.

Incest as a literary motif is something new—at least it is new when applied to the context of ordinary mortals. In ancient Egypt and in the Greek myths incest remained a prerogative of the pharaohs or gods. But here, incest is not sacred any longer: it has been secularized. In the novels and novellas of the nineteenth and twentieth centuries there are many indications of incest occurring both in highly developed civilizations[17] and in the natural world.[18] On the other hand, the love affair between brother and sister is described as an all but "divine" form of relationship between a man and woman—a kind of relationship intended only for the "chosen few." This aspect of the matter becomes particularly clear in Thomas Mann's novel *The Holy Sinner*, which tells about the legend of Saint Gregory, who is called "the chosen one." Not only is Gregory the child of a love affair between a brother and sister, but in addition to this he actually marries his own mother. This "sinner," in spite of all these apparent sins of the flesh, is chosen by God to be his representative on earth: he becomes Pope Gregory. The concept of being a "chosen one" is of course a conscious reference to the "chosen people," or the Jews.

This new literary motif is characterized initially by the fact that brother-sister love affairs are considered to be the ultimate in passion, in being prepared to give up one's life for love. Where the original Romeo and Juliet could not be together because they were members of opposing families, the lovers now are not allowed to fulfill their desires because they both come from the same family. In both the old and new versions of the legendary love story, society is denounced, as is any law acting as an obstacle to "true" love. The only thing that has changed is the kind of obstacle that stands in the lovers' way.

Even so, the story still ends in tragedy and often in death. But now death takes on a new dimension. Of course the author reviles the executioner who stands brandishing his axe over the lovers' heads and condemns the society that has no room for "pure" love. But the new dimension goes beyond all of this. The lovers' death must also prove that their passion is real, that it knows no bounds: theirs is the kind of love where one does not hesitate to go beyond the bounds of one's own self, where one is not afraid of the annihilation of personal consciousness. And the bounds of one's own self are understood in two ways: both as the boundary between life and death and as that between the self and the other. This is precisely what is new in the mythologized brother-sister love affair: there is no longer any difference between oneself and "others." Love comes to mean self-sacrifice and self-annihilation: but it also means murder.

This new ideal of love, the love that removes all limitations, is the essential theme of Goethe's *Elective Affinities*. But his interpretation was meant as a warning; he intended this work to be read as an *Erziehungsroman*.[19] In one passage, where the relations between the elements of nature are compared to those between people, the captain gives the following definition: "The tendency of those elements which, when they come into contact, at once take hold of, and act on one another, we call "affinity." And Charlotte answers that such "affinities" could develop between people as well, because "opposite dispositions are the best basis for a very close union."[20]

Charlotte resists the attraction of this "affinity" that comes from "acting on one another" and from the reconciliation of opposites. Her husband Eduard, by contrast, succumbs to a passion and to a delusion destroying all who are involved. He falls passionately in love with Ottilie, who for her part starts to write with the same handwriting as Eduard, making herself more and more indistinguishable from him. She will not regain the right to be something "other" than what he is, until she finally passes into the "other world." But until that time, she is nothing more than Eduard's alter-ego. He evokes Ottilie's presence in this way: "I write loving and confiding letters from her to me; I answer them and keep both letters together."[21]

Goethe contrasts this delusion of love with "true love," which can be seen not only in Charlotte's decision not to consummate her "passion," or in the "saintly," chaste love evinced by Ottilie, who resorts to death in order to escape a conflict she cannot resolve. But the real antithesis of Eduard's delusion of love is portrayed in a story that is incidental to the novel, that of two children from neighboring families who have grown up "like brother and sister," intimate friends since childhood, who are even engaged in sibling rivalry. Finally, after years of being oblivious to one another, they fall in love. In other words, Goethe depicts the ideal of "true love" as a deep relation similar to that between a brother and sister, although not between actual blood relations. For him, brother-sister love— the assimilation of opposites— becomes the ideal relationship between a man and woman because is not determined by passion. (The fact that Goethe did not write this didactic work until he was more or less "beyond good and evil" himself, is something we will pass over for now.)

Not only does Goethe's novel *Elective Affinities* illustrate the theme of brother-sister love in literature, but it also gives us an early indication of the fact that behind all the ideals of harmony and the demand for symbiosis and assimilation between lovers, there occurs something very violent. During the conversation about the relations between the elements of nature, the following comment is made: "You must see with your own eyes these apparently lifeless but actually very dynamic elements and observe with interest how they attract, seize, destroy, devour and absorb each other and then emerge out of that violent combination in renewed and unexpected form. Only then will you agree that they might be immortal or even capable of feeling and reasoning."[22]

In the novel these "laws of nature" are also applied to the relations between lovers. Thus Eduard, who has dissociated himself from Ottilie for a while, says: "And so her image slips into all my dreams. Everything that happened to us runs together. Sometimes we sign a contract together: there is her handwriting and mine, her signature and mine; each blots out the other; both intertwine. These delightful ephemeral fantasies are not without pain."[23]

This kind of "love," which involves intertwining with one another, being absorbed by one another, becoming as one with one another, does not mean that this is a symmetrical process, or one in which both parties are affected in the same way. This is demonstrated in the novel by the character of Ottilie. For her, the only way to resolve the conflict between her longing for this kind of love and her fear of it is self-sacrifice—giving in to a slow death that will heal Eduard and finally allow the lovers to be united (in death). Incidentally, Ottilie dies from refusing to eat. Goethe's insight was remarkable for the year 1809. He described anorexic behavior as a reaction to encroachments on female privacy, and to her individual identity being threatened both in love and in her family life. But never does "intimacy" take a more threatening form than incest.[24]

The term *self-sacrifice* is no exaggeration. The "self-sacrificing woman" is found more and more often in literature and art from about the year 1800, in images that are often quite remarkably similar to portrayals of the Crucifixion. For example, in Novalis's *Heinrich von Ofterdingen*, a woman must die before the hero can become a poet—that is, before he can achieve immortality. There are also connotations of martyrdom and "saintliness" attached to Ottilie: her grave is described as a shrine where the sick come for healing. But her slow suicide is self-sacrifice in a different sense as well: it is her way of consenting to a marriage with Eduard, and this marriage represents self-annihilation, the self-annihilation that comes from her being completely taken over by him. Here, death is the ultimate proof of "love"—and this literary motif corresponds perfectly with Christ's sacrifice, Christ as the Redeemer who gave his life out of love for humanity.

In literature, the image portrayed of marital relationships that are not based on passion relies heavily on the Christian tradition. *The Kreutzer Sonata* is another example of this. Tolstoy intended this work to be didactic, just as Goethe's intention had been with *Elective Affinities*. In *The Kreutzer Sonata*, a man murders his wife because he sees her playing music with another man. The murderer confides in a fellow traveller on a long train journey, telling him how he longs for "his relation to women" to be "simple, clear, pure, that of a brother to a sister."[25] This relationship is be characterized mainly by the fact that sexuality does not play a very important role in it. In the postscript, Tolstoy explains that "we must give up thinking of carnal love as something particularly exalted." Rather, one should realize that the union with the object of one's love "never make[s] the achievement of a goal worthy of man any easier, but always render[s] it more difficult."[26] With Tolstoy, then, brotherly and sisterly love is elevated to represent the ideal of all marital relationships. Tolstoy expresses this even more explicitly than does Goethe. He calls upon men and women to "strive together to free themselves from temptation," and to "replace carnal love with the pure relations that exist between a brother and sister."[27]

Both writers, Goethe as well as Tolstoy, attempt to counteract a trend in which emotionalism, sensuality, and the irresponsible surrender to desire were depicted as the ultimate in life. Interestingly enough, this trend is most clearly typified in the motif of a brother and sister who are passionately in love with one another. In opposing this trend, Goethe and Tolstoy also take brotherly and sisterly love as their ideal, but this time the love is free from passion. The theme of brother-sister love thus underwent a complete reversal—just like the concept of *Blutschande* itself. But a closer look at the two different approaches to this theme shows that they do have one thing in common—they both rely on the

Christian tradition. Naturally, the ways in which they relate to Christianity are very different, in fact irreconcilably so. While Tolstoy and Goethe demonstrate the value of asceticism in a Christian marriage by advocating a form of transcendence, the other approach, in allowing the brother-sister love to become "consummated," represents a form of secularized Christianity. This persistent use of Christian metaphor and Christian constructs is also the reason for the close connection between the incest theme and anti-Semitic imagery. They both represent, in their different ways, the secularization of Christianity.

In the course of the nineteenth century, the theme of "ascetic" brother-sister love rapidly became obsolete, and in its place the theme of incestuous love gained more and more significance as it became one of the central motifs in literature by the early twentieth century. I have already mentioned Thomas Mann's novel *The Holy Sinner*. I should also mention his novella, *The Blood of the Walsungs*, as well as Frank Thiess's novel *Die Verdammten* (The Damned), Leonard Frank's *Bruder und Schwester* (Brother and Sister) Jean Cocteau's *Les Enfants terribles* (The Holy Terrors), and lastly, Robert Musil's *The Man without Qualities*.

In the case of Musil it is quite clear that the theme of brother-sister love is closely linked to religious tradition. Musil's hero, Ulrich, is searches for a religious experience. He wants to experience that "other state of being" being spoken of by all mystics. According to Ulrich, this "other state of being" involves a force that should be considered an older, more unadulterated force than all the world's religions. For him, this other state of being involves not sublimation or asceticism but something that could be described as a "religious drive." Therefore, Ulrich continues, "civilized communities of religious people have always treated this condition with pretty much the sort of mistrust a bureaucrat has for any individual spirit of enterprise."[28] His relationship with his sister Agathe is an intellectual and spiritual union that eventually becomes sexual union as well—the sexual union takes place in a section entitled "The Journey to Paradise." For Ulrich, this relationship becomes a kind of secular unio mystica: in his "other state of being," he is united not with God but with a mirror image of himself—his sister. He and his sister call themselves "Siamese twins." But this experience of worldly love is intended to be understood as a mystical experience, and Musil makes this explicit in certain passages of the novel, such as the following: "He [Ulrich] and Agathe found themselves on a path that had a great deal in common with the ways taken by those who are possessed by God; they went along it without a faith, without believing in God or the soul; indeed without even believing in a beyond or another life. They had entered upon it as children of this world and went along it as such: and precisely that was the significant thing."[29]

This secular religion has an inherent significance, not only regarding relationships between men and women but also in terms of German history; this is illustrated by the fact that almost all the great German authors, as well as many of those who were less well-known, at some point took up the theme of brother-sister love. There was one major collective exception: that of the Jewish authors; and, as you know, there were many Jewish authors within the German-speaking world, some of whose works became classics of world literature. In the rare cases in which a Jewish writer would take up this subject, it was to emphasize not the erotic element of incest but its more sinister aspects. In retrospect, many of these texts seem a metaphorical premonition of the disastrous consequences of the German-Jewish symbiosis. An example of this is the work of Kurt Münzer, who is hardly known today. He wrote a better class of light fiction. In 1907 he used the incest theme in his novel *Der Weg nach Zion* (The Road to Zion).[30] This novel takes up a subject matter better belonging to a Germanic race mythology and transports it into a story about Jewish identity. Not only the title but also many other aspects of this novel demonstrate that the author is conscious of the anti-Semitic dimension of the incest mythology, and that he uses this motif to expound the view that assimilation could lead only to disaster. In Germany, the concept of 'assimilation,' which seemed to imply the convergence of two differing principles, in fact exclusively referred to the extinction of Jewish otherness. When dealing with this particular subject matter, it seems to be very difficult to make a distinction between the issue of brother-sister love, on the one hand, and the question of the brotherly-sisterly coexistence of Jews with Germans on the other. This is one of the keys to understanding this mythology of incestuous love and its impact on German race ideology.

The Jewish authors, then, developed no affinity for the theme of brother-sister love, which only made it all the more popular among the anti-Semites. To name one example I will mention Frank Thiess's best-selling novel *Die Verdammten* (The Damned), which appeared in 1922. Within a few years there were hundreds of thousands of copies in print and in circulation, just as was the case of Dinter's *Die Sünde wider das Blut*. *Die Verdammten* takes place in the Baltic countries somewhere around the year 1900. The novel is filled with images that prefigure the

October Revolution. Johannes, one of the principal characters, experiences visions of blood-red revolutionaries during brief moments of
insanity. Johannes is in love with Ursula, but she is then reunited with
her brother and finds the latter to be the man she has always been
waiting for. The brother gets a separation from his American wife.
"There's an emptiness there" because she's "from a different bloodline,
a different race." He and his sister say it is not possible to love those "of
another kind." True love, union, in terms of being "kindred spirits"
with nature, can only be found in the "other self," or in "treading the
earth of one's homeland," or in music (his sister is a pianist): only these
things can create the "infinity made for two," eternal "harmony," the
"end of all time." Springtime and a piano sonata, the lake and the
boundless countryside: everything combines into one whole and holy
entirety. Ultimate fulfillment comes with the love of brother and sister, a
fulfillment that by no means involves any kind of renunciation of
sensuality; but rather, sensuality becomes a part of the grand design.
Johannes, finally understanding that he cannot compete with Ursula's
brother, tells her:

> The unutterable can become reality. When a man finds a point
> of contact with the universe, he becomes ethereal; he is released
> almost completely from pain. He is not able to see God, but he
> is aware of His presence, because the breath of infinity surges
> through this man's life. Don't you see, Ursel, I was wrong when
> I thought you and I were one another's other half, that we were
> destined to find each other here on earth. That was just a sweet
> fantasy. I was carried away by it because it was too beautiful to
> give up at first. Everything is so much greater than that....Why
> are you afraid? You believe in the power of things, but your
> soul knows better—your soul has a presentiment of the
> invisible forces deep within. Ursel, don't imagine that I thought
> all this out in sleepless nights. The truth can't be thought out. It
> can only be experienced. I thought the truth was that we were
> meant for one another, but I was wrong. We aren't closely
> enough related to be chosen ones, to be near to God.[31]

Johannes is not the only one unable to compete with the brother. Ursula
is also loved by a Jew from the village, who functions in the novel as the
antithesis of her brother. Of course, he is ugly, and so we can tell he is
not one of the "chosen ones" simply by the way he looks; he also

betrays his former benefactors. Every passage of the novel indicates that he can never be part of the grand design in which it is possible for a man to unite with his sister, his homeland, the earth, and God. Johannes "finds God" in his own way, even without Ursula's help—he goes mad and ends up taking his own life. But the Jew, of course, joins the Bolshevik revolution, the revolution of which Johannes had such blood-red visions.

Jews play an important role in many works addressing the issue of brother-sister love. This is even true in cases where the author is not anti-Semitic. In Cocteau's *Les Enfants terribles*,[32] the Jewish character is Michael, an American who falls in love with and marries the principal female character, Agathe. Although he is not permitted to join the "sect" composed of Agathe and her brother, he is tolerated as an outsider because he provides the sect's financial support. He is not fully accepted until after he dies in a car crash. In contrast to Goethe's Ottilie, Michael, the Jew, achieves in death the right to no longer be considered an outsider (once he crosses over to the "other world" he is no longer considered "other").

In *The Man without Qualities*, it is a Jew, the pragmatist Arnheim, who represents the antithesis of Ulrich, the researcher in matters of mystic experience. The brother and sister in Thomas Mann's *The Blood of the Walsungs*, meanwhile, are themselves members of a Jewish family, a family that has taken the notion of assimilation so far as to name their children Siegmund and Sieglinde. Mann's story of these two creatures of luxury becomes a parody both of assimilation itself and of the characters in Richard Wagner's opera. The author is ambiguous concerning what it is he parodies—the lives of the brother and sister, or the Germanic mythology. But this particular subject matter has always been treated in two contradictory ways. Either it is used to define the Aryan identity in terms of non-Jewishness—in other words to support the presumption of the Germanic master race. Or it can demonstrate the parallels between the claim of the Germanic race to be the chosen people based on their Aryan blood and that of the Jewish tradition in which religious affiliation and the identity of a people go hand in hand.

Musil's brother and sister set out to find the "millenium" through sexual union. But for the lovers, attaining God's kingdom on earth proves to be anything but a heavenly experience. The attainment of paradise, the fulfillment of desire, brings with it, at best, the feeling of emptiness that comes over Ulrich and Agathe after they experience being as one, each of them seeing themselves embodied in the other.[33]

Usually, however, the drama ends not with this kind of sobering insight but in a different kind of "paradise": in the death of all concerned (Cocteau), in the death of a child (Thiess), or in the death of one of the two lovers, and this almost always means the death of the woman, or rather the sister. Here again, the death of these female characters is clearly reminiscent of Christ's own sacrifice. It is perhaps the clearest indication that this subject matter must be interpreted as the transfer of a religious mythology to the secular level. In both the ascetic version of brother-sister love and the passionate version, it is always the woman who must give up her life before the man (the brother) can be "redeemed" and find "eternal peace"—or, as the case may be, revert to being the "eternal Jew," as in Münzer's novel.

The sacrificial death of the sister can take many different forms. It does not always involve her actual, physical death. It is often death on a spiritual level, which is represented by her willingness to sacrifice her inner self, her "identity." Leonard Frank's novel *Bruder und Schwester* (Brother and Sister) can be cited as an example of this. Here the lovers are a "divine couple," which the secondary characters sometimes call them. Soon after they get married they find out they are brother and sister. To be more precise, it is the mother who finds out, and after telling her children the unbearable news, she dutifully takes her own life. The author thus conveniently removes from the scene the only witness to the "sin." Konstantin has no problems with the fact that he knows his wife to be his sister as well. As he says, it is only "one more blossom on the tree of his love for Lydia."[34] Lydia, on the other hand, is horror-stricken. She runs away. For months, a conflict rages within her between her love for Konstantin and "this feeling of horror, worse by far than mere aversion or disgust." It is a "dark something" that "cannot be comprehended, nor analyzed" and for that very reason, it takes on "overwhelming dimensions."[35] Finally, her love for Konstantin conquers the "feeling of horror." The novel ends as Lydia returns, like a priestess or saint coming to sacrifice herself to the dreaded "something" on the altar of love. It now becomes clear, if it was not so before, that Lydia's dread of incest is really a fear of death, of personal annihilation, and it is also clear that this is how it is meant to be understood. Conquering this fear means both her own death and the fulfillment of this one, true love—the love of the chosen ones, the "divine couple." The novel ends with the following passage:

> With a lover's instinct, Konstantin felt that Lydia had to make
> up her own mind to take that last step across the invisible line

between them, towards a new togetherness with him....For several long minutes, she lay completely still, as rigid as a corpse. So beautiful! . . . She must take that next step alone; nothing in the world could help her with it. The only thing that could make the difference was the greatness of her soul. It must be no less great than her love for him. . . . Konstantin heard a gentle clicking noise. He saw the door handle move. The door opened. / She was wearing a nightshirt that came down to her ankles. She came in, white and stiff, a walking corpse. And then he was with her.[36]

Murder and suicide—to lose one's self-identity or to destroy the identity of the other: These are concepts that, in all their various forms of expression, are all hidden factors in the change in the meaning of *Blutschande* during the nineteenth century. The word *love* itself was to take on a whole new meaning, becoming synonymous with *death*. This becomes especially clear in Dinter's "racial novel," to which I now return. Hermann can really love Elisabeth only once she is dead. But then he loves her with all his heart:

He had such a strong sensation of her physical presence that he would ask her to come and sit with him on the sofa and talk with him for a little while, as evening was coming on—just as they used to do. Then he would take her on his arm and let her rest her charming head on his chest. He would dream away the winter evenings with her in front of the fire. . . . No, the woman he loved was not dead! She was closer to him than ever, now that she had been freed from all earthly cares, released from the material nature of physical existence. In fact, his happiness in love and in marriage would have been quite perfect now, at last, if only the physical presence of that unnatural child had not embittered his happiness, and ruined everything for him time and time again. But that was how he must atone for the rest of his life for the grave sin he had committed against the sacred blood of his race.[37]

For some, 'love' entails an expansion of one's being, purification, and the achievement of immortality, the release from mortality that is made possible by the other's sacrifice. For others, however, the concept of love means self-sacrifice, self-annihilation, as when Lydia sacrifices her "self" to her brother on the altar of love, giving up her own "otherness" for his sake. This concept of love as self-sacrifice is also inherent in the words of Richard Wagner as he calls upon the Jews to annihilate themselves as such and to become "one with us in a single and inseparable whole."[38] Again and again, there are close similarities in the process of annihilation that both women and Jews must undergo. This can be seen in the case of Wagner, as well as in Dinter's novel, in the work of Weininger, and many other instances. And yet I would like to point out some definitive differences in the literary treatment of women and Jews.

Women are only loved after undergoing a metamorphosis into an imaginary creature, be it a Muse, a metaphor, or any other form of immaterial being. The real woman, with real otherness, must disappear. This corresponds to the demand for complete symbiosis within the romanticized ideal of marriage, where the feminine ego must be sacrificed. In order to become eligible for love, a woman must be prepared to become a "sister" and sacrifice her otherness. She must become an element, "attracted, seized, destroyed, devoured and absorbed," so that a new element can emerge "out of that violent combination in renewed and unexpected form." The new element is either the mature man, the lover, or the immortal poet: "only then will you agree that they might be immortal or even capable of feeling and reasoning." It can almost be said that the woman is transformed into a kind of diary, where one can confide one's most intimate secrets: she represents the other self, which is actually nothing more than a dialogue with one's own self.[39]

This attraction to one's own kind, to a conception of love that means loving one's own self-image, is linked to the exclusion of everything that represents otherness. But this otherness, with its concepts of 'the other race', or 'the other blood', is just as contrived as is the transformation of a woman into a sister figure. The hatred of the other race is the conditio sine qua non of any definition of one's own race. The "Jew" of nineteenth-century racial theory never existed in real life. Never does this become more clear than in the inconsistencies in the definitions of the Jewish race provided by authors like Dinter or Chamberlain. Both describe a monstrosity that owes its existence not only to an excessive admixture of foreign blood but also to too much inbreeding.[40] It is, by the way, worth mentioning that one of the typical clichés of anti-Semitic racism was that the Jews practiced incest.[41] In other words, the sexual fantasies of the time were being applied to the Jews in a process of inversion that also characterizes many other anti-Jewish beliefs.

However, the very fact that these concepts of 'Jewish blood' and 'Jewish race' were products of the anti-Semitic imagination is what gave anti-Semitic racism its own characteristic violence. The physical persecution of the Jew, the blood spilled in real life was supposed to make the imaginary figure, "the Jew," come to life, paradoxical as this may seem. It was meant to make his otherness become visible. (It is worth pointing out that in the German language the word *verschieden* means both "different" and "dead".) I would like to suggest a parallel here that could be outlined as follows: While a real woman, in order to undergo a metamorphosis into an imaginary figure, was destroyed whether in body or soul, the imaginary figure of the Jew underwent physical persecution so that the fictional figure could be experienced as a real person.

Incest between a brother and sister became a motif for a Utopian ideal of "love," whereas anti-Semitic racism was a concrete expression of hatred. But both these products of the imagination have something in common, and this is that they both demonstrate a very complex change in the concept of 'self', evincing a self whose existence is based not only on a union with "the other" where "the other" is consumed by the self, but also on a process of segregating that "other" that it has itself created. This "other," in turn, was understood to have originally been a part of one's own self, as is demonstrated by the anti-Semitic metaphors depicting Jews as "vampires sucking at the heart's blood"[42] or as "the enemy within."

The concept of 'the Jew' became a determining factor in the creation of German symbiosis, of the German homeland, and of German identity. But Weininger has made it clear that this applies not only to the German Reich but also to a sense of personal identity. For Weininger, "the Jew" is seen as the other self, as something within oneself that does not belong there: "it is, as previously stated, perhaps its great significance in the world's history and the immense merit of Judaism that it and nothing else, leads the Aryan to a knowledge of himself and warns him against himself. For this the Aryan has to thank the Jew that, through him, he knows how to guard against Judaism as a possibility within himself."[43]

Finally, the literary motif of brother-sister incest provides evidence of two closely connected historical developments. The first is that certain things that had been part of the "unknown" were so no longer, and this applies not only to the dark continent on the other side of the world but also to the "dark continent" of a woman's being with all the secret depths that Freud longed to recreate. And the second of these two developments, which are both very closely connected to one another, is the decline of religion, which in this context means not the disappearance but rather the secularization of Christian metaphors and teachings. I will try to explain this briefly.

Nature and women—everything we call "the other" in fact—had for centuries been mistreated, burned at the stake and reduced to ashes. By the nineteenth century, the two had finally become domesticated. They had been vanquished, but at the same time they had also lost their otherness and were no longer seen as threatening. This created a vacuum that had to be filled by something new. And so there arose, on the one hand, the ideal of being in love with one's sister, that fragment of one's own self. But on the other hand, there flourished the notions of unfettered passions and all-powerful, bloodthirsty Nature, which were expressed in fiction in the relentless women, the Carmens, Salomes, Medusas, and Lulus who were so popular towards the end of the nineteenth century. But these overpowering female figures do not have anything to do with conceptions of femininity; in fact, they represent fantasies of male femininity, and so once again it is a question of the disappearance of otherness.[44] In fact, in counterpoint to these images of female passion, there emerged numerous "scientific" theories that contrasted the deficit in the female sex drive with the unbridled passion of the male sex drive. This represents the first time in the history of Western civilization that such theories emerged (and they were voiced exclusively in the industrialized nations). Even in pre-Christian times, and to an even greater extent after Christianity became a prevailing force, women were always considered to be the embodiment of sexual desire, and men, at best, the victims of it. In other words, men, who for centuries had defined themselves in terms of the difference between themselves and animals, finally discovered that they were all lions at heart—but not until the end of the nineteenth century, by which time one could see lions in zoos.

The mythologizing of brother-sister love exhibits many of the elements of a "secular religion," and this explains the power and fascination it held for so many people. It helps us understand why *Blutschande* became one of the central concepts of anti-Semitic racism. The "blood shame" of nineteenth-century racial theories was a logical continuation of traditional Christian anti-Semitism. According to Christian dogma, Christ was nailed to the cross by the Jews, who thus embodied the Antichrist. Now, the sacrifice of the Redeemer and the pure, innocent blood of Christ became the sacrifice of the sister's blood—blood that derived its purity from the natural, biological laws of incest. To consume this blood was to achieve immortality. And taking his own part in this phantasmagoria, it is once again the Jew who carries out the sacrificial death (this time, the woman's) and he does so by means of sexual intercourse, by means of *Blutschande*.

Notes

Translated by Elizabeth Naylor Endres.

1. See also Colette Piat, *Julien et Marguerite: Les amants maudits de Tourlaville* (Paris: Fayard, 1985).

2. See also Michel Carmona, *Une affaire d'inceste: Julien et Marguerite de Ravalet* (Paris: Perrin, 1988).

3. Artur Dinter, *Die Sünde wider das Blut*, 1917; quotations are from a later edition: Leipzig: Verlag Ludolf Beust, 1927, here: 338.

4. Ibid., 237.

5. Ibid., 316.

6. Wilhelm Marr is considered the inventor of the term. See Wilhelm Marr, *Der Judenspiegel* (1862).

7. I use the concept of 'symbiosis' in the sense of merging two people or two entities.

8. The concept of 'harmony' and 'symphilosophy' played an important role in the German Romantic movement.

9. See also Edmund Leites, *Puritanisches Gewissen und moderne Sexualität*, trans. Friedrich Griese (Frankfurt am Main: Suhrkamp 1988).

10. See also Georg Denzler, *Die verbotene Lust: 2000 Jahre christliche Sexualmoral* (Munich and Zürich: Piper, 1984). Michel Foucault, *Histoire de la Sexualité*, vol. 2, *L'Usage des plaisirs*; vol. 3, *Le Souci de soi* (Paris: Gallimard, 1984).

11. Richard Wagner to Mathilde Wesendonck, trans., prefaced, etc. William Ashton Ellis, (New York: Scribner's, 1905), 165.

12. Leo Tolstoy, *The Kreutzer Sonata and Other Stories*, trans. with an introduction by David McDuff (New York: Penguin Books, 1985), 96.

13. See also Erich Schön, *Der Verlust der Sinnlichkeit, oder Die Verwandlungen des Lesers: Mentalitätswandel um 1800* (Stuttgart: Klett-Cotta, 1987).

14. Jules Barbey d'Aurevilly, *Une Page d'histoire, 1603* (Paris, 1886).

15. Georg Trakl, *Selected Poems*, trans. Robert Grenier et al. (London: Jonathan Cape, 1968), 17.

16. Georg Trakl, *Offenbarung und Untergang: Die Prosadichtungen* (Salzburg: Müller, 1947).

17. See also Leonhard Frank, *Bruder und Schwester* (1929; Munich: Langen-Müller, 1985), 160.

18. See Johann Wolfgang Goethe, *Wilhelm Meister's Lehrjahre* (Wilhelm Meister's Apprenticeship [1795]).

19. See also Paul Stöcklein, ed., *Die Wahlverwandtschaften*, by Johann Wolfgang von Goethe (Munich: dtv, 1965), 227.

20. Johann Wolfgang von Goethe, *Elective Affinities*, in *The Sufferings of Young Werther, and Elective Affinities*, ed. Victor Lange, trans. Elizabeth Mayer and Louise Bogan (New York: Continuum, 1990), 158.

21. Goethe, *Elective Affinities*, 225.

22. Ibid., 160.

23. Ibid., 226.

24. See also Christina von Braun, "Inkarnation und Desinkarnation," in *Nicht Ich: Logik Lüge Libido* (Frankfurt am Main: Neue Kritik, 1985) and Christina von Braun, "Die Frau, das Essen und der Tod: Zur Geschichte weiblichen Fastens," in *Weibliche Adoleszenz*, ed. Karin Flaake and Vera King (Frankfurt am Main: Campus, 1991).

25. Tolstoy, *Kreutzer Sonata*, 41.

26. Ibid., 271.

27. Ibid., 280.

28. Robert Musil, *The Man without Qualities*, trans. E. Wilkins and E. Kaiser (London: Secker and Warburg, 1953), 3:117.

29. Musil, *Man without Qualities*, 3:111.

30. Kurt Münzer, *Der Weg nach Zion* (Berlin: Axel Junckers, 1907).

31. Frank Thiess, *Die Verdammten* (Berlin: Gustav Kiepenheuer, 1922), 410ff.

32. Jean Cocteau, *The Holy Terrors*, trans. Rosamond Lehmann (New York: New Directions, 1957).

33. Robert Musil, *Der Mann ohne Eigenschaften*, in *Gesammelte Werke*, ed. Adolf Frisé (Reinbek bei Hamburg: Rowohlt, 1978.), 1420.

34. Frank, *Bruder und Schwester*, 151.

35. Ibid., 179.

36. Ibid., 210ff.

37. Dinter, *Sünde wider das Blut*, 264.

38. Richard Wagner, *Das Judentum in der Musik*, in *Gesammelte Schriften*, ed. by Julius Kapp (Leipzig: Verlagsbuchhandlung J. J. Weber, 1914) vol. 13:29.

39. See also Vladimir Nabokov, *Ada or Ardor: A Family Chronicle* (New York: McGraw-Hill, 1969).

40. See also Dinter, *Sünde wider das Blut*, 210.

41. Marr, *Judenspiegel*, 43; Dinter, *Sünde wider das Blut*, 210; H. S. T. Chamberlain, *Die Grundlagen des XIX. Jahrhunderts* (Munich: F. Bruckmann, 1909), 441.

42. Dinter, *Sünde wider das Blut*, 320.

43. Otto Weininger, *Sex and Character* [no trans. named] (New York: Putnam's, 1906).

44. See Christina von Braun, "Männliche Hysterie—Weibliche Askese: Zum Paradigmenwechsel der Geschlechterrollen," in *Die schamlose Schönheit des Vergangenen: Zum Verhältnis von Geschlecht und Geschichte* (Frankfurt am Main: Neue Kritik, 1989).

CHAPTER 8

The Jewish Nose: Are Jews White?
Or, The History of the Nose Job

SANDER L. GILMAN

The personals columns in *Washingtonian*, the local city magazine in Washington, D.C., are filled with announcements of individuals "in search of" mates. ("In search of" is the rubric under which these advertisements are grouped.) These advertisements are peppered with various codes so well known that they are never really explained: DWM [Divorced White Male] just recently arrived from Boston seeks a non-smoking, financially secure 40+ who loves to laugh" . . . or "SJF [Jewish Single Female], Kathleen Turner type, with a zest for life in search of S/DJM . . . for a passionate relationship." Recently, I was struck by a notice which began "DW(J)F [Divorced White (Jewish) Female]—young, 41, Ph.D., professional, no kids . . . seeks S/D/WWM, exceptional mind, heart & soul . . . "[1] What fascinated me were the brackets: advertisements for "Jews" or for "African Americans" or for "Whites" made it clear that individuals were interested in choosing their sexual partners from certain designated groups within American society. But the parentheses implied that here was a woman who was both "White" and "Jewish." Given the racial politics of post–civil rights America, where do the Jews fit in? It made me ask the questions, which the woman who placed the personals advertisement clearly was addressing: are Jews White? and what does "White" mean in this context? Or, to present this question in a slightly less polemical manner, how has the question of racial identity shaped Jewish identity in the Diaspora? I am addressing not what the religious, ethnic, or cultural definition of the Jew is—either from within or without Judaism or the Jewish community—but how the category of race present within Western, scientific, and popular culture has shaped Jewish self-perception.

My question is not merely an "academic" one—rather I am interested in how the representation of the Jewish body is shaped and, in turn, shapes the sense of Jewish identity. My point of departure is the view of Mary Douglas: "The human body is always treated as an image of society and . . . there can be no natural way of considering the body that does not involve at the same time a social dimension. Interest in its apertures depends on the preoccupation with social exits and entrances, escape routes and invasions. If there is no concern to preserve social boundaries, I would not expect to find concern with bodily boundaries."[2]

Where and how a society defines the body reflects how those in society define themselves. This is especially true in terms of the "scientific" or pseudoscientific categories such as race that have had such an extraordinary importance in shaping how we all understand ourselves and each other. From the conclusion of the nineteenth century, the idea of "race" has been given a positive as well as a negative quality. We belong to a race and our biology defines us is as true a statement for many groups as is the opposite: you belong to a race and your biology limits you. Race is a constructed category of social organization as much as it is a reflection of some aspects of biological reality. Racial identity has been a powerful force in shaping how we, at the close of the twentieth century, understand ourselves—often in spite of ourselves. Beginning in the eighteenth century and continuing to the present, there has been an important cultural response to the idea of race, one that has stressed the uniqueness of the individual over the uniformity of the group. As Theodosius Dobzhansky noted in 1967: "Every person has a genotype and a life history different from any other person, be that person a member of his family, clan, race, or mankind. Beyond the universal rights of all human beings (which may be a typological notion!), a person ought to be evaluated on his own merits."[3] Dobzhansky and many scientists of the 1960s dismissed "race" as a category of scientific evaluation, arguing that whenever it had been included over the course of history, horrible abuses had resulted.[4] At the same time, within Western, specifically American culture of the 1960s, there was also a transvaluation of the concept of "race." "Black" was "beautiful," and "roots" were to be celebrated, not denied. The view was that seeing oneself as being a part of a "race" was a strengthening factor. We at the close of the twentieth century have, however, not suddenly become callous to the negative potential of the concept of "race." Given its abuse in the Shoah[5] as well as in neocolonial policies throughout the world,[6] it is clear that a great deal of sensitivity must be used in employing the very idea of "race." In reversing the idea of "race," we have not eliminated its negative implications, we have only masked them. For it is also clear that the meanings associated with "race" impact on those included within these constructed categories. It forms them and shapes them. And this can be a seemingly positive or a clearly negative response. There is no question that there are "real," that is, shared genetic distinctions within and between groups. But the rhetoric of what this shared distinction comes to mean for the general culture and for the "group" so defined becomes central to any understanding of the implications of race.

Where I would like to begin is with that advertisement in the *Washingtonian* and with the question that the "(J)" posed: are Jews White? To begin to answer that question we must trace the debate about the skin color of the Jews, for skin color remains one of the most salient markers for the construction of race in the West over time. The general consensus of the ethnological literature of the late nineteenth century was that the Jews were "Black" or, at least, "swarthy." This view had a long history in European science. As early as 1691 François-Maximilien Misson, whose ideas influenced Buffon's *Natural History*, argued against the notion that Jews were Black:

> 'Tis also a vulgar error that the Jews are all black; for this is only true of the Portuguese Jews, who, marrying always among one another, beget Children like themselves, and consequently the Swarthiness of their Complexion is entail'd upon their whole Race, even in the Northern Regions. But the Jews who are originally of Germany, those, for example, I have seen at Prague, are not blacker than the rest of their Countrymen.[7]

But this was a minority position. For the eighteenth- and nineteenth-century scientist the "Blackness" of the Jew was not only a mark of racial inferiority but also an indicator of the diseased nature of the Jew. The "liberal" Bavarian writer Johann Pezzl, who traveled to Vienna in the 1780s, described the typical Viennese Jew of his time:

> There are about five hundred Jews in Vienna. Their sole and eternal occupation is to counterfeit, salvage, trade in coins, and cheat Christians, Turks, heathens, indeed themselves. . . . This is only the beggarly filth from Canaan which can only be exceeded in filth, uncleanliness, stench, disgust, poverty, dishonesty, pushiness and other things by the trash of the twelve

tribes from Galicia. Excluding the Indian fakirs, there is no category of supposed human beings which comes closer to the Orang-Utan than does a Polish Jew. . . . Covered from foot to head in filth, dirt and rags, covered in a type of black sack . . . their necks exposed, the color of a Black, their faces covered up to the eyes with a beard, which would have given the High Priest in the Temple chills, the hair turned and knotted as if they all suffered from the *plica polonica*.[8]

The image of the Viennese Jew was that of the eastern Jew, suffering from the diseases of the East, such as the *Judenkratze*, the fabled skin and hair disease also attributed to the Poles under the designation of the *plica polonica*.[9] The Jews' disease was written on the skin. It was the appearance, the skin color, the external manifestation of the Jew that marked the Jew as different. There was no question for a non-Jewish visitor to Vienna upon first seeing the Jew that the Jew suffered from Jewishness. The internal, moral state of the Jew, the Jew's very psychology, was reflected in the diseased exterior of the Jew. *Plica polonica* was a real dermatologic syndrome. It resulted from living in filth and poverty. But it was also associated with the unhygienic nature of the Jew and, by the mid-nineteenth century, with the Jew's special relationship to the most frightening disease of the period, syphilis.[10] For the non-Jew seeing the Jew it mirrored popular assumptions about the Jew's inherent, essential nature. Pezzl's contemporary, Joseph Rohrer, stressed the "disgusting skin diseases" of the Jew as a sign of the group's general infirmity.[11] And the essential Jew for Pezzl is the Galician Jew, the Jew from the eastern reaches of the Hapsburg Empire.[12] (This late-eighteenth-century view of the meaning of the Jew's skin color was not only held by non-Jews. The Enlightenment Jewish physician Elcan Isaac Wolf saw this "black-yellow" skin color as a pathognomonic sign of the diseased Jew.[13]) Following the humoral theory of the times, James Cowles Pritchard (1808) commented on the Jews' "choleric and melancholic temperaments, so that they have in general a shade of complexion somewhat darker than that of the English people."[14] Nineteenth-century anthropology as early as the work of Claudius Buchanan commented on the "inferiority" of the "black" Jews of India.[15] By the mid-century, being Black, being Jewish, being diseased, and being "ugly" came to be inexorably linked. All races, according to the ethnology of the day, were described in terms of aesthetics, as either "ugly" or "beautiful."[16] African Blacks, especially the Hottentot, as I have shown elsewhere, became the epitome of the "ugly" race.[17] And being ugly, as I have also argued, was not merely a matter of aesthetics but was a clear sign of pathology, of disease. Being Black was not beautiful. Indeed, the blackness of the African, like the blackness of the Jew, was believed to mark a pathological change in the skin, the result of congenital syphilis. (And, as we shall see, syphilis was given the responsibility for the form of the nose.) One bore the signs of one's diseased status on one's anatomy, and by extension, in one's psyche. And all of these signs pointed to the Jews being a member of the "ugly" races of mankind, rather than the "beautiful" races. In being denied any association with the beautiful and the erotic, the Jew's body was denigrated.[18]

Within the racial science of the nineteenth century, being "Black" came to signify that the Jews had crossed racial boundaries. The boundaries of race were one of the most powerful social and political divisions evolved in the science of the period. That the Jews, rather than being considered the purest race, are because of their endogenous marriages, an impure race, and therefore, a potentially diseased one. That this impurity is written on their physiognomy. According to Houston Stewart Chamberlain, the Jews are a "mongrel" (rather than a healthy "mixed") race who interbred with Africans during the period of the Alexandrian exile.[19] They are "a mongrel race which always retains this mongrel character." Jews had "hybridized" with Blacks in Alexandrian exile. They are, in an ironic review of Chamberlain's work by Nathan Birnbaum, the Viennese-Jewish activist who coined the word "Zionist," a "bastard" race, the origin of which was caused by their incestuousness, their sexual selectivity.[20]

The blackness of the Jew was associated very early with the meaning of the Jew's physiognomy. At the close of the eighteenth century, the Dutch anatomist Petrus Camper came to describe the meaning of the facial angle and its reflex, the nasal index. The nasal index was the line that connected the forehead via the nose to the upper lip; the facial angle was determined by connecting this line with a horizontal line coming from the jaw. This line came to be a means of distinguishing between the human and the other higher anthropoids. The importance of Camper's distinction between the line that determines man from ape is that it was also used by many of his contemporaries, such as Theodor Soemmering, and by most of his successors as a means of distinguishing among the races on the basis of the perceived aesthetics of the facial angle. Camper himself presents criteria for the beautiful face in his study. Indeed, he defines the "beautiful face" as one in which the facial line creates an angle of 100° to the horizontal.[21] The African is the least beautiful because he/she is closest to the ape in his physiognomy, went the later reading of Camper. And the Jew was virtually as ugly because the Jew's physiognomy was understood to be closer to that of the African than to that of the European. Camper also saw the physiognomy of the Jew as immutable:

> There is no nation which is as clearly identifiable as the Jews: men, women, children, even when they are first born, bear the sign of their origin. I have often spoken about this with the famed painter of historical subjects [Benjamin] West, to whom I mentioned my difficulty in capturing the national essence of the Jews. He was of the opinion that this must be sought in the curvature of the nose. I can not deny that the nose has much to do with this, and that it bears a resemblance to the form of the Mongol (whom I had often observed in London and of which I possess a facial cast), but this is not sufficient for me. For this reason, I feel that the famed painter J[acob] de Wit has painted many men with beards in the Meeting Room of the Inner Council [in Amsterdam] but no Jews.[22]

It was the nose that made the Jewish face and it was this quality that was closest to that of the face of the African. It was the nose that related the image of the Jew to the image of the Black, not because of any overt similarity in the stereotypical representation of the two idealized types of noses, but because these qualities were seen as racial signs and as such reflected as much the internal life ascribed to Jew and African as their physiognomy. The most widely read physiognomist of the eighteenth century, Johann Caspar Lavater, quoted the Storm and Stress poet J. M. R. Lenz to the effect that: "It is evident to me the the Jews bear the sign of their fatherland, the orient, throughout the world. I mean their short, black, curly hair, their brown skin color. Their rapid speech, their brusque and precipitous actions also come from this source. I believe, that the Jews have more gall than other people."[23] It was the character ascribed to the Jews that is written in the nose and on their skin. Jews bore the sign of the Black, "the African character of the Jew, his muzzle-shaped mouth and face removing him from certain other races," as Robert Knox noted at in the mid-nineteenth century.[24] The physiognomy of the Jew which was like that of the Black: "the contour is convex; the eyes long and fine, the outer angles running towards the temples; the brow and nose apt to form a single convex line; the nose comparatively narrow at the base, the eyes consequently approaching each other; lips very full, mouth projecting, chin small, and the whole physiognomy, when swarthy, as it often is, has an African look."[25] This assumption that the Jewish prognathism was the result of the Jew's close racial relationship to or intermixing with Blacks became a commonplace of nineteenth-century ethnology. Both Aryan and Jewish anthropologists of the fin de siècle wrote of the "predominant mouth of some Jews being the result of the presence of Black blood" and the "brown skin, thick lips and prognathism" of the Jew as a matter of course.[26] It was, therefore, not only the color of the skin that enabled the scientist to see the Jew as black, but also the associated anatomical signs, such as the shape of the nose. The Jews were quite literally seen as Black. Adam Gurowski, a Polish noble, "took every light-colored mulatto for a Jew" when he first arrived in the United States in the 1850s.[27]

This view dominated the readings of the Jew's nose well into the early twentieth century. The German popular physiognomist Carl Huter, who evolved his "psycho-physiognomy" at the turn of the twentieth century under the influence of spiritualism, presented his representation of the scale of the nose (1904).[28] It was the "socially dangerous" nose that marked the Jew. In 1941 one of Huter's most ardent followers, Walter Alispach, described the nose reflecting "coarse and bad character."[29] According to the interpretation, the nose showed an exaggerated "sexual area." The cropped image is a photograph of the German-Jewish novelist Stefan Zweig.

The immutability of the Jew was tied to the Jew's physiognomy, which reflected the Jew's mentality. If the Germans (Aryans) were a "pure" race—and that was for the turn-of-the-century science a positive quality—then the Jews could not be a "pure" race. But what happened when the Jew attempted to stop being a Jew, to marry out of the "race"? Their Jewishness, rather than being diminished, became heightened. Their status as a mixed race became exemplified in the icon of the *Mischling*, the member of the mixed race.[30] The term *Mischling* in late-nineteenth-century racial science referred to the offspring of a Jewish and a non-Jewish parent. The Jewishness of the *Mischling* "undoubtedly signifies a degeneration: degeneration of the Jew, whose character is much too alien, firm, and strong to be quickened and ennobled by Teutonic blood, degeneration of the European who can naturally only lose by crossing with an 'inferior type.'"[31] They can have "Jewish-Negroid" features.[32] Language and, therefore, thought processes were a reflex of the racial origin of the "Black" Jew. And their "Blackness" appeared even more strikingly in mixed marriages, almost as nature's way of pointing up the difference and visibility of the Jew. This "taint" could appear among families "into which there has been an infusion of Jewish blood. . . . [It] tends to appear in a marked and intensely Jewish cast of features and expression."[33] As early as Edgar Allan Poe's "The Fall of the House of Usher," (1839) itself indebted to German literary models, the description of Roderick Usher, the last offspring of a highly inbred family (Poe hints at an incestuous relationship between him and his sister) is visualized as degenerate: "A cadaverousness of complexion; an eye large, liquid, and luminous beyond comparison; lips somewhat thin and very pallid, but of a surpassingly beautiful curve; *a nose of a delicate Hebrew model*, but with a breadth of nostril in similar formations; a finely moulded chin, speaking, in its want of prominence, of a want of moral energy."[34] It was in the "mixed" breed, therefore, that these negative qualities were most evident. As an anti-Semite said to the German-Jewish writer Jacob Wassermann during the 1920s, "whether, after conversion, they cease to be Jews in the deeper sense we do not know, and have no way of finding out. I believe that the ancient influences continue to operate. Jewishness is like a concentrated dye: a minute quantity suffices to give a specific character—or, at least, some traces of it—to an incomparably greater mass."[35] Crossing the boundaries of race presented the potential of highlighting the inferiority of the Jews.

So even when the Jew wished to vanish, by marrying out of the "race," his or her blackness was not diminished. Indeed, it was heightened. The power of the image of the "Black Jew," the product of crossbreeding Jew with Black, was a powerful one in nineteenth-century Europe, especially for those Jews who desired to see themselves as "White." When, for example, Sigmund Freud, half a century after Knox's work, compared the unconscious with the preconscious he evoked the image of the *Mischling* or "half-breed": "We may compare them with individuals of mixed race who, taken all round, resemble white men, but who betray their colored descent by some striking feature or other, and on that account are excluded from society and enjoy none of the privileges of white people."[36] The Jew remained visible, even when the Jew gave up all cultural signs of his or her Jewishness and married out of the "race." It was the inability to "pass," as well as the image of the mixed race, that was central here. But what is the "striking feature" that marked the Jew as different, what marked the Jew as visible, even in the Jew's desired invisibility?

Jews look different, they have a different appearance, and this appearance has pathognomonic significance. Skin color marked the Jew as both different and diseased. For the Jewish scientist, such as Sigmund Freud, these "minor differences in people who are otherwise alike . . . form the basis of feelings of strangeness and hostility between them."[37] This is what Freud clinically labeled as the "narcissism of minor differences." But are these differences "minor" either from the perspective of those labeling or those labeled? In reducing this sense of the basis of difference between "people who are otherwise alike," Freud was drawing not only on the Enlightenment claim of the universality of human rights but also on the Christian underpinnings of these claims. For this "narcissism" fights "successfully against feelings of fellowship and overpower[s] the commandment that all men should love one another." It is the Christian claim to universal brotherly love that Freud was employing in arguing that the differences between himself, his body, and the body of the Aryan, are trivial. Freud comprehended the special place that the Jew played in the demonic universe of the Aryan psyche. But he marginalized this role as to the question of the Jew's function "as an agent of economic discharge . . . in the world of the Aryan ideal" rather than as one of the central aspects in the science of his time.[38] What Freud was masking was that Jews are not merely the fantasy capitalists of the paranoid delusions of the anti-Semites; they also mirror within their own sense of selves the image of their own difference.

By the close of the nineteenth century, the "reality" of the physical difference of the Jew as a central marker of race had come more and more into question. Antithetical theories, such as those of Friedrich Ratzel, began to argue that skin color was a reflex of geography and could and did shift when a people moved from one part of the globe to another. Ratzel built on earlier work by the president of Princeton University at the close of the eighteenth century, Samuel Stanhope Smith (1787). For Smith the Jews came to be seen as the adaptive people par excellence: "In Britain and Germany they are fair, brown in France and in Turkey, swarthy in Portugal and Spain, olive in Syria and Chaldea, tawny or copper-coloured in Arabia and Egypt."[39] William Lawrence commented in 1823 that "their colour is everywhere modified by the situation they occupy."[40] The questionability of skin color as the marker of Jewish difference joined with other qualities that made the Jew visible.

By the latter half of the nineteenth century, western European Jews had become indistinguishable from other western Europeans in matters of language, dress, occupation, location of their dwellings and the cut of their hair. Indeed, if Rudolf Virchow's extensive study of more than ten thousand German school children published in 1886 was accurate, they were also indistinguishable in terms of skin, hair, and eye color from the greater masses of those who lived in Germany.[41] Virchow's statistics sought to show that wherever a greater percentage of the overall population had lighter skin or bluer eyes or blonder hair there a greater percentage of Jews also had lighter skin or bluer eyes or blonder hair. But although Virchow attempted to provide a rationale for the sense of Jewish acculturation, he still assumed that Jews were a separate and distinct racial category. George Mosse has commented, "the separateness of Jewish schoolchildren, approved by Virchow, says something about the course of Jewish emancipation in Germany. However, rationalized, the survey must have made Jewish schoolchildren conscious of their minority status and their supposedly different origins."[42] Nonetheless, even though they were labeled as different, Jews came to parallel the scale of types found elsewhere in European society.

A parallel shift in the perception of the Jewish body can be found during the twentieth century in the United States. In 1910 the famed German-Jewish anthropologist (and the founder of modern American anthropology) Franz Boas authored a detailed report for Congress on the "Changes in Bodily Form of Descendants of Immigrants."[43] This report documented the change in body size, cephalic index, even hair color of the offspring of Jews, Sicilian, and Neapolitan immigrants born in the United States. Unlike their siblings born abroad first-generation immigrants were bigger, had greater brain capacity, and lighter hair color. Boas attempted to argue that racial qualities, even to the color of hair, changed when the environment shifted and that racial markers were at least to some degree mutable. Needless to say this view was contested in the science of his time—arguments against this view ranged from the impact being merely the shift from rural to urban life to the reversal of the "degenerate" types that developed in Europe and the reemergence of the "pure" and therefore healthier original European types. The image that there could be a "new human race" evolving under American conditions startled European scientists. But it was not only that these eastern European Jewish immigrants were physically becoming more and more like other Americans—they were also growing into American culture.[44] As the body type altered, their culture also changed.

It was not merely that second- and third-generation descendents of eastern European Jewish immigrants do not "look" like their grand-parents; they "looked" American. The writer and director Philip Dunne commented on the process of physical acculturation of Jews in southern California during the twentieth century:

> You could even see the physical change in the family in the second generation—not resembling the first generation at all. Of course, this is true all across the country, but it is particularly noticeable in people who come out of very poor families. . . . One dear friend and colleague of mine was a product of a Lower East Side slum. He was desperately poor. And he grew up a rickety, tiny man who had obviously suffered as a child. At school, he told me, the goyim would scream at him. Growing up in California, his two sons were tall, tanned, and blond. Both excelled academically and in athletics. One became a military officer, the other a physicist. They were California kids. Not only American but Californian.[45]

But the more Jews in Germany and Austria at the fin de siècle looked like their non-Jewish contemporaries, the more they sensed themselves as different and were so considered. As the Anglo-Jewish social scientist Joseph Jacobs noted, "it is some quality which stamps their features as distinctly Jewish. This is confirmed by the interesting fact that Jews who mix much with the outer world seem to lose their Jewish quality. This was the case with Karl Marx."[46] And yet, as we know, it was precisely those Jews who were the most assimilated, who were passing, who feared that their visibility as Jews could come to the fore. It was they who most feared being seen as bearing that disease, Jewishness, which the mid-nineteenth-century German-Jewish poet Heinrich Heine said the Jews brought from Egypt. For Heine, too, in his memorial of the German-Jewish writer Ludwig Börne, it is the body, specifically the "long nose which is a type of uniform, by which the King-God Jehova recognizes his old retainers, even if they had deserted."[47] Conversion is not an answer to this immutable marking of the Jewish body and the Jewish soul.

In the 1920s, Jacob Wassermann chronicled the ambivalence of the German Jews toward their own bodies, their own difference.

Wassermann articulated this difference within the terms of the biology of race. He wrote: "I have known many Jews who have languished with longing for the fair-haired and blue-eyed individual. They knelt before him, burned incense before him, believed his every word; every blink of his eye was heroic; and when he spoke of his native soil, when he beat his Aryan breast, they broke into a hysterical shriek of triumph."[48] Their response, Wassermann argued, is to feel disgust for their own body, which even when it is identical in *all* respects to the body of the Aryan remains different: "I was once greatly diverted by a young Viennese Jew, elegant, full of suppressed ambition, rather melancholy, something of an artist, and something of a charlatan. Providence itself had given him fair hair and blue eyes; but lo, he had no confidence in his fair hair and blue eyes: in his heart of hearts he felt that they were spurious."[49] There are older examples of the Jew's internalization of the image of his/her body, an image which is "dark and ugly." In the *Nizzahon Vetus*, the high medieval Jewish response to the Christian discourse about Judaism, the author wrote that: "The heretics ask: Why are most Gentiles fair-skinned and handsome while most Jews are dark and ugly?" The Jewish author, while never countering this assertion, answered that the Jews are "dark and ugly" because of their more hygienic and more discrete sexual practices: "Gentiles are incontinent and have sexual relations during the day, at a time when they see the faces on attractive pictures; therefore, they give birth to children who look like those pictures, as it is written, 'And the sheep conceived when they came to drink before the rods.'"[50] The Jew's experience of his or her own body was so deeply impacted by anti-Semitic rhetoric that even when that body met the expectations for perfection in the community in which the Jew lived, the Jew experienced his or her body as flawed, diseased.[51]

If only one could change those aspects of the body that marked one as Jewish! For it is these aspects that are associated with specific qualities. Thus the famed German artist and poet Wilhelm Busch, in his best known work *Pious Helene* (1872) read the Jew's usurious soul into the image of the Jew's nose:

Und der Jud mit krummer Ferse
Krummer Nas' und krummer Hos',
Schlängelt sich zur hohen Börse
Tiefverderbt und seelenlos!

[And the Hebrew, sly and craven,
Round of shoulder, nose, and knee,

Slinks to the Exchange, unshaven
And intent on usury.][52]

The nose was a sign not merely of the difference and illness of the body but also of the social illness represented by the Jew in German society, an illness of the body politic. The Jew's nose came to represent the Jew's sick soul.

This awareness was projected not merely onto but also into the Jew. There was a startling series of studies undertaken during the 1940s and 1950s in the United States concerning the visibility of the Jew. Raphael Isaacs in 1940 discussed the "so-called Jewish type" in a Jewish medical journal and his focus was on the "so-called 'hooked' nose." For him the "hooked nose, curling nasal folds (ali nasal)" were the salient markers in the representation of the Jew. He cited a University of Michigan study in which "only 51 per cent showed a definite convex nasal outline." Isaacs's work, like earlier work by Jacobs and Fischberg, argued against the centrality of "nasality" as a marker of the Jew while illustrating the central importance of this sign for the culture in which he lived. The more analytic work of the Harvard psychologist Gordon Allport in 1946, followed by a series of papers, attempted to understand what was being measured when Jewish and non-Jewish judges were asked to sort images into the category "Jewish" and "non-Jewish."[53] It was clear that Jews had a higher rate of positive identification as did those non-Jewish judges who showed a higher index for anti-Semitism. Was it that these two groups were more closely attuned to what the subliminal signs of Jewishness were or was it that they simply judged more of the images to be Jewish? The former seemed to be the case.[54] What was clear was that the Jewish judges "tended to give more false positives and were more accurate than non-Jews." The conclusion was that they "were particularly sensitive to possible cues in others which would enable them to ascribe group membership to these others and that this disposition was directly related to the degree of acceptance of the majority stereotype."[55] In other words, Jews were attuned of the meaning of the image of the Jew because of the culture in which they lived. As Nietzsche noted, one is never aware of one's own body until one is ill; one is also never aware of the difference of one's body—whether it is real or constructed—until one learns about it. This difference is associated with the exotic and the distanced, as the contemporary British novelist Julian Barnes has his protagonist note in one of his early novels about one of his Jewish friends:

Toni far outclassed me in rootlessness. His parents were Polish
Jews and, though we didn't actually know it for certain, we
were practically sure that they had escaped from the Warsaw
ghetto at the very last minute. This gave Toni the flash foreign
name of Barbarowski, two languages, three cultures, and a
sense (he assured me) of atavistic wrench: in short, real class.
He looked an exile, too: swarthy, bulbous-nosed, thick-lipped,
disarmingly short, energetic and hairy; he even had to shave
every day.[56]

Barnes romanticizes all of the negative images associated with the Jew
but still associates them with the physical difference of the Jew. This is
not all that far from the aspect of Dickens's Fagin (with his "villainous
and repulsive face") or du Maurier's Svengali (whose "Jewish aspect
[was] well featured but sinister"). It is associated with the difference and
the distance of the Jew in British society.[57] The actual acculturation of
the Jew into British society could in no way mask the Jew's visibility.

But nothing, not acculturation, not baptism, could wipe away the
taint of race. No matter how they changed, they still remained diseased
Jews. And this was marked on their physiognomy. Moses Hess, the
German-Jewish revolutionary and political theorist, commented in his
Rome and Jerusalem (1862) that "even baptism will not redeem the
German Jew from the nightmare of German Jew-hatred. The Germans
hate less the religion of the Jews than their race, less their peculiar
beliefs than their peculiar noses. . . . Jewish noses cannot be reformed,
nor black, curly, Jewish hair be turned through baptism or combing
into smooth hair. The Jewish race is a primal one, which had reproduced itself in its integrity despite climactic influences. . . . The Jewish
type is indestructible."[58] The theme of the Jew's immutability was
directly tied to arguments about the permanence of the negative features
of the Jewish race.

On one count, Hess seemed to be wrong—the external appearance
of the Jew did seem to be shifting. His skin seemed to be getting whiter,
at least in his own estimation, though it could never get white enough.
Jews, at least in western Europe, no longer suffered from the disgusting
skin diseases of poverty that had once marked their skin. But on
another count, Hess was right. The Jew's nose could not be "reformed."
Interrelated with the meaning of skin was the meaning of the Jew's
physiognomy, especially the Jew's nose. And it was also associated with
the Jew's nature. George Jabet, writing as Eden Warwick, in his *Notes*

on Noses (1848) characterized the "Jewish, or Hawknose," as "very convex, and preserves its convexity like a bow, throughout the whole length from the eyes to the tip. It is thin and sharp." Shape also carried here a specific meaning: "It indicates considerable Shrewdness in worldly matters; a deep insight into character, and facility of turning that insight to profitable account."[59] Physicians, drawing on such analogies, speculated that the difference of the Jew's language, the very mirror of his psyche, was the result of the form of his nose. Thus Bernhard Blechmann's rationale for the *Mauscheln* of the Jews, their inability to speak with other than a Jewish intonation, is that the "muscles, which are used for speaking and laughing are used inherently different from those of Christians and that this use can be traced . . . to the great difference in their nose and chin."[60] The nose becomes one of the central loci of difference in seeing the Jew.

It is the relationship between character and physiognomy which led Jewish social scientists, such as Joseph Jacobs, to confront the question of the "nostrility" of the Jews. He (and other Jewish scientists of the fin de siècle) saw that "the nose does contribute much toward producing the Jewish expression."[61] But how can one alter the "nostrility" of the Jewish nose, a sign which, unlike the skin color of the Jew, does not seem to vanish when the Jew is acculturated. Indeed, a detailed study of the anthropology of the *"Mischlinge* born to Jews and non-Jews" published in 1928 summarized the given view that there was a "Jew nose" and that this specific form of the nose was dominant in mixed marriages and was recognized to be a fixed, inherited sign of being Jewish.[62] In popular and medical imagery, the nose came to be the sign of the pathological Jewish character for Western Jews, replacing the pathognomonic sign of the skin, though closely linked to it. For the shape of the nose and the color of the skin, as we have seen, are related signs.

It seemed that one could "cure" the skin, one could make it less "black" by eliminating the skin diseases that haunted the poverty of the ghetto, or, one could simply see oneself as "white." With this, the "disease" of Jewishness could no longer be seen on the skin. But how could one eliminate the symptom of the "nostrility" of the Jew, that sign that everyone at the close of the nineteenth century associated with the Jew's visibility? An answer was supplied by Jacques Joseph, a highly acculturated young German-Jewish surgeon practicing in fin-de-siècle Berlin. Born Jakob Joseph, the physician had altered his Jewish name when he studied medicine in Berlin and Leipzig. Joseph was a typical acculturated Jew of the period. He had been a member of one of the conservative dueling fraternities and bore the scars of his sabre dueling with pride. Like many acculturated Jews, such as Theodor Herzl, Joseph "relished the test and adventure of the duel, the so-called *Mensur*, which was considered manly and edifying."[63] The scars (*Schmisse*) from the *Mensur* were intentionally created. Students challenged each other to duels as a matter of course, without any real need for insults to be exchanged. Being challenged was a process of social selection. "Without exclusivity—no corporation" was the code of the fraternities as late as 1912.[64] The duelists had their eyes and throat protected, but their faces were purposefully exposed to the blade of the sabre. When a cut was made, there were guidelines as to how to repair it so as to maximize the resulting scar. The scar which Joseph bore his entire life marked him as someone who was *Satisfaktionsfähig* (worthy of satisfaction), someone who had been seen as an equal and had been challenged to a duel. Marked on the duelist's face was his integration into German culture. And the more marginal you were the more you wanted to be scarred. In 1874 William Osler, then a young Canadian medical student visiting Berlin, described "one hopeful young Spanish American of my acquaintance [who] has one half of his face—they are usually on the left half—laid out in the most irregular manner, the cicatrices running in all directions, enclosing areas of all shapes,—the relics of fourteen duels!"[65] While such scarring was extreme among the medical students of the day, it was not unknown. The scar marked the individual, even within the medical faculty, who was seen as a hardy member of the body politic. Being a member of a Jewish fraternity (most of which did not duel) could reconstitute the sickly Jewish body into what Max Nordau called the "new muscle Jew." The Jewish fraternity organization stated in 1902, that "it desires the physical education of its members in order to collaborate in the physical regeneration of the Jewish people."[66] A dueling scar marked the socially healthy individual.

The social status of the fraternity member, like that of the military officer, was contested for Jews at the close of the nineteenth century. In 1896 the following proposal was accepted by the dueling fraternities: "In full appreciation of the fact that there exists between Aryans and Jews such a deep moral and psychic difference, and that our qualities have suffered so much through Jewish mischief, in full consideration of the many proofs which the Jewish student has also given of his lack of honor and character and since he is completely void of honor according to our German concepts, today's conference . . . resolves: "No satisfaction is to be given to a Jew with any weapon, as he is unworthy of it."[67] Jews are different. But with their facial scars, they look just like us. The visibility of the scar is meant as an assurance of the purity of the group. But Jews cannot be pure, so they must be excluded. For a Jew to bear a facial scar is to hide his sickly essence from us. And that is "mischief."

The scarred Jacques Joseph was a trained orthopedic surgeon who had been the assistant of Julius Wolff, one of the leaders in that field. Among Wolff's most important findings was the establishment of the "law of the transformation of the skeleton," which argued that every function of the skeleton could be described through the laws of mechanics and that any change of the relationship between single components of the skeleton would lead to a functional and physiological change of the external form of the entire skeleton.[68] Wolff's major contribution to the treatment of diseases of the leg was his development of a therapeutic procedure by which a club foot could be corrected through the use of a specialized dressing that altered the very shape of the foot.[69] Orthopedics, more than any other medical speciality of the period, presented the challenge of altering the visible errors of development so as to restore a "normal" function. Wolff's approach also stressed the interrelationship among all aspects of the body. Among his procedures were corrective surgery and the use of appliances. Joseph's interests lay not with the foot, another sign of Jewish inferiority, but elsewhere in the anatomy. In 1896 Joseph had undertaken a corrective procedure on a child with protruding ears; while successful, it caused him to be dismissed from Wolff's clinic. This was cosmetic, not reconstructive, surgery.[70] One simply did not undertake surgical procedures for vanity's sake, he was told. This was not a case of a functional disability, such as a club foot. The child was not suffering from any physical ailment that could be cured through surgery. Here reconstructive surgery became aesthetic surgery.

Joseph opened a private surgical practice in Berlin. In January 1898, a twenty-eight-year-old man came to him, having heard of the successful operation on the child's ears. He complained that "his nose was the source of considerable annoyance. Wherever he went, everybody stared at him; often, he was the target of remarks or ridiculing gestures. On account of this he became melancholic, withdrew almost completely from social life, and had the earnest desire to be relieved of this deformity."[71] Joseph took the young man's case and proceeded to perform the first modern cosmetic rhinoplasty. On May 11, 1898, he reported on this operation before the Berlin Medical Society. In that report Joseph provided a "scientific" rationale for performing a medical procedure on what was an otherwise completely healthy individual: "the psychological effect of the operation is of utmost importance. The depressed attitude of the patient subsided completely. He is happy to move around unnoticed. His happiness in life has increased, his wife was glad to report; the patient who formerly avoided social contact now wishes to attend and give parties. In other words, he is happy over the results."[72] The patient no longer felt himself marked by the form of his nose. He was cured of his "disease," which was his visibility. Joseph had undertaken a surgical procedure that had cured his patient's psychological disorder!

Here we can evoke Jean-Jacques Rousseau, who commented in his novel of education, *Emile* (1762), that "the way in which the Author of our being has shaped our heads does not suit us; we must have them modelled from without by midwives and from within by philosophers."[73] For Joseph articulated the basic premise of modern aesthetic surgery, that the correction of perceived physical anomalies (not pathologies) was a means of repairing not the body but the psyche. And this at exactly the same moment in modern history that Sigmund Freud had begun to understand the basis for his own approach to curing the hysterical body, with all of its physical signs and symptoms, through the treatment of the psyche! Aesthetic surgery comes to be understood as "organopsychic therapy" in which "it is exclusively the altered or defective form of the pathologically and anatomically normal organ that causes psychic conflicts."[74] We see at the close of the nineteenth century a "modeling from within" by surgeons rather than philosophers, but surgeons whose role is to cure not the body but the psyche. But what if the source of the dis-ease with one's body comes as much from an internalization of the society's image of oneself as from any private cause? What if the anti-Semitic representation of the Jewish nose —so widely present in the literature of the fin de siècle—itself shaped the Jew's response to the Jew's own nose? Thus the French turn-of-the-century anti-Semitic pamphleteer "Dr. Celticus" presented an anatomy of the Jew in which the "hooked nose" represented the "true Jew." "Nasality" here became the first visual representation of the "primitiveness of the Semitic race."[75] It is in this context that the damaged psyche of the Jew was to be repaired. But it was not unique within the annals of nineteenth-century medicine.

Joseph's procedure was not the first reduction rhinoplasty. Cosmetic nose surgery had been undertaken earlier in the century in

Germany and France, before the introduction of modern surgical techniques of anesthesia and antisepsis, by such surgeons as Johann Friedrich Dieffenbach. In the 1880s, John Orlando Roe in Rochester, New York, had performed an operation to "cure" the "pug nose."[76] Based on the profile, Roe divided the image of the nose into five categories: Roman, Greek, Jewish, Snub or Pug, and Celestial. Roe cited the "snub-nose" as "proof of a degeneracy of the human race." It is, of course, the Irish profile that is characterized by the snub-nose in the caricatures of the period.[77] Roe's procedure turned the Irish nose into "a thing of beauty."[78] (In addition, work on reshaping the nose had been done by Robert Weir in New York, Vincenz von Czerny in Heidelberg, George Monks in Boston, and James Israel in Berlin. All of these had been primarily forms of reconstructive surgery with the emphasis on correcting underlying somatic rather than aesthetic problems.[79]) However, Joseph's was the first procedure of the type still carried out today. The climate was ripe for the development of a quick and relatively simple procedure to alter the external form of the nose. The earlier procedures not only were more complicated (as well as dangerous) but also did not come at a time when the need to "cure" the disease of the visibility of the Other was as powerful. Central to Joseph's process of nasal reduction was the fact that there was "no visible scar."[80] Joseph's procedure began the craze for nose jobs in fin-de-siècle Germany and Austria. In the history of medicine, Joseph was the "father of aesthetic rhinoplasty." He came to be nicknamed "Nase-Josef = Nosef" in the German-Jewish community.[81]

It is unclear whether Joseph's first patient was Jewish, but the depiction of his psychological sense of social isolation due to the form of his nose certainly mirrors the meaning associated with anti-Semitic bias at the fin de siècle. It is clear, however, that Joseph's initial clientele was heavily Jewish and that he regularly reduced "Jewish noses" to "gentile contours." Many of his patients underwent the operation "to conceal their origins."[82] In justifying the procedure, Joseph called upon the rationale of the psychological damage done by the nose's shape. He cured the sense of inferiority of his patients through changing the shape of their nose. His primary "cure" was to make them less visible in their world. This was one of the rationales cited by the other German-Jewish cosmetic surgeons of the period, such as the art historian–physician Eugen Holländer.[83] Joseph's orthopedic training served him well. He could holistically cure the ailments of the entire patient, including the patient's psyche, by operating on the patient's nose. Here was an extension of Wolff's law into the realm of the psychological. Joseph noted, at the conclusion of his first annual report (1917) as the director of the first department for "facial-plasty" at the Charité, the major teaching hospital in Berlin, that "the discharged patients have all been cured of their psychic depression which the consciousness of bodily deformity always involves."[84] These were for the most part patients horribly maimed in the war who were made whole, both physically and psychologically. How equally true of his private patients.

We have one very late case description of one of Joseph's rhino-plasties, dating from January 1933, soon after the Nazi seizure of power and after Jewish physicians were forbidden to operate on non-Jewish patients except with special permission. The sixteen-year-old Adolphine Schwarz followed the lead of her older brother and had "her nose bobbed." She commented that her brother had written to Joseph and informed him that he had very limited means. "Joseph was very charitable," she later said, "and when he felt that someone suffered from a 'Jewish nose,' he would operate for nothing."[85] The image of "suffering from a 'Jewish nose'" is a powerful one. Young men and women needed to become invisible, needed to alter their bodies, as their visibility became even more marked. For the virtual invisibility of the Jews in Germany vanished with the introduction of the yellow "Jewish star." "Nosef" died in February 1934 from a heart attack, before he was forbidden to practice medicine completely. His scarred face, at the last, did not make him invisible as a Jew, nor did his surgical interventions make those Jews whose noses he "bobbed" any less visible.

But Jacques Joseph was not the only Berlin physician who was operating on noses in the 1890s. Two Jewish scientists of fin-de-siècle Europe who were preoccupied with the nose argued that there is a direct relationship between the "nose" and the "genitalia." For Wilhelm Fliess and his Viennese collaborator, Sigmund Freud, the nose came to serve as a sign of universal development rather than as a specific sign of an "inferior" racial identity.[86] The nose was the developmental analogy to the genitalia. Evolving embryologically at the same stage, there was a shared relationship between the tissue of the nose and that of the genitalia. And, for Fliess and Freud, this was true of all human beings, not merely Jews. Thus one cure for sexual dysfunction, according to Fliess, was to operate on the nose, and that he regularly did. Fliess's views were shared by other physicians of the time, such as John Noland Mackensie at The Johns Hopkins University.[87] But their interest was hypothetical; Fliess acted on his theories by operating upon the nose in order to cure perceived "nervous" illnesses. In reviewing the records, it is clear that Fliess's patients did not make up a cross section of society. Of the 156 cases he records (some from the medical literature of the time), only a dozen were men.[88] All of the rest were women, who were operated upon for numerous complaints, primarily psychological ones. Fliess treated a wide range of mental illnesses, including hysteria, through the extensive use of cocaine, but he also applied acid to the internal structures of the nasal passages or surgically removed them. What Fliess managed to do in these years was to convert a quality of race into an attribute of gender. While his theoretical material covered both males and females, his clinical material (and one assumes this reflected his clinical practice) focused on the female's nasal cavities as the clinical substitute for the Jew's nose.

It was not merely that in turn-of-the-century Europe there was an association between the genitalia and the nose; there was, and had long been, a direct relationship drawn in popular and medical thought between the size of the nose and that of the penis. Ovid wrote: "Noscitur e naso quanta sit hast viro." The link between the Jew's sexuality and the Jew's nose was a similarly well established one at century's end, but here the traditional pattern was reversed.[89] The specific shape of the Jew's nose indicated the damaged nature, the shortened form, of his penis. The traditional positive association between the size of the nose and that of the male genitalia was reversed, and this reversal was made a pathological sign.[90] The association between the Jewish nose and the circumcised penis, as signs of Jewish difference, was been made in the crudest and most revolting manner during the 1880s. In the streets of Berlin and Vienna, in penny-papers or on the newly installed *Litfaßsäulen* (advertising columns), caricatures of Jews could be seen.[91] An image of the essential Jew, little "Mr. Kohn," showed him drowned, only his nose and huge, over-sized feet showing above the waterline.[92] These extraordinary caricatures stressed one central aspect of the physiognomy of the Jewish male, his nose, which represented that hidden sign of his sexual difference, his circumcised penis. The Jews' sign of sexual difference, their sexual selectivity, as an indicator of their identity was, as Friedrich Nietzsche strikingly observed in *Beyond Good and Evil*, the focus of the Germans' fear of the superficiality of their recently created national identity.[93] This fear was represented in caricatures by the elongated nose. It also permeated the scientific discussions of the time. In the "anatomical-anthropological" study of the nose by Viennese anatomist, Oskar Hovorka (1893), the form of the nose was seen as a sign of negative racial difference, as well as a sign of the "idiot and the insane."[94] Look at the nose of the Other and you will see the basic sign of the atavism. Thus, when Wilhelm Fliess attempted to alter the pathology of the genitalia by operating on the nose, at a point in time when national identity was extremely unsure of itself and scapegoats easy to find, he joined together the Enlightenment universalist theory to the German biology of race. Fliess's desire was to make this into a quality of all human beings, male and female, Jew and Aryan, not merely of Jewish males. He succeeded in generating an image of the woman as the sufferer from the pathologies of the nose which was equivalent to the general cultural view of the Jewish male.

Fliess's goal—as that of so many others of the time—was to alter the Jewish body so that the Jew could become invisible. Some Jews, such as the Berlin literary critic Ludwig Geiger, rebelled against this desire for a Jewish invisibility: "If one desires assimilation—and that can only mean becoming German in morals, language, actions, feelings —one needs neither mixed marriages nor baptism. No serious person would suggest an assimilation which demanded that all Jews had straight noses and blond hair."[95] But, of course, in arguing the point this way Geiger was reacting to precisely those pressures that caused Jews to dye their hair and "bob" their noses. Geiger implied that the changes are primarily for cosmetic purposes, vanity's sake. What he pointedly avoids discussing is the fact that they were actually meant to "cure" the disease of Jewishness, the anxiety of being seen as a Jew. Being seen as a Jew meant being persecuted, attacked, and harassed. The "cure" for this was the actual alteration of the body. The Jewish mind, which German culture saw as different from that of the Aryan, is afflicted by its sense of its own difference. In order to cure the Jew's mind, Joseph and Fliess had to operate on the Jew's nose.

One can cite another case of the severe psychological damage done by the internalization of this sense of the "Jewish nose," not from the surgical literature, but from the psychoanalytic literature of the fin de siècle. It comes from the case file of Freud's first biographer and one of the first psychoanalysts, the Viennese-Jewish physician Fritz Wittels. At the meeting of the Viennese Psychoanalytic Society on December 9, 1908, Wittels recounted a case of a patient who had come to him specifically because of the publication of his polemical work on baptized Jews, on Jews who were trying to pass as Christians.[96] Wittels saw this as a form of insanity. It was a young man of about thirty who suffered from "anti-Semitic persecution, for which he holds his inconspicuously Semitic nose responsible. He therefore plans to have the shape of his nose changed by plastic surgery."[97] Wittels attempted to persuade him that his anxiety about his nose was merely a displacement for anxiety about his sexual identity. "This the patient declared to be a good joke." The evident analogy of Wittel's suggestions does not occur to him. If a patient comes to him expressly because of his writing about the neurosis of conversion and wishes to have his nose rebuilt to hide his Jewishness, then the question of his own "paranoid" relationship to his own circumcised penis, that invisible but omnipresent sign of the male's Jewishness is self-evident. Freud picked up on this directly and notes that "the man is evidently unhappy about being a Jew and wants to be baptized." "At this point Wittels remarks that the patient is an ardent Jew. Nevertheless, he does not undergo baptism. In this fact lies the conflict that has absorbed the meaning of other conflicts." To be a Jew and to be so intensely fixated on the public visibility of that identity is to be ill. Then Wittels revealed the name of the patient to the group and Freud recognized from the name that the patient's father was an engaged Zionist. He then read the desire to unmake himself as a Jew as a sign of the rejection of the father. Freud, however, did not comment on the link between a strong Jewish identity and the rejection of the visibility that that identity entailed. There was a real sense in Freud's comment that the Jewish body, represented by the skin or the nose, could never truly be changed. It was a permanent fixture, forever reflecting the Jew's racial identity. Altering the Jew's external form may have provided a wider margin in which the Jew could "pass," but the Jew could never be truly at peace with the sense of his or her invisibility.

But the Jew's internalization of society's image of the Jew's body leads to psychic damage according to Joseph if not Freud. In post-Shoah Jewish tradition this connection is acknowledged in a straightforward manner. Traditional Judaism rejects surgical alteration of the body except for reconstructive surgery. (Circumcision is a religious and not a medical practice for traditional Jews.) Yet what is striking is that Halakhic traditions would permit the alteration of the shape of the nose for men and for women. For such a procedure would fall within the interpretation that sees "a state of mind which prevents a person from mingling with people" as "pain." Joseph's rationale—that the reshaping of the nose cures the psyche—has become accepted among traditional Jews who in general would reject any merely cosmetic alteration of the body.[98] And this to what the Talmud sees as one of the central organs of the body. Abba Saul notes "that when an embryo is formed it is formed from the center, but with respect to existence all agree that its source is in the nose; for it is written, *All in whose nostrils was the breath of the spirit of life.* [Gen. 7: 22]."[99] The alteration of the nose is a serious procedure, but it is permitted if it eliminates "psychological anguish."

The image of a literally scarred Jacques Joseph operating on the literal image of the Jew is powerfully disturbing. Joseph reshapes the image of the Jew, but even that is not enough. The more the Jew desires to become invisible, the more the Jew's invisibility becomes a sign of difference. We can see this operation in effect once again in the writings of Walter Lippmann, one of the leading American-Jewish intellectuals of the first half of the twentieth century, who commented in the late 1920s that "the rich and vulgar and pretentious Jews of our big American cities are perhaps the greatest misfortune that has ever befallen the Jewish people. They are the fountain of anti-Semitism. When they rush about in super automobiles, bejeweled and furred and painted and overbarbered, when they build themselves French chateaux and Italian palazzi, they stir up the latent hatred against crude wealth in the hands of shallow people; and that hatred diffuses itself."[100] The Jew remains a Jew even when disguised. It is in their "painted and over-barbered" essence. One cannot hide—nose job or no nose job—from the lessons of race. And the Jew is the most aware of this. Lippmann creates in his mind's eye the image of his antithesis, the "bad" Jew to his "good" Jew. And this Jew is just as visible as he believes himself to be invisible. Lippmann, in his Wall Street suit and carefully controlled manners and appearance, looks just like everyone else—or so he hopes. But there is no hiding from the fact of a constructed difference. There is no mask, no operation, no refuge.

But the desire for invisibility, to "look like everyone else" still shaped the Jew's desire to alter his/her body. The greatest growth in rhinoplasties in the United States was in the 1940s, at the point where the awareness of the dangers of being seen as a Jew was at its peak.[101] And indeed through the 1960s as many as more than half of the patients seeking rhinoplasty were first- or second-generation Americans.[102] In 1960 a Johns Hopkins survey of predominantly Jewish female adolescents saw their desire for rhinoplasty as rooted in their ethnic origin. Indeed, the assumption of this study was that these young women were articulating their negative identification with their parents, specifically their desire to alter the appearance of their noses, which they said seemed to resemble those of their fathers. But it was the image of their father as a Jew and its associations that they were attempting to mask. But like Fritz Wittel's patient, these young women gave no sign of wishing to abandon their Jewish identity, only their Jewish visibility: "We were interested to know whether the quest for rhinoplasty was perceived as a disavowal or disassociation from a Jewish identity. Whereas this would seem to be true at a superficial level, the patients came from practising religious homes and there was no hint they wished to marry or have male friends outside of their religion or that they contemplated any deviation from the patterns of religious beliefs of the family. In the attitudes and response of parents also, there was no evidence of their being perceived as a desertion of religious or racial identifications."[103] It was the internalization of the negative image of the Jew, the desire to not be seen as a Jew, while retaining one's own identity as a Jew, that is one model of response to the sense of being seen as "too Jewish" or, indeed, being seen as Jewish at all.

The overt motivation for rhinoplasty still seemed to be "ethnocultural considerations." "On a conscious level," wrote the best sociologist to deal with this question, Frances Cooke Macgregor, in 1989, "prejudice and discrimination—real or imagined—and the desire to 'look American,' played a substantial role in [the patients's] motivation for surgery."[104] And indeed almost 40 percent of Macgregor's 1989 sample were Jews. In another study Macgregor pointed out the radical impact of the image of the nose on patients whose own psychic makeup predisposed them to focus on their own inadequacies. Thus in one case, an eighteen-year-old male student who focused on his nose, a "typically Jewish nose," as the source of his social failings.[105] While this patient was advised not to have surgery, it was clear from the detailed case description that the social environment in which he had been raised marked his nose as the appropriate focus for his status anxieties. Such patients, who see their own sense of inadequacy mirrored in the society's image of the inadequacy of the Jew, as is shown in another of Macgregor's case studies, rarely see their surgery as successful. Yet for Jews in general the level of satisfaction with rhinoplasties is higher than the norm. John M. Goin and Marcia Kraft Goin illustrated a significantly lower index of negative responses to rhinoplasty among Jews, with some 84 percent of their Jewish patients expressing a sense of the improvement of their appearance as opposed to approximately 50 percent of the other control groups.[106] Paul Schilder, one of Freud's original collaborators in Vienna, recounted in 1935 a case of a twenty-nine-year-old man whose "nose was particularly offensive to him since it was in his opinion too Jewish."[107] He associated this with "his father's family because of their very Semitic appearance and specific Jewish qualities." Appearance became associated for Schilder's patient with a specific negative disposition and this in turn with his own ugliness and his sexual rejection by a young woman. Jewishness sensed on the body becomes converted into the ugliness of the spirit. Schilder sees the patient only after his rhinoplasty. The patient "quoted others who said that before his operation his face was more characteristic [read: Jewish] than it was now, but seemed on the whole rather contented with the result." This patient eventually broke with his religious identity and converted to Catholicism, the ultimate form of invisibility in Catholic Vienna.

While in the course of the mid-twentieth century in the United States the "nose job" came to represent as much a gender distinction, its roots remained within the internalization of the meaning of the Jew's body in Western culture. With the rise of a heightened feminist and Jewish consciousness during the late 1980s this association became the focus of some concern. This is nowhere better illustrated than in the feminist "Wimmen's Comix" entitled "Little Girls" (1989) and sub-titled "Case Histories in Child Psychology." One of the most striking of these case histories is Aline Kominsky-Crumb's "Nose Job." Aline Kominsky-Crumb was one of the founders of the feminist comic book movement with her creation in the late 1970s of *Twisted Sisters* and is presently the editor of *Weirdo* magazine. "Nose Job" is a cautionary tale about a young woman "growing up with cosmetic surgery all around [her]" who avoided cosmetic surgery in her forties by recalling her earlier temptation as a teenager on Long Island in 1962. There "prominent noses, oily skin & frizzy hair were the norm . . . (No, we Jews are not a cute race!)" This self-conscious admission of the inter-nalization of the norms of her society even in 1989 underlies the dangers lurking even for those who can articulate the meaning ascribed to the Jew's body. As all about her teenagers were having their noses restructured she held out. She eventually fled to Greenwich Village, where she "felt hideously repulsive." Her "sensitive folks kicked this already beaten dog" by pushing their daughter to have a nose job. After she ran away, her parents agreed to postponing the procedure. And she "manages to make it thru High School with [her] nose." The story, at least in the "comix" has a happy end: "6 months later styles had changed and she looks like the folk singers Joan Baez or Buffy St. Marie." In other words one could look as "beat" as one wanted, as long as one did not look "Jewish." The "Jewish" nose came to signify the outsider, but that outsider was never identified as Jewish. The moral of Aline Kominsky-Crumb's tale is that fashions in appearance change and that women should not succumb to the pressures of fashion to homogenize their bodies. But the hidden meaning was—it is alright to look Jewish as long as you are visible as anything but a Jew. What is still left within the memory of Aline Kominsky-Crumb is the sense that looking Jewish is still looking different, looking marginal, not "looking cute." Even the heightened awareness of feminism does not dismiss the power of the internalization of a culture's sense not only that one looks different but, like Julian Barnes' portrait of the Jew, that that is associated with marginality, with being a beatnik folk singer who could in no way be understood as being "cute." This sense of the negative aspects of the body leads to the sense that some type of alteration of the body is a potential need, even if it is rejected.

Indeed, as the plastic surgeon Mark Gorney has recently noted: "Patients seeking rhinoplasty . . . frequently show a guilt-tinged, second generation rejection of their ethnic background masked by excuses, such as not photographing well. Often it is not so much a desire to abandon the ethnic group as it is to be viewed as individuals and to rid themselves of specific physical attributes associated with their particular ethnic group."[108] It is in being visible in "the body that betrays" that the Jew is most uncomfortable.[109] This is still the case even among the new "ethnic specific" aesthetic surgery of the 1980s—for the fear there is not looking Jewish but looking "too Jewish."[110] Ethnic identity—whether being Jewish-American or Asian-American or African American—is validated as long as the general aesthetic norms of the society are not transgressed. For being too visible means being seen not as an individual but as an Other, one of the "ugly" race.

Notes

1. *Washingtonian* 26, 4 (January 1991): 196.

2. Mary Douglas, *Natural Symbols* (New York: Pantheon Books, 1970), 70.

3. Theodosius Dobzhansky, "On Types, Genotypes, and the Genetic Diversity in Populations," in *Genetic Diversity and Human Behavior*, ed. J. N. Spuhler (Chicago: Aldine, 1967), 12.

4. See, for example, Peter A. Bochnik, *Die mächtigen Diener: Die Medizin und die Entwicklung von Frauenfeindlichkeit und Antisemitismus in der europäischen Geschichte* (Reinbek bei Hamburg: Rowohlt, 1985).

5. Robert Jay Lifton, *The Nazi Doctors: Medical Killing and the Psychology of Genocide* (New York: Basic Books, 1986).

6. See Oliver Ransford, *"Bid the Sickness Cease": Disease in the History of Black Africa* (London: John Murray, 1983).

7. François-Maximilien Mission, *A New Voyage to Italy* (London: R. Bonwicke, 1714), 2: 139.

8. Johann Pezzl, *Skizze von Wien: Ein Kultur- und Sittenbild aus der josephinischen Zeit*, ed. Gustav Gugitz and Anton Schlossar (Graz: Leykam-Verlag, 1923), 107-8.

9. On the meaning of this disease in the medical literature of the period see the following dissertations on the topic: Michael Scheiba, *Dissertatio inauguralis medica, sistens quaedam plicae pathologica: Germ. Juden-Zopff, Polon. Koltun: quam . . . in Academia Albertina pro gradu doctoris . . . subjiciet defensurus Michael Scheiba. . . .* (Regiomonti: Litteris Reusnerianis, 1739) and Hieronymus Ludolf, *Dissertatio inauguralis medica de plica, vom Juden-Zopff. . . .* (Erfordiae: Typis Groschianis, 1724).

10. Harry Friedenwald, *The Jews and Medicine: Essays* (Baltimore: Johns Hopkins University Press, 1944), 2:531.

11. Joseph Rohrer, *Versuch über die jüdischen Bewohner der österreichischen Monarchie* (Vienna: n.p., 1804), 26. The debate about the special tendency of the Jews for skin disease, especially *plica polonica*, goes on well into the twentieth century. See Richard Weinberg, "Zur Pathologie der Juden," *Zeitschrift für Demographie und Statistik der Juden* 1 (1905): 10–11.

12. Wolfgang Häusler, *Das galizische Judentum in der Habsburgermonarchie im Lichte der zeitgenössischen Publizistik und Reiseliteratur von 1772–1848* (Vienna: Verlag für Geschichte und Politik, 1979). On the status of the debates about the pathology of the Jews in the East after 1919, see *Voprosy biologii i patologii evreev* (Leningrad: State Publishing House, 1926).

13. Elcan Isaac Wolf, *Von den Krankheiten der Juden* (Mannheim: C. F. Schwan, 1777), 12.

14. James Cowles Pritchard, *Researches into the Physical History of Man* (Chicago: The University of Chicago Press, 1973), 186.

15. Claudius Buchanan, *Christian Researches in Asia, with Notices of the Translation of the Scriptures into the Oriental Languages* (Boston: Samuel T. Armstrong, 1811), 169. On the background to these questions see George W. Stocking, Jr., *Victorian Anthropology* (New York: Free Press, 1987).

16. Léon Poliakov, *The Aryan Myth: A History of Racist and Nationalist Ideas in Europe* (New York: Meridan, 1977), 155–82.

17. Sander L. Gilman, *On Blackness without Blacks: Essays on the Image of the Black in Germany*, Yale Afro-American Studies (Boston: G. K. Hall, 1982).

18. See Cheryl Herr, "The Erotics of Irishness," *Critical Inquiry* 17 (Winter 1990–91): 1–34.

19. Houston Stewart Chamberlain, *Foundations of the Nineteenth Century*, trans. John Lees (London: John Lane, Bodley Head, 1913), 1:389.

20. Nathan Birnbaum, "Über Houston Stewart Chamberlain," in *Ausgewählte Schriften zur jüdischen Frage* (Czernowitz: Verlag der Buchhandlung Dr. Birnbaum & Dr. Kohut, 1910), 2:201.

21. Peter Camper, *Der natürliche Unterschied der Gesichtszüge in Menschen verschiedener Gegenden und verschiedenen Alters*, trans. S. Th. Sömmering (Berlin: Voss, 1792), 62.

22. Camper, 7.

23. Johann Caspar Lavater, *Physiognomische Fragment zur Beförderung des Menschenkenntnis und Menschenliebe* (Leipzig: Weidmann, 1775–78), 3:98 and 4:272–74. This reference is cited (and rebutted) in Paolo Mantegazza, *Physiognomy and Expression* (New York: Walter Scott, 1904), 239.

24. Robert Knox, *The Races of Men: A Fragment* (Philadelphia: Lea and Blanchard, 1850), 134.

25. Ibid., 133.

26. A summary of this literature is offered in the chapter "Die negerische Rasse," in the standard racial anthropology of the Jew written during the first third of the twentieth century, Hans F. K. Günther, *Rassenkunde des jüdischen Volkes* (Munich: J. F. Lehmann, 1930), 143–49. These two quotes are taken fron von Luschan and Judt.

27. Adam G. de Gurowski, *America and Europe* (New York: D. Appleton, 1857), 177.

28. Carl Huter, *Menschenkenntnis: Körperform- und Gesichts-Ausdruckskunde* (1904; Schwaig bei Nuremberg: Verlag für Carl Huters Werke, 1957). See the partisan discussion in Fritz Aerni, *Carl Huter (1861–1912): Leben und Werk* (Zurich: Kalos, 1986) and his *Huter und Lavater: Von der Gefühlsphysiognomik zur Psychologie und Psycho-Physiognomik* (Zurich: Kalos, 1984).

29. Walter Alispach, *Nasenform und Charakter* (1941; Zurich: Helioda, 1960).

30. On the question of the definition and meaning of the *Mischling* see Paul Weindling, *Health, Race and German Politics between National Unification and Nazism, 1870–1945* (Cambridge: Cambridge University Press, 1989), 531–32.

31. Chamberlain, *Foundations of the Nineteenth Century*, 1: 332.

32. W. W. Kopp, "Beobachtung an Halbjuden in Berliner Schulen," *Volk und Rasse* 10 (1935): 392.

33. Joseph Jacobs, *Studies in Jewish Statistics, Social, Vital and Anthropometric* (London: D. Nutt, 1891), xxiii.

34. Edgar Allan Poe, *Poetry and Tales*, ed. Patrick F. Quinn (New York: Library of America, 1984), 321. My emphasis.

35. Jacob Wassermann, *My Life as German and Jew* (London: George Allen & Unwin, 1933), 72.

36. All references are to *Standard Edition of the Complete Psychological Works of Sigmund Freud*, ed. and trans. J. Strachey, A. Freud, A. Strachey, and A. Tyson (London: Hogarth, 1955–74), 14:191. Henceforth cited as *SE*.

37. *SE*, 11:199; 18:101; 21:114.

38. *SE*, 21:120.

39. Samuel Stanhope Smith, *An Essay on the Causes of the Variety of Complexion and Figure in the Human Species* (Cambridge: Harvard University Press, Belknap Press, 1965), 42.

40. William Lawrence, *Lectures on Physiology, Zoology, and the Natural History of Man* (London: James Smith, 1823), 468.

41. Rudolf Virchow, "Gesamtbericht über die Farbe der Haut, der Haare und der Augen der Schulkinder in Deutschland," *Archiv für Anthropologie* 16 (1886): 275–475.

42. George L. Mosse, *Toward the Final Solution: A History of European Racism* (New York: Howard Fertig, 1975), 90–91.

43. This report was submitted to Congress on December 3, 1910 and issued on March 17, 1911. A full text was published by Columbia University Press in 1912. Boas summarized his findings (and chronicles the objections to this report) in his *Race, Language and Culture* (New York: Macmillan, 1940), 60–75.

44. Boas, *Race, Language and Culture*, 83.

45. Cited from an interview by Neal Gabler, *An Empire of Their Own: How the Jews Invented Hollywood* (New York: Crown, 1988), 242–43.

46. "Types," *The Jewish Encyclopedia* (New York: Funk and Wagnalls, 1906), 12:295.

47. Heinrich Heine, *Werke*, ed. Klaus Briegleb (Berlin: Ullstein, 1981), 7:31.

48. Wassermann, *My Life*, 156.

49. Ibid.

50. David Berger, trans. and ed., *The Jewish-Christian Debate in the High Middles Ages* (Philadephlia: Jewish Publication Society of America, 1979), 224.

51. On the cultural background for this concept see Jacob Katz, *Out of the Ghetto: The Social Background of Jewish Emancipation 1770–1870* (Cambridge: Harvard University Press, 1973), and Rainer Erb and Werner Bergmann, *Die Nachtseite der Judenemanzipation: Der Widerstand gegen die Integration der Juden in Deutschland 1780–1860* (Berlin: Metropol, 1989).

52. Wilhelm Busch, *Gesamtausgabe*, ed. Friedrich Bohne (Wiesbaden: Emil Vollmer Verlag, n.d.), 2:204; the English translation, which is very accurate to the tone, but not to the order of the parts of the Jew's body, is from Walter Arndt, comp. and trans., *The Genius of Wilhelm Busch* (Berkeley and Los Angeles: University of California Press, 1982), 42.

53. Gordon Allport and Bernard M. Kramer, "Some Roots of Prejudice," *Journal of Psychology* 22 (1946): 9–39. See also Frederick H. Lund and Wilner C. Berg, "Identifiability of Nationality Characteristics," *Journal of Social Psychology* 24 (1946): 77–83; Launor F. Carter, "The Identification of 'Racial' Membership," *Journal of Abnormal and Social Psychology* 43 (1948): 279–86; Gardner Lindzey and Saul Rogolsky, "Prejudice and Identification of Minority Group Membership," *Journal of Abnormal and Social Psychology* 45 (1950): 37–53; Donald N. Elliott and Bernard H. Wittenberg, "Accuracy of Identification of Jewish and Non-Jewish Photographs," *Journal of Abnormal and Social Psychology* 51 (1955): 339–41.

54. Leonard D. Savitz and Richard F. Tomasson, "The Identifiablity of Jews," *American Journal of Sociology* 64 (1958): 468–75.

55. Alvin Scodel and Harvey Austrin, "The Perception of Jewish Photographs by Non-Jews and Jews," *Journal of Abnormal and Social Psychology* 54 (1957): 278–80.

56. Julian Barnes, *Metroland* (London: Jonathan Cape: 1980), 32.

57. See the discussion in Hyman L. Muslin, "The Jew in Literature: The Hated Self," *Israel Journal of Psychiatry and Related Science* 27 (1990): 1–16.

58. Moses Hess, *Rom und Jerusalem*, 2nd ed. (Leipzig: M. W. Kaufmann, 1899), Brief 4. Cited in the translation from Paul Lawrence Rose, *Revolutionary Antisemitism in Germany from Kant to Wagner* (Princeton: Princeton University Press, 1990), 323.

59. Eden Warwick, *Notes on Noses* (1848; London: Richard Bentley, 1864), 11. On the general question of the representation of the physiognomy of the Jew in mid-nineteenth-century culture, see Mary Cowling, *The Artist as Anthropologist: The Representation of Type and Character in Victorian Art* (Cambridge: Cambridge University Press, 1989), 118–19, 332–33.

60. Bernhard Blechmann, *Ein Beitrag zur Anthropologie der Juden* (Dorpat: Wilhelm Just, 1882), 11.

61. Jacobs, *Studies in Jewish Statistics*, xxxii.

62. Hans Leicher, *Die Vererbung anatomischer Variationen der Nase, Ihrer Nebenhöhlen und des Gehörorgans* (Munich: J. F. Bergmann, 1928), 80–85.

63. Amos Elon, *Herzl* (New York: Holt, Rinehardt and Winston, 1975), 63.

64. Quoted from Konrad H. Jarausch, *Students, Society and Politics in Imperial Germany: The Rise of Academic Illiberalism* (Princeton: Princeton University Press, 1982), 350. See also his *Deutsche Studenten 1800–1970* (Frankfurt am Main: Suhrkamp, 1984), 82–93 as well as Michael Kater, *Studentenschaft und Rechtsradikalismus in Deutschland 1918–1933: Eine sozialgeschichtliche Studie zur Bildungskrise in der Weimarer Republik* (Hamburg: Hoffmann und Campe, 1975), 145–62.

65. W[illiam] O[sler], "Berlin Correspondence," *Canada Medical and Surgical Journal* 2 (1874): 308–15; 310.

66. Jarausch, *Students*, 272.

67. Quoted by Peter Pulzer, *The Rise of Political Anti-Semitism in Germany and Austria* (London: Peter Halband, 1988), 246.

68. Stephan Mencke, *Zur Geschichte der Orthopädie* (Munich: Michael Beckstein, 1930), 68–69.

69. Bruno Valentin, *Geschichte der Orthopädie* (Stuttgart: Georg Thieme, 1961), 101–2.

70. The traditional histories of reconstructive surgery still do not cover cosmetic surgery. See, for example, Joachim Gabka and Ekkehard Vaubel, *Plastic Surgery, Past and Present: Origin and History of Modern Lines of Incision* (Munich: S. Karger, 1983), which mentions Joseph in passing but does not even supply his biography in their biographical appendix. The only comprehensive history of cosmetic surgery discusses his role, without any social context: Mario González-Ulloa, ed., *The Creation of Aesthetic Plastic Surgery* (New York: Springer, 1985), 87–114.

71. "Über die operative Verkleinerung einer Nase (Rhinomiosis)," *Berliner klinische Wochenschrift* 40 (1898): 882–85. Translation from Jacques Joseph, "Operative Reduction of the Size of a Nose (Rhinomiosis)," trans. Gustave Aufricht, *Plastic and Reconstructive Surgery* 46 (1970): 178–81; 178; reproduced in Frank McDowell, ed., *The Source Book of Plastic Surgery* (Baltimore: Williams and Wilkins Co., 1977), 164–67. See also Paul Natvig, *Jacques Joseph: Surgical Sculptor* (Philadelphia: W. B. Saunders, 1982), 23–24. On the general history of rhinoplasty see Blair O. Rogers, "A Chronological History of Cosmetic Surgery," *Bulletin of the New York Academy of Medicine* 47 (1971): 265–302; Blair O. Rogers, "A Brief History of Cosmetic Surgery," *Surgical Clinics of North America* 51 (1971): 265–88; S. Milstein, "Jacques Joseph and the Upper Lateral Nasal Cartilages," *Plastic and Reconstructive Surgery* 78 (1986): 424; J. S. Carey, "Kant and the Cosmetic Surgeon," *Journal of the Florida Medical Association* 76 (1989): 637–43.

72. Joseph, "Operative Reduction," 180.

73. Jean-Jacques Rousseau, *Oeuvres completes*, ed. V. D. Musset-Pathay (Paris: F. Didot, 1823), 3:20.

74. Alfred Berndorfer, "Aesthetic Surgery as Organopyschic Therapy," *Aesthetic and Plastic Surgery* 3 (1979): 143–46; 143. For a good critique of this problem see David A. Hyman, "Aesthetics and Ethics: The Implications of Cosmetic Surgery," *Perspectives in Biology and Medicine* 33 (1990): 190–202.

75. Docteur Celticus, *Les 19 Tares corporelles visibles pour reconnaitre un juif* (Paris: Librairie Antisemite, 1903), chap. 1.

76. John O. Roe, "The Deformity Termed 'Pug Nose' And its Correction, by a Simple Operation," (1887) reprinted in McDowell, *Source Book of Plastic Surgery*, 114–19; 114.

77. Cowling, *Artist as Anthropologist*, 125–29. The image of the nose reproduced by Cowling from the physiognomic literature of the nineteenth century representing the Irish is identical with those in the "before" images reproduced by Roe.

78. Blair O. Rogers, "John Orlando Roe—Not Jacques Joseph—The Father of Aesthetic Rhinoplasty," *Aesthetic Plastic Surgery* 10 (1986): 63–88.

79. See the papers reproduced in McDowell, *Source Book of Plastic Surgery*, 136–64.

80. Jacques Joseph, "Nasenverkleinerungen," *Deutsche medizinische Wochenschrift* 30 (1904): 1095–98; 1095; trans. Frank McDowell in McDowell, *Source Book of Plastic Surgery*, 174–76; 184.

81. Natvig, *Jacques Joseph*, 94.

82. Ibid., 71.

83. See the comments by Eugen Holländer, "Die kosmetische Chirurgie," in Max Joseph, ed., *Handbuch der Kosmetik* (Leipzig: Veit & Comp., 1912), 669–712; 673.

84. Natvig, *Jacques Joseph*, 179.

85. Ibid., 95.

86. See Sander L. Gilman, *Disease and Representation: Images of Illness from Madness to AIDS* (Ithaca: Cornell University Press, 1988), 182–201.

87. Frank J. Sulloway, *Freud, Biologist of the Mind: Beyond the Psychoanalytic Legend* (New York: Basic Books, 1979), 148–50.

88. Wilhelm Fliess, *Die Beziehungen zwischen Nase und weiblichen Geschlechtsorganen: In ihrer biologischen Bedeutung dargestellt* (Leipzig: Franz Deuticke, 1897).

89. "Nase," in *Handwörterbuch des deutschen Aberglaubens*, ed. Hanns Bächtold-Stäubli (Berlin and Leipzig: Walter de Gruyter & Co., 1934–35), 6:970–79 and Havelock Ellis, *Studies in the Psychology of Sex*, Vol. 4, *Sexual Selection in Man* (Philadelphia: F. A. Davis, 1905), 67–69.

90. On this principle of reversal and the meaning of the nose as a symbol of the castrated penis see Otto Fenichel, "Die 'lange Nase,'" *Imago* 14 (1928): 502–4.

91. John Grand-Carteret, *L'affaire Dreyfus et l'image* (Paris: E. Flammarion, 1898); Eduard Fuchs, *Die Juden in der Karikatur* (Munich: Langen, 1921); and Judith Vogt, *Historien om et Image: Antisemitisme og Antizionisme i Karikaturer* (Copenhagen: Samieren, 1978).

92. See Dietz Bering, *Der Name als Stigma: Antisemitismus im deutschen Alltag 1812–1933* (Stuttgart: Klett/Cotta, 1987), 211.

93. Friedrich Nietzsche, *Beyond Good and Evil*, trans. Marianne Cowan (Chicago: Henry Regnery, 1955), 184–88.

94. Oskar Hovorka, *Die äussere Nase: Eine anatomisch-anthropologische Studie* (Vienna: Alfred Hölder, 1893), 130–40. On the pathological meaning of the nose in German science for the later period, see Leicher, *Vererbung anatomischer Variationen der Nase*, 81.

95. Arthur Landsberger, ed., *Judentaufe* (Munich: Georg Müller, 1912), 45.

96. See Sander L. Gilman, *Jewish Self-Hatred: Anti-Semitism and the Hidden Language of the Jews* (Baltimore: The Johns Hopkins University Press, 1986), 193–94.

97. *Protokolle der Wiener Psychoanalytischen Vereinigung*, ed. Herman Nunberg and Ernst Federn, 4 vols. (Frankfurt am Main: Fischer, 1976–81), 1:66–67; translation from *Minutes of the Vienna Psychoanalytic Society*, trans. M. Nunberg (New York: International Universities Press, 1962–75), 2:60–61.

98. See J. David Bleich, *Judaism and Healing: Halakhic Perspectives* (New York: KTAV, 1981), 126–28.

99. Sotah, 45b.

100. Ronald Steel, *Walter Lippmann and the American Century* (Boston: Little, Brown, 1980), 192.

101. Frances Cooke Macgregor, "Social, Psychological and Cultural Dimensions of Cosmetic and Reconstructive Plastic Surgery," *Aesthetic Plastic Surgery* 13 (1989): 1–8; 1.

102. See the discussion in Joseph G. McCarthy, ed., *Plastic Surgery* (Philadelphia: W. B. Saunders, 1990), 1:122–24.

103. Eugene Meyer, Wayne E. Jacobson, Milton T. Edgerton, and Arthur Canter, "Motivational Patterns in Patients Seeking Elective Plastic Surgery," *Psychosomatic Medicine* 22 (1960): 193–203; 197.

104. Macgregor, "Social, Psychological and Cultural Dimensions," 2.

105. Frances Cooke Macgregor and Bertram Schaffner, "Screening Patients for Nasal Plastic Operations," *Psychosomatic Medicine* 12 (1950): 277–91; 283–84.

106. John M. Goin and Macia Kraft Goin, *Changing the Body: Psychological Effects of Plastic Surgery* (Baltimore and London: Williams and Wilkins Co., 1981), 133.

107. Paul Schilder, *The Image and Appearance of the Human Body: Studies in the Constructive Energies of the Psyche* (London: Paul, Trench, Trubner, 1935), 258.

108. Mark Gorney, "Patient Selection and Medicolegal Responsibility for the Rhinoplasty Patient," in *Rhinoplasty: Problems and Controversies*, ed. Thomas D. Ress (St. Louis: C.V. Mosby, 1988), 2.

109. Jean-Paul Sartre, *Anti-Semite and Jew*, trans. George J. Becker (New York: Schocken Books, 1965), 119.

110. For example, see the discussion of "special considerations" in Eugene H. Courtiss, ed., *Male Aesthetic Surgery* (St. Louis: C. V. Mosby, 1991), 159–88 as well as "Ethnic Ideals: Rethinking Plastic Surgery," *The New York Times*, September 25, 1991, C1.

CHAPTER 9

It Has, Like You, No Name:
Paul Celan and the Question of Address

JASON M. WIRTH

For Clyde V. Pax

Handwerk ist . . . die Voraussetzung aller Dichtung. Dieses Handwerk hat ganz bestimmt keinen goldenen Boden—wer weiß, ob es überhaupt einen Boden hat. Es hat seine Abgründe und Tiefen—manche (ach, ich gehöre nicht dazu) haben sogar einen Namen dafür. Und diese Hände wiederum gehören nur einem Menschen, d.h., einem einmaligen und sterblichen Seelenwesen, das mit seiner Stimme und seiner Stummheit einen Weg sucht.

   Nur wahre Hände schreiben wahre Gedichte. Ich sehe keinen prinzipiellen Unterschied zwischen Händedruck und Gedicht.

   . . . Wir leben unter finsteren Himmeln, und—es gibt wenig Menschen. Darum gibt es wohl auch so wenig Gedichte. Die Hoffnungen, die ich noch habe, sind nicht groß; ich versuche, mir das mir Verbliebene zu erhalten.

[Handiwork is . . . the presupposition of all poetry. This handiwork has most certainly no "golden ground"—who knows if it has a ground at all? It has its abysses and depths—some (alas, I do not belong to them) even have a name for it. And these hands once again belong only to a single person, that is, to a unique and mortal human essence (Seelenwesen) that seeks a way with its voice and speechlessness.

   Only true hands write true poems. I see no principle distinction between a handshake and a poem.

   . . . We live under sinister heavens and—there are few humans. That is why there are probably so few poems. The hopes that I still have are not great; I am attempting to preserve what was left for me.]
   —Paul Celan, Brief an Hans Bender (May 18, 1960)

Insomnia in the bed of Being, the impossibility of curling up in order to forget oneself. Expulsion out of the worlding of the world.
   —E. Levinas, "Paul Celan: De l'être a l'autre," *Noms Propres*

183

> May it be a question of Nothing, ever, for anyone.
> —M. Blanchot, *The Writing of the Disaster*

Paul Celan wrote poetry with his hands. This writing resembled a kind of handiwork, a kind of work involving the hands, but not in the sense of a Greek *cheirotechnia* or handicraft that already pre-possessed the image or *eidos* according to which the work would become the instantiation. He represented no essential pictures with words. He shook hands—moving towards "unrecognizable" destinies. His poems were his hands, bottomless perhaps, sent underway to a "you" [du] that, "who knows," might not receive it. His poems suggest the mobile asymmetry of address[1] as they become hands underway to a place that is not a place in what Celan called not the event but the "mystery of encounter" [im Geheimnis der Begegnung].[2] The poem lacks the craftsperson's self-assurance. It is language with dialogical design but without the security of an interlocutor or the preview or even the attainability of its goal. It is "desperate" and it is "impossible" and it is "lonely" [einsam] and it is "unterwegs" [underway], with the one "who writes it remaining given with it."[3] The poem, concerned with the conditions of its own possibility, conceives of itself "in the light of U-topia"[4] as the preservation of a temporality that paradoxically fixes the poem as always on the move, being nowhere and heading nowhere, with "all of its tropes and metaphors wanting to be led *ad absurdum.*"[5] "The poem," Celan writes in an essay entitled "Der Meridian," "intends another, it needs this other [Andere], it needs an opposite [ein Gegenüber]. It seeks it and speaks itself to it. For the poem which heads for the other, each thing, each person is a Gestalt of this other."[6] As Levinas described Celan's poetic address: "The poem moves toward the other. It would hope to catch up to it set free and empty" [délivré et vacant].[7] It is the desperate attempt of someone learning to speak with nothing and no one and perhaps asking that he be addressed likewise.

In this light, Celan, when giving a "Speech on the Occasion of Receiving the Literature Prize in Bremen," claimed that the handiwork of a poem, "being a form of the appearance of language," [eine Erscheinungsform der Sprache] can be a Flaschenpost,[8] (a message in a bottle), sent out to sea, destination (addressee) unknown, the author not knowing where, if anywhere, her or his work will land. Perhaps in a *Herzland* (heartland). "Who knows?"[9] But just as the hand is a moving toward, the poem appears as a "headed toward" [halten auf etwas zu] and hence "according to its essence dialogical."[10] As Celan remarks in

"Der Meridian," "often is it a desperate dialogue" but that "only in the space of this dialogue is the addressee constituted, gathering it around the I that speaks to it and names it. But the addressee brings along its being other [Anderssein] into the present through its having become Du through naming as it were."[11] In this present moment of being addressed through the poem's dialogical gesture toward its unforeseen and unrecognizable interlocutor, the poem lets the other "speak with what is most its own [das Eigenste]: its time."[12] The other is preserved as other in what Levinas called its "finality without end" [finalité sans fin].[13] The other, by always remaining an unreachable no where and no one, does not become lost to the past as an "already no more" when it becomes subsumed by a name; it is preserved in the immediacy of the moment as "still here" when addressed as the always not yet, the still to come. The poem is a handshake that reaches out to no one and no thing.

It does not perpetually reach towards the other as a *quidditas*, as a "what" that can be held with a name. Celan's poetry dis-figures language, reaching towards its other disarticulately "in the swell of wandering words" with unrecognizable and variable keys. The inability to recognize a usage of language protects it as still not yet. Language, "which had to go through its own lack of answers, through terrifying silence, through the thousand darknesses of murderous speech," works with what little remains. Adorno had, at least for awhile, proclaimed that poetry could no longer be written after the Holocaust.[14] As Celan attempted to "project" [entwerfen] what was actual for him, "it meant Ereignis, movement, being underway [Unterwegsein] toward something standing Open [etwas Offenstehendes], inhabitable [Besetzbares], an addressable you perhaps [ansprechbares du], towards an addressable reality."[15] In the poem "ES WAR ERDE IN IHNEN," Celan asks, "To where did it go when it went nowhere?" [Wohin gings, da's nirgendhin ging?] One grubs, one digs, one ponders[16] in the ruins of language and rehabilitates the corpses of words ("Ein Wort—du weißt: / eine Leiche"),[17] turning them "heavenward," toward, "who knows," "perhaps an altogether other."[18] It goes toward, Celan writes in a later poem, the *Unverklungen,*[19] toward what has not subsided or become extinct, toward what and who remains, which may mean toward no one and no thing, toward what Levinas described in Celan as "the place towards the non-place" [le lieu vers le non-lieu].[20]

In what now follows, I hope, as Levinas put it, to "flush out a face to face" [débusquer un vis-à-vis] with this paradoxical du. It will be an address of Celan's address of what Gadamer describes as "simply the

One addressed" [der Angeredete schlechthin] who remains "unde-cidable" [ist nicht auszumachen][21] yet still the "intimate, unknown Du" [das vertraute, unbekannte Du].[22] This task, if it is to be faithful to its own law, must adhere to the temporality that it invokes. It must remain content merely to move toward that which gives itself as always not yet and forever beyond. Paul Celan's poetry was not written so that the most clever could "get it" by decoding its ciphers. Celan's recuperating language splays itself in multiple directions without unveiling a hidden source. "Who speaks shadows, speaks true" [wahr spricht, wer Schatten spricht].[23] The notorious difficulty of Celan's writing has led many to resist it as private and closed even though Celan insisted that he was in no way hermetic[24] and that poetry "no longer imposes itself, it exposes itself."[25] Celan placed his own writing under the laws of the mobility it invokes. As his poetry moves toward its other, so we move toward it, never to see it directly, lest we repeat Orpheus's mistake and lose it forever. I would like to proceed remembering that, as Gadamer said of Celan, the "expectation of meaning [Sinn] in every encountered obscuration of meaning has withdrawn itself."[26] In "light" of all this, I will briefly look towards this perhaps imperceptible du in two poems in Celan's 1963 *Die Niemandsrose* that I hope will be somehow suggestive of my above comments.

ES IST NICHT MEHR
diese
zuweilen mit dir
in die Stunde gesenkte
Schwere. Es ist
eine andre.

Es ist das Gewicht, das die
        Leere zurückhält,

die mit—
ginge mit dir.
Es hat, wie du, keinen Namen.
        Vielleicht
seid ihr dasselbe. Vielleicht
nennst auch du mich einst
so.

[IT IS NO MORE
this
occasionally with you
sunken into the hour
gravity. It is
an other.

It is the weight that
        holds back the emptiness

that would go
along with you.
It has, like you, no name
        Perhaps
you two are the same. Perhaps
one day you will also name me
so.][27]

I will not aim here at a detailed treatment of this poem but rather, in a preliminary fashion, simply point to some resonances. The poem interrelates four pronouns: *I*, *it* (es), *you* (du], and *me*. The du is the first-person familiar mode of address often employed by Celan. It can connote an intimate address (as opposed to the more formal *Sie*) or it can connote the most formal of addresses: the thou that is invoked when one addresses the holy. One might note that nowhere in the poem does Celan make it evident whom he is addressing or in which of the two modes he is using the du.

What we do learn about this du, however, comes from its relationship to the it [es]. Both the es and the du are related to each other by having no name. Perhaps this relationship makes them *dasselbe* [the same]. This es, on the other hand, is "other" than what it once was. It is "no more" "with you" in the way it once was but has become "the weight that holds back the emptiness that goes along with you." The emptiness of the es holds back the concurrent emptiness of the du. This nameless es somehow keeps this du weighted.

Perhaps this es reaches toward the nameless es in the German phrase "es gibt," which, as Martin Heidegger thought, names no thing but rather marks "ein Anwesen von Abwesen,"[28] a coming to presence of a withdrawal of presence, an es that gives but withdraws itself in this giving. As such, it cannot be subsumed under either time or being. It is *das Ereignis*, the moment of presencing-withdrawal of which one can only say, "das Ereignis ereignet."[29] Being itself "would be a type of Ereignis" [wäre das Sein eine Art des Ereignisses][30] and *Ereignis* "the self-withdrawing" [das Sich-entziehen] and, as such, also belonging to Enteignis,[31] or "dis-occurrence," "disappropriation." The es is without name, without why, presencing in the withdrawal of presencing. The du thought as the place or the clearing (Lichtung) of the Ereignis/Enteignis of this es cannot be brought to full presence as subsumed under a name-giving substratum. "The Ereignis neither is nor does it give the Ereignis" [Das Ereignis ist weder, noch gibt es das Ereignis.].[32] The es as the horizon of the du will not provide the du with a name, a raison d'être, a static topos to call its home. The du is preserved from emptiness precisely as that which is ek-static and has no name and no topos. The du thought in light of the es is the du "In the light of U-topia."[33] Addressed as such, it remains deferred as not yet.

This poem, furthermore, is found in a book of poems rich with religious allusions and paradoxically psalmlike threnodies. Perhaps this is a prayer to be no one by someone whose experiences would not let him forget who he was. "Perhaps one day you will also name me so." All poetry, Celan wrote, "is marked [eingeschrieben] by its own '20th of

January,'" a date from which one writes in the hope of somehow
transcending it. "But do we not write out of [sich herschreiben] such
dates? And to which dates do we ascribe [zuschreiben] ourselves?"[34] For
Celan, this date quite literally marked the Wannsee Konferenz in which
Celan was to find himself bearing a name as a Rumanian Jew that
threatened to silence language altogether.[35]

PSALM

Niemand knetet uns wieder
      aus Erde und Lehm,
niemand bespricht unsern Staub.
	[Nobody molds us again
	      out of earth and clay,
	nobody speaks for our dust.

Niemand.	Nobody.
Gelobst seist du, Niemand. Dir zulieb wollen wir blühn. Dir entgegen.	Praised be you, Nobody. We want to blossom for your sake. Towards you.
Ein Nichts waren wir, sind wir, werden wir bleiben, blühend: die Nichts-, die Niemandsrose.	A Nothing were we, are we, will we remain, blossoming: the rose of Nothing, of Nobody.
Mit	With
dem Giffel seelenhell, dem Staubfaden himmelswüst, der Krone rot von Purpurwort, das wir sangen	the pistil soul-bright, the stamen heaven's desert, the crown red with the purple (pure pure) word which we sang
über, o über dem Dorn.	over, o over the thorn.][36]

Prima facie the first sentence seems to be a variation of Genesis 2.7:
"Then the Lord God formed a man out of the dust of the earth." Yet "a
man" is now "us," the ones who have once been formed but who now
seek re-formation. That "we" need this reformation presupposes,
somehow, that "we" have been de-formed and returned to the materials

out of which "we" were once formed. Who, one might already ask, is this "we" that in its deformation seeks reformation? To respond to this question from an oblique angle, Celan claimed that the poet can only write from the "angle of inclination of one's existence" [Neigungs-winkel seines Daseins],[37] which, for Celan, suggests the camps where his family, his race, his country people, perhaps his own psyche, have been deformed into earth, clay, and dust. Celan's traumatic experiences as a Rumanian Jew during the war (the loss of his parents, his internment in work camps, the association of his "mother" tongue with the murderers of his mother, etc.), allusions to which re-occur throughout his oeuvre, suggest that it may be addressed to "you" who can hear "your" com-plicity in the painful remnant of Celan's life. If one listens to the first stanza, it can sound like a threnody sung by the ashen earth to an unconcerned you:

Nobody kneads us again out of earth and clay,
Nobody speaks for our dust.
Nobody.

Heard this way, the psalm begins as a songful cry of abandonment and a refusal of theodicy: No one cares! As one could hear in the opening poem of the collection, "ES WAR ERDE IN IHNEN," God knew and willed their return to the ash from which God had kneaded them. ("And they / did not praise God / who, they heard, wanted all of / this, / who, they had heard, knew of all of this.")[38] That such a deformation could manifest itself as the systematic cremation of an entire race pro-voked a sense of utter forlornness. In their pain, in their having been reduced to dust, nobody redeems them. Nobody intervenes and proclaims that it should not have happened. The Holocaust destroyed the possibility of a theodicy.

A psalm, however, is a prayer and a song to the sacred. Does the threnodic quality of this poem mock this and, as some have suggested, render the book a kind of "anti-Bible"?[39] I do not think so in the sense that Celan places the addressee in a place otherwise than the Bible or its inverse. He places "it" otherwise than place itself. No one is found either in the Bible or its opposite. You are found no where. Celan, elsewhere in *Die Niemandsrose*, places himself between the polar slopes of abandonment and hope. ("BY WINE AND FORLORNNESS, by both declivities . . . " [BEI WEIN UND VERLORENHEIT, bei beider Neige . . .]).[40] As such, one could perhaps hear the faint hope underlying what little remained after the Holocaust, perhaps in the mood of Psalm 61.1: "Hear my cry, O God, listen to my prayer." In this light, it is an address in the form of a prayer to the (no)one(s) who left "us" In the paradox of silenced, singing prayer. It is sung to the nobody to whom all address is a *Flaschenpost*; the nobody who answers with silence. It is in this middle place between two polar declivities, wine and forlornness, the hope implicit in prayer and utter abandonment, that I would like to call attention to Celan's employment of some devices from the cabalistic strategy of language. This world, these stories, these poems and prayers are, as appearances of language, but garments and coverings that, as such, necessarily occlude. At the same time, however, they move, albeit inadequately and disarticulately but counter to language's tendency toward sclerosis, toward that which remains other than the cover. Garments do not have a naming function, but in their failure to name, they can somehow invoke their other.[41] In the *Zohar*, an important text in the Kabbalah, the directions for How to Look at Torah assert that "the stories of this world" are mere "garments" and

As wine must sit in a jar,
so Torah must sit in this garment.
So look only at what is under the garment!
So all those words and all those stories—
they are garments![42]

But whose garments? What wine is hidden in the flask of ashen earth? Nobody's garments of course! The wine is nothing. We point to nobody. It is, if you will, the rose of Nothing and Nobody. Relocating ourselves between the declivities of forlornness and wine, we can begin to hear an expansion of the paradox of Niemand. Tucked away beyond the range of naming to circumscribe, of speaking to comprehend, of words to exact a meaning, of stories to explain, is nothing. That is to say, beyond language one finds nothing. One finds Niemand. That is to say, one finds the wine in the flask. One enjoins, through the preserving power of language, the silence at the edge of language, the "counter-word" [Gegenwort] beyond each word. In the "desperate," alchemical dialogue of poetry, Celan experiments with lifeless, leaden words, attempting to free them up as he grubs through the ruins of language for wine and gold. And he finds: Nothing, No one, Nobody. He succeeds and he fails. He finds silence. As the call of address sings forth in "ES WAR ERDE IN IHNEN," the first poem in *Die Niemandsrose*:

O einer, oh keiner, o niemand, o du
[O one, O not one, o no one, o you].[43]

Just as the alchemists sought to turn lead into gold (a journey, one might remember, which was religious in orientation), Celan "combs" and "washes" dead words and finds a golden silence, if you will, cooked (perhaps cremated) in the oven of the earth. To cite a couple of lines from "Alchemical" [*Chymisch*], another poem in *Die Niemandsrose*:

Schweigen, wie Gold gekocht, in verkohlten, verkohlten Händen.
Finger, rauchdünn. Wie Kronen, Luftkronen um—

[Silence, cooked like Gold, in charred, charred hands.
Fingers, thin with smoke, like crowns, air-crowns about—

Große. Graue. Fährte- lose.
König- liche.

Great One. Grey One. Trace- less One.
King- ly One.][44]

These are not poems of redemption if the copula "are" denotes an identitarian relationship between the Celan's poetic handshakes and redemption. Silence is what little remains as one grubs through the ruins of language and, as such, seems to manifest itself as the crowns of the Great, Grey, and Traceless One. As Celan says in another poem in *Die Niemandsrose*: "Snuggled up to nobody cheek to cheek / To you—Life. / To you—found with the / stump of a hand."[45] It is an encounter with another sense of Niemand, who, like the pre-Socratic *apeiron* (no limit/ *peras*) emerges at the boundaries of determination:

Nobody kneads us again out of earth and clay,
Nobody speaks for our dust.
Nobody.

Praised be you, Nobody.

In this second gestalt, concomitant with the forlorn quality of the first, Nobody takes the form of an Other that is being addressed and, as such, suggests another relationship to the Kabbalah. In this light,

Niemand suggests an affinity with the Ein-Sof, a word meaning
"infinite" or "having no limit." It is the boundlessness, the nothing and
no one, fetched back and preserved by language but always remaining,
in another way, beyond language. About the Ein-Sof, which is invoked
with Du, the *Zohar* says:

> There is none that knows anything of You, and besides You
> there is no singleness and no unity in the upper or the lower
> worlds, and You are acknowledged as Lord over all. As for the
> sefirot, each one has a known name, and the angels are desig-
> nated by them, but You have no known name, for You fill all
> names, and You are the perfect completion of them all. And
> when You remove Yourself from them, all the names are left
> like a body without a soul.[46]

The very name *Ein-Sof*, one might infer, already harbors the seeds of its
own overcoming and deferral.[47] The Ein-Sof is other than any of its
names and its effability as ineffable and its determination as indeterminate was its first and highest emanation but was other than the
Ein-Sof itself. As Scholem explains, "Although there were widely
differing views on the nature of the first step from concealment to
manifestation, all stressed that no account of this process could be an
objective description of a process in Ein-Sof; it was no more than could
be conjectured from the perspective of created beings."[48] The Ein-Sof
remains always otherwise than our thoughts of "it" and gives itself in a
hierarchized relay of ten emanations or *sefirot*, or what Scholem calls
the "progressive manifestation of the names of God."[49] Despite its
names, including the supreme name which marks it as unnameable, the
Ein-Sof remains wholly effaced. As the *Zohar* phrases it, "the concealed
within the concealed of the mystery of the Infinite [Ein-Sof]."[50]

In the second stanza, this doubling of Niemand emanates as the You
toward which we want to blossom, but instead of singing "Gelobt sei
der Herr, der Gott Israels" [Praised be the Lord, the God of Israel]"
(Psalm 41.14), as Luther's Bible does, Celan addresses Nobody: "Praised
be you, Nobody." Praised be the Nobody that left "us" forlorn. Praised
be the nothing beyond the wine vessels.

The third stanza links the "we" that wants reformation and
blossoming to the rose of nothing and Nobody. The image of a rose, of
course, is one of the most perennial in the Western literary imagination.
In Ecclesiastes 39.13 we are advised to "listen to me, my devout sons,

and blossom like a rose planted by a stream."[51] If one listens to Nobody and nothing—and perhaps that is all that is left after the deformation of the Holocaust—one remains a blooming nothing. The rose was also a favored image in Rilke's poetry, of which Celan was said to be a careful reader. In the sixth poem in the second part of the *Sonnets to Orpheus* we read: "Rose, you being enthroned . . . the full, countless flower, the inexhaustible thing . . . Yet we do not know what to name it, we guess" [Rose, du thronende. . . . die volle zahllose Blume, der unerschöpfliche Gegenstand. . . . Dennoch, wir wissen ihn nicht zu nennen, wir raten].[52] And the rose was again mentioned on Rilke's epitaph in Raron: "Rose, oh pure contradiction, desire to be Nobody's sleep under so many lids." [Rose, oh reiner Widerspruch, Lust, Niemandes Schlaf zu sein unter soviel Lidern].[53] "We" remain nameless, paradoxical roses; perhaps as roses of no one, one refracts the "light of no place" [U-topie].

This rose has a red crown, perhaps the crown of thorns used to mock and deform Jesus but also the crown of thorns that became an emblem of his overcoming.[54] The crown is perhaps also *keter elyon*, the "supreme crown" that was the first and supreme emanation of the Ein-Sof. "It is called Ein-Sof internally and Keter Elyon externally."[55] Although it is the first *sefirot* from which all other *sefirot* flow, it manifests itself not determinately but rather as no thing or no body—as "ayin" [nothing] or "afisah" [nothingness]. As Scholem explains, "Essentially, this nothingness is the barrier confronting the human intellectual faculty when it reaches the limits of its capacity. In other words, it is a subjective statement affirming that there is a realm which no created being can intellectually comprehend . . . God who is called Ein-Sof in respect of Himself is called Ayin in respect of His first self-revelation."[56] This is not an ontological theory of creation. Rather, creation becomes the creation of temporality as the arena for the emanations of the Ein-Sof or the "dark flame" as it became set in a crown while remaining beyond time and being. Within time it is preserved as always not yet in time. To quote from elsewhere in *Die Niemandsrose*, it is: "YOUR BEING-BEYOND this night. With words I fetched you back, there you are, / everything is true and a waiting for the true" [DEIN HINÜBERSEIN heute Nacht. Mit Worten hole ich dich wieder, da bist du, / alles ist wahr und ein Warten auf Wahres].[57]

However, ayin is still a point or a place in which the Ein-Sof can somehow be thought. Since the Ein-Sof remains beyond even its supreme manifestation, it is the failure of nothingness to invoke the infinite that comes paradoxically closer to invoking it. This paradoxical

use of language in which the Other of the du is preserved in its
"counter-word," in its always being not yet in language, was described
as *zimzum*, or the du's "contraction" or "concentration." Keter, as the
first emanation, was not a manifestation of the Ein-Sof, after all, but a
concealment in order that it might appear at all. The "du" must in part
withdraw for any of "it" to manifest itself. Zimzum suggests, then, the
withdrawal of the du from a place in order to emanate even as nothing.
Keter, as the crown of nothingness, is the place from which the Ein-Sof
emanates as having already withdrawn into no place. It is the place of
contraction. The place towards no place. As Harold Bloom phrases it:
"Zimzum is initially a rhetorical irony for the act of creation, in that it
means the opposite of what it appears to 'say.' It says 'withdrawal' and
means 'concentration.' God withdraws from a point only to concentrate
Himself upon it. The image of His absence becomes one of the greatest
images ever found for His presence, a presence which is intensified by
the original metaphor of mezamzem, His holding in of His breath.[58] It is
with this impossible alchemical magic of the zimzum of address to an
utopian du that "we sang over, o over the thorn."[59]

And what of my own attempts here to counter Wittgenstein and say
the ineffable? Have I not just given voice to Celan's carefully preserved
silences? Perhaps in addressing Celan's mode of poetic address is an
invitation to reflect further on the goals of critical address and perhaps
let them lead us nowhere. Celan called his poetry an "Atemwende," a
turning of the breath, a holding of the heath, if you will, perhaps to
speak old words in new ways, to hold on to whatever was left, to speak
with words as well as silences, to walk the meridian "way of the
impossible" [Weg des Unmöglichen],[60] or, as Levinas said of Celan, "to
say without saying" [Dire sans dit]:[61]

I see you, you pluck them with my
new, my every person's hand, you put them
in the Brightness-Once-More, that nobody
needs to weep or to name.[62]

Notes

1. On this point, Maurice Merleau-Ponty makes the striking claim in his essay
"Hegel's Existentialism" that "the only experience which brings me close to an authentic
awareness of death is the experience of contact with another. . . ." (*Sense and Non-Sense*,
trans. Hubert and Patricia Dreyfus [Evanston: Northwestern University Press, 1964],
68).

2. *Paul Celan: Gesammelte Werke*, ed. Beda Allemann and Stefan Reichert under the collaboration of Rolf Bücher (Frankfurt am Main: Suhrkamp, 1983), 3:198. Henceforth cited as *GW*. The translations throughout this essay, despite Celan's own contention that poetry, like du, is "das schicksalhaft Einmalige der Sprache" (*GW*, 3:175), are my own responsibility. To compare translations, see R. Waldrop, *Collected Prose* (Manchester: Carcanet Press, 1985), 49. Henceforth cited as *CP*. With respect to the paradoxical, or, perhaps more accurately, the differential, nature of the du, one could keep in mind Celan's attack upon the "alter Identitätskrämer" [old identity monger] in his 1948 essay "Der Traum von Träume."

3. *GW*, 3:198/*CP*, 49.

4. *GW*, 3:199/*CP*, 51.

5. *GW*, 3:199/*CP*, 51.

6. *GW*, 3:198/*CP*, 49.

7. Emmanuel Levinas, "Paul Celan: De l'être a l'autre," in *Noms Propres* (Paris: Fata Morgana, 1975), 51. Hence, Levinas collects this movement of Celan as "language of proximity for the sake of proximity" [langage de la proximité pour la proximité], 50. Translations of this short yet extraordinary essay are my own.

8. *GW*, 3:186/*CP*, 34–35. This suggestion that a poem is like a "message in a bottle" possibly owes some of its roots to the poetry of Ossip Mandelstamm (to whose memory *Die Niemandsrose* is dedicated) or Alfred de Vigny's contention found in an 1842 diary entry in which he wrote that "a book is a bottle thrown in the midst of the sea" ["Un livre est une bouteille jetée en pleine mer"]. See Amy Colin, *Paul Celan: Holograms of Darkness* (Bloomington: Indiana University Press, 1991), 191. This text is an interesting exploration of some of Celan's themes as well as an overview of much of the literature on Celan and contains a lot of important biographical materials. As Colin quite perceptively notes: "His verses resemble Kafka's castle, for the closer the reader approaches them, the further they recede into darkness" (xxiii).

9. Celan often intersects this "wer weiß?" throughout the Meridian Rede. As Celan himself addresses his use of this phrase: "This 'Who knows' which I have now reached, is all that I am able to add today and here to the old hopes" (*GW*, 3:196/*CP*, 48).

10. *GW*, 3:186/*CP*, 34.

11. *GW*, 3:198/*CP*, 50.

12. *GW*, 3:199/*CP*, 50.

13. Levinas, "Paul Celan," 54.

14. For a discussion of this comment and Adorno's later repeal of the statement in his *Negative Dialectics*, see Colin, *Paul Celan*, xvii. There is a sense, I suspect, that Adorno's concept of the non-concept, of the "vertiginous," a-teleological, fluid movement ("performance") of the non-identity principle and its invocation not as subsumed under a concept but as a monadological impulse refracted in a "constellation" could be one of the devices that might allow one to glimpse indirectly the forever elusive *du*.

15. *GW*, 3:186/*CP*, 34–35.

16. This calls to mind a new, perhaps more radical sense of the Jewish tradition of Talmudic exegesis or *midrash*—a word whose root means "to search." In "ES WAR

ERDE IN IHNEN," quoted below, Celan uses the word *graben*, which not only means to dig, including to dig graves, but to grub in the sense of pondering—perhaps in the sense of the melancholy *Grübler* in Walter Benjamin's *Ursprung des deutschen Trauerspiels*.

17. "A word—you know / a corpse." All Celan poems are from *Paul Celan: Gedichte in zwei Bänden* (Frankfurt am Main: Suhrkamp, 1975). Henceforth cited as *Celan*. (*Celan*, 1:125.)

18. *GW*, 3:196/*CP*, 48.

19. *Wohin gings? Gen Unverklungen*. From a poem in *Die Niemandsrose* beginning "WAS GESCHAH?" (*GW*, 1:269).

20. Levinas, "Paul Celan," 52.

21. Hans-Georg Gadamer, *Wer bin Ich und wer bist Du? Kommentar zu Celans 'Atemkristall'* (Frankfurt am Main: Suhrkamp, 1973), 12. Translations of this extremely thoughtful text are my own responsibility. Gadamer holds that the du is the figure of the du itself and cannot be correlated to this or that du: "Die Figur dieses Du ist sie selbst und nicht dieser oder jener, ein geliebter Mensch, ein anderer oder das ganz Andere" (118).

22. Gadamer, *Wer bin Ich*, 112.

23. From "Sprich Auch Du" in *Von Schwelle zu Schwelle* (*Celan*, 1:135).

24. "Ich bin ganz und gar nicht hermetisch," quoted in *Paul Celan: Last Poems*, trans. Katherine Washburn and Margret Guillermin (San Francisco: North Point Press, 1986), vi.

25. *CP*, 29.

26. Quoted in Véronique Foti, "Celan's Challenges to Heidegger," in *Festivals of Interpretation*, ed. Kathleen Wright (Albany: SUNY Press, 1990), 192. Foti observes: "Such a poetics outstrips mimetology in that the same becomes unrecognizable and cannot be brought to a standstill or kept in memory" (200).

27. *GW*, 1:238.

28. Martin Heidegger, "Zeit und Sein," *Zur Sache des Denkens* (Tübingen: Max Niemeyer Verlag, 1969), 19. My translations. The essay has been translated by Joan Stambaugh in *On Time and Being* (San Francisco: Harper Torchbooks, 1972), 1–24. In this context, one might remember that Celan was a careful student of Heidegger's writings and that he met with Heidegger twice. The poem "Todtnauberg" is a result of one of those encounters.

29. Heidegger, "Zeit und Sein," 24. Heidegger himself notes the inappropriate nature of the essay style (including my present efforts here) to say these thoughts: "Ein Hindernis dieser Art bleibt auch das Sagen vom Ereignis in der Weise eines Vortrags. Er hat nur in Aussagesätzen gesprochen" [A hindrance of this kind also remains for the saying of Ereignis in the fashion of a lecture. It has only spoken in propositions] (25).

30. Ibid., 22.

31. Ibid., 23.

32. Ibid., 24.

33. *GW*, 3:199/*CP*, 51.

34. *GW*, 3:196/*CP*, 47.

35. It is interesting to note here that Paul Celan changed his name shortly after the war. Celan is an anagram of his original name Ancel.

36. *GW*, 1:225. One can find three other attempts to translate this poem (one in French, two in English) in *Argumentum e Silentio*, 402–4.

37. *GW*, 3:147/*CP*, 49. Celan once remarked that "The silence is the same . . . Who isn't alone? Who isn't overwelmed by all kinds of fears, nuclear threats and others?" (Quoted in Colin, *Paul Celan*, xvi).

38. Cf., the opening, unnamed (untitled) poem in *Die Niemandsrose*, *GW*, 1:211.

39. Marlies Janz, quoted in Bernd Witte, "Der Zyklische Charakter der Niemandsrose von Paul Celan" in *Argumentum e Silentio*, ed. Amy D. Colin (Berlin: Walter de Gruyter & Co., 1987), 75.

40. *GW*, 1:213.

41. Gershom Scholem once claimed that reading Kafka is the best way to understand the cabalistic theory of language today. *Walter Benjamin: The Story of a Friendship*, trans. Harry Zohn (New York: Schocken Books, 1981), 125.

42. *Zohar—The Book of Enlightenment*, trans. Daniel Chanan Matt (New York: Paulist Press, 1983), 45.

43. *GW*, 1:211.

44. *GW*, 1:228.

45. *GW*, 1:245.

46. *Zohar*, 2nd preface, 17a–17b in *The Wisdom of the Zohar*, Isaiah Tishby ed. (Oxford: Oxford University Press, 1989), 1:261. In this respect, see Martin Buber, from whom Levinas remarks that Celan derived his "categories" of poetry as "l'acte de débusquer un via à vis" [the act of flushing out a face to face] (Levinas, "Paul Celan," 51). Buber writes: "Extended, the lines of relationship intersect in the eternal You (Du) every single You is a glimpse of that" (*I and Thou*, trans. Walter Kaufmann, [New York: Scribners, 1970], 123). Buber later continues: "The It-world coheres in space and time. The You-world coheres in neither. It coheres in the center in which the extended lines of relationship intersect in the eternal You" (148).

47. Levinas uses a similar device in *Totalité et Infinité* with "infinition" in "l'idée de l'infini . . . déborde la pensée qui le pense" such that infinition is "dans ce débordement." As such, it is "nonenglobable dans une totallté" and an "au-delà." Ethics becomes eschatological as a "signification sans contexte" and a "vision sans image." Celan's saying without saying or his saying without names and with silence seems to me to have a affinity with Levinas's strategy. As such, it may force us to think more carefully even of ontological privilege.

48. Gershom Scholem, *Kabbalah* (New York: Dorset Press, 1987), 90.

49. Ibid., 107.

50. *Zohar*, trans. Matt, 49.

51. I owe this reference to Joachim Schulze, *Celan und die Mystiker* (Bonn: Bouvier Verlag Herbert Grundmann, 1976), 26. This text supplies some very informative source materials.

52. Rainer Maria Rilke, *Sonnets to Orpheus*, a bilingual ed., trans. C. F. MacIntyre (Berkeley and Los Angeles: University of California Press, 1961), 66–67. I altered the translation slightly.

53. *The Selected Poetry of Rainer Maria Rilke*, a bilingual ed., ed. and trans. Stephen Mitchell (New York: Vintage, 1984), 278. My translation.

54. For an interesting reference to this image, see Amy Colin's discussion of Celan's early poem "Dornenkranz" in Colin, *Paul Celan*, 70–74.

55. Scholem, *Kabbalah*, 92.

56. Ibid., 94.

57. *GW*, 1:218.

58. Harold Bloom, *Kabbalah and Criticism* (New York: Continuum, 1984), 74. For a discussion of *zimzum*, see Scholem, *Kabbalah*, 129–35. As Scholem describes it: "Some part of the Godhead therefore withdraws and leaves room, so to speak, for the creative processes to come into play. Such a retreat must precede any emanation. . . . [I]t is not the concentration of God's power in a place, but its withdrawal from a place. The place from which He retreats is merely a "point" in comparison with His infinity, but it comprises from our point of view all levels of existence, both spiritual and corporeal" (129–30).

59. It is with "purple word" that we sang. The Christ imagery of the poem seems to suggest that the "purple"—a color of splendor—is, as Colin notes, "the scarlet cloak . . . in which the soldiers wrapped Christ to mock him (Matt. 27:28)" (71). Again, what was used to mock is what is used to go over the thorn. The *Zohar* speaks of "sowing a seed for its glory like the seed of fine purple silk" (*Zohar*, trans. Matt, 50). *Purpur* is also a pun. It also sounds like "pure pure."

60. *GW*, 3:202/*CP*, 54.

61. Levinas, "Paul Celan," 49, 52.

62. *GW*, 1:255.

CHAPTER 10

The Malady of Community

MICHAEL STRYSICK

Traditionally, the notion of community is concerned with what is shared or common among individuals. Unfortunately, it then becomes far too easy to privilege one type of characteristic over another through so-called terminal truths. In short, a malady of community arises that can be diagnosed as inattention to difference by opposing same against other. Such totalizing severely discounts the degree to which difference among people might be considered more essential. By emphasizing our radical difference, infinite in nature, and then structuring our sense of community anew, the hegemony of totality can be challenged.

I would like to address such a task through a palimpsest of literary and critical texts whose themes and very language work to expose such totalizing gestures within community, most specifically in terms of gender issues. Throughout, I will operate on the assumption that a cure may be possible for such a malady, but that it is predicated upon our ability to not only re-think but un-think community as conceived through the convenience of terminal and totalizing truths. This altered philosophy of community—more a wisdom of love than a love of wisdom, to play upon philosophy's etymological roots— operates in order to achieve the dissolution of a Manichean ordering of relations.

Perhaps the most provocative lines on love arise in Marguerite Duras's *The Malady of Death*: "You ask how loving can happen—the emotion of loving. She answers: Perhaps a sudden lapse in the logic of the universe. She says: Through a mistake, for instance. She says: Never through an act of will."[1] Or maybe the proper adjective is not *provocative* but *arresting*, for these are lines that charge, indict, and condemn. Duras asserts this in *Practicalities*, a collection of thoughts on a variety of topics, when she says flatly that "*The Malady of Death* is an indictment."[2]

199

But let me begin to pursue this by a diversion. Kathy Acker, in her equally dystopic novel, *Don Quixote*,[3] also presents arresting thoughts on love. In typical Acker fashion, several different pre-existent textual strands are woven together to create a coat of quite a different color. In one particular section, entitled "Wedekind's Words,"[4] she has constructed a patchwork consisting of references to Wedekind's Lulu plays,[5] G. W. Pabst's film *Pandora's Box*,[6] and the Pygmalion myth.[7]

While the texts referenced in this section may appear on the one hand confusing, just the opposite is the case; that is, the many elective affinities among the references are shown. In Acker's treatment, the Prof. Henry Higgins and Dr. Schön characters are collapsed into that of Prof. Schön, and Lulu is both the Wedekind earth-spirit and the young girl who apparently needs to be saved by a man and turned into a lady.

Upon meeting Lulu, selling flowers and trying to lift his wallet, Prof. Schön—representing, beauty, culture, and order—says, "You do not know who you are because you do not know how to speak properly" (*Quixote*, 78). After deciding to take her home and give her proper speech, he declares: "By George, the streets will be strewn with the bodies of men shooting themselves for your sake before I'm done with you" (*Quixote*, 78). Thus, Acker mocks the presentation of woman as object, as thing to be molded into a something by the Pygmalion figure of man, to be educated in such a way as to incite murder.

Two hundred years earlier, in her *Vindication of the Rights of Woman*, Mary Wollstonecraft discussed a similar situation; her criticism, however, is less implicit: "The education of woman has, of late, been more attended to than formerly; yet they are still reckoned a frivolous sex, and ridiculed or pitied by the writers who endeavor by satire or instruction to improve them. . . . The instruction which women have hitherto received has only tended, with the constitution of civil society, to render them insignificant objects of desire."[8] While the problematic is clearly stated, its alleviation appears elusive—historically (that is, will such a critique be written again in another two hundred years?). "Many are the causes that, in the present corrupt state of society, contribute to enslave women," Wollstonecraft writes, "One, perhaps, that silently does more mischief than all the rest, is their disregard for order" (*Vindication*, 22). But the disregard for order, one of the attributes of the beautiful (*das Schön*),[9] is perhaps better stated as disregard for the imposed order in which, Wollstonecraft asserts, woman—categorically reduced—"was created to be the toy of man, his rattle, and it must jingle in his ears whenever, dismissing reason, he chooses to be amused" (*Vindication*, 34). This "prevailing opinion," Wollstonecraft surmises, "may have taken its rise from Moses's poetical story . . . that Eve was, literally speaking, one of Adam's ribs" (*Vindication*, 26).

Acker's text takes on such opinions by circulating around a critique, hardly nostalgic, that love is not present in the world—or is not present enough. Her character Lulu suggests, "Since love is sympathy or communication, I need an object which is both subject and object: to love, I must love a soul" (*Quixote*, 10). But she then exclaims, "To survive I must not love." She is talking about survival, however, under the current structure or grammar of so-called order. Prof. Schön cannot tolerate her sarcasm and says, holding a gun to his head, "What you call 'love', if I paid any attention to it, would rip me (and this world) apart" (*Quixote*, 90).

With this Schön recognizes that this thing called "love" does not fall within his realm, whose order and presence is felt strongly in countless ways—some overt, others covert.[10] Prof. Schön continues: "You are nothing, nothing. I will not have you break into my world, break me up, destroy me." To which Lulu replies: "You're mad. This is a world of madness" (*Quixote*, 90).[11]

But what is this thing called love?

In Duras's *Malady of Death* it is defined more through its absence, as that which is pursued by the male character through the female character. The tale opens with the establishment of a contract. But the transaction's economy is such that the man contracts the woman. Maurice Blanchot, who provides a reading of Duras's text in the second part of his *Unavowable Community*, describes the opening as indicating a so-called homosexual economy that marks its own failure by the economical-material nature of the man's request. Blanchot writes of

> a man, who has never known anybody but those like him, that is to say only other men who are nothing but the multiplication of himself, a man thus, and a young woman bound to him by a paid contract for a few nights, for a whole life, which has led hasty critics to talk about a prostitute though she herself makes clear that she is not, although there is a contract—a relationship that is purely contractual (marriage, money)—because she has felt from the beginning, without knowing it clearly, that, incapable of loving, he can only approach her conditionally, after concluding a transaction.[12]

Blanchot is careful to point out that the apparent power exercised by one being able to contract another "measures only his impotence" (*Unavowable*, 36). For his worth is measured by her ability to contribute to the contract. He may possess the agency to initiate the contract, but she has what he desires.[13] The contract itself constitutes what I would call an "avowable structure,"[14] which has its own defense built in and is deaf to the feebleness of its manner of placing value on things other than itself upon the basis of its own self.

Duras presents this in terms of an avowable request to the woman by the man: "She asks: What other conditions? You say she mustn't speak, like the women of her ancestors, must yield completely to you and your will, be entirely submissive" (*Malady*, 4). The woman's reply is "in that case it'll be even more expensive" (*Malady*, 5). But the real expense is the further damage of the relation by the increased intensity of its avowability and manifest impotence.

Other conditions follow along the way: she must surrender the power of discourse, must not act as if things are shared, for if things were shared, a radical equality— that is, an unavowability[15]—would have to be recognized and practiced; but the avowable community will not allow this, for it will tolerate defense of only a single position.

Duras declares this a sickness, a malady. It is a power (*puissance*) whose sickness is revealed as impotence (*impuissance*), as reduction to a criminal, violent state; an impotence, as well, that manifests itself through ignorance. "Because you know nothing about her," Duras writes, "you'd say she knows nothing about you. You'd leave it at that" (*Malady*, 15). But of course it is she who does know, who is coming to know, is coming to understand the nature and depth of the malady through her treatment.

It is at this point in the text when the woman understands the nature of their relation and its malady as perversely economical. After all, she accepted the contract "Because as soon as you spoke to me I saw you were suffering from the malady of death" (*Malady*, 18). Importantly, she recognizes the malady through his speech and its very grammar, for the man is unable to speak from any position other than that of a privileged same.

Charlotte Perkins Gilman's *The Yellow Wallpaper* raises similar issues, but here things are somewhat reversed. The female protagonist— as in Duras, never specifically named—is supposedly sick; though one might argue that all she ultimately suffers from is the malady of death carried by her husband, John, a doctor, man of science, healer. We read of him, "John is a physician, and *perhaps*—(I would not say it to a living soul, of course, but this is dead paper and a great relief to my mind)—*perhaps* that is one reason I do not get well faster."[16] Gilman presents a doctor who cannot heal someone else because he must first heal himself of a disease he is unable to diagnose.

The woman is interned in "A colonial mansion, a hereditary estate, I would say a haunted house" (*Yellow*, 9), which describes the political-economical condition—patriarchal, colonizing—as much as the physical structure itself. John decides on a particular bedroom for them in this hereditary estate, that of an old nursery in the house's top floor, a room covered with a strangely yellow wallpaper patterned with bars and rings. At first repulsive, the jaundiced surroundings ultimately become a point of fascination. She recognizes that "On a pattern like this, by daylight, there is lack of sequence, a defiance of law, that is a constant irritation to a normal mind" (*Yellow*, 25). The element of light, of daylight, is important here, suggesting as it does a critique of reason and enlightenment; especially since she says, "There is one marked peculiarity about this paper, a thing nobody seems to notice but myself, and that is that it changes as the light changes" (*Yellow*, 25). In other words, the illogic of the wall paper's order (its pattern or grammar)[17] is able to conform itself to varying degrees of light and dark. Even further, it is able to control such variations by virtue of a presumed universality that assumes all can be totalized. But it is at night that its true nature is revealed: "At night in any kind of light, in twilight, candle light, lamp-light, and worst of all by moonlight, it becomes bars! The outside pattern I mean, and the woman behind it is as plain as can be" (*Yellow*, 26). The very basis of the pattern is predicated upon an imprisoning notion of difference that moves beyond regulation to incarceration.

In the end, she sees the destruction of this prison as the only prescription to this sick pattern and begins tearing off the wallpaper. It is at this moment that her so-called madness sets in, at the moment when she is able to tear down the imprisoning paper and its pattern; at the time, one might say, that her love for the others imprisoned—in its madness—manifests itself.

Duras's character, like Gilman's, lives a sleepy existence. In Gilman, sleep is imposed by the husband, John, as a way of preventing the woman from writing.[18] In Duras, sleep appears to be an almost natural condition. But here, too, it is a state imposed by the very conditions of the relation. She is to be on call for him to attempt to love, but the attempt itself marks the inability Duras describes as "that deadly routine of lovelessness" (*Malady*, 48). This malady causes him to "ask her why she sleeps, what weariness she has to rest from, what monumental weariness." To this she can only reply: "The fact that you ask the question proves you can't understand" (*Malady*, 49). This lack of understanding Duras portrays later as not recognizing "The marvelous impossibility of reaching her through the difference that separates you" (*Malady*, 54). This misunderstanding on his part is indicative of a grammar of avowability where the other is merely the lesser pole in a conveniently binary relation.

But can one order community upon the basis of love and lovers?

In "The Sorcerer's Apprentice," his inaugural text for the College of Sociology, Georges Bataille calls the world of lovers (friends or couples) the "true world."[19] Blanchot, in *The Unavowable Community*, describes this world as "a world that is, precisely, the oblivion of the world" (*Unavowable*, 34), that "the community of lovers no longer cares about the forms of the tradition or any social agreement" (*Unavowable*, 47), and that "The community of lovers . . . has as its goal the destruction of society," achieved by their creation of a united "war machine" (*Unavowable*, 48).

But what is especially important is that despite the apparent primacy of the elective community of lovers over traditional community, Bataille moves away from centering this relation, limiting the so-called foundational quality of this true world. In a footnote to "The Sorcerer's Apprentice" he writes: "The description of the 'lovers' world' in this text, however, has only a *demonstrative* value. This world constitutes one of the rare possibilities in actual life, and its realization presents a character far less distant from the totality of existence than are the worlds of art, politics or science. It is not, however, the fulfillment of human life. In any case it would be a mistake to consider it as the elementary form of society. The idea that the couple is at the base of the social phenomenon has had to be abandoned for reasons that seem conclusive."[20] The conclusive reason is, essentially, based on the character of the unavowable. To reductively prescribe the community of lovers—friends or couples—as the basis of society would be to set it up as a complete and avowable structure, which is the very thing it is working toward destroying and undoing.

Blanchot, following Bataille, points out that community, the question of community, is itself a response to the fact that "'There exists a principle of insufficiency at the root of each being . . . ' (the principle of incompleteness)" (*Unavowable*, 5).[21] For Bataille, connected to this insufficiency is incompletion, his beloved state of *inachevement*.[22] Importantly, Bataille works never toward overcoming this incompleteness and unknowability but rather toward un-working[23] notions of completion and knowability. This is for him, undoubtedly, the basis of what I would call his "Zarathustrian project." A prototypical Antichrist who wishes nothing but to return creativity—the breaking of rules, the setting out on a thousand paths—and overcome the avowable structures of the Higher Men, the great doctors and Fathers of reason, completion, and order. This overcoming can be accomplished only through what Blanchot used to describe the lovers' world: oblivion, indifference, destruction.

In his short narrative, *The Madness of the Day*, Blanchot critiques such Fathers and theologues: "I liked the doctors quite well, and I did not feel belittled by their doubts. The annoying thing was that their authority loomed larger by the hour. One is not aware of it, but these men are kings. Throwing open my rooms, they would say, 'Everything here belongs to us.' They would fall upon my scraps of thought: 'This is ours.' They would challenge my story: 'Talk,' and my story would put itself at their service."[24] He then goes on to say "Behind their backs I saw the silhouette of the law" (*Madness*, 14). But a silhouette only; a shadow, a phantom. Blanchot's character in this tale is receiving treatment for his eyes, which have been recently impaired. But after being asked to narrate events leading up to the accident—and fully aware that all would be put at their service—he admits: "I had to acknowledge that I was not capable of forming a story out of these events" (*Madness*, 18). Yet he reports that "This explanation only made them more insistent" (*Madness*, 18). This realization is then followed by another: "Then I noticed for the first time that there were two of them and that this distortion of the traditional method, even though it was explained by the fact that one of them was an eye doctor, the other a specialist in mental illness, constantly gave our conversation the character of an authoritarian interrogation, overseen and controlled by a strict set of rules" (*Madness*, 18). This points to what could be called the avowable's "optical imperative."[25] Importantly, the doctor in Blanchot's *Madness of the Day* is an optician, a doctor whose goal is to achieve perfect vision in the patient, just as the specialist helps achieve a kind of universal reason. Read metaphorically, the correct vision is ultimately the proper vision put at their service, conforming to their strict rules and strict order.

In such a setting, the them, operating as a same, determines the other, but determines the other according to the order of their same; not merely through specific discourse, but through the structure of speech itself; not only through specific institutions, but through the structure of institutions themselves; not only through specific thinking, but through the structure of thought itself. Therefore, the defense of the structure is implicit, confessed to (avouer),[26] its avowability untouchable within its own structure.[27]

The fault of this structure is its notion of vision whose optical orientation is based on totality and not infinity. Totality is tied to this optical imperative as the idea that all can be seen, as a whole, and must be defined within this totality, completely. In Totality and Infinity, Levinas concludes that "we can proceed from the experience of totality, back to a situation where totality breaks up, a situation that conditions the totality itself. Such a situation is the gleam of exteriority or of transcendence in the face of the other [autrui]."[28] A gleam of that which has, thus, fallen outside, exists outside, the totality. Levinas claims that "The rigorously developed concept of this transcendence is expressed by the term infinity" (Totality, 25).

As such, totality functions as a kind of lithographic thinking where the primacy of the same—as supreme panopticon—stands as a kind of stele marking the boundaries of its own interiority around which everything must be oriented. The texts of both Acker and Gilman present implicit criticisms of how this operates, chiefly in terms of speech itself. Prof. Schön will teach Lulu how to speak properly, while in Gilman the phrase "John says" is repeated over and over, emphasizing that within the economy of even her own home—or especially within that economy—she has no voice. John relates to his wife paternally and patriarchally such that the managing (nemein) of the house (oikos) bears the character of a theological economy (oikonomia). Gilman's female protagonist attempts to speak and to write but is foreclosed by John the physician, husband, and father. Finally, Acker's Lulu must have proper speech taught to her by Prof. Schön.[29] This hearkens back to the very foundation of our earliest literary criticism, I am thinking especially of Horace, which consistently manifests its optical imperative as pedagogy via the dictum that poetry must delight and instruct. But instruct upon what basis? One that is avowable or one that is unavowable?

Levinas offers such a contrast in his distinction between morality and ethics, identifying the former with totality, the latter with infinity.[30] He opens Totality and Infinity with the powerful statement "Everyone will readily agree that it is of the highest importance to know whether we are not duped by morality" (*Totality*, 21). Levinas discusses this so-called duping in harsh language, speaking of its excess as violence in these terms:

> violence does not consist so much in injuring and annihilating persons as in interrupting their continuity, making them play roles in which they no longer recognize themselves, making them betray not only commitments but their own substance, making them carry out actions that will destroy every possibility for action. (*Totality*, 21)

Levinas opts for an eschatology that he says, "institutes a relation with being *beyond the totality* or beyond history," which is "a relationship with *a surplus always exterior to the totality*, as though the objective totality did not fill out the true measure of being" (*Totality*, 22). In short, Levinas states, this is because "beings exist in relationship, to be sure, but on the basis of themselves and not on the basis of the totality" (*Totality*, 23). From this standpoint, the totalizing structure fails to recognize that being-together, community, is a multiplicity of infinities (as separate beings) encountering one another. Thus, imperatives—optical, categorical or otherwise—fail as they imply a universal notion that does not respect the other in its infinition.

Levinas refutes the ability of totality to fully totalize everything:

> the radical separation between the same and the other means precisely that it is impossible to place oneself outside of the correlation between the same and the other so as to record the correspondence or the non-correspondence of this going with this return. Otherwise the same and the other would be reunited under one gaze, and the absolute distance that separates them filled in.
>
> The alterity, the radical heterogeneity of the other, is possible only if the other is other with respect to a term whose essence is to remain at the point of departure, to serve as *entry* into the relation, to be the same not relatively but absolutely. (*Totality*, 36)

The word "between" is very important here. Individuals are separate and the infinite space of their separation is the between. It is, in the end, the neutral space from which critique can and must take place; neither the one nor the other, but the space—difference itself—that separates.

Levinas presents several indictments of his own that support such a change: "The relation with Being that is enacted as ontology consists in neutralizing the existent in order to comprehend or grasp it. It is hence not a relation with the other as such but the reduction of the other to the same" (*Totality*, 45–46). Rather, the approach must be to think the absolutely other, to think *autrui*,[31] since, as Levinas writes, "the infinite is the absolutely other" (*Totality*, 49). Therefore, the other (*autrui*), in its own terms, not regulated or neutralized by a same, is the true state of the other.[32] It is a relationship Levinas talks of in terms of "a face to face" (*Totality*, 39), and he says explicitly "*We call justice this face to face approach, in conversation*" (*Totality*, 71).

The just relation is thus marked, in discourse, as conversation. The French is very important here: *entretien*, literally, "a holding between."[33] There is no conversation in the dystopic novels of Acker, Duras, Gilman, or Blanchot to make the point of such an absence. There is merely a holding forth, not a holding between. The effort must be for nothing short of pluralism—pluralism thought of as irreducibility, as a kind of unknowability, and one structured by unavowability. Pluralism, which Levinas writes, "implies a radical alterity of the other, whom I do not simply *conceive* by relation to myself, but *confront* out of my egoism" (*Totality*, 121).

While radical alterity may perhaps appear redundant, it is necessary in respecting the other qua other, the other regulated by its own terms rather than mediated—and hence neutralized—by a same. A pluralism that requires responsibility. Levinas writes, in *Time and the Other*:

> The relationship with the other is not an idyllic and harmonious relationship of communion, or a sympathy through which we put ourselves in the other's place; we recognize the other as resembling us, but exterior to us; the relationship with the other is a relationship with a Mystery. The other's being is constituted by its exteriority, or rather its alterity, for exteriority is a property of space that leads the subject back to itself through light.[34]

He then adds: "The very relationship with the other is the relationship with the future" (*Other*, 77). But the future is to be understood in terms of a task of infinite attention and unknowability. Denis Hollier sums this fact up well in his introduction to *Against Architecture*, the English translation of his study on Bataille: "The concept of heterology, a neologism invented by Bataille, does not simply indicate a warm, euphoric relationship to otherness. Otherness, in other words, is not simply a matter of pleasure and enjoyment."[35] It is this face to face, this relation that Blanchot in *The Unavowable Community* so eloquently, and so simply, describes as "infinite attention to the other [*autrui*]" (*Unavowable*, 43), that will help to break through the madness of sham pluralism.

The best hope—a word used reservedly—is to keep this holding-between open, to keep the conversation between others, in their infinition, going; the conversation really began only recently. In the process, we must address the malady of community by hacking away at totalizing discourse, specifically by being attentive to how its grammar has oriented our very thinking. A task then of working, as an unworking (*désoeuvrement*),[36] toward respect and infinite attention to the unavowability of the other, working toward an unavowable community which, as Blanchot writes, "evasively consecrates *the always uncertain end* inscribed in the destiny of community" (*Unavowable*, 56).

Notes

This paper is a condensed version of issues raised in my dissertation, The Malady of Community (Binghamton University, State University of New York, 1994).

1. Marguerite Duras, *The Malady of Death*, trans. Barbara Bray (New York: Grove Press, 1986), 49–50. Henceforth cited parenthetically in the text as *Malady*.

2. Marguerite Duras, *Practicalities: Marguerite Duras Speaks to Jérôme Beaujour*, trans. Barbara Bray (London: Collins, 1990), 33.

3. Kathy Acker, *Don Quixote* (New York: Grove Press, 1986). Henceforth cited parenthetically in the text as *Quixote*.

4. This is a subsection of her novel's second section, entitled "The Second Part of Don Quixote: Other Texts." "Text 4: Wedekind's Words," a further subsection, can be found on pp. 77–97. I am limiting my references to this section of Acker's text for the purposes of my discussion. For a fuller treatment of the novel as a whole, which seems pertinent to my brief reference, see Douglas Shields Dix, "Kathy Acker's *Don Quixote*: Nomad Writing," *Review of Contemporary Fiction* 9, no. 3 (fall 1989): 56–62. Here Dix discusses the truly revolutionary character of love.

5. Specifically his *Earth-Spirit* and *Pandora's Box*. Cf. Frank Wedekind, *The Lulu Plays & Other Sex Tragedies*, trans. Stephen Spender (New York: Riverrun Press, 1978).

6. Pabst's last two silent films deal with the Wedekind plays: *Pandora's Box* (Die Büchse der Pandora), 1929; and *Diary of a Lost One* (Tagebuch einer Verlorenen), 1929. Both films featured Louise Brooks, an American actress.

7. Acker is playing on the Bernard Shaw play and the film versions.

8. Mary Wollstonecraft, *A Vindication of the Rights of Woman* (New York: Norton, 1975), 10–11. Henceforth cited parenthetically in the text as *Vindication*.

9. See the distinctions between the sublime and the beautiful in Immanuel Kant, *Critique of Judgment*, trans. Werner S. Pluhar (Indianapolis: Hackett, 1987).

10. A realm, perhaps, as fortress surrounded by a great wall similar to that described in Kafka's "The Great Wall of China," in *The Complete Stories*, ed. Nahum N. Glazer, trans. Willa and Edwin Muir (New York: Schocken Books, 1971). Here he writes very critically, for example: "In those days many people, and among them the best, had a secret maxim which ran: Try with all your might to comprehend the decrees of the high command, but only up to a certain point; then avoid further meditation" (240).

11. Here I cannot help but recall those powerful lines of Michel Foucault in *Madness and Civilization*, trans. Richard Howard (New York: Vintage, 1988), where he talks of our world as one which "constitutes a milieu favorable to the development of madness" (217).

12. Maurice Blanchot, *The Unavowable Community*, trans. Pierre Joris (Barrytown, NY: Station Hill Press, 1988), 35. Henceforth cited parenthetically in the text as *Unavowable*.

13. I am grateful to Monica Chiu for pointing this out.

14. Avow has feudal connotations deriving from *avouer*, "to call to" or "to call upon," especially to call on as a defender or patron, derived from the Latin *advocare*. The term *avoué* refers to this patron and defender as advocate. To avow is thus a call in which one will be put under the protection or patronage of this *avoué*. In the process, individual sovereignty is lost as authority is transferred to the *avoué*, with individual identity sacrificed to an immanent totality. I employ this characterization in order to suggest the metanarrative character of the avowable structure. I make this connection precisely because I see the avowable as a story which the *avoué* demands others to defend and vow allegiance to. In an immanent, avowable structure the ends are always certain, with individuals merely ends themselves, understood as means of profit (as support) of this end. The unavowable would be more attentive to loss.

15. The term *unavowable* is abundantly meaningful and may be described as an indefensible state—that is, a state which is not oriented by prescribed or pre-defined statutes—because of the fact that there is no central grand narrative that one vows to uphold. The form of the respective community is based upon the zero-point created by the collision of two in the sense of *partager*, "sharing" and "dividing." Given the disparity that exists from one individual to another, and, in a sense, the precariousness of identity itself, community must be based less upon a sense of the same than a sense of difference.

16. Charlotte Perkins Gilman, *The Yellow Wallpaper* (New York: Feminist Press, 1973), 9–10. Henceforth cited parenthetically in the text as *Yellow*.

17. Much of this language about order, pattern, and grammar is informed by a powerful quote from Nietzsche's *The Will to Power*, ed. Walter Kaufmann, trans. Walter Kaufmann and R. J. Hollingdale (New York: Vintage, 1968): "We are prisoners of a grammar invented at an early stage of human evolution, and it seems that, since we can think only by using language, our reason too is conditioned by the most primitive notions of reality" (sec. 522).

18. The very act which Hélène Cixous describes as "precisely *the very possibility of change*." See Hélène Cixous, "The Laugh of the Medusa," trans. Keith Cohen and Paula

Cohen, *Signs* 1, no. 4 (1976): 879. This text as a whole is pertinent to the issues presented in Gilman's *The Yellow Wallpaper.*

19. See Georges Bataille, "The Sorcerer's Apprentice," in *The College of Sociology* (1937–1939), ed. Denis Hollier, trans. Betsy Wing (Minneapolis: University of Minnesota Press, 1988).

20. Bataille, "Sorcerer's Apprentice," 20 n. 2.

21. This quote is taken from Bataille's *Inner Experience*, trans. Leslie Anne Boldt (Albany: SUNY Press, 1988), specifically the section entitled "The Labyrinth (Or the Constitution of Beings)," 81–93. I slip back and forth between Blanchot and Bataille, given the great proximity between their thinking and writing.

22. Patterned after his appreciation of Nietzsche's dictum, in *The Gay Science*, "I love the unknowability of the future" (slightly altered translation). See Friedrich Nietzsche, *The Gay Science*, trans. Walter Kaufmann (New York: Vintage, 1974), sec. 287, *Delight in Blindness*, 230–31. The phrase, in German, is "*Ich liebe die Unwissenheit um die Zukunft.*" I have translated *Unwissenheit* very literally, preferring *unknowing* over the word *ignorance* (used in both English and French translations) to emphasize an active character to the privative prefix *Un-*.

23. This term is *désoeuvrement* in French. It is important to the work of Maurice Blanchot (see especially his sections on Mallarmé in *The Space of Literature*, trans. Ann Smock [Lincoln: University of Nebraska Press, 1982]) and in Jean-Luc Nancy's study on Bataille, *The Inoperative Community*, ed. Peter Connor, trans. Peter Connor, Lisa Garbus, Michael Holland, and Simona Sawhney (Minneapolis: University of Minnesota Press, 1991).

24. Maurice Blanchot, *The Madness of the Day*, trans. Lydia Davis (Barrytown, N.Y.: Station Hill Press, 1981), 14. Henceforth cited parenthetically in the text as *Madness.*

25. Blanchot speaks to this directly in *The Infinite Conversation*, trans. Susan Hanson (Minneapolis: University of Minnesota Press, 1993). Here he criticizes "the optical imperative that in the Western tradition, for thousands of years, has subjugated our approach to things, and induced us to think under the guaranty of light or under the threat of its absence. I'll let you count all the words through which it is suggested that, to speak truly, one must think according to the measure of the eye" (27).

26. The two French terms, *avouer*, "to defend," "to confess to," and *inavouable*, "unavowable," are key here. I would suggest that *avowable* be understood as inattention to difference and support of a notion of the same, while *unavowable* marks a very specific attention to difference, attempting to unwork the hierarchical structure of same-other where the same always holds the upper hand.

27. Which is what Audre Lorde's statement that "the master's tools will never dismantle the master's house" seems to be all about. See Audre Lorde, "The Master's Tools Will Never Dismantle the Master's House" in *Sister Outsider* (Trumansburg, N.Y.: Crossing Press, 1984), 112.

28. Emmanuel Levinas, *Totality and Infinity: An Essay on Exteriority*, trans. Alphonso Lingis (Pittsburgh: Duquesne University Press, 1969), 24. Henceforth cited parenthetically in the text as *Totality.*

29. Here I would associate avowability with totality, unavowability with infinity.

30. Teresa de Lauretis makes the point with equal force in describing the writing of Monique Wittig, which, she says, "has stressed the power of discourse to 'do violence' to people, a violence which is material and physical, although produced by abstract and scientific discourses as well as the discourses of mass media" (*Technologies of Gender: Essays on Theory, Film, and Fiction* [Bloomington: Indiana University Press, 1987], 17).

31. This very particular French term denotes others generally, and is here understood as the Other itself. This term has been central to the discussions of both Levinas and Blanchot, especially prominent in the latter's *The Infinite Conversation*. In the foreword to her translation of this text, Susan Hanson defines this term as "other people" generally (xxxiii n. 1), as well as "the site of a between-two, between appearing and disappearing" (xxxi).

32. This is the crux of a new way of thinking. We must move beyond thinking of the other as regulated by or mediated through a privileged same. This means working toward a hyper- or radical alterity where other is mediated by other, understood in itself, by itself. The goal would be achieving a displacement of traditional relations and proximities previously oriented around a grammar of avowability.

33. From *entre*, "between," plus *se tenir*, "to hold."

34. Emmanuel Levinas, *Time and the Other*, trans. Richard A. Cohen (Pittsburgh: Duquesne University Press, 1987), 75–76. Henceforth cited parenthetically in the text as *Other*.

35. Denis Hollier, *Against Architecture: The Writings of Georges Bataille*, trans. Betsy Wing (Cambridge: MIT Press, 1989), xxiii.

36. See Blanchot, *Infinite Conversation*: "Unworking is at work, but does not produce the work" (418). Following the language of this paper, the work is a negative notion (see, for example, Roland Barthes, "From Work to Text" in *Image—Music—Text*, trans. Stephen Heath [New York: Noonday, 1977]). The unworking is directed at undoing the (pan)optical imperative so inherent in totalizing structures.

CHAPTER 11

Andean Waltz

LEO SPITZER

*As a very young child, I am told that my grandfather died on the
ship when he, my grandmother, and my parents were on the way
from Austria to Bolivia. I am shown photos of the ship, the Italian
passenger liner "Virgilio," and of my parents with other passengers.
The ship, I eventually find out, is transporting over a thousand
refugees from Nazi Germany, Austria, Czechoslovakia, and the
civil war in Spain. My mother has a big belly in the photographs,
and my parents explain jokingly that I am "in there"—a stowaway
on the voyage. I am also told that the Virgilio's captain wanted to
bury my grandfather at sea. This would have been a violation of
orthodox Jewish law mandating the interment of a body in the
ground. My grandmother and father objected—less, my mother
tells me, from religious conviction than from some elemental
unwillingness to have his final resting place be an unmarked spot in
the ocean. Their protestations and pleas were to no avail until a
Jewish fellow passenger, with personal financial resources, made an
arrangement for the ship to make an unscheduled landing in La
Guaira. There the body was dressed in a shroud and buried in
earth, in the Jewish cemetery in Caracas.*

*When I am born in La Paz some months later I am named
Leopoldo, after my grandfather, given his Hebrew name, Gershon,
and nicknamed Poldi: the same diminutive that had been his during
his lifetime. While I am still a young child, my parents tell me that
they have given me my grandfather's names to honor the departed
and to maintain a continuity between the past and the present.
Only many years later, in hindsight, do I realize that their effort to
maintain continuities—to perpetuate something of the lost in the*

213

*new—was manifested in many different ways during their years in
Bolivia. Indeed, I realize that this effort was a central characteristic
of the Jewish refugee experience in that Andean land.*

Before the rise of Nazism in Central Europe, very few Jews, perhaps
fewer than a hundred from Alsace, Poland, and Russia had settled in
Bolivia. In the early 1930s, this relatively isolated landlocked republic of
some three million persons—the site of great pre-Hispanic Indian
civilizations—was inhabited by a ruling minority claiming Spanish
descent, a larger mestizo population, and a subordinated Aymara and
Quechua Indian majority. European travellers visiting Bolivia in the
early decades of the twentieth century considered it as among the least
"Europeanized" of the South American nations.[1]

But in the mid-1930s, and until the end of the first year of World
War II, thousands of refugees from Nazi-dominated Central Europe, the
majority of them Jews, fled to Bolivia to escape the increasingly
vehement persecution. Wealthier or "better connected" refugees, who
emigrated soon after the Nazis came to power, had acquired visas and
found a haven in "countries of choice"—Great Britain, the United
States, Australia, Palestine, Argentina, Brazil. The tightening of immigration to these countries, however, virtually closed off entry for the
large number of persons desperate to leave in the late '30s.[2] By the end
of the decade Bolivia was one of very few places to accept Jewish immigrants. Some twenty thousand refugees from Germany, Austria, Czechoslovakia, and Hungary arrived between 1938 and 1940—a number
that, when calculated as a percentage of Bolivia's total "non-Indian"
population at the time, gives some sense of how substantial the demographic impact of this Central European immigrant influx must have
been. The new arrivals settled primarily in La Paz, 12,500 feet above
sea level, as well as in Cochabamba, Oruro, Sucre, and in small mining
and tropical agricultural communities throughout the land.

*It is July 1941 in Cochabamba. Dr. Heinrich Stern, born in
Nordhausem am Harz and a recent immigrant to Bolivia, reflects in
a note written to himself:*

*The path was rocky and rough, steep and lonely. Now I sit on a
rock and look about me. Thorny shrubbery, thicket, tall cactus,*

*stones and stones. In the distance, two, no three wretched huts;
mountains all around, giant, furrowed mountains. The sun sinks
lower; its rays bring a magic glow to the peaks. Loneliness, frightful
loneliness; and strangeness. In the far distance two women,
wrapped in red ochre shawls, climb uphill. Their appearance
increases my sense of loneliness, of abandonment.*
Indianerlandschaft! *Indian landscape! My new homeland! Is this
my new homeland?*

*Dark thoughts waltz through my brain. They torment me, they
repeatedly knock and sting against my forehead. They circle about
the horizon and want to penetrate the distant mountain wall; and
they search and inquire: The sky above me, is it not the sky of the
old homeland? No, it seems to be—or am I only imagining it—
more glaring, more poisonous. Only the clouds cast a smile of
friendliness on me, reminders of other environs. But the land
remains hostile. A landscape of the uncivilized*—Indianerlandschaft,
Indian landscape. Gigantic, strange, melancholy and lonely.[3]

Bewilderment. Nostalgia. Yearning. Difference. An alien world—a world
of others. *Indianerlandschaft.* These impressions were widely shared by
the immigrants after their arrival in Bolivia. Could one have expected
anything else? Before leaving Europe, Bolivia had been little more than a
place on a map of South America. Many of the refugees knew virtually
nothing about its physical geography, climate, history, government, or
economy. In their eagerness to find a country that would accept them,
they were ready to go anywhere that would permit them to live in safety.
"Bolivia—quick, where is it?" was Egon Schwarz's response on receiving
his visa through the *Hilfsverein* (Refugee Aid Society) from the Paris
consulate. "We would have gone to the moon," Andres Simon recalled.
"Bolivia was a closer possibility, but the moon we saw every night. It
was more real to us." "I knew about Bolivia what you know about the
North Pole," Renata Schwarz said to me. "Maybe you know more
about the North Pole."[4]

If the refugees knew anything at all about the inhabitants of the
country to which they were emigrating, it was either extremely limited
or stereotypical. Some of them, having lived in the larger European
cities or travelled to them in their search for visas, had briefly encountered Bolivian consular officials or representatives—the first Bolivian

nationals they had ever met. Many, perhaps most, had only a remote sense of the cultural and ethnic milieu into which they were entering. Spanish-speaking, Catholic, Indian: these were the terms they vaguely associated with the Bolivians. But these terms were broad, generic identifiers that hardly prepared the refugees for the immense cultural and social differences they would have to face. Their preconceptions of the land and its people were shaped by information that varied greatly in reliability and perspective. Some of it came from old, half-forgotten, world-geography and world-culture lectures they had received back in school. More up to date, but not necessarily more trustworthy information came in letters from those who had preceded them to Bolivia, or from the second- and third-hand retelling of the contents of such letters. Some was acquired "post visa," by reading the entry "Bolivia" in encyclopedias and geographical atlases. And a certain, surely not insignificant, amount was derived from accounts in popular literature—a literature that routinely represented the landscape and people of South America as mysterious, exotic, if not forbidding, and that simplified or blurred the particularity and diversity of both.

Werner Guttentag, for example, emigrated from Germany to Bolivia via Holland in 1939. Before leaving Europe, he decided he would move to Cochabamba (where he still resides) simply on the basis of its relatively central location on the map of Bolivia—which, he maintains, he examined closely for the first time only after learning that he and his parents had received visas to go there. His predeparture image of Bolivia's indigenous populations, he recalls, came from reading "the Inca novels" of the immensely popular German author of adventure books, Karl May—a writer who had never set foot in South America and whose colorful and seemingly authentic ethnographic representation of its people was largely invented, the imaginary creations of a fertile mind.[5]

> *We absolutely didn't know what was awaiting us. We didn't know about the people, or their customs, or traditions. We did not expect the altitude to be so oppressive. On the train from Arica to La Paz, people's noses and ears were bleeding. Some were hemorrhaging. . . .*[6]

> *The Indios. We never had seen anything like them. Already on the train, at stops, a real novelty: we looked at them; they looked at us. . . .*[7]

What immediately impressed me about La Paz was the smell—a terrible impression. The streets smelled horrible. The Indians urinated and defecated in the streets. The women squatted right down in the street, lifted up their skirts, and did their thing. There were no public sanitary facilties. And they brought their llama herds through the streets. And the llamas spit and left their little traces. . . .[8]

The Indian women wore multiple skirts and colorful mantas. *They were sometimes beautifully dressed, richly dressed, with gold and silver pins and gold earrings. But they had no culture. They had no civilization. . . .*[9]

I noticed that I was in a black land. Not that the people were Negroes, but so many men and women were dressed in black or dark clothing. Only sometime afterwards did I learn that they were still in mourning clothes—mourning their dead, casualties in the disastrous Chaco war that Bolivia had fought with Paraguay. . . .[10]

Music . . . the noise of a never-before-heard, never-ending, melancholy Indian music, whose monotone initially grates the nerves, but which one never again forgets after hearing it played night after night for months on end. . . .[11]

. . . [Here] practically nothing is as one knows it, either in society or in nature. The person who applies middle-European standards to what is seen and experienced will never understand. . . .[12]

"Nothing is as one knows it, either in society or nature"—that was said by Egon Schwarz soon after arriving in Bolivia. Indeed, there was little in the Central European cultural background or experience of the refugees that would echo sympathetically and provide a familiar referent to help ease their integration. Neither the cities nor the country-side reminded those who had left Germany, Austria, or any of the Central European countries of the Austro-German *Kulturkreis*, of places they had known before.

For the refugees, the harsh physical environment in which they now found themselves was the first impediment to adjustment. When they arrived in La Paz, or anywhere in the Andean highland (some twelve to fourteen thousand feet above sea-level) many came down with altitude sickness—*Soroche*—and suffered shortness of breath, sleeplessness, and aches in the head and body. Those with lung or heart problems generally found the altitude unbearable. If they moved to the sub-tropical or tropical lowlands, they encountered high temperature and humidity and faced the danger of contracting illnesses for which the temperate-climate disease environment from which they had emigrated had provided no immunity or tolerance. But aside from the adjustment difficulties and medical dangers associated with their natural sur-roundings, it was the immense *foreignness* of the cultural environment that compounded feelings of alienation—the refugees' sense of being distinct "outsiders," truly strangers in a strange land. The various indigenous people looked different, they dressed differently, their customs, practices, festivals, and foods were unfamiliar, they com-municated in languages that none of the immigrants had ever heard before, their psychology and worldview seemed unfathomable.[13]

The refugees, of course, were themselves not a homogeneous group. Their origins and social status had been diverse in Central Europe, ranging across generational, educational, political, and class lines and incorporating various professional backgrounds. They included persons who had at one time been engineers, doctors, lawyers, musicians, actors, and artists, as well as a large number of both skilled and unskilled workers whose living had been interrupted by Nazi exclusionary decrees. The majority who came to Bolivia were Jews or married to Jews. Some, however, were non-Jewish *political* refugees: communists, socialists, and others persecuted by the Nazi regime. The Jews themseves differed greatly in the degreee of their identification with their religion and its traditions. There were Zionists among them, atheists, orthodox believers, "High Holiday" Jews, and nonpracti-tioners. They shared a common identity as Jews only in the sense, perhaps, that they had all been defined as "Jews" from the outside— that the Nazis had "othered" them as Jews.

No matter what their background differences had been in Europe, however, the vast majority of refugees arrived in dire straits, with few personal possessions and very little money. This in itself had a leveling effect, cutting across previous class distinctions. But there were other factors too that helped the refugees to create a sense of collective identity, aiding their adjustment and survival. Despite differences of detail, their common history of persecution was certainly one of these. Each and every one of the refugees had been identified as undesirable, stripped of citizenship and possessions. They were all "in the same boat." The war back in Europe, and the fact that so many of them had relatives and friends from whom they had been separated, was also an ever-present reality of which they were collectively conscious and that bonded them together. They kept themselves—each other—informed of news about the war from accounts in the press and radio, and, they shared efforts to discover the fate of those left behind. In this regard, the German language (which they still spoke at home and among themselves), served as a vehicle of inquiry, information, and unity. It allowed them to communicate intimately and to express themselves with a degree of familiarity that most could never attain in the Spanish of their surroundings. German permitted them to maintain a wider connection with refugees and immigrants in other countries and throughout Bolivia—by means of their own newspaper, the *Rundschau vom Illimani*, which Ernst Schumacher established in La Paz in 1939, or the important *Aufbau* of New York, or *Jüdische Wochenschau* in Buenos Aires.[14]

But it was memory—the employment of memory by the refugees to connect their present to a particular version of the past—that served as the creative tool of adjustment, helping to ease cultural uprootedness and alienation. No sooner had they arrived in Bolivia when a process began by which the immigrants recalled, negotiated, and reshaped their memories of Europe. They employed elements of these memories to re-create institutions, symbolic practices, and a style of life which they had previously shared. Collective memory became the basis on which they built a communal "culture" to serve their changing needs.

It was no doubt from their recollections of the *Israelitische Kultusgemeinden* of Berlin and Vienna that one of the first centers of collective immigrant activity, the Comunidad Israelita, was founded in La Paz in 1939 by refugees from Germany and Austria. This communal organization established a Jewish temple in which religious services were held, an old people's home, a *Kinderheim* serving as kindergarten, boarding, and day-care center, and a school, La Escuela Boliviana-Israelita. But, from its inception, the Comunidad also fulfilled a very different social function. Its quarters became a clubhouse where people could gather, eat meals, read newspapers, play cards, chess, or ping-pong—where they could gossip, socialize, exchange information, and reminisce about their lives, loves, and the past.[15] The Comunidad became a version of an institution that many of the immigrants would have remembered with nostalgia: the *Klublokal* or coffee house of Central Europe.

And, within a relatively short period, in 1939 and the early 1940s, the refugees created other organizations, established shops and restaurants, and developed cultural activities that reconnected them to a way of life from which they had been forcibly detached. A glance through the pages of the *Rundschau vom Illimani* and *Jüdische Wochenschau* of these years provides illustrative examples. The "Hogar Austriaco" ("Austrian Home," as the Austrian Club was called), the associations *Das Andere Deutschland* and *Freies Deutschland* (the "Other Germany" and "Free Germany"), the League of Women of the Comunidad and the Macabi Sports Club; the Cafe Viena, Club Metropol, Cafe-Restaurant Weiner; the Pension Neumann, Pension Europa; the Haberdashery Berlin, Casa Paris-Viena, Peleteria Viena; the "Buchhandlung La America" advertising German editions of Franz Werfel, Paul Zech, Bruno Weil; the *Kleinkunstbühne* (cabaret theater) presenting scenes from Schnitzler, von Hoffmansthal, Beer-Hoffmann, as well as readings of German classics; the Colegium Musicum with its chamber-music concerts and recitals featuring Mozart, Beethoven, and Schubert played by musicians trained at conservatories in Vienna, Prague, and Berlin: these, and many others, attest to the range of the immigrants' economic and institutional adjustment in Bolivia and confirm the character of their symbolic reconnection with Central Europe.[16]

Children of the refugees—especially during the early years of the immigration—received both formal and informal tuition strongly influenced by cultural memories of Europe. The intended purpose behind the establishment of the Escuela Boliviana-Israelita, for example, was twofold: the school offered courses in Spanish, so that recently arrived children might learn the language of the land, and it instructed them in the three Rs as well as in Jewish religion and history. From its inception, moreover, Bolivian officials also required the school to hire a Bolivian teacher to instruct its pupils in local and national history—in what the Bolivians called "*educación cívica.*"[17] Apart from the Spanish language classes and *educación cívica*, however, the pedagogical methods and general curriculum of the Escuela Boliviana-Israelita differed little from those employed in elementary schools in Germany and Austria before the rise of Nazism. The referent examples the immigrant teachers used in their subjects of instruction derived, as one might have expected, from their Central European cultural background and experience.

ℭ

*Sifting through memorabilia of which I became the keeper when
my mother died—*

I look at my report cards for grades one through four from the
Escuela Boliviana Israelita. *Seeing my grades in geography and
music, I try to recall if I was in my first or second school year when
Dr. Asher first taught us to locate the Danube, Rhein, and the Alps
on a map of Europe, and when it was that Mr. Aaron, who played
a portable piano and the accordion, taught us to sing the* Hatikvah
as well as German folk songs . . .

I find five of my childhood books. Two of them, Max und Moritz:
eine Bubengeschichte in sieben Streichen [Max and Moritz: a Boys
Tale in Seven Episodes] *by Wilhelm Busch (my copy published in
Santiago de Chile) and H. Hoffman's* Der Struwwelpeter, *are
cautionary tales that my parents and grandmother read aloud to
me dozens of times. They contain my scribblings and, probably, the
earliest existent sample of my nickname, Poldi, printed in pencil in
my own handwriting. It is, I am quite certain, because of the
horrible penalty paid by Konrad, in* "Die Geschichte vom Daumen-
Lutscher," [The Story of the Thumb-Sucker] *and Paulinchen, in*
"Die gar traurige Geschichte mit dem Feuerzeug" [The Truly Sad
Story With the Lighter], *that I never sucked my thumbs and was
fearful about playing with matches. Two other books—an
illustrated German children's edition of* Grimm's Fairy Tales *and
Frida Schanz's* Schulkindergeschichten—*were also read to me by
my grandmother Lina. The fifth, a children's book in Spanish and
printed on wartime paper now yellowed by time, is* Beethoven, El
Sacrificio de Un Niño. *Beethoven and Johann Strauss were my
father's favorite composers. . . .*

*I discover that an undated Hogar Austriaco cabaret-program is also
among the memorabilia. It introduces a show,* "Radio Wien Sendet:
Ein Wunschkabarett" [Radio Vienna Broadcasts: A Cabaret on
Demand], *and lists, among its entertainment numbers,* "In einem
Wiener Vorstadtvarieté" [In a Viennese Suburban Music Hall],
"Ein Maederl aus Moedling," [A Lass from Moedling], "Frauen
sind zum Küssen da" [Women are Made to be Kissed], *and various
other skits in Viennese dialect.*

In spite of the persecution they had endured, therefore, and Nazi efforts to depict them as the "other," it was Austro-German culture—and, in particular, Austro-German Jewish bourgeois culture as it had existed in the capital cities—that provided the refugees with a model for emulation and a common locus for identification. This held true even for persons, like my parents and others, who had come from a working-class background and whose political sympathies lay with Marxism. Commenting on the character of this identification with some irony, Egon Schwarz noted how often the immigrants began their sentences with the phrase "Back home in Germany" or "Back home in our country," and how one man, in a conversation with him, had actually exclaimed: "Back home in our concentration camp."[18] At the very time when that dynamic social and cultural amalgam, European Jewish bourgeois culture, was being ruthlessly and systematically destroyed by the Nazis, these refugees attempted to revive aspects of it in an alien land thousands of miles from their home: in a country that offered them a haven, but in which many—perhaps most—of them felt mere sojourners.

☙

"I never thought our family would stay in Bolivia," Julius Wolfinger *recalls. "I really believed Hitler would lose, that the Nazis would be destroyed, and that we would return to Vienna to help rebuild a Social Democratic Austria."*[19]

"For me," Max Gans *observes, "Bolivia was temporary, a sort of bridge to somewhere else. I didn't know if I thought of returning to Germany. I thought of Argentina, maybe. Or the U.S."*[20]

I think back: Even when my father began to make a reasonably good living, we never acquired anything—furniture, apartment, auto—which would appear as if we were putting down permanent roots in the land. My parents were always waiting for their quota number to come up so they could go to the United States.[21]

"We didn't know where we would end up." Julio Meier *notes, "Maybe permanently in Bolivia. But we needed to maintain what we prized. We couldn't let Hitler obliterate our past."*[22]

☙

As many of them phrased it in their recollections, "their need" to reestablish and maintain a Central European identity had discernible consequences even within the immigrant community. It maintained an old rift imported to Bolivia from Europe between the then numerically much larger German-speaking group from the Austro-German *Kulturkreis* and the smaller, predominantly Yiddish-speaking, Jewish group from Poland, Russia, and other parts of Eastern Europe.[23] The German speakers, who were considered "highly assimilated" and referred to as "*Yekkes*" by the East Europeans, tended to fraternize with each other, keeping their social distance from the *Polacos* (as the East Europeans were called), whom they often viewed as "more primitive," "less cultured." This division—effectively bridged in the realm of economic interaction and on occasions when the immigrants, *as Jews*, rallied together in celebration or against some "outside" threat—was maintained institutionally, in the establishment, for example, of the Círculo Israelita of the Polacos as an organization with distinct cultural offerings separate from the Austro-German Comunidad Israelita.[24]

But the communal identity constructed by the refugees had an especially profound and enduring influence on relationships between them and native Bolivians. Refugees recalling their emigration to Bolivia in writing or oral testimony, have been universally grateful to Bolivians for saving their lives.[25] From the earliest days of their arrival, moreover, they began to develop business relationships with Bolivians that were frequently based on mutual trust and good will. Bolivians, in this respect, "made space" for the immigrants, allowing them to set up businesses and to enter and participate in every imaginable entrepreneurial—but not professional—activity. Bolivians also "made space," physically and culturally, so the immigrants could establish their own social and cultural institutions. Paradoxically, however, the very institutions the refugees created, and the cultural symbols and memories on which they relied for their collective identity, were also instrumental in maintaining barriers between the refugees and the Bolivians. Culturally and, in many respects, socially Bolivians and refugees began their encounter, and remained, as each other's "other."

The cultural distance seemed most unbridgeable between refugees and "Indians"—the Aymara and Quechua in the highlands, and the people belonging to the smaller indigenous groups in the tropical lowlands of the country. Although the contact between refugees and individual *Indios* could be quite intimate, their relationship was always a hierarchical one: master-servant, employer-laborer. Aymara and Quechua women worked as domestic servants and took care of the children of even the poorest immigrants; while the men were hired for various menial tasks on an hourly basis, as carriers of heavy loads, as day laborers, or, on rarer occasions, as shop assistants and unskilled workers. Many of the refugees did show admiration for the cultural achievements of the pre-Columbian Tiahuanaco and Inca ancestors of the Aymara and Quechua; they did value indigenous craft skills, particularly weaving and gold and silver jewelry, and they purchased items for personal use. But it was unusual for any refugee to make the effort to learn more than a few words of an indigenous language or to engage in any informal intercourse with people who, numerically, made up the vast majority of Bolivia's population.

One might have expected some greater interchange between the refugees and those Bolivians closer to them in social background: with the Spanish-speaking White and mestizo middle classes, and with members of the professional and ruling elites. But here the immigrants' selectively remembered and reconstituted culture—based on Central European-Jewish bourgeois values, on the German language, on a certain conception of "modernity," on literature, music, and hygiene, and on their generally more liberal and materialistic world-view—proved irreconcilable with what many of them perceived as the deeply rooted Catholicism, intensely private family life-style, social conservatism, and technical and industrial "backwardness" of middle- and upper-class Bolivians.

Middle- and upper-class Bolivians, of course, also maintained largely impermeable barriers between themselves and the immigrants. Flirtations and sexual encounters between Bolivian men and European women, and between immigrant men and Bolivian women, did occasionally occur. But marriages between Bolivians and refugees were extremely rare and, in the few instances where they did take place, were viewed by members of both groups as eccentric departures from the communal fold.[26] Despite business and professional dealings with the immigrants, moreover, it was highly uncommon for Bolivians to invite any of them to their house for dinner or for informal social events.

Indeed, expressions of anti-Semitic prejudice by Bolivians were not unusual. Rooted in religious biases derived from the Spanish-Catholic popular tradition blaming Jews for the killing of Christ, and in stereotypes depicting Jews as unscrupulous money-grubbers in league with the Devil, the epithet *Judio* (Jew) was sometimes hurled contemptuously at immigrants, or scrawled as grafitti on their doors and walls. More ominously, virulent anti-Semitism, inspired by Nazi propaganda, found its way into Bolivia as well. In a Bolivian Chamber of Deputies' debate of 1942 over an immigration bill seeking the exclusion of Jews, Deputy Zuazo Cuenca read aloud portions from *The Protocols of the Elders of Zion,* that scurrilous forgery implicating Jews in acts of ritual murder—a copy of which, it was revealed later, Zuazo Cuenca had received from the German Office of Propaganda. The newspaper *La Calle,* in one of its many editorials on the bill, lamented the "inundation" of the country by immigrants "with very beaked noses": by members of the "Jewish race" who were waiting "to fall like a ravenous invading horde upon the cities of Bolivia," and who were planning to gain control of the government. Jews, as "a race," some Bolivians in influential positions argued, posed a danger to Bolivia's "nationality" and should be expelled.[27]

It is of course important to contextualize Bolivian anti-Semitism in perspective. Throughout the war years, many Bolivians also forcefully attacked anti-Semitism and came to the defense of the immigrants. Their voices and opinions, expressed in forums and in print, provided a strong counterpoint to the hatemongering and presented the immigrants with a more positive image.[28] But the existence and expression of anti-Semitism in Bolivia certainly contributed to the fears and insecurities that inspired the refugees to maintain close-knit institutional bonds and a collective identity. It also helped to convince many of them that Bolivia could never be their permanent home—that their future lay elsewhere.

In view of the immigrants' awareness of the potential threat that Bolivian anti-Semitism posed for their safety, it is remarkable that, in *the present-day memory* of the refugees, Bolivian anti-Semitism does not play an important role. This, of course, is a clear illustration of the constructed nature of memory—of the ways in which individuals and groups recall, reorganize, and distort their present memory to represent the past. Quite possibly, for present-day survivors of the immigration still living in Bolivia, the memory of that virulent anti-Semitism in the past might awaken old insecurities and stir up unpleasant communal tensions better left dormant. Having settled in Bolivia, found acceptance for their communal existence, and prospered economically, they recall their past selectively, reconstructing it to safeguard their current well-being. And for those who left Bolivia to settle elsewhere, Bolivian anti-

Semitism is usually remembered as a relatively minor episode within a sojourn fraught with challenges and difficulties but also characterized by relative tolerance. No matter how short their residence in Bolivia had been, this Andean land inserted itself into the memory of these emigres as the place that gave them refuge when all others had rejected them. "For better or for worse," Ilse Hertz observed in her recollection of the emigration, "Bolivians permitted us to live."[29] It was in Bolivia that the refugees survived the horrors of the Nazi Holocaust. Consciousness of that overwhelming reality is the background against which their present-day memories have been constructed.

But might the refugees adjustment in Bolivia have been different, had they been more willing to modify their cultural memories and integrate more completely into Bolivian society? Would their cultural memories of the European world into which Jews had become assimilated—and with which they had tried to identify so fully before the rise of exclusionary anti-Semitism and Nazi persecution—have been less likely to inspire revival and recreation if news of death camps and the extent of Austrian-German responsibility for the Holocaust been confirmed earlier?

Two recollections:

In my most vivid memory of early childhood I return home from the Kinderheim one day in 1945 and meet my father hurrying up the stairs with a letter in his hand. He gathers us together in the kitchen—my mother, grandparents, Uncle Ferri, Uncle Julius—and tells us that Frieda—Ferri's sister, my father's niece—is alive; that she survived a series of concentration camps; that she is free, and has reestablished contact. But the letter he reads from Frieda is frightening as well. It describes how her mother, father, and younger sister were shot before her eyes by the Germans, and how she was selected to work while others were marched off to die. I recall the scene in the room while he read; I still hear, as though it occurred yesterday, the crying, everyone in the room weeping, embracing, shouting. Included with the letter is a photograph: Frieda as lonely and lone survivor, smiling at the photographer, reconnecting with us who are together, comforting each other. . . .

Looking through family albums and loose pictures, I find photos taken at the Austrian Club in La Paz in 1947, two years after the war. Some show my mother and other women at a Dirndl ball dressed in Austrian folk costumes and my father, my uncle Ferri, and other men wearing lederhosen, Alpine knee-socks, and Tyrolean hats. Other pictures of the same vintage from an Hogar Austriaco banquet. In their background one can clearly see the Club's wallhangings: two Austrian flags, a lithograph of Old Vienna,and lamps with shades emblazoned with the Austrian republican coat of arms.

Notes

A slightly longer version of this paper was published in Holocaust Remembrance: the Shapes of Memory, ed. Geoffrey Hartman (Oxford: Blackwell, 1993).

1. For early Jewish settlement in Bolivia see Jacob Beller, *Jews in Latin America* (New York, 1969), 211–12; Judith Laikin Elkin and Gilbert W. Merkx, eds., *The Jewish Presence in Latin America* (Boston, 1987); Marc J. Osterweil, "The Meaning of Elitehood: Germans, Jews and Arabs in La Paz, Bolivia" (Ph.D. diss., New York University, 1978), 55–58; Jacob Shatzky, *Comunidades Judias en Latinoamerica* (Buenos Aires, 1952), 100–101.

2. See the detailed account by Herbert A. Strauss, "Jewish Emigration from Germany, Nazi Policies and Jewish Responses," pts. 1 and 2, in *Leo Baeck Institute, Yearbook* 25 (1980) and 26 (1981), respectively. Although a large number of refugees were admitted to Bolivia conditionally, as *agricultores*—with visas stipulating that the immigrants settle in rural areas and engage in agriculture or related occupations—the majority, coming from urban backgrounds, managed to remain and settle in the country's urban centers.

3. Dr. Heinrich Stern, "Indianer-Landschaft" (Cochabamba, Bolivia, July 1941, typescript). My translation.

4. Egon Schwarz, *Keine Zeit für Eichendorff: Chronik unfreiwilliger Wanderjahre* (Königstein, 1979), 58; Andres J. Simon, interview by author, videotape, La Paz, Bolivia, July 22, 1991; Renate Schwarz, interview by author, videotape, Teaneck, N.J., May 2, 1991.

5. Videotaped interview with Werner Guttentag, Cochabamba, Bolivia, July 31, 1991. For Karl May, see Christian Heermann, *Der Mann, der Old Shatterhand war: Eine Karl-May-Biographie* (Berlin, 1988) and Martin Lowsky, *Karl May* (Stuttgart, 1987).

6. Heinz Pinshower, interview by author, videotape, Chicago, April 10, 1991.

7. Hanni Pinshower, interview by author, videotape, Chicago, April 10, 1991.

8. Renate Schwarz, interview by author, videotape, Teaneck, N.J., May 2, 1991.

9. Ibid.

10. Werner Guttentag, interview by author, videotape, Cochabamba, Bolivia, July 31, 1991.

11. Schwarz, *Keine Zeit für Eichendorff,* 66.

12. Schwarz, *Keine Zeit für Eichendorff*, 65–66.

13. For an articulation of this feeling in a refugee memoir, see Schwarz, *Keine Zeit für Eichendorff*, 72–73. For a discussion of climatic adjustment problems see von zur Mühlen, *Fluchtziel Lateinamerika: Die deutsche Emigration 1933–1945: politische Aktivitäten und soziokulturelle Integration* (Bonn: 1988), 54–55.

14. For a discussion of the *Rundschau vom Illimani* and Ernst Schumacher, see Patrik von zur Mühlen, *Fluchtziel Lateinamerika*, 217–19, 221–26. The importance of the *Aufbau* as a vehicle for refugee communication and as an instument fostering a refugee communicty during the war, see Schwarz, *Keine Zeit für Eichendorff*, 79. The Wiener Library in London has a complete run of the *Jüdische Wochenshau* on microfilm.

15. The Circulo Israelita, founded in 1935 by Polish and Rumanian Jews, was the first Jewish community organization in Bolivia. Although it would continue to exist as a separate entity throughout the war years and, in the 1950s, would absorb the, by then, much diminished Comunidad, it was the Comunidad, with its (at the time) larger Central European membership and its affiliated institutions, that dominated Jewish-immigrant community life. For a history of the Circulo Israelita, see Circulo Israelita, *Medio Siglo de Vida Judia en La Paz* (La Paz, 1987). Also see Schwarz, *Keine Zeit für Eichendorff*, 81.

16. *Jüdische Wochenschau* (monthly "Bolivia" sections of the Buenos Aires newspaper), and *Rundschau vom Illimani* (1939–42).

17. Circulo Israelita, *Medio Siglo de Vida Judia en La Paz*, 171–75.

18. Schwarz, *Keine Zeit für Eichendorff*, 73.

19. Julius Wolfinger, interview by author, videotape, Queens, N.Y., July 2, 1991.

20. Max Gans, interview by author, New York, June 26, 1991.

21. Leo Spitzer, in a discussion with Heini and Liesl Lipczenko, videotape, August 12, 1990.

22. Julio Meier, interview by author, videotape, La Paz, Bolivia, August 5, 1991.

23. A second wave of Jewish immigration to Bolivia, consisting largely of persons of Eastern European origin, many of whom were concentration camp survivors, occurred after the end of the war. Ironically, ex-Nazis like the notorious Claus Barbie also found refuge in Bolivia in the late 1940s. See Marcel Ophuls's award-winning documentary film, *Hotel Terminus: The Life and Times of Klaus Barbie.*

24. Circulo Israelita, *Medio Siglo de Vida Judia en La Paz*, 30–42; Max Gans, interview by author, New York City, June 26, 1991; Heini Lipczenko and Liesl Lipczenko, interview by author, videotape, August 12, 1990.

25. See, for example, Schwarz, *Keine Zeit für Eichendorff*, and author's interviews with Hanni Pinschower and Heinz Pinschower; Heini Lipczenko and Liesl Lipczenko;Werner Guttentag; Julius Wolfinger; Renate Schwarz; Trude Hassberg, Queens, N.Y., May 4, 1991.

26. Many of the persons I interviewed have referred to these. For example: Julius Wolfinger; Heini Lipczenko and Liesl Lipczenko; Heinz Pinshower and Hanni Pinshower; Werner Guttentag; Walter Guevarra, La Paz, July 14, 1991; Willi Becker, Los Angeles, March 16, 1991. Also see Schwarz, *Keine Zeit für Eichendorff*, 82–83; Arthur Propp memoirs, Leo Baeck Institute, New York.

27. Jerry W. Knudson, "The Bolivian Immigration Bill of 1942: A Case Study in Latin American Anti-Semitism," *American Jewish Archives*, 20, no. 1 (April 1968), 138–59.

28. Ibid.

29. Ilse Herz, interview by author, videotape, Arsdale, N.Y., February 26, 1991.

CHAPTER 12

The East Indian Presence in Jamaican Literature: With Reference to "The Arrival of the Snake Woman" by Olive Senior

VELMA POLLARD

Jeremy Poynting in a well-researched paper, "African Indian Relations in Caribbean Fiction," citing Trinidad and Guyana as the locations under consideration, concludes from his data that "Afro-Creole writing has tended to ignore the Indian presence" and suggests that the fiction "echoes the political and cultural marginalisation of Indians in the Caribbean."[1] More recently Jeffrey Robinson reviewing Roy Heath's novel *Shadow Bride* takes the opportunity to make a somewhat similar comment. "Novels set in the Indian communities of the Caribbean," he says, "are in the minority but novels about the situation of women in those communities are exceedingly rare."[2]

While both remarks are generally accurate in terms of Caribbean literature, they are even more so when applied to Jamaican literature. Indeed when one considers the quantity of writing that has emanated from Jamaica within the last fifty years or so, and the variety of themes treated, the East Indian is indeed conspicuous by his absence.

The accuracy of the remarks quoted above makes the work about to be appreciated in this paper doubly worthy of our attention. "The Arrival of the Snake Woman" by Olive Senior[3] is the story of the entrance into, and adjustment to, a rural Jamaican village by an East Indian woman, typically named Miss Coolie ("coolie" being a colloquial term for "East Indian").

Academic research into the East Indian presence has been equally neglected. Outstanding here is the work of Verene Shepherd, the source of much of the historical information contained in this paper.[4]

231

Historical Background

East Indians were brought to Jamaica to supplement a labor force that had been depleted with the abolition of slavery and the resultant unwillingness of negroes to work on the plantations where they had been slaves. Indians were brought to the Caribbean "indentured," meaning they came under contract to work for a certain number of years after which they could be repatriated or given land to work if they decided to remain. Indentureship began in 1845 and ended in 1921. The majority of those imported into Jamaica failed, for one reason or another, to return to India.[5]

Like other minority people in the island, the East Indian became part of the folklore of the largely African population of the island. That is to say that people who did not know them well wove myth and lore around them. The imagination of the native population allowed the spirit of an Indian child who died ("coolie baby duppy"), for example, to be more powerful than other spirits and much sought after by obeah men who were required to do harm to offending colleagues. Habits of thrift, practiced especially by the women, were frowned upon. The wearing of jewelry particularly gold bangles of great value was particularly offensive to a population recently proselytized by fundamentalist Christian churches preaching against gold and silver.

The cultural habits of the Indians, which were different from those of the ex-slaves, inspired strange interpretations. The newcomers were different not only in appearance, which included dress, but in eating habits, language, and religion. The following comment from Ehrlich with regard to the Negro/Indian interaction as he perceived it as late as the mid-seventies is instructive in that it attests to the pervasiveness of some of these myths and to their endurance even after a century: "Much stereotypical thinking goes on in people's minds. The Indians characterize Negroes as being lazy, argumentative, wasteful of their resources, and wanting only to sport and drink rum. The Negro villagers' stereotype of Indians is that they are prolific, frugal and always hiding their money so that others will not know how wealthy they really are."[6] Poynting comments on similar stereotyping in Trinidad and Guyana and sees its origins in the "attempts of Europeans in the nineteenth century to justify the indenture system and in Afro-Creole fears of Indian competition."[7]

Shepherd makes a similar comment and substantiates it with reference to official documents. She offers the following quotation from parliamentary "Papers Relating to the West Indian Colonies and Mauritius (1858)" emanating from the Baptist Union: "[T]he immigration of a number of heathen and pagan foreigners with their religious superstitions, idolatry and wickedness, will act most injuriously on the morals of the [Black] inhabitants of the island and hinder very much the efforts that are now in operation for their moral and religious improvement."[8] The view of the Indians by Blacks, formulated even before they arrived, must have been affected in no small way by this attitude offered by the official church and the individual preacher alike.

That the antipathy was not a one-sided phenomenon has been attested to by history. Indians came to the Black communities with their own built-in bias. Note, for example, the following reference to Speckman's (1965) comment in Ehrlich's essay: "Speckman has noted that indentured Indians came to the West Indies with a built-in negative bias towards the freed slave population. 'These views were mainly based on an aversion to the black colour of their skins, an aversion which dates back to the Vedic time when 'black skin' (krsna tyac) was used as a denigratory name in order to designate the dark-complexioned, hostile population of the country.'"[9] It is against this socio-historical background that the story "The Arrival of the Snake Woman" must be seen.

Fiction and History—The Story

Senior's unusually long short story identifies several of the myths and prejudices and exposes them in the normal run of the lives of significant characters. Miss Coolie's interaction with the villagers as she comes in contact with them forces the reader not only to see some of the more despicable aspects of the classical village characters but also to appreciate the positions of ignorance from which two populations, the African ex-slaves and the East Indian indentured laborers, operated.

Very few people in Mount Rose, the hill village in which the story is set, had ever seen an Indian before Miss Coolie arrived. Only the young men who had been privileged to go to "Bay," a name given to any seaport town in Jamaica, would have seen one. One of these sages explained that 'snake woman' was the name given to Indian women "from the way their body so neat and trim and they move their hip when they walk just like a snake and they don't wear no proper clothes just these thin little clothes-wrap, thinner than cobweb, yu [*sic*] can see every line of their body when they walk" (2–3).

The folk perception of historical fact made explicit in the story allows for an understanding of some of the prejudices that came with the interaction of the two races of laborers. "Indenture," which saved the planter from loss when slavery ended, is viewed in quite a different way by the ex-slave who had hoped to improve his bargaining position when the estate owners fell on hard times. Ex-slaves were not happy with these people the government had "brought from a place call India fe work in the cane fe nutten." Moses, the young man doing the explaining, adds his own comment to this fact: "Imagine come from so far to tek way black man work. The man dem is a wicket set a beast them." His antipathy however does not run to the women for he finishes "but the woman them! Whai!" (3).

Miss Coolie's selection of the village, or indeed its selection of her at the very outset, is carried out in the most unlikely and flippant manner possible. The story begins with the boy narrator watching young men pull straws to decide who will entice the "Snake Woman" from the coast to come to live with him in the mountain village. There is mystery behind this woman. The reader is told that snake women are anxious to get away from men of their own race partly because of the woman's place in that culture (she is not allowed to say 'kemps' lest she lose her life). They also want to get away from the Bay where the sea is there as a painful reminder of the home they left behind. Snake women are said to hate the sea "like pisen for is the sea that carry them away from India" (3).

This is the Black man's account of the historical fact that while Indian men seldom took Negro women, Indian women entered into unions with Black men. Shepherd, making a point about the lack of interaction between the races, supports her position by quoting Comins's note in the India Office's 1893 records, which reported that sexual union between the races was rare and that when it did take place it was between Black men and Indian women and scarcely ever vice versa.[10]

In the story, one of the straw lottery competitors already has three children with two different women, but he is prepared to incur the wrath of these women and bring Miss Coolie to the village, so obsessed is he; and he wins her. This aspect of the portrayal of the Indian female in the eyes of the Black male is similar to what Poynting found in his survey of Caribbean novels referred to above. He reports that "(t)he Indian woman is invariably portrayed in a stereotyped way as a creature of Eastern allure."[11]

Senior exploits the accepted stereotypes to destroy them in the unfolding of her story. It is Miss Coolie's composure throughout the different experiences the reader is called upon to observe that is most noteworthy. Her coming is predicted, it seems—almost as if Parson, the religious bigot, had had wind of it, for he preached in his church, the Sunday before her arrival, against the daughters of Zion who are haughty and "walk with stretched forth necks and wanton eyes, walking and mincing as they go, and making a tinkling with their feet" (5).

The Boy Narrator

It is significant that the character Senior makes into Miss Coolie's guide and friend from the moment she enters the village is a child, Ish. The implication is that he will not have been tainted by all the prejudices the adults had internalized. It is he who tells Miss Coolie's story, reflecting as he tells it on the surprising pettiness and hate evidenced in the non-Indian villagers' behavior.

Through him Senior unobtrusively goes about displacing the negative myths folklore has woven around the people who came indentured from the East. Through his outraged reaction to the extreme positions taken for example, by the parson, God's representative on earth and the trend setter in the district, against Miss Coolie (the heathen), the reader is made to appreciate the poisonous nature of bigotry.

Miss Coolie, whose infant is refused treatment at a clinic set up by the church, must take her child miles away (to Bay) to be hospitalized. The parson's outburst at the approach of woman and child is hysterical: "Get that woman out of here! We cannot have her here! Unclean!" (29). The young narrator, observing this action, comes to question the faith into which he has been socialized. Miss Coolie has to take her child to the coast town (Bay). She rushes from the clinic and makes her preparations with great speed and efficiency and is off to the doctor. Ish, the young narrator, eventually rushes to tell her husband the story. The husband packs food and goes immediately to catch up with her.

Ish falls into a kind of stupor, probably the result of a virus but definitely brought on by the trauma of his attempts to come to terms with the parson's philosophy outlined in his teachings and his unchristian treatment of the sick child and his mother.

Ish notices that among the few things Miss Coolie takes with her on the journey, which is to be very significant in her development, are "several of the bangles she had taken off before" (30). The bangles represent wealth to be used in just such an emergency as Miss Coolie is about to face. Gold is easily convertible to cash.

This is the first of the examples of the financial canniness frequently spoken of disparagingly by Blacks discussing the cultural traits of Indians. Later in the story, bangles are brought into play again, this time in a way directly related to Ish's future. After completing a brilliant school career, Ish is about to leave home to study medicine. Miss Coolie gives him a heavy gold bangle with the words: "Ish, never sell this. Keep it and anytime you need money go and pawn it but never never sell" (43). In the years to come, Ish uses the bangle in this way several times over and learns that shrewdness is different from thievery. He learns too that, contrary to what some believe, money management is a skill that can be learned. It is interesting that Ehrlich, quoted above, comments that many of the Negro villagers he interviewed in his sample thought the money-saving trait to be genetic to the Indian but that it could be acquired by association as in marriage to an Indian.[12]

Integration

The birth of her child brings Miss Coolie a few steps toward integration into the village. Ish reports that attitudes toward her begin to soften then. Nana the village midwife delivers the child, and men and women come bearing gifts of food. And the child, as affable as his father and as gentle as his mother is soon "all over the district even in the homes of Jestina and Dina, Son-Son's other baby mothers" (26).

The child also gives Miss Coolie an obvious stake in the community. Her ambition for him is to become a lawyer. One of the things she wants him to do is to get titles for all the district people for land to which they have only squatters' rites. And Biya eventually does that and more, remaining faithful to the district and its mores even more so than Ish, who, as Miss Coolie (again) predicts, becomes a doctor but chooses to live in the city after honoring his promise to marry her daughter Najeela.

Senior's Miss Coolie combines traits associated with woman with traits associated with the Indian. She is far seeing in terms of the district and individual futures, and she has the resourcefulness to help with the achievement of community aspirations.

The story of Miss Coolie is the story of integration. It had to be achieved slowly and at great pains by the first generation. The reader is made to watch Miss Coolie easily make decisions that could not have been painless. Seeing that her child's education is at stake, she joins the official church whose parson treated her so badly before. She arrives in church one Sunday without her sari and without her offending bangles and with her son at her side. (He is five years old and ready to go to the village school.) As she stands at the church door, Parson forgets the order of service and intones. "Praise God from whom all blessings flow." When school opens, Biya is among the screaming children experiencing first-day nerves.

Miss Coolie's arrival at church is a significant event. It underlines the extreme nature of her compromise. That events like these are examples of her ability to do what is expedient and necessary becomes clear at the end of the story. At that point the few dry goods she used to sell from her house have grown into a big business place and her children have qualified and are gone. Miss Coolie reverts to her saris, to tilak, the red spot on her forehead, and to her bangles.

Near the end of the story, too, Senior takes the opportunity to do what she seldom does, to preach. Her medium is the cogitation of the adult Ish on matters of social history. Among other pieces of wisdom, Ish the adult is made to say that Miss Coolie is "our embodiment of the spirit of the new age, an age in which sentiment has been replaced by pragmatism and superstition by materialism" (44). The next generation could hardly feel these pains. Biya fathers a number of children in the district, children of mixed race, Jamaican children. Ish the narrator, and his wife, Najeela, add to Miss Coolie's and Son-Son's cadre of grandchildren of mixed race as well. These children are heirs, one hopes, to the better traits of both races.

Notes

1. Jeremy Poynting, "African Indian Relations in Caribbean Fictions," *Wasafiri* 5 (1986): 15.

2. Jeffrey Robinson, "Roy Heath's Novel *Shadow Bride*," *Journal of West Indian Literature* 4, no. 1 (1990): 63.

3. All quotations are taken from: Olive Senior, *Arrival of the Snake Woman and Other Stories* (London: Longman, 1989).

4. Verene Shepherd, "Transients to Citizens," *Jamaica Journal* 18, no. 3 (1985); and "The Dynamics of Afro-Jamaican–East Indian relations in Jamaica, 1838–1917," *Caribbean Quarterly* 32, nos. 3 and 4 (1986). Shepherd herself comments on the preoccupation of the research with Black-White relations and mentions Johnson's research on the Chinese and Ehrlich's on the East Indian as notable exceptions.

5. Shepherd, "The Dynamics," 17.

6. Allen S. Ehrlich, "Race and Ethnic Identity in Rural Jamaica: the East Indian Case," *Caribbean Quarterly* 22, no. 1 (1976): 22.

7. Poynting, "African Indian Relations," 16.

8. Shepherd, "Transients to Citizens," 15.

9. Ehrlich, "Race and Ethnic Identity," 25.

10. Shepherd, "Transients to Citizens," 18.

11. Poynting, "African Indian Relations," 16.

12. Ehrlich, "Race and Ethnic Identity," 25.

CHAPTER 13

The "Other's Others": Chicana Identity and Its Textual Expressions

ELIANA S. RIVERO

Even from a surface reading of Chicana texts, it becomes evident that the writers are engaged in the quest for an identity. They are searching for an artistic configuration that will express a valid sense of their profile, both as ethnic females inserted in a particular social and historical milieu and as human beings. The real-life experiences of Chicanas have molded a consistently repeated "otherness," nurtured by attempts at differentiation from both Mexican and Anglo-American cultural modalities. Beyond coming to terms with the conflicts inherent in the quest for personal definition, Chicana writers have also concerned themselves with class and race struggles. And although she defines herself in her writings very frequently as a woman of La Raza,[1] the Mexican-American woman often asks to be thought of as a very personal being who is not only molded by color or subculture or gender, but woven out of her individual fibers:

don't call me for the chicanos,
nor for my parents,
nor for women
summon me for myself.
      (Marina Rivera, "iv. what i want . . .")[2]

It is not surprising that Chicana texts should exhibit this characteristic; neither is it that literature—written by women or by men—does so. In the annals of universal writing, beginning with the canonized classics of Western civilization, an ontological search for both individual and collective nature, for a personal essence, is evidenced. From Homer to Borges, from national epics in the Far East to existentialist literature

239

in modern European countries, the quest for the self is portrayed in all manner of symbolic and artistic forms. Critical analyses of literary narrative modes and lyrical expressions in fictional texts all over the world demonstrate this commonality of pursuit: the journey without and the journey within inform literary texts and give shape to profiles of male and female heroes. The exploration of unknown territories is often a metaphor for the inner voyage into the self: Ithaca for the Greeks and Aztlán for the Chicanos are both mythical lands of origin and return, the spiritual mother lode of personal and cultural identities. Whether the voices are those of the young man's musings in Thomas Mann's *Buddenbrooks*, the male child's recollections in Rudolfo Anaya's *Bless Me, Ultima*, or the adolescent inner monologues of the female protagonist in Sandra Cisneros's *The House on Mango Street*, they all call out of a cross-cultural longing for self-knowledge, definition, and affirmation. Undoubtedly, expressions of identity are molded by the social, cultural, class, and gender determinants pointed out before. Nevertheless, critical textual readings indicate that one of the universal functions of the cultural artifact is to reveal its maker by the contour and the space that it delineates.

Definitions and expressions of self-identity are especially central to the emergence and development of a minority literature. A group which is not part of the mainstream society struggles to claim validity for itself by affirming *sui generis* values. This affirmation of idiosyncratic features defines the group's uniqueness and legitimizes its claims for acceptance, on its own terms, by the larger society. Of particular interest in this respect is the study of ethnic minority literatures, which express a national culture through ideological confirmation of their very existence, especially when those groups face cultural annihilation and their only means of survival is through resistance.[3] Another language and another perspective on the world, different from those of the dominant culture in which they are submerged, is the ground for much of what is produced by those literatures, in both the oral and the written modes.

In the 1960s, the blossoming of ethnic literatures in the United States signaled the answers by cultural subgroups to questions such as, What *are we* as a group, or even as a "class"? How do *we see* ourselves? How do we define who *we are*? In their development toward maturity, the arts and literatures of these groups have seen individual artists and writers ask these questions and affirm the answers through images of the self. Ralph Ellison, in *The Invisible Man*, illustrated the point of social and political nonexistence for African Americans, as the

Black movement in those years made a poignant example of the quest for an identity.[4] The women's movement produced a similar awareness and a similar development; by means of new creations, and especially through historical writings, Anglo-American women searched for their own traditions. Critics have pointed out analogies among groups of marginalized artists:

> Like the minority writer, the female writer exists within that inescapable condition of identity which distances her from the mainstream of the culture and forces her either to stress her separation from the masculine literary tradition or to pursue her resemblance to it. In either case, like writers who belong to ethnic and racial minorities, she carries with her a special self-consciousness.[5]

Other female subgroups, such as "women of color," experienced the emergence of a new conciousness that was primarily woman oriented, but also race and class oriented. Theirs was, indeed, the special self-awareness of being doubly different.[6] The quest for self-definition could be found in women's literature from France to Mexico, from Australia to Puerto Rico. Feminist criticism itself arose out of just such a process, with the intention of finding corroboration for the existence of the self-conscious female in its examination of the literature written by women which was being published across the continents. It was the "story of women's emergence from colonization under patriarchy, and thus this emergence was as close to universal as patriarchal systems are."[7]

Since the beginning of the literary reawakening described as the "Chicano Renaissance" of the mid-sixties, Chicano writers have dwelled on the ways in which they see themselves individually and as a group as well as on the nature of their relationship to the dominant culture of the society in which they live. The first significant affirmation of *Chicanismo* in an artistic sense was the narrative poem "I am Joaquín/Yo soy Joaquín," by Rodolfo "Corky" Gonzales, a political activist who founded the Crusade for Justice in Denver. Born in the midst of the movement struggle, in the wake of Chicano manifestos such as the Plan of Delano, the Plan Espiritual de Aztlán, Cesar Chavez's organization of the United Farm Workers, and the "artistification" of the labor strike in California fields by means of the Teatro Campesino of Luis Valdez,[8] "I am Joaquín" is a long bilingual poem that affirms uniqueness through an ethnic, cultural definition of both the individual and the collective self, mostly in terms of a Chicano nationalistic conciousness.

The resounding cadences of the "I am, I am . . ." found in the original verse narrative by Gonzales has its counterpart in quite a few of the early Chicana texts. Some critics are acutely perceptive of this phenomenon, and they agree that the language of identification is a means to express sentiments brought on by generation after generation of cultural invisibility: "in the language of the Self, through the images of affirmation, in Spanish, the Chicano sees himself and herself" [sic].[9] Both as an affirmative expression of an individual conciousness and as a collective vision, Chicana poetry—since its inception—has been predominantly defined by the writers' perceptions of who they are as women and as members of the largest Hispanic minority in the United States. Several texts are significant in this respect, among them two poems: Lorenza Calvillo Schmidt's "soy" (I am . . .) and Adaljiza Sosa Riddell's "Como duele (ser Malinche)" (How it hurts [to be a traitor]) first appeared in the special issue "Chicanas en la literatura y el arte" (Chicanas in Art and Literature) published by El Grito in September 1973.[10] Other texts of the seventies, such as Dorinda Moreno's "My son, my daughters,"[11] are significant to the study of Chicana self-definition, but the two chosen for analysis here are distinctive in their characterization of several categories for self-definition. An examination of their salient features begins to clarify the paradigms within which our perspective of Chicana textual identity emerges.

These texts are indeed cultural artifacts, noncanonical forms of discourse that have been "minorized" or erased within their own subculture. Their contouring differences, based on gender, set these productions apart from the prevalent Chicano canon, a construct containing mostly male figures.[12] The poems under consideration here, moreover, are discursive formations characterized by their double degree of "minorityhood": they exist outside the dominant cultural canon and on the fringes of their own subcultural paradigm. "Soy" and "Como duele" are, above all, configurations of self-otherness, expressions of a desire to mark and to define a hybrid self-alterity.

Identity through Language: The Poem as Quest

It has been no secret to feminist critics that language and language use are not neutral but instead imbued with sex-inflected cultural values as well as with patterns that bespeak of structures based on race and class: "Language conceals an invincible adversary because it is the language of men and their grammar."[13] Women writers themselves have become very aware of the realities of language to express structures of a patriarchal culture, which is universal in nature: Tillie Olsen calls attention to the danger of "perpetuating—by continous usage—entrenched, centuries-old oppressive power realities, early-on incorporated into language."[14] In this sense, women who are coming into a tradition of literary language and forms already appropriated by male expression will be forced to wrestle with language in an effort to remake it as a language adequate to their conceptual processes.[15]

Women writers who create literary constructs from an experience of cultural ethnicity, as well as "femaleness," are particularly affected when confronted with an inadequate language. Their creation must confront other realities not relevant to White women writers, especially when trying to configure a literary identity that will define who they really are. Some critics who write about Third World discourses have pointed this out, mostly in relation to male authors: "Minority discourse borrows the language of the dominant world, which in its purely dominant form negates or diminishes the minority subject . . . the minority writer must eventually attempt to cast away the cultural burden that the language of the majority . . . imposes."[16]

The concept of 'women's bilinguality', which has long preoccupied female authors, is even more relevant to minority writers. Dorothy Richardson has written in *Tunnel*: "In speech with a man, a woman is at a disadvantage—because they speak different languages. She may understand his. Hers he will never speak or understand. . . . He listens and is flattered and thinks he has her mental measure when he has not touched even the fringe of her consciousness."[17] Chicana writers, as African American or Asian American or Native American female writers, can recognize that the White majority does not touch "even the fringe of their consciousness" and in many cases does not even listen, as men must listen to women for their own survival. The language of the ethnic minority person is a silent one when disregarded by the mainstream listener; even more so when the speaker is a woman. In this context, Chicanas are doubly disregarded in their own language forms: by the Chicanos and by the White majority.

The issue of women's "bilinguality" has also been dealt with by the critics: women are bilingual, alternating between the two dialects of "neutral language" [read "male conceived and male oriented"] and "women's language," argues Robin Lakoff.[18] In addition, women have always been subject to stricter verbal codes than men; words and expressions are traditionally forbidden to them, even in liberal environments. These linguistic cultural taboos become particularly binding when women writers attempt to express their (different) sexual realities in the literary text. But even though the problem of gender-differentiated language is a real one for Anglo female writers, one can find an understandably more complex set of circumstances affecting the works of Chicanas. For them, the strictures of a proudly patriarchal, inwardly and outwardly conservative, avowedly religious culture, which has generated a set of mores specifically designed to keep women in rein, constitutes yet another challenging limitation.

The texts in question are particularly well suited to an exploration of the Chicanas' main focus on self-definition. In reading them, we distinguish two particular speech acts which are generated by two separate textual views of self, or personae. By examining surface features of morphology, syntax, lexicon, and even diction, conciousness of self is found in the text; deep structures, such as intentional modes, reveal a vision of self intimately related to the variables of gender, race, and culture.

A common and distinct stylistic feature of Chicana poetic texts is their use and mixture of two different linguistic codes, Spanish and English, and this characteristic trait of much of Chicano poetry can be considered as revealing an awareness of dualism or pluralism.[19] The poetic "I," in correspondence with the authorial experience that is mediated by the conventions of literary language, can be said to belong to two (or more) coexisting cultural systems: Anglo versus Mexican American, male versus female, working class versus middle class. When the reader is confronted by Calvillo Schmidt's text, for example, realization arises that biculturalism, as well as bilingualism, are textual determinants of reading:

soy hija de mis padres
meta de mis abuelos
hermana de mis hermanos
prima de mis primos
amiga de mis amigos
soy
lencha
lorraine

wa
panzas y
"mija"
yo soy
soy
yo

Language clues allow the reader to perceive mediatized "living" experiences, attitudes, subjective perspectives on other objects or beings: the use of a Spanish nickname, for example (*"lencha"*), gives the reader access to a funny tenderness that is also captured by a self-deprecating physical humor (*"panzas"* /bellies). Ultimately, the composite of attitudes, emotions, relationships, and visions describe the background out of which a sense of self is formed for the poetic speaker, indeed the literary persona of the author.

Schmidt's text has all the characteristics of an assertion: the speaker addresses an implied listener, or reader, without giving any hints of an expected reply. The poetic persona is concerned with getting the addressee to believe or to know something; this direct purpose is served by the simplicity of the communication, couched in terms that share the characteristics of ordinary language. The speech of direct affirmation, in the first grammatical person, has the weight and the nakedness of a revelation: "I am / am / I."[20]

But before this plainly stated definition of "one" is given, the poetic speaker resorts to describing the net of relationships that define her personhood, in connection with others. The first and second stanzas, although beginning by the same verb of being, "soy" (am), contain very different paradigms. The first is relational, the second is nominational: one connects, the other names, the speaker. It is interesting to note that the relational definitions of self are particular to female discourse, or to discourse about women. Whether in the East or in the West, and certainly in the Judeo-Christian tradition, a woman has been historically described in relation to her father, her husband, her children.[21]

A woman even loses her name, her social identity, to be known under her spouse's name. Chicana poets in the seventies explored this facet of their "borrowed" identity. Miriam Bornstein's "Toma de nombre" offers a classic example of this:

soy
fulana de tal

esposa de fulano
madre de zutano
y algunas veces presiento que solamente soy
mujer de sola

[I am
Mrs. So-and-so
wife of So-and-so
mother of So-and-so
and sometimes I feel that am only
woman of "alone"][22]

    A reader would not be likely to find such forms of self-description
in the discourse of a male poet or the speech of a male narrator. But
even when discourse does not refer specifically to women's identity and
related themes, critics seem to distinguish a female "expressive" mode
from a male "linear and dualistic mode," as evidenced in female (and
feminist) writers' use of specific organic verbs, run-on syntax, and a
"discursive, conjunctive" style.[23] The syntactic fluidity created by lack of
punctuation in the texts above would seem to point to such a writing
mode, although the departure from standard grammar and word order
does not fully explain what these particular features have to do with a
female worldview. A rejection of male aesthetics could be functioning in
these texts, affirming—as do Stanley and Robbins—that a feminist
aesthetics results from the adoption of a linguistic mode defined as
"female." Still, what I posit here is the idea that female experience
generates a different kind of discourse, while a feminist aesthetics
embodies a critical consciousness of women's situation in patriarchy.
Moreover, women of Hispanic heritage, who come from traditional
backgrounds, use kinship and friendship ties not only to acquire a sense
of their identity but also to gain access to certain language and speech
modes that allow them to survive and thrive in a male-dominated
society. This they do by learning certain modes and structures of speech,
whether for social or inner exchanges—talk and thought.[24]
    In the first stanza of Calvillo Schmidt's poem, an interesting
dichotomy is observed. Due to Spanish language rules of grammatical
agreement and generic-inclusive usage, all feminine gender nouns
describing the relational identity of the speaker are directly opposed by
the masculine plural forms of generic nouns:

I am
daughter of my parents
granddaughter of my grandparents
sister of my brother and sisters
cousin of my cousins
friend of my friends
I am *lorenza*
lencha
lorraine
wa
bellies and
"*mija*"[25]

The words for parents, grandparents, siblings (brother/sisters), cousins, and friends (*hija, nieta, hermana, prima, amiga*) subsume the feminine/ grammatical gender category of the "I." The persona is a female within the male "groupings," distinct by virtue of her selfhood but dependent in relation to a generic group that engulfs her. This is a very particular trait of Chicana literature, and all through its texts the identity formulae are repeated: Chicanas see themselves as daughters (mostly of mothers), grandaughters (especially of *abuelitas*, "grandmothers"), sisters, mothers, and friends, and they construct their literary self-images accordingly. Many poems and short stories by Cervantes, Cota Cárdenas, Villanueva, Cisneros, Chávez, and Bornstein present this same relational network.

The second stanza shows very distinctive features. Names that others call the speaker are underlined, their original Italics setting them off as identity labels by which the "I"—homologous to the real poet and as such its namesake in the text—is known to the world outside her inner concious self. The list of names itself is revealing. "Lorenza" is the Spanish name, the official label for social relations, self-naming, identification in the public sphere. "Lencha" is a familiar nickname, peculiar to Mexican rural culture, constructed by the imitation of childish speech; there is usually a smaller sibling or a doting parent who produces babbling sounds for naming others in the immediate circle of the nuclear family.[26] "Lorraine" is the Anglo adaptation of the Spanish name, whether self-adopted or given; many Hispanics solve the drudgery of spelling their names for the Anglo-speaking ear by adopting a similarly sounding English name. The resulting self-images and identities are markedly different; Lorraine can be associated with Hollywood stars, with French names, even with saints, and it has a glamorous connotation of is own. Lorenza, however, is a common peasant name in Spanish, unsophisticated and plain. In the Chicano family circle, "lencha" and "lorenza" serve an everyday function of simplicity; in the outer world dominated by Anglo culture, those two labels are a hindrance, because of their difficulty (in spelling and pronouncing) and their "strangeness" to mainstream individuals and institutions. Hence, the elegance and functionality of "lorraine." "Wa" is a totally childish form, with the interesting feature of a consonantal sound and spelling foreign to the Spanish alphabet (*gua* would be the rough equivalent). It connotes not only familiarity but closeness and affection, perhaps one of those shortening of names so common in closely knit units across cultures. "Panzas" and "mija" are totally different categories of naming and are perceived as such by the speaker, who places these names at the end of the list of identity labels. If "lorenza," "lencha," and "lorraine" are proper names molded to the cultural needs of the group and the individual, and "wa" is—although in the category of proper names—a monosyllabic call for the inner circle of identification, the last two Italicized "tags" represent very distinct cultural images of a female within the known nucleus of close kinship. No other individual would call a Hispanic woman "bellies" except her brothers or sisters (probably the former); the joking allusion to bodily imperfection is only allowed—if grudgingly—to immediate family members. And then, of course, the last term on the list is that well-known vocative of everyday use in Mexican and Chicano culture (more within the latter). It is a Spanish contraction for *mi* and *hija*, the feminine form of that shortened possessive used by mothers at the end of an English sentence. It is the sign for the speaker and the addressee that the conversation runs along "soft lines"; it is usually a mother's way of finishing a command, a question, a sentence, addressed to her children (although used by male parents too, is a more common word in female speech).[27] It is also used by male spouses or lovers in addressing their women; in this sense it carries a certain tone of either affection, condescension, or both.[28]

At the end of the text, there is a "yo" and "yo soy" [I, I am] presenting a stark contrast to the enumeration of functions and vocatives. It is the real "I," expressed through the simple transparency of the first person singular; "yo," detached from kinship and friendship ties, undefined by the naming of others, is the real essence of this speaker. If the identity given by names is imposed from the outside, the inner self dwells on a singularity of purpose—the simple "I" is the only sound needed in the interior recesses of knowing "who you are". Such knowledge, albeit determined outwardly by the Chicano cultural environment, is not only an affirmation but also a confirmation of femaleness. This short text, a declaration of identity configured as an assertion, stands out because it is situated among other poetic texts written in English. Its use of standard Spanish makes it into an utterance of linguistic and cultural preservation, an intimate yet powerful manifesto of identification.

Some might argue that this particular form of speech does not constitute an occurrence of poetic language: it is too simple, too transparent, too "devoid" of figurative forms. The traditional approach would even maintain that the "private speech of the household," this instance of women's speech, lacks "the form of poetry."[29] And yet, the reader's expectations upon coming before a self-declared poetic text are fulfilled: it becomes an aesthetically meaningful message through use of form, space, rhythm, and authorial attitude.

The Self through Cultural Identification

"Como duele"
Pinche, como duele ser Malinche

["How it hurts"
Damn, how it hurts to be a traitor].[30]

The most distinctive features of this Chicana text are, at first glance, its bilingualism and its mode of addressing. The poem consists of an apostrophic speech act, spoken from the first-person singular of a female persona, and directed toward a male "you" that is fictional to the reality of the situation, with the exception of seven verses where Malinche becomes the apostrophic "you."

Malinche, pinche,
forever with me;
I was born out of you,
I walk beside you,
bear my children with you,
for sure, I'll die
alone with you. (76)

As in other poetic direct discourses, the addressee is not necessarily "present" but constitutes the main object of address and embodies characteristics of an ideal "reader" or listener. Both speaker and addressee are known to be Chicanos, because of the linguistic and cultural clues and the outright "naming" of a man "Ese, vato" [Hey, dude/I saw you today]. The second addressee, centrally relevant to the poetic construction, is the sixteenth century Mexican Indian woman Malinche (Malintzin/Tenépal). The whole text is constructed around this central image, repeated in its refrains and encoded in the mother tongue of the Chicana: "Pinche, como duele ser Malinche" [Damn, how it hurts to be a crossover, a traitor [Malinche]]. The combination of a mythical/cultural figure and stereotype requires a close explanation, outside from the direct features of the utterance itself.

The Malinche image is one central and vital to Mexican culture, and it has been explored in many classic studies. Simply put, Malinche/Malintzin (her given Nahuatl name was changed to the Christian Marina at baptism) was the Indian interpreter who served Hernán Cortés in many capacities, bore him a son, and facilitated with her service the advance of Spanish conquistadores during the Conquest.[31] In Mexican culture, she represents the submissive traitor, the ultimate villainess, who by her acquiescence allowed the Aztec empire to be raped, pillaged, and conquered. She has been dubbed the "ethnic traitress supreme."[32] In addition to its treachery connotations, the Malinche name evokes "selling out to foreigners" and is specially caustic when used to denigrate a person of Mexican origin for his or her association with non-Mexicans. The usual manner of referring to Malinche in popular, profane speech, is by a taboo word that doubles as an insult.[33] Feminist writers and critics, especially among the Chicanas, have rescued this much maligned figure of the Mexican Conquest, blaming misogynistic historicism for the historical abuse heaped on "la Malinche."[34]

In the poem by Sosa Riddell, the refrain repeats the painful lament: "how it hurts to be a traitor." How is the lyric speaker a traitor? The nature of the addressee reveals her "treason." At a point in her life when she should have made a Chicano her companion, she "changed her name by law" (married an Anglo) and hid behind her pale color to become a Malinche, to conform and pass as "regular," not as "other." This is the identity against which she rebels and fights, only to be ambivalent in her guilt. Many years after, the speaker still remembers the days of her youth and how family pressures to "marry well" conquered her indecision about an (idealized) young man of la Raza, her fellow ethnic. Her poetic persona is totally identified with the stereotypical Malinche of Mexican culture: she herself is a daughter of Malinche, walks daily under her shadow, and will feel the guilt of cultural treason until her death. Relational patterns are thus inscribed in the text, but under the veil of indirect speech. In this case, the traditional view is questioned sometimes in the form of ironic interrogations—"A Chicano at Dartmouth?"—only to be countered by the title refrain (Como duele) with its guilt-laden statement.

The language issues in this text are intriguing, yet predictable. A split conciousness—between the Anglo world of Riddell and the Mexican-Spanish world of Sosa—is at work through and behind the linguistic structures: the dichotomy of codification, a split format on the page, the dual addressee (Chicano and Malinche), the interlingualism that slides between codes at the sentence level. Still, the main image-refrain is codified in the mother tongue, aided by the rythmic sound and alliterative power of the *ch*: pin*che*—Malinche, which brings the reader to the sounds of cursing with euphemisms.[35] The first stanzas are reminiscent of the Movimiento poetry that proliferated in the early seventies; made popular by the linguistic codeswitching of poets like Alurista, José Montoya, and Raúl Salinas, in Sosa Riddell it is framed within a very distinct female conciousness of cultural "duty" toward la Raza. It is a woman's experience, her historical guilt; no other persona in Chicano texts deals with the problematic issue of mixed marriages, of "selling out" to an Anglo name during the heyday of the activist struggle. But no male poetic persona had to reflect the vital experience of a name change through marriage, a powerful indication of cross-cultural assimilation. The experience of cultural "treason" is then distinctly female, aided by the powerful mythic stereotype of la Malinche, tainted mother and slut according to *machista* interpretations of history.

The basic structure of the text is given by a division of the speech act in two parts, corresponding to two addressees (the young Chicano man and the Malinche figure), united by the introspective refrain— "Pinche, como duele ser Malinche" [Damn, how it hurts to be a traitor]. This refrain is actually the only instance of textual self-address; in uttering the alliterative phrase, the poetic persona reminds herself of her painful guilt at being considered a traitor to her ethnic culture. Although one addressee is part of empirical past reality and the other a mythic motif, both are equally "absent" from the utterance situation;

their presence is due only to an act of willful memory on the part of the speaker. The language chosen to address the Chicano is heavily "interlingual": it slides between English and Spanish, producing a constant tension between two languages being used at once.[36] There seems to be, however, a consistent pattern for the choice of words or phrases that are uttered in standard Spanish, in Chicano Spanish, in Pachuco/Caló,[37] or in standard English.

Standard Spanish appears as part of sentences that carry an affirmation or an emotional message; "como duele ser" [how it hurts to be] in the refrain, "por la ley" [by law], "pobrecitos" [poor little things], "mis pobres padres" [my poor parents], and "para siempre" [forever]. The affirmation of the legality in her change of name—powerful sign of identity—is linked to traditional culture standards, to the image of the speaker's parents who wanted "the best" for their daughter. They thought she could make it in mainstream society much better if she had an Anglo name, as she was White enough; years after, she forgives the parental error with feelings of compassion. The guilt associated with treason to her race and culture is linked to parental pressure and to breaking out of the stereotype of Mexican identity—saying goodbye to the barrio, to "cruiser culture"—ruefully seen as a certain form of death. Connection with a man of her same heritage was temporary, and the finality of separation from both man and ethnic identity is emphasized in the strong Spanish phrase "para siempre" [forever]. The self that is reflected by this type of language is ultimately one of split consciousness, of torn loyalties; and this division is paralleled in a double code. Tradition, heritage, Malinche, affirmation, emotion: instances of linguistic choice that prefer standard Spanish. Not unlike in samples of oral speech, these phrases appear mostly in the context of alternating idioms, in occurrences of code-switching that are triggered precisely because of the emotional content of the utterance.[38]

There are strong indications that when poetic discourse is inscribed in a dialogue mode, and addresses a certain type of interlocutor—as the "Chicano chulo" [good looking guy] in this text—code-switching occurrences follow closely the alternation of everyday speech. Some critics have expressed this viewpoint: "The principal development of Chicano as well as Neorrican poetry is based in the appropriation of oral language as poetic language . . . popular speech, transformed into poetry by integration of metaphoric devices, alliteration, images and similes, assumes then possibilities that go beyond its function as a document of community speech."[39]

Both at the lexical and the syntactic levels, Chicano Spanish appears as selected vocabulary items in Sosa Riddell's text, mostly nouns ("rucos" [old men or people], originally a Pachuco term but widespread in usage today, "pendejadas" [stupid things], colloquial in Mexico) or discourse markers ("Pero sabes"[But you know]), exclamations/slogans ("Que viva la Raza" [long live the Raza]); and emphatic, vocative phrases (such as "chicano chulo" [good looking Chicano (young man)]). In addition, the presence of Chicano idiom is marked by untranslatable cultural icons, borrowed from slang: "grifa y peleonera" [for (being) a dope addict and a (street) fighter]. This phrase (which explains why the young man had to do time in jail while the female "Malinche" was spared that type of life), is a whole clause in Chicano Spanish that incorporates the Caló Pachuco (street or gang slang) word *grifa* in seemingly adjectival form.[40] In a sentence like "I said goodbye *al barrio y al Cruiser*," the complement contains two nouns that are also Chicano cultural icons, and whether Spanish or English, they require prepositions and articles in Spanish.[41] Hence the code-switching so typical of intrasentence alternation, where the word in Spanish/English "triggers a change" for the preceding part of speech and this is then inscribed in the other code.[42] Exactly the same happens in the expression "returned wrapped *como* enchiladas / in red, white, and blue" (in reference to Chicano casualties in Korea and Vietnam) and in the last line of the poem, "you are *muy* gringo too." All three utterances are a good example of Chicano idiom.[43] Geographic names that have become stock part of a Chicano topography also appear in this variety of Spanish: "Los" (Los Angeles), "Sacra" (Sacramento), "Sanfra" (San Francisco).[44]

The speech addressed to the Chicano in Sosa Riddell's text utilizes many of the slang words that are part of a young man's street vocabulary, and are taken from the stock of Pachuco Spanish. From the greeting "Ese, vato"—Hey, man—to the farewell—"Pero sabes, ése" [standard Spanish plus Caló/But you know, man], which are both identity discourse markers, to loaned cultural signs ("rucos," "grifa"), the chosen code is *Caló* because it denotes the familiarity of student days in the 1960's, when "carnales/carnalas" (brothers/sisters) were involved in the struggle of the Chicano rights movement. The female poetic persona begins to address her former young man in this code because it is the idiom of urban male Chicano youth, often connoting virility;[45] it is the outward linguistic system for identification in the Chicano movement, in addition to the visual signs exhibited in the dress code—"eagle on your jacket."[46]

The Malinche incarnation of Sosa Riddell's text is a social and ideological indictment of the present-day persona. At the time she was supposed to forge a profile of her own self in the political arena, she found the Chicano labeling unsuitable. In the reverie of this poetic discourse, her language choice reflects a direct concern with the proper vehicle for expressing those memories of guilt and/or reaffirmation; whether she engages defensively in a direct confrontation with her past, or whether she returns to the realization of her guilt—facets of her conflicting identity—the poetic speaker chooses the linguistic code that best suits the textual situation. In either case, standard English functions as a pivot for syntactical and lexical departure; it is the language used as basis for the entire speech act.

The poems by Calvillo Schmidt and Sosa Ridell constitute quite a different modality of Chicana literary expression, one that flourished in a period when the need for cultural identification and affirmation superseded the search for individual craft. Chicana texts in the 1980s and 1990s are produced by authors who are more critically aware of their unique craft—many of them in possession of sophisticated writing skills—and who also respond to different readers. Even if still limited, the audience of Chicana literature is starting to include monolingual feminists and members of other English-speaking ethnic minorities. The publishing market is also opening its doors, even if still on a reduced scale, to minority writers. The very circumstances of the Chicanas' training as wordsmiths, and the necessity to reach a larger audience of readers, may well be helping to produce a type of literary text that—although evidently bicultural—is decidedly not interlingual or bilingual in the interpenetration of its codes.

Nevertheless, Chicana writers are still engaged in the process of defining and affirming their own ethnic and class identity, although their cultural and linguistic relationships with society at large, captured in their texts, bring them into closer and closer contact with the realities of *women* in America. The Chicanas' literary selves, as seen both in poetry and prose works, are portrayed out of an experience of cultural otherness; but the terms in which such an experience is couched refer quite often to the female condition.[47]

Again, in the words of a prominent critic of minority discourse: "Minority literature is not just jettisoned against the dominant canon, but is also *immersed in those linguistic forms customarily thought to be outside the possibilities of creativity.*"[48] In this sense, Chicana writers are doing not only the seemingly unprecedented but also the impossible.

The "otherness" of the cultural objects examined here is defined by the hybridity of the subjects. Their bilingualism and biculturalism become textual determiners of how to read these different products of culture, which within their minority group have come to be the "other's others."

Notes

1. Literally, "the race." A term used by Chicano movement activists and supporters to signify all members of their ethnic minority group.

2. Marina Rivera, *Mestiza* (Tucson: Grilled Flowers Press, 1977).

3. Illustrations can be found, for example, in the Palestinian literature written in Jordan or even within the borders of Israel, or the bilingual/bicultural literature of Native Americans in both North and South America (Navajo, Quechua).

4. Another interesting symbolic insight into the issue of ethnic invisibility is given by the Chicana writer Sylvia Lizárraga, in her short story "¿Don?" *Maize* 1, no. 2 (1977): 20–22.

5. Lynn Sukenick, "On Women and Fiction," in *The Authority of Experience: Essays in Feminist Criticism,* ed. Arlyn Diamond and Lee Edwards (Amherst: University of Massachusetts Press, 1977), 28–29.

6. Anthropologist Margarita Melville has referred to Chicana identity as determined by a condition of double oppression; see her *Twice A Minority: Mexican American Women* (St. Louis: C. V. Mosby, 1980). Other critics insist on the class factor as a determinant in the cultural identification of women of color; Cordelia Candelaria labels this the "triple jeopardy" experienced by Chicanas in her book *Chicano Poetry: A Critical Introduction* (Westport, Conn.: Greenwood Press, 1986), 172 n. 22.

7. For a typology of this process, see Sharon S. Mayes, "Sociology, Women, and Fiction," *International Journal of Women's Studies* 2, no. 3 (May–June 1979): 203–20. For a historical and cultural study of the same process in a classic woman writer, see Madelyn Gutwirth, *Madame de Staël, Novelist: The Emergence of the Artist as Woman* (Urbana: University of Illinois Press, 1978). The subject is well covered by Cheri Register in her important review essay "Feminist Criticism," *Signs* 6, no. 2 (1980): 268–82, which also suggests the application of fruitful feminist models to "women who are doubly colonized" (279).

8. For a simplified, accessible compilation of the Chicano Movement actions between 1965 and 1969, the manifestos and their cultural and political repercusions, see Luis Valdez and Stan Steiner, "La Causa: In the Beginning," and "La Causa: The Chicanos," in *Aztlan: An Anthology of Mexican American Literature* (New York: Alfred A. Knopf, 1972), 197–224 and 283–323, respectively.

9. Michael Sedano, "Toward a Rhetoric of Chicano Poetry: Publication and Linguistic Strategies," *Papeles de la Frontera*, 1 (1978): 4–5.

10. For a reproduction of these texts in their entirety, see Tey Diana Rebolledo and Eliana S. Rivero, eds., *Infinite Divisions: An Anthology of Chicana Literature* (Tucson: University of Arizona Press, 1993), 83–84, 213–15. Calvillo Schmidt's name is changed now to Calvillo-Craig.

256 ELIANA S. RIVERO

11. "Yo soy Chicana
de las montañas de Nuevo Mejico.
My skin is dark. My hair is black.
My nipples are dark brown. . . .
My people have been harvesters of cotton,
of chili, of corn.
We, native to the Southwest, were long ago overtaken
by a people whose military strength overpowered ours.
Today I speak their languages, both English and Spanish,
but still I am neither, nor do I want to be. . . .
I am Chicana"

Although compiled in Moreno's *La Mujer es la tierra* (1975), it had been first published in *Los Poetas del barrio de la misión* (San Francisco: Casa Editorial, 1973). This is a text best remembered for its historical rather than for its aesthetic value, but still it carries echoes of the epic *I Am Joaquín.*

12. See Juan Bruce-Novoa, "Canonical and Non-canonical Texts," in his *Retrospace: Collected Essays on Chicano Literature* (Houston: Arte Público Press, 1990), 132–45.

13. Hélène Cixous, "The Laugh of the Medusa," trans. Keith Cohen and Paula Cohen, *Signs* 1, no. 4 (1976): 87. A good discussion of this important point can be found in Nelly Furman, "The Study of Women and Language: Comment on vol. 3, no. 3," *Signs* 4, no. 1 (1978): 184ff.

14. Tillie Olsen, *Silences* (New York: Delacorte Press/Seymour Lawrence, 1978), 239–40.

15. Annette Kolodny, in her now classic article "Dancing through the Minefield: Some Observations on the Theory, Practice and Politics of a Feminist Literary Criticism," *Feminist Studies* 6, no. 1 (spring 1980): 1–25, offers some very pertinent observations on the subject and indicates the appropriateness of applying the same criteria to the work of Black and Third World women critics of literature.

16. See Josaphat Kubayanda, "Minority Discourse and the African Collective: Some Examples from Latin American and Caribbean Literature," *Cultural Critique* 6 (spring 1987): 117.

17. Dorothy Richardson, *Pilgrimage* (London: J. M. Dent, 1967), 2:210.

18. Robin Lakoff, *Language and Woman's Place* (New York: Harper and Row, 1975), 7.

19. Of the several important critical studies on bilingualism in Chicano and Hispanic literature in the United States, see especially Guadalupe Valdés, "The Socio-linguistics of Chicano Literature: Towards an Analysis of the Role and Function of Language Alternation in Contemporary Bilingual Poetry," *Point of Contact/Punto de Contacto* 1, no. 4 (1977): 30–39; Gary Keller, "The Literary Stratagems Available to the Bilingual Chicano Writer," in *The Identification and Analysis of Chicano Literature*, ed. Francisco Jiménez (Binghamton, New York: Bilingual Press, 1979), 263–316; and John Lipsky, "Spanish-English Language Switching in Speech and Literature: Theories and Models," *The Bilingual Review* 9, no. 3 (September–December 1982): 191–212. Most literary studies on the subject, however, deal with Chicano male discourse, with

exceptions such as Marta Sanchez' brief approaches to language alternation in Chicana poets, as seen in her *Contemporary Chicana Poetry* (Berkeley: University of California Press, 1985). Useful to our study is also Guadalupe Valdés, "Code-Switching among Bilingual Mexican American Women: Towards an Understanding of Sex-Related Language Alternation," *International Journal of the Sociology of Language*, 17 (1978): 65–72.

20. The directness of speech in the first person is even related to a sacred code of biblical epiphany; in the Judeo-Christian tradition, the divinity chooses to reveal itself (himself or herself have a very narrow meaning in this context, hence my use of the neuter pronoun) with the most simple of verbal conjugations—the all inclusive *belam*. The act of self-naming, on the other hand, has traditionally corresponded to the Western "Adamic" function, which lyric poets, from the psalmists to Walt Whitman—and indeed Corky Gonzales—have utilized in the context of declarative affirmation.

21. "In the Tenth Commandment, the male is instructed not to covet his neighbor's house or his wife or his ox or his ass. . . ."; both quotations from Rachel Conrad Wahlberg, *Jesus According to a Woman*, 2nd ed., rev. (New York: Paulist Press, 1986), 61.

22. In *Siete Poetas*, ed. Margarita Cota Cárdenas and Eliana Rivero (Tucson: Scorpion Press, 1978), 1. The word *alone* is really not an accurate rendering because of its lack of grammatical feminine ending in English. It also corresponds, in Spanish, to the first two syllables of *only* (*sola/solamente*), as well as to *lonely*. Hence, the poet's play with meaning—"I am only woman [wife] of [female] alone/only/lonely"—is basically untranslatable.

23. See Julia Stanley and Susan W. Robbins, "Toward A Feminist Aesthetic," *Chrysalis* 6 (1977): 63.

24. Cf. the research conducted by Susan Harding on the language of women in Hispanic and French cultures; partial results are published in her article "Women and Words in a Spanish Village," in *Towards an Anthropology of Women*, ed. Rayna A. Reiter (New York: Monthly Review Press, 1975), 283–308.

25. This is my own version of the original Spanish, as translated in Rebolledo and Rivero, *Infinite Divisions*, 83.

26. Many times the resulting nickname converts *s* sounds into *ch*: Ten*ch*a from Hortensia, Chu*ch*o or *Ch*uy for Jesús, Len*ch*a from Lorenza (the Latin American pronunciation of the intervocalic *z* is just like that of an *s*).

27. See Wendy Redlinger, "Mothers' Speech to Children in Bilingual Mexican American Homes," *International Journal of the Sociology of Language*, 17 (1978): 80.

28. The expression *mija* (sometimes spelled as a true contraction, *m'ija*) is even converted into a verb to point out its precise connotation of paternalism. The female speaker in a poem by Lorna Dee Cervantes tells a man whom she addresses: "You 'mija' / 'mija' 'mija' me / until I can scream" ("You Cramp My Style, Baby," *El Fuego de Aztlán*, 1, no. 4 [summer 1977]: 39).

29. For a revealing summary of classical (male) ideas on women's speech, see Jean Bethke Elshtain, "Feminist discourse and Its Discontents: Language, Power, and Meaning," *Signs*, 7, no. 3 (1982): 603–21.

30. Published originally in "Chicanas en la literatura y en el arte," special issue of *El Grito* 7, no. 1 (September 1973): 61, 76.

31. For the best known of the "official" interpretations of the Malinche myth, and the most widely used perpetuation of this infamy in Mexican and Latin American lore, see Octavio Paz, "The Sons of La Malinche," in his *The Labyrinth of Solitude*, trans. Lysander Kemp (New York: Grove Press, 1961), 65–88.

32. T. R. Fehrenbach, *Fire and Blood: A History of Mexico* (New York: Macmillan, 1973), 131, as cited in Cordelia Candelaria, "La Malinche, Feminist Prototype," *Frontiers* 5, no. 2 (summer 1980): 1.

33. The taboo word is *chingada*, roughly translated by the English "screwed." A whole host of euphemisms ending in *-ada* (*-ed*) can be substituted for it in popular speech: *tiznada* (sooty), *fregada* (bothered, disturbed), all referring indirectly to the image of Marina, raped Indian mother of the Mexican nation, ravaged by the Spaniards. The word *malinchista* refers to one who associates with foreigners, or "sells out" to them.

34. See Adelaida R. del Castillo, "Malintzin Tenépal: A Preliminary Look into a New Perspective," in *Essays on La Mujer*, ed. Rosaura Sanchez and Rosa Martinez Cruz (Los Angeles: Chicano Studies Center, University of California, 1977), 124–29.

35. Gary Keller has pointed out the significance of alliteration as a rhetorical device used by code-switching poets; see "Literary Stratagems," 307.

36. This phenomenon, which the linguists call "code switching," has been studied for its importance in the Hispanic literatures of the United States; see Gary D. Keller, "Toward a Stylistic Analysis of Bilingual Texts: From Ernest Hemingway to Contemporary Boricua and Chicano Literature," in *The Analysis of Hispanic Texts: Current Trends in Methodology*, ed. Mary Beck et al. (New York: Bilingual Press, 1976), 130–49. In the specific instance of Chicano literature, Juan Bruce-Novoa refers to it as "interlingualism," explaining that in the speech of Chicanos linguistic codes of English and Spanish are, "not separate, but intrinsically fused"; see his Introduction to *Chicano Authors: Inquiry by Interview* (Austin: University of Texas Press, 1980), 29. In this context, Bruce-Novoa disagrees with the concept of bilingualism as it had been explained previously by Tino Villanueva: a "bisensitivity" that comes from the feeling of experiencing something "from two points of reference" (see Villanueva, "Apuntes sobre la poesía chicana," *Papeles de Sons Armadans* 271–73 [October–December 1978]: 51).

37. Although the term *Caló* originally referred to the language of Spanish gypsies, today it is used to indicate a particular variety of Chicano slang that had its origins in the Pachuco speech of the 1940s. The ethnically rebellious groups known as "Zoot Suiters," who became the target of racial xenophobia during World War II, popularized this highly colloquial form of "street" language, which survives in popular culture and in art. For an in-depth study of the pachuco, see Arturo Madrid, "In Search of the Authentic Pachuco: An Interpretive Essay," *Aztlán*, 4, no. 1 (spring 1973): 31–62; for research on the dialect, consult George C. Baker, *Pachuco: An American-Spanish Argot* (Tucson: University of Arizona Press, 1950). Although some critics confuse Caló with Chicano Spanish, the former is more reduced in scope and used less by women speakers.

38. In language choices for the bilingual, one of the variables at work in code switching "is the degree of emotional involvement" (see Redlinger, "Mothers' Speech," 81).

39. See Frances R. Aparicio, "Nombres, apellidos y lenguas: la disyuntiva ontológica del poeta hispano en los Estados Unidos," *The Bilingual Review* 13, no. 3 (September–December 1986), 47–58. My translation. Gary Keller has argued, however, that literary code-switching does not necessarily follow bilingual alternation patterns of ordinary language and that code-switching that reflects communal speech norms but does not create "powerful bilingual images" is not aesthetically valuable ("Literary Stratagems," 268–69). Carmen Salazar, on the other hand, affirms that code switching in the literary text works best when it follows the patterns of ordinary language, not when it is contrived as part of a literary (supposedly different) discourse: "in some authors, it simply does not 'sound right' because they do not know the bilingual/interlingual code well, but it flows naturally for some other authors because they really know how to use the language, as, for example, José Montoya" ("Introducing Chicano Authors in a Spanish Language Program" [paper presented at the "Symposium on the Teaching of Hispanic Literatures," Northeast Conference on the Teaching of Foreign Languages, New York, April 1987]).

40. *Grifa* is a common word for marijuana, chosen here to represent its user; *peleonera*, from the Spanish *pelear*, "to fight," should actually have the masculine ending *-o*, i.e., a man who likes a good fight or brawl; but it is apparently used in its feminine form for phonetic and morphological reasons (it looks and sounds better than *peleonero* alongside *grifa*).

41. In speaking about these significant cultural items in bilingual poetry, Efraín Barradas refers to them as "Proustian objects"; that is, "supporting points" that enable the poet to "reconstruct an individual or collective personality." See Efraín Barradas and Rafael Rodríguez, *Herejes y mitificadores: muestra de poesía puertorriqueña en los Estados Unidos* (San Juan: Ediciones Huracán, 1980), 23. My translation.

42. The concepts and terminology for much of this discussion ("intrasentential" code-switching as typical of a compound bilingual, and "intersentential" code-switching as denotative of a coordinate bilingual) are taken from John Lipsky, "Spanish-English Language Switching in Speech and Literature: Theories and Models" (see note 19, above).

43. Sometimes—both in ordinary language and in literary texts—the preceding word (article/preposition) belongs to the main discursive code of the utterance, or base language: "to the barrio," "for the barrio." An excellent, comprehensive study of these characteristics of Chicano Spanish can be found in Rosaura Sánchez, *Chicano Discourse: Socio-Historic Perspectives* (Rowley, Mass.: Newbury House, 1983), especially the chapter "Code-switching Discourse," 139–76.

44. Chicanos have "renamed" most places in the Southwest and the West heavily populated by Mexican Americans (the original site of Aztlán) with terms that are used for in-group communication, and sometimes even for addresses: "Sanjo" (San Jose), "Califas" or "Califaztlán" (California), "San Anto" (San Antonio), "E.P.T." (El Paso, Texas), "Ariztlán" (Arizona).

45. See Rosaura Sánchez, *Chicano Discourse*, 128–29.

46. This is not, of course, the American eagle; but neither it is the Mexican *águila* of the flag, symbol of Aztec legends for the foundation of that pre-Hispanic empire. Rather, it is the red and black stylized logo of Cesar Chavez's United Farm Workers union (an Aztec thunderbird, according to some) very much present on California campuses during the late sixties and early seventies.

47. Marta Sánchez has dealt partially with this issue in "The Birthing of the Poetic 'I' in Alma Villanueva's *Mother, May I?*" in "The Search for a Female Identity," in her *Contemporary Chicana Poetry*, 24–28. She has also referred, in the same chapter, to the question of a specific audience for Chicana poetry, emphasizing the authors' intentionality in reaching an audience as superseding their development of a certain linguistic competence (20–22).

48. Kubayanda, "Minority Discourse and the African Collective," 118. My emphasis.

CHAPTER 14

Poetry

ABENA BUSIA

Migrations

for homi, because I changed his words—

We have lived that moment of the scattering of the people—
     Immigrant, Migrant, Emigrant, Exile,
     Where do the birds gather?
That in other nations, other lives, other places has become:

The gathering of last warriors on lost frontiers,
The gathering of lost refugees on lasting border-camps,
The gathering of the indentured on the side-walks of strange cities,
The gathering of émigrés on the margins of foreign cultures.

     Immigrate, Migrate, Emigrate, Exile,
     Where do the birds fly?

In the half-life, half-light of alien tongues,
In the uncanny fluency of the other's language,
We relive the past in rituals of revival,
Unravelling memories in slow time; gathering the present.

     Immigrant, Migrant, Emigrant, Exile,
     After the last sky, Where do the birds fly?*

---

*This last phrase is an echo of the line from Mahmoud Darwish's poem "The Earth Is Closing In On Us."

261

Petitions

And we have asked for courage Not
to belong, Not
to identify, Not
to regret.
Not to confine the spaces of our souls
        to the places of our first heart beat
Not to let withering umbilical cords
        keep us parched
making more barren
the strangeness of our foreign homes.

Achimota: *From The Story My Mother Taught Me*

There is a place between Accra and the Legon hills
where they built the famous school.
Everyone thinks of that
today
when the name Achimota
is heard.
Yet the new school takes the name
of the place
but does not reveal what that name means.
The name is A-chee-mo-ta.
It is a forest still, beside the school,
the roads, the railways, and the streetside markets.
But the forest came first,
and has always been there.
The trees still stand,
but they do not speak the history they have seen;
A-chee-mo-ta-no, not at all.
And only the name remains the reminder
of who we are, what we have been,
and what we have been through.

Sometimes it seems we are forgetting,
but so long as there are people alive who remember,

we will remember the meaning:
Here we came, fleeing
to a place of shelter,
escaping the chains and lash
we would not submit to,
and these trees hid us.
So, when travelling through
here, searching,
you do not call
by name
in this place.
A-chee-mo-ta;
you do not call,
by name,
out loud,
no, not here.

The "underground railroad" had its precursor,
long, long before, on this side of the world.
No one will tell you that today.
We too have been taught forgetting.
We are schooled in another language now
and names loose their meanings, except
as labels.

We are being taught forgetting.
But some remember still
Achimota, and its history
a forest, and its meaning—
the place, and its silence.

PART III

The De/Colonized Other/s

CHAPTER 15

Domesticating the Other:
European Colonial Fantasies
1770–1830

SUSANNE ZANTOP

Virgen del mundo, América inocente!
Tú, que el preciado seno
al cielo ostentas de abundancia lleno,
y de apacible juventud la frente . . .
  —Manuel José Quintana, *A la expedición española*, 1806

Love, the fatal enemy to repose and innocence, love like mine, the inhabitants
of these regions have never felt. The habit of desiring only what is permitted,
conducts them quietly along the narrow path which their laws prescribe. But
how cruel are those laws, to which youth, beauty, and love, are the sorrowful
victims! How just and generous would it be to set them free!
  —Marmontel, *Les Incas*, 1777

After denouncing, over and over again, the "countless unheard-of . . .
cruelties, the violence and sinfulness"[1] committed by the Spaniards
against God, the king of Spain and the innocent peoples in the New
World—in that order—Bartolomé de las Casas, the outraged Dominican friar, approvingly quotes a letter by another witness of atrocities,
the bishop of Santa Marta. Referring to the Spanish conquistadors and
first colonial administrators, the bishop had written to the king of
Spain: "I wish to say, great Caesar, that the means to remedy this land is
for Your Majesty to remove from power these rascally stepfathers and
to give the land a husband who will treat her with the reasonableness
she deserves. And this must be done rapidly, for otherwise, the way she
is being harassed and fatigued by these tyrants that have charge of her, I
hold it a certainty that very soon she will die."[2]

269

The bishop's emotional plea is remarkable for a variety of reasons. If read within the context of Las Casas's 1542 narrative, it lends further support to his project: to denounce the "devastation of the Indies" by ruthless conquerors; to affirm the humanity of the indigenous peoples, as opposed to their "bestiality"; to reject current theory that the "Indians" are "born slaves"; and to accept them into the family of Christians—not as servants, as his opponent Sepúlveda had suggested,[3] but as full-fledged members. If read against Las Casas's text, however, the passage stands out in all its strangeness. Rather than proposing to substitute the "padrastro," the stepfather, with a natural father—a simile suggested by Las Casas's insistence throughout his text on the natives' childlike innocence and docility[4]—the Bishop imagines a "husband," who will treat his wife reasonably and "as she deserves" [*que la tracte como es razón y ella merece*].

To envisage the relationship between colonizer and colonized in terms of matrimony, that is, in terms of an indissoluble sacrament or a legal contract, seems a bold step forward, if we consider, for example, Sepúlveda's equation, with which he attempted to define the inferiority of the Native Americans vis-à-vis the Spaniards in order to "prove" the latter's right to dominion. "The Spaniards rule with perfect right over those barbarians of the New World and adjacent islands," Sepúlveda stated in 1550, "since they are *as inferior* to the Spaniards in wisdom, intelligence, virtue and humanity, *as are children to adults and women to men* and since they differ from the latter as savage and cruel people differ from benevolent people, or as excessively violent people differ from restrained and moderate people, *or, I am inclined to say, as monkeys differ from humans.*"[5] Whereas Sepúlveda and the bishop coincide in their gendered perception of colonial relations, they diverge as to how they weigh the supposed femininity of the other. While Sepúlveda confirms the hierarchy between colonizer and colonized on the basis of their unsurmountable difference—the other, likened to children, women, and monkeys, is closer to beasts than to humans—the bishop seems to posit a hierarchical relationship on the basis of sameness: although feminine, the other is of the same species, man, and therefore able to engage in a relationship of reciprocity.

Upon closer scrutiny, however, the bishop's fantasy of colonial redemption through marriage reveals its own ideological investment. He does not really propose a matrimonial relationship between conqueror and conquered: the conqueror is to be wedded to *la tierra*, "the land." In fact, the Native Americans who suffered the assault and

ill-treatment of the conquistadors in the first place are both erased from
and subsumed by the bishop's evocation of an erotic union between
European man and American continent. As part of, and indistinguishable from, the land, the natives are not conceived of as humans; they
are identical with the "nature" the colonists are in the process of
transforming into "culture."

Thus, what at first glance seemed to be a critique of previous
approaches to colonialism, of the pillaging and brutal subjection of the
natives in the name of God, reveals its complicity with the colonial
project. What looked like the assimilation of the other into a partner-
ship between equals turns out to be the other's erasure. The shift from
stepfather to husband marks the shift from conquest to colony, and
from one form of justification of appropriation to another. Former
violence is redeemed by present care, yet the masters remain the same.

I have spent so much time on the bishop's quote—although my
paper supposedly focuses on eighteenth- and nineteenth-century
colonial fantasies—because this early vision of matrimonial bliss forms
the ur-narrative of much of later representations. It contains, in a
nutshell, the rudiments of both the gendered relationship between self
and other constitutive of colonial discourse and the colonial "romance"
so popular in subsequent centuries. What is more, the juxtaposition of
Las Casas's scathing indictment of the exploitation and destruction of
native peoples with the bishop's "concrete" but "empty" utopia of a
loving union literally reenacts the split between "habits of action" and
"habits of the mind" (Kolodny), thus reenforcing the patterns of
displacement that make up the discourse of colonialism. In other words,
the fantasy of a legitimate, blissful bond contained in an account of
unheard-of violence both highlights and facilitates the repression of
actual rapes and massacres of native women and men and the ruthless
usurpation of their territories. As a means of repression of facts, and as
a model for successful, "humane" colonization, the matrimonial
metaphor thus points both backward and forward, connecting, like a
bridge, the writings of conquest in the fifteenth and sixteenth centuries
with the discourse of imperialism in the eighteenth and nineteenth
centuries.

Taking Possession

As Annette Kolodny has demonstrated in her landmark study *The Lay
of the Land* (1975), the tendency to conflate the land with woman is as

old as the Conquest itself, if not older.[6] Continents were given feminine names; their "discovery" was depicted in terms of male-female sexual encounters, for example in Stradanus's much-discussed depiction of Vespucci's discovery of America (1589), where the new continent, a naked woman, rests in a hammock opening her arms invitingly to the dressed European conqueror, who carries with him the instruments of knowledge and power, the astrolabe and the banner. From the very first accounts of discovery onward, conquerors and explorers saw their task in terms of "penetrating" virgin territory and taking possession, while colonists either praised the bounty of "Mother" nature, or placed their seeds in her fertile soils, hoping for rich returns. As Kolodny observes: "It is America's oldest and most cherished fantasy: a daily reality of harmony between man and nature based on an experience of the land as essentially feminine—that is, not simply the land as mother, but the land as woman, the total female principle of gratification—enclosing the individual in an environment of receptivity, repose, and painless and integral satisfaction" (4). And referring to the term *virgin* (territory), Peter Hulme asserts: "Probably no single word has had to bear so heavy a weight in the construction of American mythology from the moment when, in Samuel Eliot Morison's immortal words, 'the New World gracefully yielded her virginity to the conquering Castilians.'"[7]

Yet this eroticized image of the land as nurturing mother or alluring mistress is incomplete. That the New World did not yield her virginity as gracefully as Morison claimed[8] is addressed in allegorical representations of America, from Philippe Galle's late-sixteenth-century allegory to the famous Tiepolo frescoes in Würzburg in the mid-seventeen hundreds: the many bare-breasted Indian queens in feather headdresses, armed with spears, bows, and arrows and sitting on ferocious animals, surrounded by the vestiges of cannibalistic orgies also attest to the fears the exotic new continent inspired.[9] Indeed, visions of loving embrace and blissful ecstasy must be seen in juxtaposition to and in constant tension with nightmares, in which a savage, devouring, "phallic" femininity, in the form of impenetrable jungles, engulfing swamps, and orifices, threatens to annihilate the innocent European traveller. Where he hopes to find a nurturing mother or alluring mistress, he may well encounter cannibals, amazons, or other "monsters."[10]

Whether the land is allegorized as yielding virgin or as threatening amazon, whether it is represented as nurturing Nature or devouring Jungle, it is the dual femininity of the other that dominates the imagination of actual and would-be colonizers and induces fantasies of erotic attraction and subjection, of yielding and resistance, surrender and mastery. The pervasiveness of this erotic fantasy of conquest extends even to the realm of philosophy. In order to prove the natural inferiority of the Amerindians once and for all, the influential eighteenth-century *philosophe* Cornelius de Pauw, for example, developed a theory of degeneracy according to which pre-Columbian men had become so weak and effeminate that their frustrated wives felt the urge to surrender en masse to the more potent Spanish conquistadors, thereby opening the land to foreign invasion and control.[11] "Be it as it may," de Pauw concluded after weighing all the "evidence,"

> all narratives agree that the Indian women were exceedingly pleased at the arrival of the Europeans who—because of their sexual prowess, compared to that of the natives—resembled satyrs. If this strange paradox were not proven by a multiplicity of facts, one would not believe that they would have been able to surrender themselves willingly to the barbaric companions of the Pizarros and the Cortezes, who but marched over dead bodies . . . and whose hands were dripping with blood. Despite all the good reasons they had to hate those cruel people, the three hundred wives of the Inca Atabaliba [Atahualpa] who were taken prisoner with him at the battle of Caxamalca [Cajamarca], threw themselves at the feet of the victor, and the morning thereafter more than five thousand American women came to the Spaniards' camp and surrendered voluntarily, while the unfortunate remains of their vanquished nation escaped more than 40 miles into the woods and deserts. (1:69–70)

De Pauw's "philosophical investigations" into this titillating subject matter are only one in many instances—but one of the more perfidious and obvious ones—of theory in the service of colonial practice. It is not surprising that backed by philosophically proven "facts," fictions would turn the story of voluntary surrender of the women to the conqueror and the "disappearance" of their emasculated men into the central plot elements of the "colonial romance" that came to dominate representations of colonial relations in the eighteenth century. It is to these colonial romances and their function in a period of decolonization that I will now turn my attention.

One Happy Family

As Peter Hulme has pointed out, violent colonial encounters were represented as love stories from the seventeenth century onward—and well into the nineteenth century, I might add. The difference between earlier and later romances lies in their resolution: the early romances tend to have tragic, the later ones happy, endings. Thus, the early colonial master-plot, familiar to us through the stories of John Smith and Pocahontas or Inkle and Yariko, is a tale of "shipwreck, hospitality, and ingratitude" (246) or, from the perspective of the American protagonists, rescue, love, and betrayal: the European colonizer, cast by a tempest against foreign shores, is saved and sustained by a native woman, who becomes his natural wife. He abandons her and (in the case of Inkle and Yarico) their child—even sells her into slavery—as soon as he has an opportunity to return to Europe and his former trading occupation.[12] The innumerable revisions and productions of this master narrative throughout the seventeenth and eighteenth centuries, in a variety of genres, attest to the narrative's central significance within the colonialist imagination.

In all versions of this colonial romance the European is cast as male, the native as female; in each case, the American, an "Indian princess," falls in love with the "superior" European and relinquishes her "savage ways" in order to live with and serve him. In all instances, however, the European is unwilling to settle down and fulfill his new responsibility; instead, he abandons her and the child she has borne him.

The ideological implications of this story are obvious. It not only rewrites the violent dispossession of the natives as the woman's voluntary surrender, thereby making it palatable to European readers, but, as in the bishop's or de Pauw's passages quoted above, the Euro-American couple assumes center stage, completely displacing the native man, not to mention the European woman, who is absent from the scene to begin with. In the moral outrage over the European's inability to reciprocate love and form a permanent bond that informs these early texts, one might detect the first stirrings of colonial guilt.[13] In light of subsequent colonial love fantasies, however, one might also interpret these earlier versions as articulations of a desire to move from conquest and pillaging or trading to permanent colonial settlement and long-term economic exploitation. In any case, the initial infraction, the "destruction of the Indies," that is, the violent appropriation of territory and subjugation of its population, is repressed, recast, substituted by a new infraction: the lack of commitment to the conquered territory.

This desire for a long-term commitment on foreign soil is apparent in a colonial romance Hulme mentions only in passing because it is outside his Caribbean focus, a romance that becomes the master narrative for the latter half of the eighteenth century: the love story of Cora and Alonzo at the center of Marmontel's sentimental novel *Les Incas; ou, La Destruction de l'Empire du Pérou* (1777).[14] This popular, widely imitated tale marks the beginning of a new phase in colonialist discourse and colonial activity. Not only does Marmontel allude in his title to Las Casas's treatise on the destruction of the Indies and to a tradition of moral outrage over Spanish atrocities, but his tale is a literal elaboration on the bishop's matrimonial metaphor contained in Las Casas's text.

In Marmontel's sentimental rewriting of the conquest, the two familial models for the conqueror-conquered relationship that I briefly mentioned in my introduction—the Lascasian educational paternalism of the father-child model and the erotic patriarchalism of the conjugal model—make their concerted reappearance: Alonzo Molina, a "good conquistador," educated in Las Casas's humanitarian tradition, goes to Peru to help the natives prepare against the Spanish onslaught and to educate the Incas in modern warfare and Christian thought. He falls in love with Cora, a "virgin of the Sun," and seduces her when a natural event, an earthquake, breaks down the walls of the temple in which Cora is kept. When Cora's pregnancy is discovered and the trial begins—according to Inca law any infraction of the vow of chastity is punished with the death of all her family members—Alonzo comes forward, and, admitting his responsibility, makes an eloquent and convincing plea for a new order, in which "natural" feelings and Christian forgiving, not revenge, reign supreme. Alonzo and Cora's subsequent marriage would be blissful and everlasting, were it not for Pizarro and his lot, the murderous, greedy "stepfathers" who conquer by force. Alonzo perishes on the battlefield, while Cora dies of grief on his grave, together with her newborn child.

The story shares with previous colonial romances the myth of the women's natural surrender, as well as the subsequent displacement of native men. For example, earlier in the novel, after another conveniently placed earthquake, Alonzo is rescued from the wrath of a "tribe of man-eaters" by their women, who, recognizing his natural superiority, "devour him with their eyes" (192):

His auburn locks waving in long ringlets over the ivory of his captive shoulders, served as a foil to their enchanting white; and his shape, in which all the charms of elegance, grace, and majesty, were combined, completed every thing that was wanting to make a perfect model. In the court of Spain, in the midst of the most brilliant train of youth, Molina would have outshone all competitors. How much more rare and striking among those savages must have been the spectacle of such beauty? (191)

The European male is the object of the eroticized gaze of the native women, who, rising above their savage men, establish the new bond between European and American. Not only the cannibal "mothers" but also Cora, the "Virgin" of the Sun, fall for this natural conqueror of hearts, as her first thoughts upon setting eyes on him reveal:

Happy would she have been had her timid eyes been never raised on Alonzo! One glance destroyed her; this imprudent glance presented to her view the most formidable enemy to her repose and her innocence. If he, by his grace and beauty had melted the hearts even of cannibals when thirsting for his blood, what must have been their influence on the breast of a virgin, simple, tender, ingenuous, and made for love! This sentiment, the germ of which nature had planted in her bosom, disclosed itself at once. (2:6)

This encounter marks the moment, however, when Marmontel's romance departs from previous models: Alonzo does not abandon, but stands by his woman and, once her "condition" is known, even accepts to exchange vows, "until death." Despite the parallels to previous fantasies, Marmontel's colonial love story thus pushes the narrative of colonial desire one step further: not only does "nature"—natural passions and natural catastrophes—rather than convention (e.g., hospitality) cooperate in, or even cause, the subjection of the woman/land to the virtuous conqueror, thereby introducing an element of colonial determinism or "natural law"; but the conqueror accepts his charge, decides to stay, be fertile and multiply, thus atoning for his past "guilt." While the story of rape is, again, rewritten as one of "natural surrender," *any* past infraction or vestiges of guilt are once and for all expiated through the vows of marriage. By marrying Cora, Alonzo gives their union ex post facto legitimacy, divine sanction—and permanence.

This integration of conqueror and conquered into a new, permanent colonial order is underscored by Las Casas's role in the romance. The ailing Las Casas, venerated teacher and father figure throughout, becomes the child of the New World, when, in a much depicted scene, he is revitalized by mother's milk, offered to him from the breasts of Enriquillo's wife (Enriquillo was the *cacique* whose successful, albeit shortlived, rebellion against the Spaniards Las Casas had described in his *Historia de las Indias*).[15] It is the body of the native virgin, in the case of Alonzo, and the body of the native mother, in the case of Las Casas, that become the vehicles for redemption and that provide "good" foreign conquerors with legitimate access to the New Continent. Voluntary surrender to the stronger, the better, the good European, and voluntary acceptance of the responsibility for the new continent's welfare combine in creating the new, mixed Colonial Family.

The degree to which the matrimonial fantasy takes over and displaces stories of unrequited love and abandonment becomes even more pronounced in subsequent adaptations of Marmontel's and other romances. It is a curious phenomenon, for example, that from the mid-1700s onward, writers in France, England, and Germany try to revise the tragic ending of the traditional Inkle-Yarico narrative to allow for a final reconciliation, with the result that, from 1780 onward, practically all Inkle-Yariko plays have happy endings.[16] In one particularly popular French version, Yariko is released from slavery, Inkle repents, and together, they rule over a Caribbean Island.[17] Likewise, the tragic ending of the Cora-Alonzo story turns to comedy in all subsequent adaptations, culminating in August von Kotzebue's much performed play *The Virgin of the Sun* (1789). Kotzebue literally reenacts the exclusion of the native male in the play's 1795 sequel when he introduces, and then kills off, Alonzo's only rival, the native warrior Rolla, who had loved Cora since childhood (*The Spaniards in Peru; or, Rolla's Death*, 1795). Rolla must die so that the Euro-American family, Alonzo, Cora and their child, can live happily ever after—until the final breakdown of the traditional colonial system in the 1820s. In fact, as European imperialism enters a new stage, a new master narrative appears on the scene: one that does not advocate commitment, restraint, and legality but allows for the uninhibited release of pent-up colonial desire.

Marriage and Otherness

This leads me to my final questions, for which I try to present some tentative answers: Why did the matrimonial metaphor come to dominate colonial representations in the late 1700s? What were or are its implications for the relationship between Europe and its American others? And why was "matrimony" displaced by other metaphors in nineteenth-century literature?

It has been suggested that the drive toward conciliatory romances followed a typical sentimentalist impulse that affected much of late-eighteenth-century popular literature: as avid consumers of plays or trivial literature, the public, it was argued, craved happy endings. While there may be some truth to the argument (although I don't like its implicit elitism), it does not account for the timing, that is, the resurfacing of the matrimonial metaphor in late eighteenth-century colonial discourse and its abandonment in the nineteenth century. Nor does this explanation help us to assess the meaning of the metaphor within its historical context. In order to understand the popularity of colonial romances with happy endings, we should look at what needs these symbolic representations fulfilled within the sociopsychological structures of European nations. As Helen Callaway has convincingly argued, "imperial culture exercised its power not so much through physical coercion, which was relatively minimal though always a threat, but through its cognitive dimension; its comprehensive symbolic order which constituted permissible thinking and action and prevented other worlds from emerging" (57).

As I have indicated before, as "fantasies of natural conquest" or "fantasies of legitimacy," the Cora-Alonzo stories suggest a new indissoluble colonial order: one based on the recognition of natural superiority and on voluntary submission, on care and imperceptible rule, in one word: on mutual love. The attractiveness of this "foundational fiction" of European colonialism, to borrow Doris Sommer's phrase, is obvious.[18] Alonzo, the virtuous conqueror who, in contrast to eighteenth-century Spaniards, has not rejected Las Casas but learned from him, can become the object of identification, the model colonist, for any European nation in search of a "place in the sun." The indictment of Spain and the idea of a "conquest by virtue" (157) propagated by Marmontel's text would appeal to those bent on not repeating the mistakes of the past, those, in Marmontel's words, who want to "conquer without oppression" (150) and to rule benignly. Thus Herder can dream in 1784 of a time when, in his words, the European "genius" will espouse "the generative power of this young bride," America, and create "from her womb beautiful offspring"[19] under better, more humane colonial conditions.

The emergence of a fantasy of virtuous conquest and colony as a sacred, indissoluble bond, in which the conqueror abandons his mother country to stay with his new bride is, I would argue, intimately linked to two historical developments. On the one hand, to the revolution and subsequent independence of the British colonies in North America and, on the other, to the threat of dissolution of the Spanish colonial empire in South America and the gradual opening up of hitherto closed areas to other imperial contenders. Although they take place in different countries, Marmontel's romance, as well as the numerous rewritings of the Inkle-Yariko plot provide a model for the successful maintenance of European hegemony, a "happy revolution" with a happy ending: as settler, cultivator and "husband," the foreign intruder affirms his rights over the land, even as he breaks away from the mother country. As Egon Menz has proposed, the victory of the North American colonists over the British was seen by Europeans as an entitlement of the former to the land: by avenging the natives against the conquerors, the victorious colonists assumed their place; they became their heirs, their grandchildren.[20] From now on the colonists were the "Americans," whereas the original Americans become "Indians," a race doomed to go under. Clearly, this process from intruder to lawful owner of the "land," from "rapist" to loving "husband," is the sustaining myth in all of the romances discussed.

In addition to providing a legitimate release for colonial desire, the matrimonial fantasy suggests the possibility of permanent colonial control at a time when insubordination and revolts have become an ever-present threat to European rule. In contrast, for example, to the educational father-child model, according to which the child would eventually be released into independence by a natural transfer of power, matrimony implies permanent inequality and bondage. The promise of "eternal love" stabilizes and veils the actual power relationship among the conjugal partners: as we all know, matrimony in the eighteenth century was a contract whereby the protection of the woman by the man was bought at the expense of her permanent subjection to his tutelage. Although the conjugal model may appear to us today more "enlightened"—after all, Alonzo crosses national and racial (albeit not class) boundaries when he marries his native concubine—let us not be deceived: while this marriage channels sexual drives into legitimate forms, the genealogical and the generative claims remain firmly in European hands (or other body parts). Nor does the model provide for any resistance to this heterosexual libidinal determinism. Cora clearly

recognizes Alonzo's "invincible attraction," his unquestioned superiority and rights to her over any native competitors (= Rolla).

The colonial romance, then, constructs a controlled three-step
process of colonial takeover: first, as bride, the "other" is familiarized;
she becomes part of the same species; second, as wife, the other is
assimilated into the family and subjected to patriarchal control; and
third, as "land," the other becomes depopulated, de-humanized, an
empty space that yearns to be filled, a blank spot on the map that
demands inscription by its new occupant and master. Whatever was
"savage" or "monstruous," resisting domination is thus tamed, domesticated, integrated. The native woman, in a reversal of Sigrid Weigel's
formulation, becomes the "territory of the familiar far away," that is,
foreign territory turned "home" through ownership and cultivation.
"Otherness" ceases to exist; as it becomes the space for the projection
of the self, differences are absorbed into a monocultural paradigm—
they cease to exist.

The wish-fulfilling, fear-exorcizing quality of this familial fantasy of
permanent mastery at a time of colonial dissolution is obvious. For a
relatively brief time in history, the years 1750 to about 1820, the
matrimonial metaphor could capture the imagination of European
would-be conquerors and colonists. With the independence of the
colonies from Spanish rule and their opening up to commerce with
other European nations, however, this conciliatory master narrative that
veiled its own aggressiveness became obsolete. As imperial powers
began to compete openly for supposedly unclaimed "virgin territories,"
atavistic rape fantasies reappeared in public discourse. Thus Heinrich
von Treitschke, one of the most outspoken advocates of unrestrained
imperialism, could write: "When once the trained resources of labour
and capital of a civilized nation are poured forth upon the virgin soil of
a savage country and there (are) allied with Nature, the three great
forces of production co-operate so effectively that colonies progress
with incredible rapidity."[21] And he asserts: "All great nations in the
fulness of their strength have desired to set their mark upon barbarian
lands. All over the globe to-day we see the peoples of Europe creating a
mighty aristocracy of the white races. Those who take no share in this
great rivalry will play a pitiable part in time to come. The colonizing
impulse has become a vital question for a great nation" (115–16).
Treitschke's vision of imperial expansion, although it echoes former
familial models, no longer disguises the brutality of the conquest and
the material interests at play. Dehumanized generative forces, labor and

capital, sown into virgin soil, produce the "child," the new colony. Although this child is supposedly bound to its "mother country" by indissoluble blood ties, Treitschke does not trust these "natural" familial relations, or the familial metaphor, for that matter. In fact, in order to prevent coming of age and separation, Treitschke suggests the child's complete absorption into the maternal body, or, in his words, his "absorption into the conquering race" (121).

Clearly, by the late nineteenth century, the "irresistible romance" between European colonizer and foreign territories is over. Instead, we find the European nations, backed by the "natural right" of the stronger, involved in or advocating outright acts of cannibalism. The matrimonial fantasy of a reconciliation between self and other, meanwhile, in another curious transfer or reversal, has moved to South America, where it serves as foundational myth for the new nation states and their internal colonial projects.

Notes

1. "Las maldades, matanzas, despoblaciones, injusticias, violencias, estragos y grandes pecados que los españoles en estos reinos de Sancta Marta han hecho e cometido contra Dios, e contra el rey, e aquellas innocentes naciones." "Brevíssima relación de la destruición de las Indias," in, *Tratados de Fray Bartolomé de las Casas* (1542; México: Fondo de Cultura Económico, 1965), 1:118–19. The English translation is taken from Bartolomé de las Casas, *The Devastation of the Indies: A Brief Account*, trans. Herma Briffault (New York: Seabury Press, 1974), 99. Curiously, it distorts the meaning of the Spanish passage by leaving out "e aquellas innocentes naciones."

2. "Digo, sagrado César, que el medio para remediar esta tierra es que Vuestra Majestad la saque ya de poder de padrastros y le dé marido que la tracte como es razón y ella merece; y éste, con toda brevedad, porque de otra manera, según la aquejan e fatigan estos tiranos que tienen encargamiento della, tengo por cierto que muy aína dejará de ser" (119). Again, the translation leaves much to be desired: "que la tracte como es razón y ella merece" is, not "with the reasonableness she deserves," but "who treats her as it is reasonable, and as she deserves it" (see p. 99).

3. Juan Ginés de Sepúlveda, *Tratado sobre las justas causas de la guerra contra los indios*, 2nd ed. (1550; México: Fondo de Cultura Económica, 1941), 173.

4. Las Casas, *Devastation*, 38–39.

5. Sepúlveda, *Tratado*, 101. My translation; emphasis added.

6. Annette Kolodny, *The Lay of the Land: Metaphor as Experience and History in American Life and Letters* (Chapel Hill: University of North Carolina Press, 1975).

7. Peter Hulme, *Colonial Encounters: Europe and the Native Caribbean, 1492–1797* (London: Methuen, 1986), 158.

8. See one of the earliest accounts of rape in Michele Cuneo's Letter on the Second Voyage, October 28, 1495, in *Journals and Other Documents in the Life and Voyages of Christopher Columbus*, trans. and ed. S. E. Morison (New York: Heritage Press, 1963), 212.

9. See Hugh Honour, *The European Vision of America* (Cleveland: Cleveland Museum of Art, 1975), 85–95, or in his *The New Golden Land: European Images of America from the Discoveries to the Present Time* (London: Allen Lane, 1976), 84ff.

10. For a discussion of this dual image of femininity, as it translates to dual representations of explorations, see Sigrid Weigel, "Die nahe Fremde—das Territorium des 'Weiblichen': Zum Verhältnis von 'Wilden' und 'Frauen' im Diskurs der Aufklärung," in, *Die andere Welt. Studien zum Exotismus*, ed. Thomas Koebner and Gerhart Pickerodt (Frankfurt: Athenäum, 1987). The meaning of amazons and monsters in colonial discourse is discussed by Peter Mason, *Deconstructing America: Representations of the Other* (London: Routledge and Kegan Paul, 1990).

11. Cornelius de Pauw, *Recherches philosophiques sur les Américains*, 2 vols. (Berlin: Decker, 1768). See also my essay: "Dialectics and Colonialism: The Underside of the Enlightenment," in *Impure Reason*, ed. Robert Holub and C. Daniel Wilson (Detroit: Wayne State University Press, 1993), 301–21.

12. Jean Mocquet, *Voyages en Afrique, Asie, Indes Orientales et Occidentales, faits par Jean Mocquet, 1601–1614* (Paris: Gouvernement, 1830), 123–24: "elle prit son enfant, et le mettant en deux pièces, elle lui en jeta une moitié vers lui en la mer, comme voulant dire que c'étoit sa part, et l'autre elle l'emporta avec soi s'en retournant à la mercy de la fortune, et pleine de deuil et desconfort."
Hulme considers Mocquet the possible source for the later Inkle-Yariko story (256–57). For the popularity of the Inkle/Yariko plot, see Lawrence Marsden Price, *Inkle and Yarico Album* (Berkeley and Los Angeles: University of California Press, 1937), esp. 139–40.

13. See Hulme, who terms these stories "concessionary narratives" (253).

14. Jean François Marmontel, *Les Incas; ou, La Destruction de l'Empire du Pérou*, 2 vols. (Berne and Lausanne: Société typographique, 1777). I am quoting from *The Incas, or, The Destruction of the Empire of Peru* (Alston, Cumberland: John Harrop, 1808).

15. Marmontel, Incas, 153–57. "Approach, my wife, embrace my father; and let thy bosom compel his mouth to draw sustenance from it. . . . Adieu, my father, . . . I leave with you the partner of my soul; and I desire not to see her again till she shall have restored you to life and our love" (156).

16. See Price, *Inkle and Yarico Album*, 115. The most popular rewritings are Chamfort's comedy *La Jeune Indienne* (1764; see Price, *Inkle and Yariko Album*, 59); the opera *Inkle and Yarico*, by George Colman the Younger (1787); the anonymous French story *Inkle & Iarico, Histoire américaine* (1778); *L'Héroïne américaine* (1786); Salomon Gessner, *Inkel und Yariko, zweyter Theil* (1756) (Gessner cannot accept Inkle's heartlessness and proposes repentance: "So sehr kann die Güte kein Herz verlassen, daß nicht ein Rückfall der Tugend, kein Schauer der Reue, mächtig ihn fasse; daß nicht seine Fähigkeit gut zu seyn, durch das Unkraut der Leidenschaften, in seinem Busen mächtig hinaufbebe, so erzähl' ich denn Yarikons Rettung und Inkelns Reue" [Price, *Inkle and Yariko Album*, 87]); Friedrich Carl von Moser, *Ynkle und Yariko* (1762): Moser believes

in poetic justice: "Es schiene billig, daß es zwischen ihnen wieder ins gleiche käme und ihre Liebe von keinem geheimen Vorwurf mehr gestöret werde" [91].

17. This ending is proposed in the anonymous French story of 1778 mentioned above.

18. Doris Sommer, *Foundational Fictions: The National Romances of Latin America* (Berkeley and Los Angeles: University of California Press, 1991).

19. Johann Gottfried Herder, *Ideen zur Philosophie der Geschichte der Menschheit*, in *Sämtliche Werke*, ed. B. Suphan (Berlin: Weidmann, 1887), 13:289

20. Egon Menz, "Die Humanität des Handelsgeistes. Amerika in der deutschen Literatur des ausgehenden 18. Jahrhunderts," in, *Amerika in der deutschen Literatur: Neue Welt-Nordamerika-USA*, ed. Sigrid Bauschinger, Horst Denkler, and Wilfried Malsch (Stuttgart: Reclam, 1975), 58–9.

21. Heinrich von Treitschke, *Politics* (New York: Macmillan 1916), 1:113.

CHAPTER 16

Writing the Other's Language:
Modes of Linguistic Representation in German Colonial and Anti-Colonial Literature

KONSTANZE STREESE

Up to the respective periods of decolonization, the discourse on issues concerning South America, Africa, the Orient, and other "foreign parts" of the world was more or less a European monologue. From emperors and popes, chroniclers, philosophers, anthropologists, and poets to merchants, pirates, slavetraders, and mercenaries, an extended and multivociferous speech was compiled.[1] In spite of its political and cultural diversity conceptually centered in a notion of selfsameness, the Occident has amply spoken about the world as an acquirable margin. Thus, the abstract potential for a "dialogical path" in the practices of "treating, trading and conversing"[2] was desubstantiated by the very concrete disparity between the economic and military interests and means of the conquerors and those of the conquered, and limited to the monological path of one way communication. "As imperialists 'administer' the resources of the conquered country," Abdul JanMohamed writes, "the discursive practices do to the symbolic, linguistic presence of the native what the material practices do to his [and her, I might add] physical presence."[3] The respective purpose of each phase of the conquest then defines the choice of the means of political domination, and a speaker's position toward it informs the modes of representation of the colonized other and the narrative "administration" of his or her linguistic presence in the literary text.

Hence, also in German fiction, the representation of the other's language reflects the different phases of the European infatuation with or denigration of the other as they have arisen from the various stages of the economic and political utilization of the world by the colonial powers. During the eighteenth and nineteenth centuries, German principalities were still involved in territorial struggles, and their budgets and armed forces were fragmented to a degree that prevented them from joining the factual colonization of other continents. In the contributions to the aforesaid monologue by German authors of that period, we observe an almost complete absence of any attempt to represent cultural difference through linguistically differentiated codes. This holds true for poems, plays, and narratives by Gellert, Wieland, Claudius, and Herder, by Tieck, Seume, Lenau, Chamisso, and even for the respective works of the realist Keller. Most of these German-speaking authors defined themselves as critical observers of the practices of colonialism. Their position as citizens of states too poor or too small to partake in the acquisition of overseas territories allowed them to express—whatever patronizing forms that expression may have taken—sympathy with native revolts, admiration for the natural nobility that they ascribed to their savage, a yearning for beauty and sensuality, for familial and tribal loyalty and honor, and for all the bourgeois virtues reified in their image of the other and set in juxtaposition to the imperfect social practices in their own societies. This ideological appropriation then is represented in the linguistic assimilation of the other's fictional utterance into the poetic and linguistic levels of the literary text, and the imaginary other's voice is rarely discernible from that of his or her interlocutor.

Discursive strategies that denigrate the other linguistically were put into practice only at a time at which colonial novels were being published for decidedly ideological and often clearly propagandistic purposes. Notorious here are colonial authors like Frieda von Bülow, Hans Grimm, and their colleagues, whose writing is sometimes an occupation taken up as a remedial practice against the boredom generated by a privileged life in the colonies, sometimes the self-assuring reflection of the author's own colonialist experience, and always self-affirmation. The translation of Joachim Warmbold's study on German colonial literature, *Germania in Africa*,[4] has provided an English-speaking public with a symptomatic array of excerpts from these texts. As one early case in point Warmbold analyzes Heinrich Smidt's colonial narrative, *Berlin und Afrika: Ein Brandenburgischer Seeroman* from 1847. It is the first purely literary work resulting from a German colonial enterprise, the activities of the elector of Brandenburg on the Gold Coast in the beginning of the eighteenth century. At the same time, Smidt's narrative set the stage for numerous propagandistic colonial novels, poems, and plays that were to follow after 1871 with the founding of the "Alldeutsche Verein" and the anticipation and realization of

German acquisitions in Africa and in the Pacific, especially after 1884. Offering comments similar to those found in many later texts published around 1900 and to those composing the colonial reveries of the Third Reich, Smidt compares Africans to "children," their language to a "loud howling," "a singsong of inarticulate sounds."[5] The fact that such "singsong" carries the meaning of tradition, rebellion, love, and politics is ignored. A revealing episode in Jean Jacques Anneau's film *Black and White in Color* (1976), for example, comments on the syndrome of refused communication when in the opening scene the lyrics of the laboring Africans' songs are—in their dubbed version, for the spectator—recognizably satirical comments on the colonizer, while for the European masters in the film they remain inarticulate, primitive folklore and the implicit critique remains veiled. Such primitivization of the colonized is analyzed poignantly in Houston Baker's text on the strategies of linguistic mis-representation of the other in *Modernism and the Harlem Renaissance*:

> An "alien" sound gives birth to notions of the indigenous . . . as *deformed*.
>
> Two things, then, can be stated about the dynamics of deformation: first, the indigenous comprehend the territory within their own vale/veil more fully than any intruder . . . The vale/veil, one might assert, is for the indigenous *language* itself.
>
> Second, the indigenous sound appears monstrous and deformed only to the intruder. . . . In literature, the trope most frequently visited by the "alien" writers and their adversaries is the hooting deformed of Shakespeare's *Tempest* [Caliban].[6]

Accordingly, Smidt in his novel of 1847 is also not concerned with representing Africans as speaking subjects. Generally, they carry what Memmi calls the "mark of the plural."[7] Only with the slave Cunny does the author create a type whose definition allows a certain development with regard to his communicative competence. This is made possible by establishing Cunny as the epitome of the "good African" in colonial terms. Characterizing him as an overly obedient, even grateful slave, Smidt is able to ascribe to him the absence of values, knowledge, and skills that marks the paradigmatic void into which the "ennobling" influence of colonization can be written. Thus Smidt's novel can serve as a relatively early and blunt German example for Frantz Fanon's observation in *Les damnés de la terre* from 1961[8] that the topography of colonial discourse would not make sense without this imaginary void, nor would colonial economy.[9] Also the third volume of *Berlin und Afrika*, then, still insists via Cunny's stammering in the foreign tongue on his native status as essentially uncivilized. In constructing Cunny's fragmented speech as the code of incompetence—or, as Baker terms it, as "white Dada"—Smidt condemns the African, within the standards of the German speaking reader, to a second rate being, passive, awkward, defensive.[10] In the sixth and last volume, Cunny has finally risen to the humanness that was originally found lacking in him, and in his use of the colonizer's language he has become like his masters; the process of linguistic acculturation has been symbolically accomplished. Also in the later work of Lene Haase, *Meine schwarzen Brüder: Stories from the Jungle* (1916), and in Richard Küas's play *Götzen* (1907), the respective level of the African's competence in the foreign language denotes the degree of indolence ascribed to him and is meant to give indication of his "colonizability" at the same time. While such linguistic strategies of denigrating the other in order to appropriate his/her resources can be observed as common practice in colonialist literature throughout Europe, they seem to take on an especially significant and exclusionary function in the face of German history, where a national definition has often relied on the bonding faculties of a common language.

If we follow the colonialist frame of mind, however, not every African speaking the colonizer's language fluently can be trusted. The interchangeability of denigrating strategies within the "manichean aesthetics"[11] of the colonial paradigm renders suspicious especially those who speak the European language flawlessly but whose acquisition of such competence did not take place in the service of their present German master. They must be mistrusted as rebels and enemies, as in Julius Steinhardt's National Socialist novel *Wir reiten still, wir reiten stumm . . .* (1933). Whenever in colonial and fascist texts the rebellious colonized is presented as fluent in the European language, Baker's observation tends to hold true for him as well. Tearing the veil by which the colonizer's world is hidden from him, not only his own but also the colonizer's territory are accessible to his comprehension. The colonizer's arrogation, on the other hand, prevents him from mastering the difficulties of the native language, and behind its veil the "master" remains in the state of ignorance for which he then takes revenge by misrepresenting the alien culture and language and by subjugating it violently. It is obvious in such texts that a dialogue between the self and the other is not intended. Instead, the exchange takes place between the mutually alienated fantasies of the selfsame: on one side the self-aggrandizement of the colonizer within the idealized realms of the potential of his own civilization, and through its implied rigidities and exclusions on the other side the colonizer's ever increasing fears of an imploding superego, which is inscribed in the moral devalorization of the other and the primitivization of his or her language.

There is a rather significant lapse in the production of literary texts on the formerly colonized after 1945. The anti-colonial tendencies of writers like Alfred Döblin and Bruno Traven, Franz Jung, Jakob Wassermann, Reinhold Schneider, and others did not find followers after the war, when only hesitantly German authors began to write toward an understanding and acknowledgement of the sociological, political, and psychological conditions and implications of fascism. When Peter Weiss's play representing the history of the war in Vietnam was published in 1967, it contributed significantly to the political discourse of the Left that had already theoretically linked the critique of a fascist past to that of a neocolonial present. *Viet Nam Discourse* and *Song of the Lusitanian Bogey* then were, with other radio and theater plays by Schnabel, Hochhut, Enzensberger, literary expressions of a new and passionate turn toward the world beyond Europe in the declared intention of constructing solidarity among the struggles for liberation against capitalism—from Watts via Wuppertal to Maputo and Saigon. Both Weiss plays stage the dialectics of colonialism, imperialism, and neocolonialism as a dialogue of historical dimensions between the antagonistic collectives of the colonizer and the colonized as protagonists. Primarily in his *Viet Nam Discourse*, the voices of the colonized are not those of individual subjects. Conceptually located in the Marxist paradigm, "les damnés de la terre" are represented as politically unifiable classes and as such enabled to advance from being mere objects of the colonial history of oppression to becoming aware of their political subjectivity. Throughout the play they voice their changing condition in the elevated tone of their historical sufferings and their future liberation. In this the representation of their language is assimilated to the revolutionary didactics of the play. Conceptualized as an attack on the manichean economy of colonial ideology and politics, they reflect much of what Enzensberger has later criticized as the "pathos of Third Worldism," which he found characteristic of the European Left.

It is only in the seventies that the awareness of the colonial condition enters the literary writing in the Federal Republic as an awareness of the oppression or assimilation of the voices of the colonized in the text. Although the story remains helpless to propose a solution to this problem, Dieter Kühn's narrative *Festspiel für Rothäute* (1974) can be regarded as a cornerstone for the new insights. Using the historical visit of four representatives of the League of the Iroquois to London in 1710, the author ironically depicts the cultural, political, and mercantile practices of the English bourgeoisie of that time. While the Iroquois guests are subjected to a pretentiously and arrogantly conducted tour of several weeks that is supposed to impress them with the superiority of their British hosts, they themselves remain locked into absolute voicelessness. In marked contrast to previous texts, however, in *Festspiel für Rothäute* the absence of the language of the other is recognizably constructed as a linguistic void resulting from the self-inflicted European incapacity to hear the colonized. Silenced, the Iroquois are reduced to a military bulwark, to objects of popular curiosity and condescending jokes, and to models for artistic representation. In this function, their speaking is not required, since it would disrupt the self-enchanted monologue of the colonizer. Only without the subjectivity of the self, however, and its manifestation in the means of expression can the other be constructed according to the manichean economy. At the same time, the objectification of the other for the purpose of consolidating the self through the colonial process of subjugation and denigration as such destroys the potential for dialogically acquired understanding. Resisting the temptation to retrospectively reinscribe language into the colonizer's perception of the colonized, Kühn's text must be understood as an attempt to demonstrate the narrator's lack of language for the other, a lack that is pivotal for an entire tradition of colonial representation.

If the traditional forms of objective knowledge equal violence, and potentially dialogical forms have been severed in the process of domination, then the question must be asked how the European author can understand and represent the cultural separateness of the other and at the same time reestablish the respect that his and her colonialist culture has denied them. Or, how can justice be done to the other in a text that emerges—whatever its intentions—necessarily from within a neo-colonial context?

We have seen the manichean aesthetics at work in all instances of writing on colonialism. Whether through stylistic assimilation and the denial of difference in texts from the eighteenth and nineteenth centuries, through the various modes of reductive denigration in colonialist writings, through the silencing of the other in an entire host of works from all periods, or even through the idealizing appropriation of the other's language for the European critique of capitalism in the didactic texts of the sixties: the modes of representing the language of the colonized have always reflected the structural monologism of the colonizer, and in each case they have served to consolidate the respective image of the self. If language, however, is the veil[12] between the self and the other, then it can be lifted and used for communication only if the colonial object is recognized and respected as a subject, capable of speaking itself. While it is true that contemporary German novels critical of colonialism set their focus on the exploration of their colonial past and thus on the very condition of their inherited culture, they are in their inquiry necessarily confronted with this predicament. It is generated by the process of decolonization and the changing needs of the world market, which make it possible for the silenced voices of the formerly colonized to emerge independently of "their" colonizers. The presence of others as subjects with a politically and culturally defined separateness that exists in spite of European and American cultural impositions finally fosters the European culture's awareness of the historical relativity of its claim to be the dominant center of the world. Because the new paradigm cannot be approached by positioning the self outside of a dissolving but at the same time omnipresent West, the de-centering of the West then finally suggests dialogue as the adequate mode of intersubjective and intercultural relationships. For the novel on colonialism, this means the necessity to expand the linguistic system of one language beyond the horizon of the colonizer and to reflect the diversity of voices and their meaning in its own text.

Although Bakhtin's conceptualization of heteroglossia is generally applicable to all novels that take the subjectivity of the other seriously, it takes on specific and difficult relevance for the novel in which the other in question is the other whose language the narrator does not speak, who walks on different roads of sounds, context, and meaning. Uwe Timm's *Morenga*, published in 1978, is symptomatic of the disintegration of the verbal/ideological system of unquestioned Western dominance as it clearly demonstrates an attempt to construct a form of narrative "that respects the other without absorbing it into the same."[13] Like Smidt's novel, *Morenga* deals with the German presence in Africa. Here, however, it is the colonialism of the German Empire and the Nama war of liberation against it during the first decade of the twentieth century. Compiled as a montage of documents, theory, and fiction, the novel focuses on the historical and present self as a culturally, politically and economically defined construction, as the own other of a self that has become critically aware of its implications. As in Kühn's text, this distancing glance reveals the historical self's status of alterity that thus invites resistance to identification. The critical and corrective potential of the novel's intertextuality is not only based on the reference to oppositional segments of the colonizing culture and the critical consciousness accumulated within it. Most acute are the corrective semantics of the discourse in this novel where they relate the other's language as that of a separate subject, thus establishing dialogue between colonized and colonizer and their divergent modes of interpretation. Not a single African in *Morenga* is characterized through deficient means of expression. Quite on the contrary: the history of colonialism in southwest Africa is inscribed in the text through the African's accomplished use of Dutch, English, and German, that is, through their possession by and the possession of European languages, which in this novel individual Africans use (besides their native Herero and Nama) to express the African critique of and resistance to colonial subjugation. Moreover, however, the readers are introduced to the phonetic structure and the semantic intricacies of the other's language through the German protagonist's laborsome and in the end successful attempt to learn Nama. This narrative device allows the text to establish a reversal and finally the syncretic elimination of the colonialist pattern of linguistic competence. It also permits a glance at the aesthetics of the complex culture to be colonized. In the process of his language acquisition, the protagonist experiences the unveiling of the other's spiritual territory to a degree that enables him to realize his collaboration in the physical destruction and oppression of an other subject, to see through the self-consolidating function of the colonial ideology and to prepare his leave from the *"Schutztruppen."* Through its accentuated use of heteroglossia then, intercultural intertextuality here becomes symptomatic for the nonappeasing aesthetics of difference in the writing on colonialism. However, if in Timm's novel the other's language is not only a primary object of representation but rather the means through which the other's culture, material existence, and politics can be drawn for the self into the realm of the understandable, then the dimension of this understanding remains still limited to that which the author and his readers infer from *their* knowledge of the self and the other. There is no narrative technique and no intention for authentic representation that would guarantee adequacy in writing the other subject. Abdul JanMohamed acknowledges this in the closing remarks of his essay "The Economy of Manichean Allegory" when he says, "the domain of literary and cultural syncretism belongs not to colonialist and neocolonialist writers but increasingly to Third World artists."[14]

Before I close my own remarks, I should like to point out two examples of novelistic writing that may lead to an acknowledgement of the limits for interculturally dialogical writing. The German text, Hans Christoph Buch's *The Wedding of Port-au-Prince*, published in 1984, derives its perspective from the neocolonial condition. The Guadeloupian novel Daniel Maximin's *L'Isolé soleil* was published in 1981 and is centered in the context of postcolonialism. Both texts drive intertextuality to its extreme; neither one does so for the purpose of representing the other. What they succeed in showing, however, is the result of colonialism in the inevitable presence of their respective other in the construction of the self. Buch interweaves innumerable set pieces of colonialist ideology, extracted from Europe's literary and political discourse of the other throughout centuries, into a disturbing account of the endemic ever-sameness of denigration and exploitation from colonialism via imperialism and fascism to neocolonialism. Also, Maximin defies the notion of the solitary hero together with that of the individual writer. Here intertextuality serves to dialogically intertwine the many voices of the francophone postcolonial text not only to a defense of "negritude as a collective enterprise,"[15] but also to an inquiry of the possibilities for retrieving history that has been silenced through domination.

Neocolonialism, after the age of Columbus the West's prevailing mode of international interaction with the world, manipulates its hegemony via arms transfer, market expansion, labor migration, media imperialism, and so on. It continuously attempts to produce new strategies of homogenization and incorporation while maintaining and feeding on the colonially established mode of differentiation at the same time. Thus, the task to do justice to the specificity of other cultures in literary texts becomes more urgent and more difficult simultaneously. The novels by Maximin and Buch are only two examples—among many others, especially from the post-colonial context—strikingly demonstrating the literary and factual presence of separate, different, and at the same time inevitably linked subjects, speaking for themselves, speaking their own texts. They also comment on the fact that even if the representation of the other's language remains a key issue in the Western text's ability to decolonize its own paradigms, with the historical decolonization this ability has lost some of its importance for the so-called "other."

Notes

1. See also Antonio Benítez Rojo, "Alte und Neue Welt: Gestern Monolog, heute Dialog." in *Lateinamerikaner über Europa*, ed. Curt Meyer-Clason (Frankfurt am Main: Suhrkamp, 1987), 63–64.

2. José Rabasa, "Dialogue as Conquest: Mapping Spaces for Counter Discourse," in The Nature and Context of Minority Discourse, ed. Abdul JanMohamed and David Lloyd (New York: Oxford University Press, 1990), 203.

3. Abdul JanMohamed, "The Economy of Manichean Allegory: The Function of Racial Difference in Colonialist Literature," in *"Race," Writing, and Difference*, ed. Henry Louis Gates, Jr. (Chicago: University of Chicago Press, 1986), 83.

4. Joachim Warmbold, *Germania in Africa: Germany's Colonial Literature* (New York: Peter Lang, 1989).

5. Walter Hietzig, *Blaue Klippe. Farmerroman aus Deutsch-Südwestafrika* (Berlin, 1941).

6. Houston A. Baker, Jr., *Modernism and the Harlem Renaissance* (Chicago: University of Chicago Press, 1987), 51–52.

7. Albert Memmi, The Colonizer and the Colonized (Boston: Beacon Press, 1965), 85.

8. Frantz Fanon, *Les damnés de la terre* (Paris: François Maspero, 1961).

9. Presenting their version of 'the African' in a similar vein, a magazine informing in Germany about her colonies wrote in 1907, "despite their lack of spiritual needs, spiritual abilities lie dormant in them and under proper guidance they are able to achieve quite substantially." *Die Deutschen Kolonien*, 1907/2, 48.

10. In his essay "The Suit and The Photograph," John Berger observes the loss of dignity as an effect similarly caused by the standardization of the clothing of one class for all. In: *About Looking* (New York: Pantheon Books, 1980), 35.

11. JanMohamed, "Economy of Manichean Allergory."

12. The phonetically double metaphor Baker himself derived from Olaudah Equiano the African and W. E. B. DuBois.

13. Robert Young, White Mythologies. Writing, History, and the West (London, New York: Routledge, 1990), 10.

14. JanMohamed, "Economy of Manichean Allegory," 104.

15. Clarisse Zimra in the preface to the English version of the novel. Daniel Maximin, *Lone Sun* (Charlottesville: University Press of Virginia, 1989), xliv.

CHAPTER 17

Isabelle Eberhardt Traveling "Other"/wise:
The "European" Subject in "Oriental" Identity

SIDONIE SMITH

What one cannot do in one's own Western environment—where to try to live out the grand dream of a successful quest is only to keep coming up against one's own mediocrity and the world's corruption and degradation—one can do abroad. Isn't it possible in India to do everything? be anything? go anywhere with impunity?

—Edward Said, "Kim, the Pleasures of Imperialism"

And while there is nothing inherently or essentially masculine about travel (women have most certainly traveled as well as written about travel), Western ideas about travel and the concomitant corpus of voyage literature have generally—if not characteristically—transmitted, inculcated, and reinforced patriarchal values and ideology from one male generation to the next.

—Georges Van Den Abbeele, *Travel As Metaphor from Montaigne to Rousseau*

I shall start another diary. What shall I record there, and where shall I be, the day in the distant future when I shall be closing it, the way I am closing this one today?

—Isabelle Eberhardt, *Diary*, 31 January 1903

The most basic form transcendental homelessness can take is discomfort with the most visible part of the self, the body.

—Marianna Torgovnick, *Gone Primitive*

The cover of Isabelle Eberhardt's journal, recently reissued in English in an abridged version by Virago Press in its series of women's travel narratives, provides an apt if unwitting entre into the text.[1] We see an

295

impressionistically painted desert scene. The hazy dome of a mosque invokes the Islamic religion. Human figures, undifferentiated, fade into the architecture or blend into the pastoral spaces surrounding the mosque. In a cameo photograph at the bottom of the cover, Eberhardt looks out at us as the youthful figure whose portrait partially obscures the desert scene. Unlike the indigenous figures before the mosque, Eberhardt's photographic figuration is hard-edged, distinct, individualized. Even though her dress is that of a desert nomad, even though her sexual identity is indeterminable, she remains unmistakably a "European" subject cross-dressed as an "oriental."

Eberhardt, known as "la bonne nomade," left behind her when she died in the Maghreb desert a journal that tracks the literal and imaginative itinerary of a Western subject traveling through pastoralized spaces, playing out a "flamboyant artifice"[2] by dressing in the garb of the North African holy man. Crossing from Europe to the desert of North Africa, the young Eberhardt attempts to escape a certain history of the subject by divesting herself of her European identity. For she associates European "civilization" with grinding monotony, enervating self-satisfactions, and bourgeois repressions, or what she calls "the genteel pleasures": "I could never be content with the genteel pleasures of city life in Europe," Eberhardt writes: "The idea I had of heading for the desert to satisfy my strange need for both adventure and peace did require courage, but it was feasible and, as it turns out, inspired" (31). Joining other Europeans of the turn of the century, Eberhardt pursues what Laura Rice describes as "the desire . . . to escape from the disciplining institutions and ideologies of Europe—the courts of law, the churches, proper schools, *la bonne famille*—and give rein to repressed desires in a supposedly primitive and lawless space."[3] The desert becomes for her "a refuge where my tormented soul can go for relief from the triviality of modern life" (41), a refuge from what Chris Bongie calls "the constitutive mediocrity of the modern subject."[4]

Traversing the expansive spaces of the Maghreb, the nomadic peoples provide Eberhardt a metaphor for the kind of life she desired, a metaphor shared in the larger European context. "The constant displacement of nomadic peoples," suggests Rice, "symbolized freedom—the escape into a timeless otherness—for late nineteenth-century Europe. The very distance between this mirage of an eternally changing pattern of otherness rooted in a dimly biblical past and the codified everyday life of modern European cities fascinated the European subject."[5] The nomads of the desert, apparently unrooted, autonomous, and "free," capture Eberhardt's imagination because they offer her a metaphor for her essential "self," that "otherness" she feels lodged within her: "A nomad I was even when I was very small and would stare at the road . . . a nomad I will remain for life, in love with distant and uncharted places" (96).

Eberhardt's exoticist project signals her disgust with the diminished sovereignty of the individual in European cities and her desire to recover her "real" self, uncontaminated by an uncomfortable and inauthentic sojourn in an illegitimate "home," or a home of illegitimacy, which is what, literally, her home in Europe had been.[6] Born an illegitimate daughter, she can claim no "proper" name. If literally and metaphorically her European self is an illegitimate self, the "nomad" self, that "other" to the European self, becomes for her the legitimate self, proper, authentic, true, and real. In the Maghreb she attempts to get found in her new and newly proper name: Mahmoud Saadi. Adopting the name/identity of the nomad enables Eberhardt to posit her incommensurable difference from what she elsewhere calls "those idiotic Europeans" (99) and the European home she so fiercely rejects.

With other romantic intellectuals, she ascribed to the nomads what Rice calls "some essential difference,"[7] an essential difference she tapped for her true self and transformed within her imagination into a superiority, perhaps even an aristocracy, of soul. Fluent in the language of the nomads, Eberhardt intersperses Arabic phrases throughout. A devotee of Islam, she meditates upon its promises, its practitioners, and its authority and incorporates Islamic tenets and sayings into the journal. She dresses, as did Lawrence of Arabia after her, as an Arab. That is, in the (reverse) assimilation into her legitimate home, she embraces the accoutrements of essential difference, the repertoire of signifiers, the specificities of language, dress, and religious affiliation, all of which secure her essential difference from "those idiotic Europeans" with their own vitiated culture.

In this sense, Eberhardt actually constructs her travels as a "return" to a "true home" from a place that has been no home, from a place in which she has always already been a "stranger." Lost to her in Europe, she seeks to find the "true" self in North Africa. Thus, in traveling away from Europe Eberhardt travels "back home" to the "other" in herself through the identification with and identity of the "otherness" of the nomad. Through this return voyage the European woman ends up "going primitive," to invoke Marianna Torgovnick's titular phrase. "Going primitive is trying to 'go home' to a place that feels comfortable and balanced, where full acceptance comes freely and easily," writes Torgovnick: "Whatever form the primitive's hominess takes, its strangeness salves our estrangement from ourselves and our culture."[8]

In this essay, I want to consider the complexities of and contradictions in Eberhardt's "going primitive" and to do so through an analysis of the relationship of nomadic identity, subjectivity, and journalistic narrative.

The History of the Gendered Subject

While Eberhardt fashions a nomadic "identity" for herself, what kind of a subject speaks in the journal? Or to put it another way, what history of the subject does she take with her to the desert to ride along with her "nomadic self" and interpenetrate her aura of essential difference? And further, how is the identification with the essential difference of the "other" part and parcel of the constitution of the "same" old European subject?

Eberhardt takes the history of bourgeois individualism with her into the desert as she takes up the identity of the nomad. She opens the first journal with the announcement, "I am utterly alone on earth" (1); and throughout she identifies herself as the resolutely lonely subject, a "lunatic," a "pariah" (2), a "tramp" (77), as well as a "nomad." As a radically individualized subject, Eberhardt believes herself to be autonomous and "free": "Far from society, far from civilisation," she writes, "I am by myself, on Muslim soil, out in the desert, free and in the best of circumstances. The outcome of my undertaking is therefore up to me" (24). In this conception of subjectivity, Eberhardt privileges a very Western/bourgeois ideal, what Regenia Gagnier describes as "abstract individualism, or the belief that essential human characteristics are properties of individuals independent of their material conditions and social environment."[9]

Coincident with this belief in autonomous selfhood is her reification of the quest for "an 'Ideal,' something mystical and eminently desirable that fires [the] soul" (9). Through this project she would forge what she calls "character,"[10] "an awareness, an intelligence and a will" (11) that is never satisfied.

In taking this history of bourgeois individualism into the desert with her, Eberhardt assumes the nomadic subject to be male.[11] She refuses to position herself as the female nomad precisely because she discredits the "female" as subject. For Eberhardt the female can have no "character" because the two traits she allies with character, an "unflinching and invincible will" and "integrity" are, she claims, "so hard to find in women" (4). Consequently, in certain journal entries she positions herself explicitly as a man, as when she writes that "life in the Desert . . . will complete my education as a man of action, the Spartan education I need" (10). Or she positions herself in pronominal masculinity, as when she professes her desire to "write a novel, tell the unique story of a man—rather like myself—who is a Muslim and tries to sow the seeds of virtue everywhere he goes" (102). And she imagines her story through a male-identified code in which she acts the "hero" who has "faith, repentance, the desire for moral perfection, the longing for a reputation based on noble *merit*, and a thirst for great and magnificent deeds" (8). This identification with normative masculinity and with a masculine code of behavior had a long history for Eberhardt. As her biographer Annette Kobak notes, her father/tutor "kept her hair cropped, dressed her like a boy, and brought her up like a boy, in keeping with Bakunin's dictum that 'every child of either sex should be prepared as much for a life of the mind as for a life of work, so that all may grow up equally into complete men.'"[12]

Her masquerade as a nomad involves a doubled-crossing, then, from Europe to North Africa, from a female to a male identity, signified by her new name, Mahmoud Saadi. In assuming the proper name of Mahmoud Saadi, Isabelle Eberhardt rejects the name-of-the-mother, since, as an illegitimate child, she carries her mother's name, itself taken from her mother's, Eberhardt. For it is not nomadic culture per se but the culture of male nomads to which she seeks to assimilate. This disidentification with women permeates the journal, in her unsympathetic treatment of her impoverished sister-in-law and in her conventional colonialist figuration of Arab women. Eberhardt allies Arab women with animals when she describes how "the expression in their large languorous and melancholy jet black eyes is resigned and sad like that of wary animals" (3). Elsewhere she assigns them to anonymity, insignificance, and opaque massification: "The problem with Tenes is its herd of neurotic, orgiastic, mean and futile females" (98). Herdlike, inarticulate, North African women remain, to use Abena Busia's phrase, "simply not real."[13] Eberhardt's African woman is voiceless, powerless, beneath observation, outside the desire for identification. Eberhardt asserts not only her essential difference from European subjects, both male and female. She asserts also her essential difference from the mass of women, European and North African, who have no character and lead sedentary, trivial lives, uninformed by the quest for a truer self.[14]

"Woman" cannot quest precisely because, as Georges Van Den Abbeele argues, "the 'law of the home' (*oikonomia*) organizes a set of gender determinations"[15] in the economy of travel. That is, "woman" is always already "domesticated." Discourses of travel, including those informed by primitivist tropes, constitute the traveler as "male" and the one allied with the home or *oikos* as "female." Or they constitute the exotic woman as a menace to the traveler, a threat to his sovereignty and to the profit of his travels. Seduced by women and their calls to desire, he may get lost in the midst of his travels. Or those discourses constitute the landscape as a "female" space to be penetrated, explored, exploited. Or they constitute the vessel of man's travels as a kind of "womb," a source of safety and a place of male camaraderie. Profoundly influenced by this "set of gender determinations" permeating travel narratives of the late nineteenth century as well as gender ideologies generally, Eberhardt erases her identification with any women and with her female body, an erasure signified by both her male "habits" and the anorexic body those habits envelop. In effect, she has been, since childhood, a stranger in her own body/habits.

And yet Eberhardt participates in the erotic itinerary of the romantic individual's exotic sojourn. Her attraction to the Maghreb as a "home" in which she can find her true self is an attraction to a landscape saturated with erotic possibilities, a place where new landscapes of desire, new forms and gestures of sexuality, promise ecstasies beyond the conforming pleasures of the "Europeanized" body, disciplined and repressed. In this expectation of pleasure Eberhardt participates in the orientalist fabrication of the "East" as "a coffer of erotic delights and unlimited freedoms."[16] What is unknown or partially known promises what has been unexperienced. The freedom to develop a more authentic "character" implies the freedom to discover a body untouched by bourgeois repressions of desire. And her journals record the calls to and ecstasies of desire. "Day after tomorrow," she writes with anticipation, "I can give in to these physical cravings and spend whole nights in wild sensuality" (41). Paradoxically, Eberhardt erases her female body through the masculine habits and yet speaks of the desires of her body openly and assertively. She manages to straddle this paradox by carefully differentiating herself from the "herd" of women whose bodies are part of the nomadic traffic of women's bodies from one man to another, the traffic in the bodies of prostitutes. "I have now reached the depths of poverty, and may well be going hungry soon. Yet I can honestly say that I have never, not even for a moment, entertained the notion of doing what so many hundreds of thousands of women do," she writes: *"That is out of the question*, period" (71). The emphasis Eberhardt adds to the declaration reveals a fundamental discomfort. The bodies of prostitutes come too close to Eberhardt for comfort. They represent a menace, what Van Den Abbeele describes as "the disruptive liminality women are represented as occupying" (xxvi) in narratives of travel. These women and their bodies are seductive of the subject of the journal; but the seduction in Eberhardt's journal derives from the sameness of their bodies rather than the otherness of their bodies. This threat of sameness incites Eberhardt's hostility and the gesture of erasure in the journal. She refuses to be domesticated as the debased female, the prostitute.

Obviously one way to take herself outside this traffic in women and in women's bodies is to take herself outside of a woman's body[17] and outside female subjectivity and identity. She recognizes, albeit indirectly, that in her sexual freedom and experimentation she stretches the cultural borderline separating the culturally sanctioned and "promiscuous" sexual activity of women. Even speaking of sexual desire and the pleasures of the body tests the limits set between the culturally speakable and unspeakable. And so she recuperates her culturally errant sexuality through the trope of romantic exoticism. For Eberhardt sexuality functions as a "domain" of knowledge, and her pursuit of sexual experience becomes an epistemological quest. "Sexual matters will continue to hold my attention, of course, from the intellectual point of view," she explains, "and I would not give up my research in that domain for anything in the world" (79). Textually constituting sexuality as an arena for research, Eberhardt distances herself as subject from her body as object of experimentation. The body is neutralized as threat by the process of intellectualization. Masquerading as an Arab male and speaking as a male writing subject, Eberhardt finds a way to speak her body but to do so with some kind of residual legitimacy because she speaks through the voice of the ceaselessly questing artist. The body becomes a source of the heightened aesthetic experiences for the artist who pushes courageously against the mediocrities of "his" culture in pursuit of new knowledge and a "better self." In this way, the body remains appropriately "feminized," the object of intellectual contemplation, and the knower remains "masculinized," the subject who turns "his" gaze upon the object under study. "He" does not give in to the body and its seductions. "Mahmoud Saadi" puts her female identity/name under erasure in order to get to the kind of bourgeois subjectivity she wants to establish precisely because female identity blocks her entrance to the pastoral space of the exotic other and the space of the creative imagination. Masquerade as a male marabout, in contrast, promotes access to an aestheticized subjectivity, the other of the European self. For Eberhardt takes the history of the writing subject and the history of Western writing practices into the desert with her; and the journal itself becomes the means through which Eberhardt constitutes herself as an exotic subject through the play of its exoticist tropes: the trope of the quest for the truer self uncontaminated by the excesses of civilization; the trope of the sublime landscape; the trope of exotic love.

The Questing Subject

The ceaseless travel of the nomad metaphorizes the ceaseless pursuit on the part of the romantic subject for a more enlightened self. And the journal becomes the appropriate writing vehicle for the subject who "need[s] to keep searching, come what may, for new events, and flee inertia and stagnation" (36) and who wants to calibrate the increments of change in that endless quest. The "apparent egocentricity to be found on every page of this diary" signals, according to the narrator, not "megalomania" but rather the "need to compile a record that will give me, later on, a true image of my soul as it is today. That is the only way I shall be able to judge my present life and to see whether my character has progressed or not" (13). Thus the preoccupation of the journals is the experiencing subject. Georg Simmel notes that habitual impressions "use up less consciousness"[18] than strange and constantly changing impressions. While his observations are directed at the individual's experience in the modern metropolis, they are relevant to the experience of the nomadic subject in constant movement through an imaginatively exoticized space. Sojourn in the desert space of "essential difference" facilitates, intensifies, and surrounds Eberhardt's pursuit of ever-expanding/changing self-consciousness.

But progress in character requires an elusive and exacting itinerary. Catastrophe threatens to distract; fragmentation threatens to undermine any achievement of purpose. To be constantly improving becomes equivalent to be constantly coming apart, only to be drawn together again and again and again. While Eberhardt constantly alludes to the multiple splits menacing the subject, she constantly adjusts the nature of the split. At times the split is along the public/private axes as in the following passage: "[F]or I simply pay no attention to anything other than the dreams that make up my true personality. I seem to wear a mask that bespeaks someone cynical, dissipated. . . . No one so far has ever managed to see through it and catch a glimpse of the sensitive soul which lives behind it" (1). In other places the split subject breaks apart along the adventure/contemplation axes as when she delineates the attraction of two lives, "one that is full of adventure and belongs to the Desert, and one, calm and restful, devoted to thought and far from all that might interfere with it" (11). Yet another fault line for the split is that between the body and intellect/soul: "I feel more and more disgusted with my second self, that no-good oaf who rears his head from time to time, usually, if not always, under the influence of physical factors. Better health, in other words, would clearly result in an improvement in the intellectual and spiritual side of my life" (11).[19] Yet another split follows the heart/head axis: "I feel a tranquil heart is mine at last; the same cannot be said for any peace of mind, alas!" (29). There is always a split to be sutured, if not here then there. And there is always an occasion for self-scrutiny, that is, for writing. The journal promotes an aesthetics of renewable self-consciousness: "Everything is radically different now, myself included" (107).

In this questing itinerary, the subject of the journal crosses threshold after threshold. Commenting on the change in her religious attitude since she survived an assassination attempt, she notes: "Yet the fact remains that if ever there was a time when my intelligence was burning like a flame, that time is now, and what is more, I know that I am only on the threshold of a new life" (67). "Period[s] of incubation" (51) are followed by periods of "new understanding of people and of things" (51) through which she anticipates achieving her better self. Six months after the attempt on her life she writes: Even though I did not realise it then, that day was the beginning of another period of incubation, of the sort I have experienced all my life, for quite clearly my intellectual development has always been achieved by fits and starts: periods of restlessness, discontent and uncertainty have always been followed by the emergence of a better version of myself. A subject to be analysed, and described perhaps in a short story or a novel" (69). The subject is a new but not yet the true subject.

Eberhardt's nomadic life is not an adventure with a certain future and a final destination, with a sure enlightenment and a successful and profitable return home. This nomadic life is a quest that goes on endlessly,[20] and the journal its appropriate venue. Because the journal luxuriates in the quotidian, the incidental, the intimate, the "individualistic," it is a form correlative with the fragmented subject, a form in which nothing is put together finally, in which everything remains vague, unfinished, provisional. The journal places the subject constantly anew on the page, caught in the exigencies of the moment, in a nomadic context of restlessness. As the venue of nomadic restlessness and the search for the exotic/"other" in the self, the journal also reveals at every point of (journal) entry that the quest has always already failed; that the "better self" can never be realized; that "home" is nowhere. In this way, Eberhardt's journalistic practice participates in the exoticist project of the fin de siecle. "The exotic necessarily becomes, for those who persist in search of it," writes Bongie, "the sign of an aporia—of a constitutional absence at the heart of what had been projected as a possible alternative to modernity" (22). Like the texts of other exoticist writers, Eberhardt's journal "register[s] the exotic as a space of absence, a dream already given over to the past."[21]

The Sublime Landscape

This endless quest for a true self takes place against a specific landscape imagined through primitivist tropes. Thus it is necessary to consider the centrality of the sublime landscape and its spatial and temporal seductions to Eberhardt's journalistic practice. Eberhardt locates the impulse for her journal writing in her "cult of the past," that same "cult" that leaves its marks of desire in her identification of Maghreb culture with the "primitive," the "biblical," the past: "For the uninitiated reader, these pages would hardly make much sense. For myself they are a vestige of my earlier cult of the past. The day may come perhaps when I will no longer record the odd thought and impression in order to make them last a while. For the moment, I sometimes find great solace in re-reading these words about days gone by" (108). This process of aestheticization is part of what Bongie calls "the exoticizing pole" of turn-of-the-century journal writing that "ground[s] its subject in the alternative space of the Other, re-presenting him [sic] in the more heroic time of the *antique indigene*."[22]

Antique subjects inhabit antique environments. Eberhardt's "timeless desert" (38) is a prehistorical space, "inhabited," she writes, "by camels and primitive men" (23). Seeing two Arabs on top of a dune one evening, she writes that "the impression was a biblical one, and I suddenly felt as if transported back to the ancient days of primitive humanity, when the great light-giving bodies in the sky had been the object of veneration" (28). The pastoral landscape is an undomesticated space outside "history," or rather, outside the history of European "enlightenment," the progressive history of "civilization." Here history has not intervened to mediate and to blunt the intensity of connection between the subject and his/her "primitive humanity." Here life exists in its primitive "naturalness," far distant from the impositions of technology (as history) that disrupt the natural landscape, including the natural landscape within the human being. Here the writing subject projects upon the landscape a prehistoric home in which to search for her "true" and "natural" self.

Within this primitivized environment everything seems dreamlike. In fact, Eberhardt describes the desert as a dreamscape, one with which she has been imaginatively familiar since childhood: "Felt intensely happy to be here again, on this African soil to which I feel tied not only by memories but also by that strange appeal it has always had for me, even before I had ever seen it, when I was still living in that boring *Villa* of ours" (19–20). Its "mysterious voice" (10–11), "mesmerising soil" (91), and "slow dreamy life" (10) "intoxicat[e]" (1) her. Here experience is rachetted up in intensity. "I had several moments of great and altogether Oriental intensity at Algiers" (22), she writes. On her return to Africa after a forced sojourn in Europe she records how the environment goes to her head (63). The pastoral space delivers intensity because it offers an existence lived in continuous consciousness of difference and thus in continuous self-consciousness.

The exotic subject of Eberhardt's journal is constituted by means of the romantic trope of the sublime landscape, broad vistas intemperate in their calls to attention, sensual and intoxicating in their pleasures, untouched by history and technology, and, finally, unpeopled, or if peopled, peopled with *antique indigenes* (and not with "those idiotic Europeans" [99]). For the nomadic men who populate this exoticized dreamscape remain, like the landscape, inscrutable, voiceless, indistinct, primitive, mysterious.[23] When they emit any sounds, they emit the mystical sound of song and chant. When they act, they act courageously and mysteriously. They function as idealized (and voiceless) silhouettes. In a sense, then, the *antique indigene* melds into the landscape/dream: land and nomadic man are one. The exoticized other becomes an object contained in and by the dream of the observing subject.[24] The subject of the journal is the "otherness" of the subject of the journal.

Ultimately the dreamscape and the silhouette-people provide Eberhardt with the self-consolidating otherness necessary to her return home as an artist. Everything experienced is experienced as potential writing: "Would it not be a better idea to start my description of my trip through Algeria with Bone rather than Algiers? If I come across any impressions that warrant recording, I could present them as recollections from another period. That would give me the opportunity to produce some splendidly melancholy pages, in the vein of African perspectives" (17). As this passage reveals, the landscape has always already been "read" by the traveler, read through representations of representations, that is, read through previous landscape writings. The "Africa" upon which she gazes is not some "real" or unmediated landscape but the "Africa" of mediated, refracted perspectives. It is the artist's desert we see here; and it is the artist who determines what is truly "African." "The true African landscape," she pronounces, "is not to be found in any of the large cities, certainly not in those of the Tell. African perspectives are hazy with a distant horizon. Vast space and emptiness, a blinding light, are what makes a landscape African!" (92).

Eberhardt's "uncharted" spaces are not at all uncharted. They are charted or mapped by her, and by means of previous chartings. She is already prepared to "see" what she sees as "African"; and so she creates her version of "Africa" as she writes. In turn this imagined "Africa of the nomads," an Africa of mystery and inscrutability, functions as the self-consolidating other of the questing European subject/woman. She projects onto the landscape her own desire for a new home commensurate with her sense of her true self. The mystery, inscrutability, and exoticism of the dreamscape she projects before her (spatially and temporally) mirror her own desire for the otherness of mystery, inscrutability, and exoticism within her. These are her "properties," so to speak, properties that distinguish her from the prosaic and idiotic European subject.

Yet the mysteries of uncharted spaces, as they hold out the promise of endless possibilities of fulfillment, elude any finality of quest for the exiled subject. The path to the true self is ultimately an aporia, an aporia as vast as the dreamscape of the Maghreb. To paraphrase Bongie, Eberhardt's dream has always been given over to the past. However much she wants to chart the otherness inside through the otherness outside, she remains hopelessly solitary, as she admits in a particularly pessimistic and telling commentary on an earlier journal passage: "Many other corners of the African continent still hold me in their spell. Soon, the solitary, woeful figure that I am will vanish from this earth, where I have always been a spectator, an *outsider* among men" (74). The "true" self is always held in some other place, some other time.

The Exoticist Plot

As Eberhardt reifies the essential difference of the North African nomads, she nourishes an aura of her own exotic difference. She takes the language, the habits (in both senses of the word), and the profound faith of the other into herself. She speaks, dresses, and prays as one of the others. But she goes further. She marries her "native" lover and, despite her sexual infidelities, remains devoted to him, at least on the journal's pages. For Eberhardt as for Pierre Loti, whose journals she read and quoted within hers, the exotic subject becomes an actor in what Bongie calls the "quintessentially romantic, plot: one of forbidden love between a gaiour and his native paramour."[25] This plot is the means through which the European subject makes intimate contact with the other. Literally Eberhardt takes the other inside her. Through the other she comes to her very life: "simply holding him in my arms as I did yesterday and looking into his eyes brings me back to life" (41). His eyes bring her to life as an exotic subject, essentially different from "those idiotic Europeans." The more intimate and self-absorbing their relationship, the further she is drawn away from that strange identity of the European; the closer she comes to her new home.

Her participation in the exoticist plot, a common staple for travel writers, confounds the interrelationships secured through patriarchal and colonial systems of power. The traditional exoticist narrative joins the European man with the "other" woman. This union of European man and "exotic" woman maintains the hierarchy of colonialism precisely because it maintains the hierarchy of gender. The other culture (signified by the other woman) remains in the inferior position, an object of desire. But Eberhardt's participation in the exoticist plot reverses this normative paradigm. The European woman assumes the narrative privileges of the European man by engaging in a cross-cultural liaison with the "exotic" man. Now when Eberhardt takes the position of the European "man" to Slimene's exotic "woman" she confuses the location of gender. She is, after all, a woman to Slimene's man. This reversal points to the potentially subversive and the potentially recuperative dynamics of mimesis.

As she literally and symbolically "marries" difference, Eberhardt espouses a culturally transgressive love and exposes the unsatisfactory nature of love in Europe. Eberhardt figures her union with her husband Slimene as a ideal relationship, one that contrasts to the conventional European marriage with its repressed and repressive sexuality (for women). The elaboration of the details of sexual experimentation function therefore as a gesture of cultural critique of Western marriages in which young girls experience unsatisfactory sexuality at the hands of clumsy European husbands (80). She also exposes the fragility of colonial relationships of power. The discourse of romantic love through which she constitutes her exotic relationship with Slimene positions her as the enthralled dependent. She would subdue her desire for authority and power and adopt a posture of "obedience" toward her "master": "I must learn the very thing that is hardest for someone of my temperament, namely obedience (which of course has its limits and must on no account turn into servility)" (48). The reference to "obedience" interjects the trace of her position as one of the colonists, if an echo of inversion. The stable dynamics of gender and racial hierarchies collapse. Eberhardt's erotics reverse the established power relations between the colonizer and the colonized and thereby "threaten," according to Rice, "the precarious fiction of European dominance and Arab submissiveness upon which the colonial venture in Algeria was built."[26] The European woman assumes the position of obedience before the colonized man, becoming the subservient other of the colonized other.

But like the quest for a truer self, the exoticist plot of the love between the gaiour and the exotic other is qualified. While Eberhardt talks of her subdual before the "Arab" lover/other, she also reveals her desire to "subdue" Slimene. That is, throughout journal four she refers to her desire to "educate" him up out of his ignorance. To educate Slimene is to prepare him to identify with as well as be identified with European culture and values. It is to prove his educability, his "equality," his potential for Westernization. It is therefore an act whereby Eberhardt would translate him out of his otherness and difference. As Rice suggests, "to the extent that the local people became Europeanized . . . they denied their essence as the exotic other."[27] The process whereby Eberhardt seeks to draw Slimene into another history and another kind of subjectivity is the very process set in motion by the "imperializing mission," the mission justifying and sustaining the colonial project. As Gayatri Spivak argues so eloquently: "No perspective *critical* of imperialism can turn the Other into a self, because the project of imperialism has always already historically refracted what might have been the absolutely Other into a domesticated Other that consolidates the imperialist self."[28] Eberhardt's exotic plot positions Slimene as the "other" or "woman" to Eberhardt's European "man" and thus reinforces the feminization of the colonial other. After all, through her journal writing she controls his representation and the representation of their relationship.

Moreover, in her projection of the transgressive coupling between Arab and European, Eberhardt reifies "the couple" as a unit of cultural meaning by incorporating Slimene into the discourse of Western marriage. Mallek Alloula points to this cultural violence in his analysis of the colonialist framing of social relationships in postcards sent back to France from the North African colonies. "The very idea of the couple," he writes, "is an imported one which is applied to a society that operates on the basis of formations that are greater than simple twoness, such as the extended family, the clan, or the tribe. The couple, in the Western senses, is an aberration, a historical error, an unthinkable possibility in Algerian society."[29] Eberhardt participates in the very violence of the colonial regime she would escape by importing into the desert and into her journal another colonizing script of cultural identity. Love for Slimene involves Eberhardt in the domestication of the other. Transgression (in the choice of an exotic lover) becomes domestication. Figuratively, Eberhardt takes Slimene "home" to Europe with her.

The Subject of History

The tropes of Eberhardt's exoticist project complicate the schemas of time in the journals. The narrator's self-preoccupation drives the journal's continuous present tense of incident, impression, feeling, reflection, and thereby sustains an unerring focus on the experiencing subject, sustains, that is, a kind of psychological "timelessness." The tropological preoccupation with the sublime landscape and the exotic love plot also promotes a kind of timelessness, that of the prehistoric, the unchanging, unspoiled realm of experience outside history. The narrator washes everything in the plot and its backdrop with the patina of vagueness, inscrutability, mystery. The time of desire becomes the more authentic, more primitive past. Immersed at once in the timelessness of the psychological present and the timelessness of the "primitive" past, the writing subject seems to evade any totalizing History with a capital *H*, that history of the Europe she leaves behind. Travel and travel writing appear to lift the writing subject out of the time of history and thus out of complicity with colonial apparati and colonial subjects.

And in fact, the adoption of a nomadic identity and its aura of difference leads Eberhardt to take certain positions toward the culture of the desert space that distinguish her from other participants in the

French colonial regime in North Africa. These positions derive from what Rice calls Eberhardt's "reverse assimilation," a process through which the European woman seeks to assimilate into North African culture. The desire to assume the identity of the nomad leads Eberhardt to develop a critical perspective on the impact of colonization upon North Africa rather than to assume with other participants in the regime, the inferiority and inequality of the colonized subjects. Thus she countervalorizes nomadic society. "Whatever their unenlightened way of life," she pronounces, "the lowliest of Bedouins are far superior to those idiotic Europeans making such a nuisance of themselves" (99). And she bemoans the cost to the indigenous peoples of prolonged exposure to Europeans and their culture, especially in "border" cities, those seaport towns that were ports of entry for everything European, including soldiers and colonial bureaucrats/authorities. They are, she writes, "unhinged and vitiated . . . by . . . contact with a foreign world" (32).

But of course the journal fills with the history it seeks to escape; for, as Bongie notes of Loti's narrative, "the journal and the subject who is writing it are constantly being rewritten within the terms of that which they would remain outside, or to the side, of."[30] The frontier of difference Eberhardt traverses is a frontier created through the very imperial project she critiques, since "the imperialist vision shapes public opinion," observes Bongie, "offering it the possibility of boundless horizons as compensation for the dismal prospects of industrial society."[31] There can be no exotic adventure without those very border cities Eberhardt maligns, without the imperialist penetration she bemoans. Thus, the "home" of Europe has always already domesticated the exoticist voyage toward a more legitimate home because as home it serves, according to Van Den Abbeele, as "the transcendental point of reference that organizes and domesticates a given area by defining all others points in relation to itself."[32] The absent home is everywhere present. History with a capital *H* organizes the exoticist project as a project outside history. It organizes the exotic other to and in the European subject.

Eberhardt exploits the North African backdrop for her own cult of the individual. She can go about her business of cross-dressing and violate all kinds of indigenous Algerian codes, ones that Algerian women could not have violated, precisely because she carries her European identification with her into the pastoral space. The cross/cultural/dressing situates her as an eccentric whose very eccentricity protects her. She cannot go incognito, for her very subjectivity, even her life, depends upon the visibility of her masquerade. She acknowledges that the indigenous people are more afraid of a European eccentric than they are of the poverty-stricken "countryman" and that she is, for this reason, safer in the masquerade. Her identity as European is as much revealed as concealed by the masquerade. Moreover, her eccentricity as a "destitute beggar"[33] enables her to survive upon the generosity and benevolence of the indigenous population. There is thus a disturbing irony underwriting parts of the journal of this romantic artist—the "colonizer" who appropriates the identity of the "colonized" lives off the very "colonized" she mimes. Eberhardt never gives up her European identity. In fact she foregrounds nationality by playing at eliding it. The security of her European origin/identification anchors her "reverse assimilation."

However fierce her desire to separate herself from the bourgeois civilization of Europe, Eberhardt carried its ideology of romantic selfhood with her into the desert. It rode her as fast as she rode her horse across the sands. This pastoral speaker cannot leave every history behind. For a specific history of Western consciousness and its imperialistic self-consolidating practices overwrite the pastoral landscape of the Maghreb. However much she wanted to leave European history behind, that history is written on her very notion of subjectivity and its journalistic practices. In fact, Eberhardt, in leaving Europe, participates in the quintessential Western activity, she participates in the "great cultural investment" of Europe. For, as Van Den Abbeele reminds us: "The dearest notions of the West nearly all appeal to the motif of the voyage: progress, the quest for knowledge, freedom as freedom to move, self-awareness as an Odyssean enterprise, salvation as a destination to be attained by following a prescribed pathway."[34] All these meanings of travel and pursuit coalesce upon and collapse into the point of the romantic subject. Thus however much she might reject the draw of her original home in Europe, that home defines the destination of her travels. Sojourn in a space of difference, cross-dressing in sexual difference, Eberhardt in/habits an environment (geographical, sartorial, and textual) in which to assert her constant "difference from."

And so her journal celebrates not the way she assimilates into the populace, fades into the pastoral landscape as do the figures on the cover of the Virago edition, but the way in which she stands out from the populace in her radical individualism. Nor does it celebrate the way her subjectivity becomes another kind of subjectivity through what

Françoise Lionnet has called via Nancy Morejon et al., "transcultura-
tion."[35] It reveals rather the degree to which cross-cultural dressing and
movement through pastoral space sets her apart. She presents herself in
her profound particularity, a profound particularity that she argues is
recognized by those very Arab "natives" among whom she travels and
with whom she converses. In promoting an aesthetics of renewable self-
consciousness and individualism, Eberhardt's journal fashions an
"artist" in exile and thus promotes what Lillian Robinson argues is "a
fundamental precept of bourgeois aesthetics": "good art . . . is art that
celebrates what is unique and even eccentric in human experience or
human personality. Individual achievement and subjective isolation are
the norm, whether the achievement and the isolation be that of the
artist or the character."[36]

Even as she traverses the sublime landscape dressed as an Algerian
marabout, even as she masquerades in the dress of communal male
identification, even as she enacts a poetics of reverse assimilation (à la
Rice) with the "other," Eberhardt reveals the distance of essential
difference, the proximity of European sameness. She wants to have her
European history—and its privileging of the creative imagination—and
to have her nomadic experience and expressive marginality too. For
ultimately she wants to establish her legitimate claim to a place in the
brotherhood of revered travel writers, a brotherhood including such
artists as Pierre Loti. That is why she incorporates passages from other
journals into her journal. In a matrix of intertextuality, she quotes
passages from the journals of Loti and the Goncourts to create a
camaraderie of isolated subjects. By surrounding her words with the
words of other romantic artists and exiles, by writing her own narrative
through the narratives of her fellow travellers, she aestheticizes and
legitimizes her "self" and her "experience."

The Subject outside the Text

As "Si Mahmoud Saadi," Isabelle Eberhardt totally confuses the
relationships among subjectivity, identity, and the body founding the
cultural construction of the romantic artist. Here is a "woman"
adopting the identity/appearance of a "Algerian nomad/man" and
harboring the subjectivity of the "universal/masculine subject," creating
the inner as masculine, the surface as female, and the outer (sartorial
identity) as masculine. What Judith Butler suggests of cross-dressing
provides insights into Eberhardt's situation:

> The performance of drag plays upon the distinction between the anatomy of the performer and the gender that is being performed. But we are actually in the presence of three contingent dimensions of significant corporeality: anatomical sex, gender identity, and gender performance. If the anatomy of the performer is already distinct from the gender of the performer, and both of those are distinct from the gender of the performance, then the performance suggests a dissonance not only between sex and performance, but sex and gender, and gender and performance.[37]

But Eberhardt's cross-cultural dressing further complicates Butler's already troublingly complex set of relationships. Eberhardt seems to be a European woman, performing the identity of an Algerian man in order to get to the subjectivity of the universal European man/artist. Further, at a material level, Eberhardt's body itself refuses to stabilize around any clear sexual identification. The anorexic body purges itself of markers of female identity (she was reported to be flat-chested and have no menstrual periods); and even sprouts markers of masculine identity (apparently her body was covered with hair). Eberhardt's "failure" to "be" any one of these three identities exposes the difficulty of fixing identity itself, of locating it anyplace but elsewhere.

As Marjorie Garber suggests, "Eberhardt's situation was itself quintessentially that of multiple displacement; she is a 'displaced person' in virtually every sense. In fact, her cross-dressing seems to mark and make legible the condition of category crisis itself. For Eberhardt is, in a sense, an example of the *personification of displacement*."[38] Thus in questing after her true self, she destabilizes through what Homi Bhabha calls "the *menace* of mimicry"[39] the discourses that establish relationships of power through identity and difference.

And in fact, Eberhardt's actual presence in the Maghreb desert troubled, as Rice argues, the "authorities" of both the French colonial bureaucracy and the indigenous nomadic centers of power. From the point of view of the colonists and the colonized (men and women) she would have seemed exotic. She troubled everyone because she reveals, however unconsciously, the unstable, perhaps even inessential, nature of identity itself through her cross-cultural, cross-sexual dressing. Rice suggests that the subversiveness of Eberhardt's nomadic identity derives from her existence outside a system of binary opposition: "Eberhardt, whether by intention or accident, slips out from under this binary coding. In merely trying to chart her own path in life, Eberhardt managed to run afoul of everyone else's agenda. Her true offense to civilized society—be it French or Arab—was that she called the system of codification into question by her existence."[40] But in fact, Eberhardt does not so much exist outside the system of binary opposition as deeply within the system, or rather within several systems simultaneously. In negotiating competing and contradictory systems she ends up reinstalling the naturalness of some and troubling the naturalness of others. In pursuing the "other" in herself through the "other" outside, this European subject both reinforces and confuses the culturally constructed boundaries between the subject and the self-consolidating other. Her very participation in colonialist and primitivist discourses simultaneously serves to uphold and to undo the assumptions informing those discourses.

But this is to look at her impact upon the inhabitants of the land through which she traveled and the impact on certain discourses through which she wrote of those travels. I want to close, however, with a consideration of her situation as a fin de siècle traveler through the exotic. Eberhardt creates herself as the isolated individual, the romantic artist in exile. She effectively becomes, to use Spivak's phrase but with some modification, "not-quite, not-woman;"[41] but also not-quite, not-European; not-quite, not-man (or boy, as she was taken to be); not-quite, not-Muslim. Ultimately Eberhardt is not-quite anything, and not-quite not-anything. In this sense perhaps she achieves what she set out to achieve: she becomes an "exotic" subject from both sides of the colonial divide.

But she is an exotic subject in a community of one, totally isolated, entirely homeless, historically situated. Shuttling between an illegitimate but inescapable home and a truer but elusive home, she is caught in the modernist condition of "transcendental homelessness." Torgovnick, adopting the phrase from Georg Lukacs and his theory of the novel, describes the mind of the "transcendentally homeless" as "secular but yearning for the sacred, ironic but yearning for the absolute, individualistic but yearning for the wholeness of community, asking questions but receiving no answers, fragmented but yearning for 'immanent totality.'"[42] Eberhardt is forever seeking and never finding the authentic experience and self promised her in the dream of fin de siècle exoticism. She can find no place of comfort, no community of kindred souls, no alternative cultural affiliation. For she can never get to any home with "nomads" who have escaped the history of European colonialism. And she can never get to any "other" in herself not consolidated through the European identity she seeks to shed. There is no place of origin outside the history of European relationships with North Africa, colonial relationships in which Eberhardt herself plays her part.[43] Eberhardt's "better self" can never be achieved. It remains a constantly deferred destination. There is no going home precisely because there is no going primitive possible at the beginning of the twentieth century. There is only writing about what has already been written and written over.

And yet . . . in that very failure/impossibility lies a complex legacy. Writing as she crossed between Europe and North Africa, writing as she crossed the vast spaces of the Maghreb, Eberhardt wrote into her journal, as into her other writings, crossings of linguistic codes. As a result she left behind what Hedi Abdel-Jaouad describes as a palpable Babel, a polyphonic linguistic practice, incorporating the simultaneous use of two languages, multiple scripts, pidginization, indigenous words, relexification.[44] Through this polylinguism she effectively displaced the privileges of French as the monolanguage through which the colonial order was consolidated. For Abdel-Jaouad "this literary genealogy may be construed, albeit posthumously, as the culmination of her search for identity and identification."[45] As she sought to escape the enervating effects of European history in a "timeless" Maghreb, Eberhardt incorporated into the language of her journal the transcultural traces of the history of Europe's colonial engagement with North Africa.

She was, in all these contradictory ways, a subject of her times.

Notes

I am indebted for aspects of the following analysis to students in a course on travel literature I taught in the spring of 1992, specifically Christine Bucher, Dianne Fallon, Vicki Ramirez, and Steve Krempa.

1. Isabelle Eberhardt, *The Passionate Nomad: The Diary of Isabelle Eberhardt* (Boston, Beacon Press, 1988). Henceforth, quotes will cited in the text by page number only. I am indebted to Karen Lawrence for the idea of "reading" the cover of the texts as suggestive of the positioning of the Western subject, in "Always Take Measurements, Miss Kingsley, and Always Take Them from the Adult Male" (paper delivered at the 1990 Modern Language Association Meeting, Chicago).

2. The phrase is Terry Eagleton's, from "Nationalism: Irony and Commitment," in *Nationalism, Colonialism, and Literature*, ed. Terry Eagleton, Fredric Jameson, Edward W. Said, (Minneapolis: University of Minnesota Press, 1990), 31. Concerned about the ironic relationship between the specific/individual and the universal, Eagleton writes, "As Oscar Wilde well understood, socialism is essential for genuine individualism; and if Wilde's own outrageous individualism prefigures that in one sense, it also testifies in its very flamboyant artifice to the way in which any individualism of the present is bound to

very flamboyant artifice to the way in which any individualism of the present is bound to be a strained, fictive, parodic travesty of the real thing."

3. Laura Rice, "'Nomad Thought': Isabelle Eberhardt and the Colonial Project," *Cultural Critique*, no. 17 (winter 1990–91): 152.

4. Chris Bongie, *Exotic Memories: Literature, Colonialism, and the Fin de Siecle* (Stanford, Stanford University Press, 1991), 21. Bongie is here differentiating between "adventure" and "quest."

5. Rice, "'Nomad Thought,'" 151–52.

6. Eberhardt's mother, joined by her children's tutor, ran away from Russia and her husband. In Geneva, where she lived as an expatriate member of the Russian aristocracy, she and the tutor maintained their masquerade. He remained the avuncular "tutor" even though he was in fact the father of Eberhardt and her brother.

7. Rice, "'Nomad Thought,'" 154.

8. Marianna Torgovnick, *Gone Primitive: Savage Intellects, Modern Lives* (Chicago: University of Chicago Press, 1990), 185.

9. Regenia Gagnier, "The Literary Standard, Working-Class Autobiography, and Gender," in *Revealing Lives: Autobiography, Biography, and Gender*, ed. Susan Groag Bell and Marilyn Yalom (Albany: SUNY Press, 1990), 100.

10. "The farther behind I leave the past," Eberhardt writes, "the closer I am to forging my own character" (4).

11. See Abena Busia, "Silencing Sycorax: On African Colonial Discourse and the Unvoiced Female," *Cultural Critique*, no. 14 (winter 1989–90): 97.

12. Annette Kobak, *The Life of Isabelle Eberhardt* (New York: Alfred A. Knopf, 1989), 16.

13. Busia, "Silencing Sycorax," 94.

14. Only once in the journal (that we have as translated) does she identify herself specifically as female. Into the text of the diary she incorporates the two letters she wrote for the public in response to the attempt on her life. In a letter written after the verdict of the trial she admits: "Abdallah has a wife and children. I am a woman and can only feel bottomless pity for the widow and orphans" (62). But this is not the journal so much as a letter for public consumption, an explanatory epistle through which she seeks to put the record straight about the attempted assassination and the trial that followed. While she incorporates this letter in her journal, its purpose is significantly different from that of the journal. She would "normalize" herself in this letter, positioning herself not as freak but as someone who shares common, and rather more conventional, values with the reader. See also the discussion of Eberhardt's friendship with and respect for Lalla Zaynab, an Algerian saint and mystic who served as her religious mentor, in Julia Clancy-Smith, "The 'Passionate Nomad' Reconsidered: A European Woman in *L'Algérie Française* (Isabelle Eberhardt, 1877–1904)," in *Western Women and Imperialism: Complicity and Resistance*, ed. Nupur Chaudhuri and Margaret Strobel (Bloomington: Indiana University Press, 1992), 69–70.

15. Georges Van Den Abbeele, *Travel As Metaphor from Montaigne to Rousseau* (Minneapolis: University of Minnesota Press, 1992), xxv. See also Sara Mills, *Discourses of Difference* (New York, Routledge, 1992), esp. the first three chapters.

16. Rana Kabbani, Introduction, to Eberhardt, *Passionate Nomad*, xii.

17. Anorexics, after all, starve themselves out of their bodies.

18. See Georg Simmel, *The Sociology of Georg Simmel*, ed. and trans. Kurt H. Wolff (Glencoe, Ill.: Free Press, 1950), 410. Quoted in Dean MacCannell, *The Tourist: A New Theory of the Leisure Class* (New York: Schocken Books, 1989), 49.

19. Elsewhere Eberhardt writes, "the human body is nothing, the human soul is all" (45).

20. See Bongie, *Exotic Memories*, 21–22.

21. Ibid., 22.

22. Ibid., 88.

23. They are often massified. But there are differences in the way she massifies the men and the women. The men are massified as primitive and savage and courageous. The women are massified as part of a neurotic herd, beneath observation.

24. For an analysis of the imperialist practices of landscape description in travel narratives of the nineteenth century, see Mary Louise Pratt, "Scratches on the Face of the Country, or, What Mr. Barrow Saw in the Land of the Bushman," *Critical Inquiry* 12 (autumn 1985): 120, 127.

25. Bongie, *Exotic Memories*, 88.

26. Kobak, *The Life of Isabella Eberhardt*, 130.

27. Rice, "'Nomad Thought,'" 153.

28. Gayatri Chakravorty Spivak, "Three Women's Texts and a Critique of Imperialism," in *Feminisms: An Anthology of Literary Theory and Criticism*, ed. Robyn R. Warhol and Diane Price Herndl (New Brunswick: Rutgers University Press, 1991), 807.

29. Mallek Alloula, *The Colonial Harem*, trans. Myrna Godzich and Wlad Godzich (Minneapolis: University of Minnesota Press, 1986), 38. The "modern couple, itself the expression of a more rational order of which colonization is supposedly the purport, finally makes its appearance and takes the place of the 'anarchic,' irreducible, traditional family" (39).

30. Bongie, *Exotic Memories*, 87.

31. Ibid., 21. He is here summarizing Edward Said's critique of Rudyard Kipling's *Kim*.

32. Van Den Abbeele, *Travel as Metaphor*, xviii.

33. Her personal history, her roots in an aristocratic family, but one that has lost its wealth, catapults her into a position of homelessness, although her own failure to act in her interest continues a poverty that was hers to avoid.

34. Van Den Abbeele, *Travel as Metaphor*, xv.

35. See Françoise Lionnet, "Logiques Metisses: Interpretation and Appropriation in Cross-Cultural Representation" (paper delivered at the 1991 American Comparative Literature Association meeting, San Diego).

36. See Lillian Robinson, "Working/Women's Writing," *Sex, Class, and Culture* (New York: Methuen, 1986), 226. Quoted in Gagnier, "The Literary Standard," 93.

37. Judith Butler, *Gender Trouble: Feminism and the Subversion of Identity* (New York: Routledge, 1990), 137.

38. See Marjorie Garber, *Vested Interests: Cross-Dressing and Cultural Anxiety* (New York: Routledge, 1992), 328.

39. See Homi Bhabha, "Of Mimicry and Man: The Ambivalence of Colonial Discourse," *October* 28 (Spring 1984).

40. Rice, "'Nomad Thought,'" 163.

41. Spivak, "Three Women's Texts," 799.

42. Torgovnick, *Gone Primitive*, 188; the phrase comes from Georg Lukacs, *The Theory of the Novel*, trans. Anna Bostock (Cambridge: MIT Press, 1971).

43. See Clancy Smith's reconsideration of Eberhardt's complicity with colonial authorities, particularly with General Lyautey whose "accomplice" she became in his campaign to "weaken the Moroccan Sultan's authority over the truculent tribes of the ill defined border regions" (70–72).

44. Hedi Abdel-Jaouad, "Isabelle Eberhardt: Portrait of the Artist as a Young Nomad," *Yale French Studies* 83 (1993): 111–16.

45. Ibid., 117.

PART IV

Passages to Other/s' Politics

Nation as the Concept of 'Democratic Otherness': *Christopher Unborn* and the Plea for Hybrid Cultures

INEKE PHAF

In this essay I intend to construct a link between the concepts of 'modernity' and 'hybridization' as discussed by Néstor García Canclini, an Argentinian anthropologist, and Bruno Latour, a French sociologist.[1] This link will be connected with the analysis of the novel *Christopher Unborn*,[2] by the Mexican Carlos Fuentes, by analyzing the way in which he deals with understanding democracy in the Americas.

In his voluminous novel Fuentes outlines a specific type of cultural politics in Mexico in the year 1992, which was projected as the year of discovery of the *Pacífica*. He concentrates on the period from January 6 (Epiphany) until October 12 (the Day of the Encounter, as Christopher Columbus annotes his landing in his diary). Fuentes's point is that the development of Mexico as an independent republic since 1821 has led to such a fragmentation of the territory that any possibility of shared experience as a democracy now seems to be utopic. This implies that the bare result of modernity in this independent republic is the loss of mediatory capacities that could bind the nation with a sense of unity in the public space.[3] The novel is told from the perspective of the unborn fetus Christopher, who reports the story of his journey to life as a liquid adventure in which he reflects on the main problems awaiting him: change of climate, pollution, hygienic provisions, and, more specifically, the political crisis in Mexico.

Problems of modernity are also placed in the center of consideration by Latour and García Canclini, as the title of their works already suggests. In *Nous n'avons jamais été modernes: Essai d'anthropologie symétrique*, Latour begins by speaking about reading his daily newspaper. Under the label "Crisis" he exclaims that it is full of *hybrid articles* in which similar issues show up that Fuentes discusses in his

321

novel. It is obvious that the average reader finds his information on overwhelming contemporary problems disseminated by various academic fields. On the one hand, Latour argues that this is mostly the case in university matters. Those specialists are hybrids themselves, not knowing how to separate one discipline from another. On the other hand, they continue leaning on the *separation of two experiential fields*, the scientific and the human, a procedure that has its roots in the seventeenth century and figures as an underlying regularity since then. In the opinion of Latour, both arguments need to be made more transparent. Scientific inventions are no longer to be viewed as dealing exclusively with the nature or the knowledge from *things-in-themselves* but have to be understood as profoundly compromised with our collectives; they even form part of the incentives that move the inner dynamics of our societies.

According to Latour, the turning point that urges reconsideration of this procedure is the year 1989, the year the Berlin Wall crashed down and all the political, social, and economic systems based on the mere distinction between socialism and capitalism no longer made any sense. In the mainstream of general forwarding trends *networks* labeled as "modern," "postmodern," "pre-modern," and so forth appear as the only reminders of this distinction. Latour conceives the meaning of the key word for those networks—*modern*—as the designation of two ensembles of completely different practices—*translation and purification*. The procedure of translation implies a hybrid proliferation between completely new genres, whereas the procedure of critical purification points to the differentiation between two completely different onthological zones, the human and the nonhuman. In order to be efficient, both practices must remain separate. They originate from the inventors of our modern world, Boyle and Hobbes, who were the founders of the meaning of "scientific" and "political" representation respectively. According to this distinction, the representation of things through the laboratory is forever dissociated from the representation of citizens through a social contract.[4]

After having exposed the difference between both representations, Latour declares that we are *really modern* if we know how to distinguish, within the networks, between the two ensembles of practices previously mentioned. As anthropology has recognized, both poles have always existed; the question is how to understand their relationship. Here Latour adds that although the hybrids were once eliminated from the human mind, in the present situation they have increased to such a degree that it is no longer possible to extract them. Nobody knows what the consequences of this new situation will be. Latour asks himself if it will either create monsters or, simply, another understanding of democracy incorporating the role of science.

It is striking that Néstor García Canclini, in *Culturas híbridas: Estrategias para entrar y salir de la modernidad*, without quoting anything of Latour's reflections on modernity, takes up a similar argument. First of all, in the title of his book he refers to the same quotation from Nietzsche as does Latour in his essay.[5] For García Canclini, the strategies for handling modernity run parallel with the presentation of the contemporary urban society as a postmodern laboratory in a permanent borderline situation. The stability of the national patrimony and its sociocultural codes is continuously challenged from inside and outside. In Mexico, the idea of the national patrimony always coincides with the presence of the pre-Columbian past. Octavio Paz, in the *Labyrinth of Solitude*, already proclaimed in the beginning of the fifties that this presence is fundamental for the symbolic representation of Mexico in that it provides the country a unifying mask behind which its hybrid dynamics are at work. García Canclini emphasizes that these hybrid dynamics are different from syncretism and similar concepts that are barred from any sense of resistance against oppressive state procedures. As an anthropologist he makes the point that hybrid cultures refute the classical opposition between modern and traditional, urban and rural, sophisticated and popular, hegemonical and subaltern in order to display other features more relevant to contemporary situations. In this sense, García Canclini conceives them at work in the *global urban topography as a postmodern laboratory and a border line*, always challenging the immobility of any national patrimony, especially in the countries of Latin America. Its dynamics function as a selective and innovative mechanism that combines the numerous fragments of the present in a collective setting, in a nation, simultaneously giving it an historical meaning.

It is this complexity of setting into motion the concept of a nation as a New Body, formed from all possible genders, origins, and languages, which is at stake in the *Unborn Christopher*. Nobody pays the slightest attention to the government in México D. F. or Washington, D.C. Fuentes describes how it is obvious that the *capital* desperately needs a *new symbol of unity* now that Mexico and the United States are divided into different territories: the Lacandonan forest with its last surviving tribe; the territory of Yucatán, ceded exclusively to the Club

Méditerranée in order to create the Peninsular Tourism Trust (PENITT);
the Chitacam Trusteeship (Chiapas-Tabasco-Campeche), ceded to the
U.S. oil consortium called the "Five Sisters"; the besieged halfmoon of
Veracruz ceded to an incomprehensible war, an agrarian revolution
according to some, a U.S. invasion according to others; and at the
northern border Mexamérica, which is independent of Mexico and the
United States, in-bond factories, smuggling, contraband, Spanglish,
providing refuge for political fugitives and free entry for those without
papers from the Pacific Coast to the Gulf Coast. This Mexamérica, one
hundred kilometers to the north and one hundred to the south from the
old frontier, became independent without any declaration.

Such a panorama of the "mutilated fatherland" is observed by Don
Fernando Benítez as he sits in a little airplane, and looks down on this
Old Body, the "narrow, skeletal, and *decapitated nation*, its *chest* in the
deserts of the north, its *infarcted heart* in the exit point of the Gulf at
Tampico, its *belly* in Mexico City, its suppurating, venereal anus in
Acapulco, its *cut-off knees* in Guerrero and Oaxaca" (19–20). Notwith-
standing this depressing view, Don Benítez suspects that another body is
resting under its surface, one that can be reanimated by the return of a
popular symbol, something like the Virgin of Guadelupe. On December
9 and 12, in 1531, she appeared to Juan Diego, an Indian, in the
neighborhood of the city of Mexico, newly founded upon the ruins of
Tenochtitlán. Since then she has been the sustenance and hope to many
Mexicans, whatever their position in society.

In order to develop a modern version of her, Fuentes models a
nameless secretary from México D. F. into the person of Mamadoc, the
Mother and Doctor of All Mexicans. It is she who has to restore the
former brilliance and powerful appearance of the nation's capital. That
amorphous city is reminiscent of Berlin in the thirties and is at the
zenith of its powerful decadence. Fuentes characterizes its ideology as
an ambiguous variant of *Mein Kampf* (369). "Makesick City" prepares
for the symbolic celebration of October 12. On this day the government
plans the "Discovery of America Contest" (5). The winning baby, born
on this day, will be president for life and the e-lector (translated as the
"selective reader") acts as the coauthor of this important event.

In the Palace of the Citizenry, in the northern sector of the city (the
Pan-American Highway's symbolic end point, flanked on both sides by
statues of the Green Indians), pregnant women can register to participate in the contest. There are two persons in charge who check each

fetus in the womb of its mother as a possible candidate for the up-coming Contest of the Americas. Doctor Menges and the "lady who looked like one of the Bergen-Belsen jail guards in an early-forties Warner Brothers movie" convince themselves of the existence of the fetus. Of course, "impure" Christopher is explicitly denied access to this for being "not Aryan . . ., this baby has the blood of slaves, gypsies, Indians, Moors, Jews, Semites" (324). At the precise moment that "the doctor's beswastikaed branding iron approached my exit" (325), the parents, horrified, run away as they look for the exit out of the building that bears all the features of a labyrinth.

Their flight from a threatening holocaust is linked to the special situation in which Mexico finds itself as a part of the body of "sub-altern nations" with similar slogans: "Citizens . . . : industrialize! You won't live longer but you will live better" (23). By discussing statistical information, the government compares Mexico with Guinea-Bissau as being two countries in which the vast majority is *screwed* (28). The discussion flows around the issue that "one system is falling apart on us, but we have no other system to put in its place" (29), a clear allu-sion to the similarity of problems of modernization in the countries of Africa.[6] It is even mentioned that Africa begins in the Andes. In this situation, the young and dynamic minister-for-life, Ulises López, "head of the Secretariat for Patriotism and Foreign Undertakings (SEPAFU)" (28), presents *economics as an exact science that will never fall apart.* The problem is how to deal with it symbolically while imagining it as a cultural fact.

The reflection on this problem begins on January 6, when Christo-pher's parents decide to conceive a son on the beach of Acapulco. His impurity derives from his parents' mixed origin. The family of the father, Angel Palomar, is highly prestigious due to its involvement in the history of modern Mexico since the Revolution, whereas the family of Angeles, his wife, is unknown. This discrepancy in backgrounds already indicates the historically hybrid genre of the future baby and becomes increasingly important. Angel's grandfather, General Rigoberto Palo-mar, figures as a national treasure: "the last survivor of the Revolution in a political system excessively eager for legitimacy" (67). He is the only one who hears the last words of General Alvaro Obregón: "More corn muffins, more corn muffins" (67), which he keeps a secret all his life. General Rigoberto Palomar has only one son. However, this son and his wife learn his secret. Because of the combination of their humanitarian and scientific concerns they are called the "Curies of

Tlalpan," the village in the outskirts of México D. F. The Curies of
Tlalpan translate the General's secret idea by inventing the Inconsumable Taco: "a taco that, the more it is eaten, the more it grows back:
the solution to Mexico's nutrition problems! the greatest national idea!"
(56). Their death leaves their son Angel behind as the orphan of this
Inconsumable Taco.

Unlike his father, who desperately tries to be accepted by the rich
upper ten of society, the unborn Christopher follows the steps of these
Scientists,[7] who are children from the revolutionary ideals from the past.
It takes him nine months to reflect on the transformation from the image
of a "Sweet Fatherland," which is a reference to the famous poem "La
Suave Patria" (April 4, 1921), by Ramón López Velarde, on the reality
of 1992, a "No Man's Fatherland" where everybody is moving on one
of the diverse highways, the only free place to be.[8] However, this part of
the book is no new version of Jack Kerouac's *On the Road*. All truck
drivers are "screwed" by a voice on the radio claiming that "there's an
Ayatollah in your future/pass it on" (416), and "there is a nation! we are
all here!" (417). Escorted by Ayatollah Matamoros, a frustrated poet,
the Mamadoc, a mechanical puppet without memory, already waits for
them when they enter the capital. This encounter implies another
unnecessary test to Mexican history of melodrama and sacralized
violence. The people are shot by the machine guns of the army, and "on
the night of the Ayatollah, Mexico City once again witnessed everything
it could bear: only the memory (extinct) of the fall of the Aztec capital or
the forgetting (voluntary) of the memory of the earthquake of September
19, 1985, could be compared to this new disaster" (450).

As Walter Benjamin has outlined for the capital of the nineteenth
century, Paris, and for Berlin in the thirties, the advancing technological
production of symbolic representation is a feature that brings out political manipulation on a very large scale. It must be thus continuously the
subject of social criticism, which is an issue taken up by Fuentes. He
imagines Mexico's democracy in 1992 by concentrating on the role of
the Spanish language as the mediator toward democratic sensitivity.
Therefore, two uncles of Angel Palomar's become very relevant. One of
them is Uncle Homero, sixty years old, who represents a language full of
academic references introduced by the famous phrase of Don José
Vasconcelos in the twenties: "Through my race shall speak the spirit" (In
Spanish: "Por mi raza hablará el espiritu"). It is clear that Vasconcelos's
version is on the decline in a country where the words of the president of
the republic are listened to "by way of loudspeakers" (21). The other

uncle, Fernández Benítez, eighty years old, is the researcher of an opposite language that functions as a secret code. He pays a visit to a place
where he observes something never seen "in more than thirty years of
visiting the most isolated and inhospitable places in Mexico" (208). As
a scholar who has studied the Indian population of Mexico all his life,[9]
he now encounters for the first time the ritual greetings of the sun by a
group of Indians, a group of people who live in a completely different
notion of time than he does. They don't even seem to be aware of the
presence of this "invisible author."[10]

From this point one realizes that the academic and the invisible
versions of language are converted into the genes of the unborn Christopher, alias Carlos Fuentes. This Christopher/Fuentes incorporates
these as two linguistic codes into his narrative enterprise. The illustrous
and very visible family of Angel Palomar is linked with the anonymous
part of the population through the mother, Angeles. Abandoned by her
husband, she resides with the survivors of the "lost cities of Mexico" in
the "anonymous cities: larger than Paris or Rome, six, seven, eight
million inhabitants, but *no name*" (83). Mother and son share their
destiny with the Four Fuckups, a group of four young musicians:
Orphan Huerta, Hipi Toltec, Egg, and the invisible Baby Ba, whose
common concern is to survive by shaping a language that adequately
verifies their existence in the present world. They are forced to take into
account that in this overall Global Village the Spanish language is
invaded by all types of different variants of English and vice versa.[11]

The unborn Christopher perceives all these complications in the
uterus of his mother. He considers his narrative enterprise as a very
personal scientific preoccupation, a Heisenberg society, "the first club I
ever belonged to" (63). His condition as a fetus allows him to participate as an invisible observer in order to outline the logics of his novel:
"the logic of the symbol does not express the experiment; it *is* the
experiment. Language is the phenomenon, and the observation of the
phenomenon changes its nature."[12] Initially, Ayatollah Matamoros
appears as the prototype of a Spanish language that purifies without
permitting any critical view. This is transformed into a populist culture,
which is personified by his lover, a Chilean named Concha Toro. She
has found "the synthesis of her life in the resurrected bolero, the bolero
disdained by Mexican modernity, by the youth of the postpunk
rockaztec of the early nineties, [. . .] and restored to the bolero what
Homero Fagoaga could never restore to the Spanish language: bril-

liance, fame, emotion, incalculable splendor" (401–2). It is clear that
such a splendor does not provide criticism against the "enlightened"
dictatorship of Mamadoc, who, with the Ayatollah Matamoros and
Concha Toro, leads the people to their graves. The Four Fuckups and
Angeles intend to formulate a countermovement in those "desperate
outskirts of the city," "of the suffering city, the outskirts of the lost city's
garbage dump and the sand dumps and the caves and cardboard houses
of the anonymous cities inhabited by millions of people as anonymous
as the places in which they lived" (421). In the center of the conversation of these marginal inhabitants, an Aztec verse is emphasized that
says:

Ueuetiliztli!
Xocoyotzin!
Aic nel toxaxahacayan.
Olloliuhqui, olloliuhqui!

[Old folks!
Young pup!
We shall never be obliterated.
How the wheel of fortune spins!][13]

It is obvious that Fuentes here refers to the discussion on the *lost cities*
(since Tenochtitlán)), its *forgotten* youth (since the film *Los Olvidados*,
by Luis Buñuel), the *informal sector* (a sociological term distinguishing
between socially classified sectors and the large informal and unknown
sector in the increasingly expanding metropolitan areas in the world),
or the *culture of poverty* (a concept from Oscar Lewis[14]). All these
concepts are interrelated by Fuentes, who adds recent observations on
the importance of the visibility of the indigenous presence in the
contemporary setting of the country.[15] The incorporation of these
problems into a Spanish language that is able to elucidate its contemporary details is a goal pursued by *Pacífica*, the ultimate station of the
narrative journey. This novel on pregnancy ends with Christopher's
birth back at the place where he was conceived "facing the sea, at
Revolcadero beach, facing the Pacific Ocean" (511).

Surprisingly, this New Body is born as part of a twin, a girl, who
appears to be the invisible Baby Ba, the only girl in the group of the
Four Fuckups. The moment of birth symbolizes the farewell to the Old
World of division, "corruption, injustice, stupidity, egoism, arrogance,

disdain, and hunger" (512). It is within this concept that the formerly neglected Pacific Coast of this northern part of the Americas is given a new meaning.[16] It includes the Asian side of the Pacific Ocean and, in this way, contains "half the world's population, working together, three-fourths of the world's commerce, almost all of the world's advanced technology, the maximum conjunction of labor, technical know-how, and political will in human history" (513). Fuentes claims that this "Pacífica" is no Utopia but a place where the works of culture are highly considered. They are as real "as a mountain or a transistor, that there is no real life without a still life to compensate for it in art, no living present with a dead past, no acceptable future that does not allow exceptions to progress, and no technological progress that does not incorporate the warnings of art" (514).

In this *Pacífica* cultural criticism becomes extremely relevant. In the fourth chapter, the "Festive Intermerzo," Fuentes discusses this issue in full. He begins by criticizing the cultural politics in the United States, where "Ronald Ranger has destroyed higher education [. . .] with the speed of the fastest gun in the West. Among the items the President had certainly read on the hit list for budget cuts were two exotic subjects, Spanish-American Literature and Comparative Mythology. The President had wondered what earthly use they could have and marked them as definite cuts from the federal aid package" (181). This earthly use is confirmed when Professor Will Gingerich, an anthropologist from Dartmouth College, goes to Acapulco. There, precisely at 9 A.M. on Monday, January 6, 1992, Gingerich meets the Antillean critic Emilio Domínguez del Tamal, "known as the Sergeant because of his long record of denunciations, detectivelike snooping, and thundering excommunications" (192). Domínguez del Tamal is accompanied by his opponent, the eminent South American critic Egberto Jiménez-Chicharra, who is "fat and olive-complexioned, all beard, oil, and melancholic eyes" (192).

In this sense, Fuentes proclaims a renewal in cultural politics throughout the Spanish-speaking countries of the Americas, including the United States, a renewal that accompanies the demographic explosion and demands awareness of the new situation of forming part of the Earthly Global Village. As we already how from the beginning of this essay, hybrid proliferation cannot be excluded from its public representation any longer. As a consequence, the New Body of this global postmodern laboratory of small urban entities has to reveal problems belonging to the field of the exact sciences, such as pollution (present at every page of the story as it describes Makesick City) or the consequences of an economic program that proceeds according to the abstractions of the Chicago Boys.[17] Such an experiential cultural criticism contributes to a reflection on general issues of social and scientific representation, a concept that surprisingly parallels the thesis from Latour and García Canclini.

There can be no doubt that the message of Fuentes's "monument of literary invention," as the back cover of the English translation makes us believe, is a consequence of the critical discussion on problems of economic growth and democracy in Latin American countries. It began in the late sixties, and Fuentes has been one of its most ardent observers. In this novel, he presents his most recent observations on this topic as it relates to Mexico. The book is full of interpretations on contemporary political or cultural conflicts, in many cases recognizable only by a Mexican reader or by a reader who is familiar with the country. The underlying tone is, however, universal and embraces problems similar to those in other disadvantaged "subaltern nations" in the industrial world. Precisely these issues have been taken up by the magazine *Transition*, which was originally founded in 1961 in Uganda. After fifty issues it had to stop publishing, but in 1991 Oxford University Press started publishing with number 51—with Wole Soyinka as the chairman and Carlos Fuentes as the only Latin American writer on the editorial board. In the opening issue, Fuentes discusses in his article "The End of Ideologies?"[18] the consequences of the end of the cold war. He argues that the "main actor in this new project for universality is the migrant worker who arrives in our cities and challenges our prejudices, obliging us to experience a world-wide process of cultural unity that is founded not just on ideological principles, but on economic needs" (30). Fuentes imagines that it is possible to create "a model city for the twenty-first century, a multiracial and polycultural city that is a true reflection of instant communication, economic integration, and cultural diversity" (31). In *Christopher Unborn* this city presents itself in its Latin American variant. The scientific and the social presentation constantly meet each other in the culture of daily life, and they are inseparably linked to the politics of the nation. Its national patrimony implies a secret code that challenges cultural criticism. That is how Fuentes intends to make readers aware of this specific variant of modernity dealing with his narrative agenda of conflict situations in the so-called subaltern nations of the contemporary world.

Notes

1. Latour, Bruno, *Nous n'avons jamais été modernes. Essai d'anthropologie symétrique* (Paris: Editions la Découverte, 1991); Nestir García Canclini, *Culturas híbridas: Estrategias para entrar y salir de la modernidad* (Mexico: Grijalbo, 1989).

2. Published in Spanish as *Christóbal Nonato*, Fondo de Cultura Económica, in Mexico in 1987; translated into English by Alfred McAdam (New York: Vintage International, 1989). Henceforth quotations are indentified in the text by page number only.

3. Fuentes expresses this as follows: "mi padre le dio la razón a Nuestro Pariente, toda una era llamada la Modernidad (igualmente opuesta a la Mothernidad de los orígenes y a la Moderridad del pasado) que ha significado individualizarse al extremo para el futuro extremo que nos aguarda, alejarse, horror, de las abstracciones colectivas de nuestros antepasados grecolatinos y medionavales y ser tú sólo tú, yo mero petatero caracterizado hasta la incomprensión" (105). This fragment, belonging to the chapter "On Birds Who Speak Our Language," has been eliminated from the English version.

4. ". . . un monde dans lequel la représentation des choses par l'intermédiaire du laboratoire est à jamais dissociée de la représentation des citoyens par l'intermédiaire du contrat social" (43).

5. "Nietzsche disait des grands problèmes qu'ils étaient comme les bains froids: il faut y entrer vite et en sortir de même" (22).

6. This is certainly a reference to the novel *Things Fall Apart*, by Chinua Achebe from Nigeria. His book, which has been celebrated as Africa's most famous novel, was initially published in London in 1958. It tells the story of an Igbo village and its reactions when confronted with the British system of colonization.

7. "Thanks to them, I understand that whatever is provisional because the time and space that precede me and whatever I know about them I know only fleetingly, as I pass, purely by chance, through this hour and this place. The important thing is that the syntheses never finish, that no one save himself, ever, from the contradiction of being in one precise place and one precise time and nevertheless thinking about a time and place that are infinite, denying the end of experience, maintaining open the infinite possibilities for observing the infinite events in the unfinished world and transforming them as I observe them: turning them into history, narrative, language, experience, infinite reading" (63).

8. "To drive on one of these highways, the Pan-american to Mexamerica, the Christopher Columbus to Oaxaca, the Transistémica to the Chitacam Trusteeship, was like heading into a country that belonged to all and to none, a free territory. The highways of the nineties are buffer zones in which all the weight of the newly mutilated Sweet Fatherland resolves itself in a kind of rapid, fleeting freedom—a swift and ephemeral freedom, but a freedom nonetheless. The highway knows no obstacles, like an arrow piercing the air" (413).

9. "Uncle Fernando had spent half his life documenting Mexico's four or five million Indians, those who were never conquered by the Spaniards, who never allowed themselves to be assimilated into the creole or mestizo world, or who simply survived the demographic catastrophe of the conquest: there were twenty-five million of them before Cortés landed in Tabasco; fifty years later, only one million were left" (208).

10. "Night fell fatally, and the Indians, once again leaning on their plows, had to return to their domestic chores, eat hunkered down next to their dying fires, all in silence, alien to my uncle now as always, my uncle who for them had never been there, this man who traveled and wrote books invisibly, that's how he felt it that afternoon on the dry plateau in the uplands: they never saw him or greeted him. The invisible author" (213).

11. Fuentes discusses this in the following quotation, eliminated from the English version of the novel: "el tío Homero llega a su vez a la conclusión, característicamente, de que en efecto vivimos en la Aldea Global y que si el idioma de la Pérfida Albión y sus perversas colonias trasatlánticas contamina la pureza de nuestra heredad verbal castellana, no es menos cierto que sesenta millones de inmigrados aztecas, guajiros y borinqueños terminarán por envenenar las tradiciones del idioma inglés" (103).

12. "[B]ut when I emerge from the interminable river to see a time and a place (which are my own), the one who accompanies me is the young mountain climber: thanks, Werner, and because of you and for you my very personal Heisenberg Society formed in the uterus of my mother Angeles, the first club I ever belonged to and from whose fluffy (enjoyable!) armchairs I already observe the world that nurtures me and which I nurture by observing it" (63).

13. 312 (English ed.). The well-known náhuatl-specialist Francis Karttunen showed me that the English translation differs considerably from the náhuatl version in the book. We cannot discuss the differences here but can focus on the meaning of this náhuatl present in the scope of reorganizing strategies of the nation Mexico. This verse is repeated twice, on pages 312 (339 Spanish ed.) and 464 (493 Spanish ed.) of the English version.

14. The "culture of poverty" is a term specially coined by the North American anthropologist Oscar Lewis. He wrote the famous study *The Children of Sánchez: Autobiography of a Mexican Family* (1961) about the inhabitants of a poor neighborhood in México D. F. This book is continuously referred to in the presence of Colasa Sánchez, the daughter of Ayatollah Matamoros, a myth who has an "indented vagina."

15. Fernando Benítez exists in real life. He wrote ten volumes on *Los indios de México*, of which exists an anthology published by Era in Mexico in 1989. Carlos Fuentes wrote the introduction (11–21), in which he discusses the fact that modern history since 1492 made the indigenous population invisible. These people remained with their own languages, many times considering the Spanish language as an enemy that divided and threatened their own community.

16. "[O]f which a part of Mexico already belongs, the whole Pacific coast from Ixtapa north, the whole Pacific basin from California to Oregon, Canada and Alaska, all of China and Japan, the peninsulas, the archipelagos, the islands, Oceania: a basin of 108 million square miles, three billion inhabitants" (513).

17. A strong parody on the situation in Chile under Pinochet is found in this novel. The Chilean bolero singer Concha Toro is the populist variant of the cultural politics of dictatorship. At the end of the book Chile is even absorbed by the Pacific Ocean. In this way, it become integrated into *Pacífica*, the democratic alternative of modernity in the future.

18. *Transition,* 51 (1991): 26–31.

CHAPTER 19

The "Other" as the "Self" under Cultural Dependency: The Impact of the Postcolonial University

ALI A. MAZRUI

Postcolonial African universities have often been expected to serve as major instruments of development in their societies. But what if those universities also constitute links in a chain of dependency? Does the postcolonial university transform an African self into a neo-Western other?

As instruments of potential development the postcolonial universities have been called upon to produce high level human-power, "relevant" research and training, "appropriate" skills, and potential innovators. Many universities have failed to live up to those developmental ideals, but development has continued to be regarded as a relevant basis for evaluating the performance of any African institution of higher learning.

But let us again ask the basic question: What if the institution is also a link in a chain of dependency that seeks to remold the African self into a Western other? Is it possible that the developmental lapses and deficiencies are connected with the constraints of dependency? And how can the dependency be transcended? How can we prevent what was *objectively "other"* from becoming *subjectively "self"*?

Some aspects of academic dependency in Africa are clear and unmistakable. In structure virtually all universities in Africa south of the Sahara are based on one or more Western models. Virtually all these African universities use a Western language as the primary medium of instruction. Many rely overwhelmingly on books and articles published by Westerners or in the West to fill the shelves of their modest libraries. Some continue to have large numbers of Western instructors and professors on their faculty. Qualifications for student admission and staff recruitment continue to put a high premium on prior assimilation into

Western culture among the candidates. Among the most prestigious of African universities are precisely those which were at one time, or continue to be, overseas extensions of some university in Europe. Among them are the universities of Ibadan, Ghana at Legon, Dakar, and the old Makerere in Uganda. The African self then was an *extension* of the European other.

Because our concern is partly with the search for a new international cultural order in this essay, we shall go beyond examining the intrinsic academic dependency of the African university in itself. We shall also explore the wider effect of that dependency on the society as a whole. An institution can itself be dependent without necessarily spreading dependency over the wider society. But the university in Africa is not only sick itself—it is also a source of wider infection and societal contagion. That is why this paper is about *cultural* dependency, and not merely about *academic* dependency within the university structure on its own. It is the *cultural self* that is at stake.

We should thus begin with what we mean by culture and then advance some working definition of our sense of dependency.

The Seven Functions of Culture

For our purposes in this essay, culture serves seven fundamental functions in society. First, it helps to provide *lenses of perception and cognition*. How people view the world is greatly conditioned by one or more cultural paradigms to which they have been exposed. A graduate from an African university thus views the world around him qualitatively differently from how he would have viewed it had he never gone to Western or neo-Western educational institutions.

The second function of culture lies in providing *motives for human behavior*. What makes a person behaviorally respond in a particular manner is partly cultural in origin. As a member of an audience in the theatre of Accra should I laugh when King Lear goes mad? Ghanaian undergraduates have been known to laugh at Shakespearean tragedy on the stage. Is this partly because they are caught up in a cultural ambivalence of some kind? What about the students' motive for being at the university at all? Is that also a product of culture change in Ghana?

The third function of culture lies in providing criteria of *evaluation*. What is deemed better or worse, ugly or beautiful, moral or immoral, attractive or repulsive, is partly a child of culture. The evaluative function of culture need not always correspond with the behavioral. Many African university graduates would condemn ethnic nepotism or "tribalism" as immoral. This is an evaluative position derived partly from Western influence. But the same graduates may find themselves *practising* ethnic nepotism in spite of their new values. This would be a case of behavioral dissonance.

The fourth function of culture provides *a basis of identification.* Ethnic nepotism is itself a product of culture in this identity sense. Western culture as transmitted in African educational institutions provides rival forms of identification—some of them related to the emergence of new elites and new social classes.

Fifth, culture is a *mode of communication.* The most elaborate system of communication is language itself. In East Africa in the first two decades of colonial rule there was considerable debate about language policy. Should the ethnic languages be given priority in the new imperial system? Or should Kiswahili be promoted as a *lingua franca?* Or did the cultural logic of European imperialism imply the promotion of European culture and languages first and foremost?

At the level of higher education when the time came there was little debate. The relevant medium of higher education was the imperial language itself. This decision, as we shall indicate later, had fundamental consequences in matters that range from intellectual imitation to elite-formation.

The sixth function of culture lies precisely in providing *a basis of stratification.* Class, rank, and status are profoundly conditioned by cultural variables. University education in Africa became a major factor in redefining status and gradation in modern African societies.

The seventh function of culture lies in *the system of production and consumption.* In our scheme of analysis—unlike in some Marxist schools—patterns of consumption sometimes affect production as profoundly as production helps to shape consumption. Universities in Africa have played a part in distorting consumption patterns as well as in influencing productive trends.

These seven functions of culture have relevance for the new international cultural order. What lies in the way is the whole problem of dependency. Let us now turn to this.

Types of Dependency

At least in the context of our analysis in this essay, dependency involves at least one of two forms of relationship. One is a relationship of *surplus need.* Society B is dependent on Society A if B needs A more than A needs B.

The second type of dependency involves *deficit control.* B is dependent on A if B has less control over their relationship than A has. In a colonial relationship proper A is the imperial power and B is each colony. After independence A's control may decline in some spheres.

But which spheres? For analytical purposes we may distinguish between the political sphere of dependency, the economic sphere, the military sphere, and the cultural.

In terms of surplus need before B became annexed as a colony, it was A that "needed" B economically. Colonies were perceived by A as potential sources of raw materials or as potential markets or as sources of labor or as recipients of surplus population from A. Technically, therefore, England was a dependency of its own empire in this special sense of England's economic needs, real or imagined.

But in terms of deficit economic control, it was the colonies that were dancing to England's economic commands instead of the other way around.

The factors that made the difference in control at that time were political and military. By definition the colonies were political dependencies of Great Britain and subject to its monopoly of physical force over their territory.

But while the British and the French were covetous of Africa's economic resources, they had little interest in Africa's cultural resources. Indeed, the French doctrine of assimilation was even prepared to exchange French culture for African economic riches. The French purposefully sought to make Africa's cultural self renounce itself.

This introduces a fundamental difference between economic dependency and cultural dependency. While economic dependency has always included some leverage on the part of the "colony" upon the metropole (since the center needs the periphery economically), cultural dependency has been much more of a case of one-way traffic at the organized level. The imperial power was prepared to dump its cultural goods on the African market, but it was not interested in purposefully importing African culture back into Europe. Whatever African culture has penetrated Europe has been due far less to organized European policies than to the activities of individual scholars, artists, and antiquarians and to the cultural impact of African slaves imported into the Western world.

Europe on the whole was prepared to offer its religion, languages, and culture to Africans—but only in exchange for land, mines, labor, energy, and other economic riches of Africa. Jomo Kenyatta in the old colonial Kenya was more profound than even he may have realized when he observed: "When the white man came to Africa he had the Bible and we had the land. And now? We have the Bible and he has the land." It was a classic case of offering culture in exchange for material goods—exporting arts and ideas and importing economic riches.

By the time African universities were established, Africans themselves were all too eager to scramble for Western culture. On the basis of surplus need, there was no doubt at all that Africans felt they needed Western culture far greater than the West felt it needed African culture. On the basis of deficit control, Western institutions exerted disproportionate control over African institutions. Cultural dependency was becoming much more acute, and less reciprocal, than economic dependency. Africans were capitulating to the temptations of exchanging old cultural selves for new ones.

The Impact of World War II

This brings us to the strange and paradoxical role of World War II in the history of the different forms of dependency in Africa. Politically, the war weakened imperial control and prepared the way for the disintegration of the empires of France and Great Britain. But economically the war helped to integrate the colonies more firmly into the global capitalist system as the economies of the periphery were made to serve more systematically the war needs of the center. As for the cultural impact of the war, it broadened Africa's exposure to alien influences and later resulted in the new imperialism of building higher educational institutions for the colonies. Militarily the war initiated more firmly the idea of recruiting African soldiers and setting up African armies equipped with modern weapons—with all the consequences that process has had for both military dependency and the tensions of civil-military relations in the former colonies.

Our focus in this particular section is on the impact of World War II on *cultural* dependency. But that requires some understanding of the other effects of the war.

Politically, imperial control was being weakened partly because of the weakening of the imperial powers themselves. France had been humiliated and partly occupied by the Germans—putting a strain on the old mystique of imperial invincibility and the grandeur of France, which had been propagandized in the colonies. Great Britain was becoming exhausted and impoverished as the war dragged on. British India was restive, though loyal—while the Japanese played havoc with Burma and the Malayan peninsula. The British Empire in Asia was not going to last long after the war even if Britain won.

African nationalists like Awolowo, Nkrumah, Kenyatta, and Azikiwe were watching these developments in the old empires with rising hopes and aspirations for Africa's own liberation. Even for those Africans who had not been abroad, the war was helping to broaden their international horizons in the very effort to follow the fortunes of the different battles on the radio and in "vernacular" newspapers. Never before had so many ordinary Africans tried so hard to understand conflicts in such remote places as Dunkirk and Rangoon, Pearl Harbor and even El Alamein.

In addition there were the African servicemen themselves who experienced combat thousands of miles from their villages, who learned new skills and acquired new aspirations, and who witnessed the White man in a new light, both as an enemy on the other side and sometimes as a frightened comrade in the trenches.

But while the war was thus undermining the political control of the old empires, it was also increasing temporarily Europe's need for the products of the colonies. There was rationing throughout the empires—and a continuing effort to make the colonies produce what Europe most needed. New food products were cultivated with Europe's hungry mouths in mind; new raw materials were produced in the periphery with Europe's industries as the intended market. There was a war boom in the colonies, to be followed later by a new depression. The very dialectic between this kind of boom and depression in Africa was a symptom of Africa's new level of economic integration into the international capitalist system. The same war that was weakening Britain's and France's political control over their colonies was at the same time deepening Africa's economic dependency upon the Western world as a whole.

What about the cultural impact of the war on Africa? This was partly related to the other processes we have mentioned. As more and more people in Britain realized that the colonies could not be held in subjection forever and that a new timetable was needed for imperial policy, a new commitment to "colonial development and welfare" emerged. It was no longer enough merely to maintain law and order in the colonies and let social change take its own slow course. A new sense of developmental urgency began to influence policy makers at the Colonial Office in London.

It was partly out of this developmental urgency that the idea of accelerating higher education for the colonies was elaborated further. In 1945 the Asquith Report, a blueprint for higher education in the colonies, was submitted to the British government. One of its basic assumptions was that the colonies needed the kind of indigenous leadership that had acquired Western skills and a "modern" outlook. The stage was being set for new forms of cultural penetration into the colonies.

But it should be emphasized at once that the motives were often of the highest. It was true that Africa had been left behind in certain basic skills of the "modern" technological era. Unfortunately the universities that were emerging were not primarily designed to help Africa close the technological gap between itself and those countries that were more advanced. On the contrary, the new colonial universities imported the same contempt for practical subjects that had characterized the academic ethos of the West for centuries. But while the West had evolved safeguards against this academic arrogance, and produced other ways of fostering technology and engineering, the colonies imported the academic arrogance without its safeguards.

The contradiction was not always recognized either by Britain or by the new spokesmen of African aspirations in the colonies. It was an often stated British imperial policy to offer Africans the education best suited to African conditions and needs. Educators such as Carey Francis in East Africa were most anxious not to de-Africanize African youth through Western education. But as a result of the educators on the ground not being sufficiently innovative, they ended up doing what they probably knew best—duplicating what was offered in Europe. Bishop Masasi's more distinctive experiments in Southern Tanganyika stood out among the rare innovations.

In some cases the new postwar policy of "universities for the colonies" partially diluted an earlier imperial commitment to vocational and practical training. In its preuniversity incarnation, Makerere in Uganda was noted less for its liberal arts than for professional training in "MAVE" (medicine, agriculture, veterinary science, and education). While these subjects continued to be a major concern of Makerere after it attained university status (veterinary science was later transferred to University College, Nairobi), the proportion of students taking them drastically declined. The appeal of the liberal arts deprived the Faculty of Education especially of its fair share of the brightest students for many years to come. In Makerere's preuniversity days, education as a professional faculty had a significantly higher proportion of the most gifted students than it did later. The most illustrious of this earlier batch of Makerere's trained teachers turned out to be Mwalimu Julius Nyerere, destined to become the philosopher-president of Tanzania several years later.

What all this means is that the new *welfare colonialism* that ensued upon World War II gave a new impetus to liberal arts and literary education, sometimes at the expense of earlier progress in more practically oriented educational policies.

In this connection it is worth bearing in mind important differences between the Westernization of Africa and the modernization of Japan after the Meiji Restoration of 1868. Japan's original modernization involved considerable selectivity on the part of the Japanese themselves. The whole purpose of selective Japanese Westernization was to protect Japan against the West, rather than merely to submit to Western cultural attractions. The emphasis in Japan was therefore on the technical and technological techniques of the West, rather than on literary and verbal culture. The Japanese slogan of "Western technique, Japanese spirit" at the time captured this ambition to borrow technology from the West while deliberately protecting a substantial part of Japanese culture or the *Japanese self*. In a sense, Japan's technological Westernization was designed to reduce the danger of other forms of cultural dependency.

The nature of Westernization in Africa has been very different. Far from emphasizing Western productive technology and containing Western life-styles and verbal culture, Africa has reversed the Japanese order of emphasis. Among the factors that have facilitated this reversal has been the role of the African university.

In order to understand this role more fully, let us examine it in relation to those seven functions of culture that we defined earlier, though not necessarily in the order in which those functions were originally enumerated.

The African University and Dependent Paradigms

As we indicated, one primary function of culture is to provide a universe of perception and cognition; a societal paradigm, a worldview. Kuhn's work on the structure of scientific revolutions has provided new insights into the process through which scientific paradigms shift and into how new alternative systems of explaining phenomena come to dominate scientific thought.

But what about shifts in *cultural* paradigms? And how are these related to shifts in scientific ones?

Religion is often a cultural paradigm in its own right. Copernicus and Galileo between them, by helping to transform scientific thought on planetary movements, in time also helped to change the Christian paradigm of the universe. Charles Darwin, by helping to initiate a revolution in the biological sciences, also started the process of transforming the Christian concept of 'creation'. These are cases in which paradigmatic changes in the sciences have led to paradigmatic changes in religion. Historically there have also been cases where religious revolutions have resulted in scientific shifts. The rise of Islam gave the Arabs scientific leadership in the Northern Hemisphere for a while. Puritanism and nonconformity in Britain in the eighteenth century were part of the background to both a scientific and an industrial revolution in that country.

But paradigmatic changes are caused not merely by great minds like those of Copernicus, Newton, Darwin, and Einstein, nor only by great social movements like Islam and the Protestant revolution, but also by acculturation and normative diffusion.

It is in this sense that colonialism constituted a major shift in the cultural paradigm of one African society after another. Traditional ideas about how rain is caused, how crops grow, how diseases are cured, and how babies are conceived, have had to be reexamined in the face of the new scientific culture of the West.

If African universities had borrowed a leaf from the Japanese book, and initially concentrated on what is indisputably the West's real area of leadership and marginal advantage (science and technology), the resultant African dependency might have been of a different kind. But the initial problem lay precisely in the model of the university itself—the paradigm of academia, with its distrust of direct problem-solving in the wider society.

There is much in our education system (in Britain) which makes it easier to define problems in terms of narrowly scientific objectives. The existing relationship between universities (with the unidirectional flow of "experts" and advisors, the flow of overseas students to this country, etc.) have tended to transfer the same standards and expectations to the LDCs [Less Developed Countries]. . . . Technologies for the satisfaction of basic needs and for rural development have received little attention . . . curricula, text books and teaching methods are too closely imitative of practice in industrialized countries. This has spilled over from teaching into research expectations. Universities have aimed to achieve international standards in defining the criteria for staff recognition and promotion; in practice this means using the international scientific and engineering literature as the touchstone. However, applied work directed at the solution of local problems . . . can rarely be associated with publication in "respectable" journals: a far better test is the local one of success or failure of the particular project in the LDC environment.[1]

The one paradigmatic change that was necessary for the imported universities did not in fact occur. The missing factor was a change in the conception of the university itself and of its purposes.

But the "lack of change" in the conception of the transplanted university caused a lot of changes in the attitudes, values, and worldview of its products. Since the university was so uncompromisingly foreign in an African context, and was transplanted with few concessions to African cultures, its impact was more culturally alienating than it need have been. A whole generation of African graduates grew up despising their own ancestry and scrambling to imitate others. They were exchanging old selves for new. It was not the traditional African that resembled the ape; it was more the Westernized one, fascinated by the West's cultural mirror. A disproportionate number of these cultural "apes" were, and continue to be, products of universities.

Those African graduates who have later become university teachers themselves have on the whole remained intellectual imitators of the disciplines of the West. African *historians* have begun to innovate methodologically as they have grappled with oral traditions, but most of the other disciplines are still condemned to paradigmatic dependency.

This includes those African scholars who belatedly discovered Karl Marx. The genius of Marx did indeed initiate a major international paradigmatic shift in social analysis. But Marx's theories were basically Eurocentric, and his legacy constitutes the radical stream of the Western heritage. Those African scholars who have replaced a Western liberal paradigm with a Western radical paradigm may have experienced a palace coup in their own minds or a changing of the guards within the brain. But they have not yet experienced an intellectual revolution in this paradigmatic sense. The ghost of intellectual dependency continues to haunt the whole gamut of Africa's academia for the time being.

The African University and Borrowed Languages

An important source of this intellectual dependency is the language in which African graduates and scholars are taught. For the time being it is impossible for an African to be even moderately familiar with the works of Marx without the help of a European language. *Das Kapital* is not yet available in Hausa or Kiswahili, let alone in Kidigo or Lutoro. Parts of the *Manifesto of the Communist Party* have already been translated into Kiswahili and Amharic, but it may take the rest of this century before even a quarter of the literary output of Marx and Engels is available in one single African language unless there is a genuine *educational* revolution involving widespread adoption of African languages as media of instruction.

As matters now stand, an African who has a good command of a European language has probably assimilated other aspects of Western culture as well. This is because the process of acquiring a European language in Africa has tended to be overwhelmingly through a formal system of Western-style education. It is because of this that the concept of an African Marxist who is not also Westernized is for the time being a *sociolinguistic impossibility.*

This need not apply to a Chinese or Japanese Marxist, where it is possible to undergo an ideological conversation at a sophisticated level without the explicit mediation of a foreign language. Japan especially has tamed its language to cope with a wide range of intellectual discourse.

Of course the Japanese range goes beyond ideological and political literature. But in Black Africa for the time being a modern surgeon who does not speak a European language is virtually a sociolinguistic impossibility. So is a modern physicist, zoologist, or economist. In Africa to become a physicist is to abandon the self!

Nor is this simply a case of the surgeon or physicist or economist acquiring an additional skill called a "European language," which he is capable of discarding when he discusses surgery or physics with fellow professionals in his own society. Professional Japanese scientists or social scientists can organize a conference or convention and discuss professional matters almost entirely in Japanese. But a conference of African scientists, devoted to scientific matters and conducted primarily in an African language, is for the time being sociologically impossible.

Almost all Black African intellectuals conduct their most sophisticated conversations in European languages. Their most complicated thinking has also to be done in some European language or another. It is because of this that intellectual and scientific dependency in Africa is inseparable from linguistic dependency.

And since a major function of culture lies, as we indicated, in providing media of communication, the choice of European languages as media of instruction in African universities has had profound cultural consequences for the societies that are served by those universities. Foreign languages are methods of changing the self into the other in postcolonial Africa.

It is possible that outside Arab Africa and parts of Eastern Africa the imperial founders of African universities had no choice. The great majority of African languages did not have enough speakers to justify the massive financial and intellectual investment necessary for making them effective media of higher education. But even those African languages like Kiswahili that stood a chance of developing in that direction did not receive adequate imperial support. As for Arabic in the Sudan, there continues to be discordance between the English language as a medium at Khartoum University and the Arabic orientation of preuniversity education, with severe costs in quality for all levels of instruction.

What should be remembered is that by the time these African universities were being established, African intellectuals had already become so mentally dependent that they themselves insisted on con- siderable imitation of Western educational systems—including the importation of Western media of instruction for African use. Depen- dency is cumulative; cultural dependency is particularly prone to this tendency. After a while Dr. Jekyll can no longer recover his old identity— and is condemned to being permanently Mr. Hyde.

The African University and Derivative Stratification

Concurrently with these other cultural changes came changes in strati- fication. What is a social class? Some have defined it in terms of "who owns what." But in the new Africa a social class was beginning to be defined in terms of "who *knows* what." Familiarity with certain aspects of Western culture began to be particularly crucial among the new forces of elite-formation.

In most African countries independence meant *the transfer of power from the West to the Westernized*. The new politicians were those with a good command of the imperial language and a substantial imitation of the Western lifestyle. In the earlier days of colonial rule there had been a debate about which African the imperial system should support—the "native in a blanket" or the "native in trousers." Many colonial policy-makers had distrusted Western education and strove hard to protect the "native in a blanket." Lord Lugard, perhaps the greatest of British colonial administrators in Africa, was particularly concerned about the disruptive consequences of Western civilization in African societies. His philosophy of Indirect Rule as a system of governing African societies through their own institutions was partly designed to contain and regulate, and sometimes even prevent, the process of Westernization in places like Northern Nigeria.

But in much of Africa (though not necessarily in Northern Nigeria), power was finally transferred to "the native in trousers." The Westernized and semi-Westernized Africans that had once been dismissed as "arrogant upstarts" began to be taken seriously as heirs apparent to the imperial system. The founding fathers of the new independent African states were disproportionately of this category. They included such figures as Nnamdi Azikiwe of Nigeria, Kwame Nkrumah and Kofi Busia of Ghana, Jomo Kenyatta and Tom Mboya of Kenya, Felix Houphouet-Boigny of the Ivory Coast, Leopold Senghor of Senegal, and Julius K. Nyerere of Tanzania. Those who had exchanged old cultural selves for new ones became Africa's rulers.

The initial constitutional arrangements in most African states seemed designed to maintain power among the acculturated. On the whole, no African could become a member of parliament unless he had a command of the relevant European language. An African who spoke seven of the indigenous languages of, say, Nigeria but could not speak English, was *ipso facto* disqualified from representing his people in the federal Parliament. On the other hand, a Nigerian politician might hypothetically speak only English, and be incapable of using any indigenous Nigerian language, and yet still be constitutionally eligible to sit in the federal Parliament. To be authentically African was often a political disqualification.

Most of this was also true in the majority of other countries south of the Sahara. To represent an African constituency required competence in a European language. And because one could not be a member of an African parliament without a European language, one could not be a minister in an African government either. And because one could not be an African minister without such European credentials, one could not ascend to the very pinnacle of power—the presidency— without those credentials either. In other words, access to the commanding heights of African political systems was partly predicated on the prior Westernization of the candidates for office. The surrender of the cultural self was often a precondition for political supremacy.

African universities played a leading role in fostering this new basis of stratification. They helped to give Western culture as a whole greater legitimacy in African societies. They produced teachers for lower levels of education and thus helped to continue the Eurocentric tradition of the colonial educational system. The universities also produced opinion leaders in other public pursuits. The university degree itself was for a while a major passport to influence and opportunity. The class systems of African societies were in a state of flux—and cultural dependency was part of this problem of restratification.

In fairness to some African governments and educational reformers, we must recognize some of the agonized efforts that have been made to modify the colonial heritage. In Kenyatta's Kenya alone, at least three major educational commissions (Ominde 1964, Ndegwa 1971, and Gachathi 1978) each dealt with educational reforms—not to mention numerous workshops and seminars.

But reforms in Daniel arap Moi's Kenya have been faster in coming. Some important concessions have been made to Kiswahili. It enjoys more attention at the University of Nairobi and Kenyatta University than it has ever done before, though the attention is still modest by absolute standards. The status of Kiswahili at lower levels of Kenya's educational system is also modest, in spite of the elevation of the language into the "national language" of Kenya with English as the "official language." English continues to overshadow Kiswahili decisively at least from the third year of schooling onwards.

In terms of political stratification, an important step was taken when Kiswahili was adopted as the language of Kenya's Parliament from 1974 to 1979. But significant anomalies remained. Whereas legislation in Kenya's Parliament was still presented in English, the debate on that legislation was conducted in Kiswahili. The speech on the budget continued to be made in English with full political and diplomatic ceremony. The minimum qualifications required of a parliamentary candidate continued to include competence in the English language—but not necessarily competence in Kiswahili. Nowadays debate can be in either language in Parliament. The most important language of national politics is now Kiswahili—but the official language of the Kenya constitution continues to be English.

Because of these continuing anomalies, the political establishment of the country continues to consist disproportionately of those who have been initiated into the culture of the former imperial system. The University of Nairobi is central to the structure that is perpetuating the Britannic factor in Kenya's system of political stratification. The newer Kenyan universities have tried to be a little more practical.

What is true of Kenya is basically true of most of former colonial Africa south of the Sahara. Indeed, these countries which do not have the equivalent of Swahili as a *lingua franca* are condemned to even more severe cultural dependency than Kenya, with all the consequences of derivative elite-formation.

Identity, Values, Motives and Economic Culture

We have so far examined the African university in relation to three of the functions of culture—perception, communication, and stratification. The remaining four functions are culture as identification, as criteria of evaluation, as motives of behavior, and as a system of production and consumption.

These functions need more space than is available in a single paper. For the time being let us merely introduce them in relation to the influence of Western education and its tertiary extensions within Africa.

Stratification is basically a ranking of social groups. But each group has an *identity* or *self* of its own and the interaction between these groups has its *rules*. Perhaps the most elaborate of the rules of stratified identities occur in caste societies. On balance the impact of Western education on such caste systems has been progressive—since it has created doubts about the legitimacy of caste as a mode of categorizing people. This has certainly been true of India, though the problem is still acute. It is also true of those few African societies that have something approximating caste. Chinua Achebe captures these dilemmas in his second novel, *No Longer at Ease*.

Obi's education in the West creates doubts in his mind about the legitimacy of the status of Osu (Ibo's equivalent of the Harijan or untouchable caste). And yet tradition is too strong, and Obi himself is too weak to resolve the issue in a manner compatible with his affection for Clara, the Osu girlfriend. The old rules of interaction between castes are still compelling, but doubts have been created by Western education—and the Ibo mind is "no longer at ease" on this issue.

Also strained partly as a result of the Western impact are the residual caste relations between the Hutu and the Tutsi in Burundi. Things have indeed been "falling apart" since the old traditional rules of authority and deference in Ruanda-Urundi were eroded by the challenge of a new normative order from the West. The clashes of identity between the Hutu and the Tutsi are reflected in other ethnic tensions elsewhere in Africa.

Rules of interaction between the sexes in Africa have also been in the process of modification as a result of Western education. Especially striking is the status of African women with university degrees. Women's liberation in Africa, as in most other parts of the world, is at best an aspiration rather than an accomplished fact. But among the factors that are facilitating it is the emergence of women graduates from African universities; these women are asserting a greater independence than they might have done had they not received higher education in the Western idiom. In this instance the cultural dependency that has come with the Western impact on Africa is having the paradoxical side effect of facilitating greater independence for African women.

A third area of identification that has been affected by higher education in the Western idiom concerns relations between age groups in African societies—including these societies that have age-grades. Western education has eroded deference for elders and made it difficult to maintain solidarity between age peers if some are Westernized and others not.

The fourth and most comprehensive area of rules of interaction in relation to salient identification goes deep into political ideology. Universities in Africa are producing both defenders of Western liberalism and civil liberties and critics of such liberal rules. Is the individual the proper and ultimate unit of identity? The universities are also producing both the egalitarian radicals of the New Left in Africa and their ideological adversaries. Is social class the proper and ultimate unit of identity? The rules of the game in Africa are still in a state of flux, partly because of considerable cultural fluidity in this period of transition. African universities are major contributors to that cultural fluidity. The self is therefore in flux.

Culture as a set of rules is in fact inseparable from culture as a *set of standards*. This is where *criteria of evaluation* comes into being. Western education has helped to change taste, morals, and other values. Western criteria of good and bad, ugly and beautiful, have won many African converts. In the words of the late Oxford political philosopher John Plamenatz, ". . . the vices of the strong acquire some of the prestige of strength."[2]

In other words, even the evil side of the Western demonstration effect has had a considerable impact on Africa. Some might even say that Africa has in reality been readier to imitate the evil side of the Western example than the good side!

Be that as it may, there is little doubt that African concepts of what is proper or improper, just or injust, attractive or repulsive, have now been profoundly influenced by that system of education of which the university is the pinnacle. As Lawino has lamented about her Westernized Acholi husband:

You trembled [once upon a time]
when you saw the tattoos
on my breasts
And the tattoos below my belly button;
And you were very fond
Of the gap in my teeth . . .
My husband [now] says
He no longer wants a woman
With a gap in her teeth
He is in love
With a woman
Whose teeth fill her mouth completely
Like the teeth of war-captives and slaves.[3]

For better or for worse, Acholi concepts of beauty and adornment in Uganda are gradually giving way to those of Western culture. It is symptomatic of a deep normative change that Africa is experiencing— sometimes smoothly, sometimes convulsively. Western education is only part of the agony of transition. But it is a major factor in this tumult of change.

Values in turn affect another aspect of culture—motives for behavior and conduct. The pursuit of private advantage, which in some parts of Africa has been aggravated by the impact of Western individualism and the erosion of traditional restraints, has sometimes led to a reckless ethos of "get rich quick" and an escalation of corruption and greed. Part of the cultural change is due to an interaction between the money economy (which is new in many parts of Africa) and Western notions of individualism and private profit. African universities cannot be blamed for these reckless acquisitive excesses in contemporary African society. The universities are simply caught up in the contradictions between old rules and new motives, old impulses and new norms.

Sometimes even genuinely constructive changes like an increase in concern for the value of time and the need for punctuality can erode older motives for courteous behavior and social responsibility. Again Lawino is eloquent on this issue:

Time has become
My husband's master
It is my husband's husband.
Like a small boy,
He rushes without dignity.
And when visitors have arrived
My husband's face darkens,
He never asks you in,
And for greeting
He says
"What can I do for you?". . . .
Listen

My husband
In the wisdom of Acholi
Time is not stupidly split up
Into seconds and minutes . . . .
It does not get finished
Like vegetables in the dish
A lazy youth is rebuked,
A lazy girl is slapped,
A lazy wife is beaten,
A lazy man is laughed at
Not because they waste time
But because they only destroy
And do not produce.[4]

As for culture as this *system of production and consumption*, African universities have played a part in producing high-level personnel for important areas of African economies. But on balance the universities have contributed more to African bureaucracies than directly to the production processes of African economies. The bureaucratic bourgeoisie, which wields considerable political power in most African countries, is on the whole a product of Western education. The impact of this class of people on patterns of consumption in African countries is sometimes greater than their impact on levels of production. But the centrality of their position in African political systems has in many cases made them custodians of the highest levels of economic policy in their countries—for better or for worse.

Toward Decolonizing the African University

We have sought to demonstrate in this contribution that the African university is part of a chain of dependency that continues to tie Africa to the Western world. African perspectives, models of communication, structures of stratification, rules of interaction, standards of evaluation, motives of behavior, and patterns of production and consumption have all been undergoing the agonies of change partly under the disturbing impact of Western culture.

African universities have been the highest transmitters of Western culture in African societies. The high priests of Western civilization in the continent are virtually all products of those cultural seminaries called "Universities." They change African *selves* into semi-Western *others*.

On balance, the African university is caught up in the tension between its ambition to promote genuine development in Africa and its continuing role in the consolidation of cultural dependency. If genuine development has to include *cultural decolonization*, a basic contradiction persists in the ultimate functions of an African university. It may generate skills relevant for modernization and development. But it has not even begun to acquire, let alone to transmit to others, what is perhaps the most fundamental skill of them all—how to promote development in a postcolonial state without consolidating the structures of dependency inherited from its imperial past. How to make the African self prosper without making the African self atrophy.

Dependency: The Therapy of Domestication

If development for Africa means the decolonization of modernity, then three major strategies are needed for African development—two of them capable of rapid implementation and the third of slower but sustained introduction. The first strategy concerns the *domestication of modernity*: the bid to relate it more firmly to local cultural and economic needs. The second strategy is paradoxical. It involves *the wider diversification of the cultural content of modernity*. Under this approach the foreign reference-group for an African institution becomes not only the West but also other non-African civilizations. The African university is thus to be transformed *from a multinational to a multicultural corporation.* The third strategy is perhaps the most ambitious. It concerns an attempt by the African continent as a whole to *counterpenetrate Western civilization itself.*

Let us take each of these strategies, beginning with the imperative of domestication in relation to education. Until now there has been no doubt that African educational systems have entered deeply into the life-styles of local societies, for better or for worse. In the very process of producing educated manpower, creating new forms of stratification, and accelerating Westernization and modernization, African educational institutions have been major instruments through which the Western world has affected and changed the continent, often eroding the authenticity of selfhood.

In order to shift this balance, African societies must be allowed fundamentally to influence the educational systems themselves. It is not enough for an African university to send a traveling theater to perform a play by Shakespeare or even by the Nigerian playwright, Wole Soyinka, before rural audiences in different villages. This type of endeavor is indeed required, and it helps to deepen the life experiences of folk communities in the villages. But the traveling theater of a university like Makerere is one more form of academic impact on the wider society. It does not by itself constitute a reverse flow of influence.

Similarly, extramural departments and even extension services offer valuable methods of increasing skills and expanding social awareness among rural communities. Like a number of other professors at Makerere University in Uganda I traveled many miles on hard roads to address village schools and assemblies on the implications of public policies in Uganda and the nature of the political system of the country. That kind of commitment was a way of reaching out to the isolated groups of the African countryside. But once again it was much less an exercise in being affected by the society than an exercise in reaching the society. The social impact was still one-sided.

The first task, then, in decolonizing modernity is to enable the influence of the local society to balance that of the Western reference group. But how is this process to be realized in the universities? Four major areas have to be examined afresh: the requirements for admission of students, the content of courses throughout the educational system, the criteria for recruitment of teachers and other staff, and the general structure of the educational system.

University admission requirements should be reformed in the direction of giving new weight to certain subjects of indigenous relevance. Social and cultural anthropology ought to become a secondary school subject, rigorously examinable, and required for entry to university. This should help promote considerably more interest in African cultures in primary and secondary school. Secondly, admission to a university should include a requirement for a pass in an African language. There were times when many African universities required some competence in Latin for entry into some faculties; the African university of the future should require competence, formally demonstrated in an examination, of at least one African language regardless of the subject that the student proposes to study once admitted.

African dance and music should be given a new legitimacy in all primary and secondary schools, regardless of the sensitivities of the missionary authorities in power. Investigation should be undertaken into whether dance and music should be competitive and into what way the ethnic diversity of musicological experience can be made creative rather than disruptive in an African school. These problems are far from insurmountable and could add a new richness to African aesthetic experience alongside the imported recreations of sports and athletics.

Progress has already been made in the teaching of African history and literature. Further progress can be made, including more effective utilization of oral literature, duly transcribed, as an introduction to the preliterate aesthetic creativity of African societies. The recovery of the African self requires it.

The university in turn should reexamine the content of its courses, permitting indigenous culture to penetrate more into the university and non-Western alien contributions to find a hearing at African universities.

Recruitment of faculty will in turn be affected by these considerations. Must all teachers at an African university have formal degrees from Western or Western-type educational institutions? Or should there be areas of expertise where lecturers or even professors could be appointed without the degree requirement so characteristic of Western institutions? Okot p'Bitek once compared the recruitment requirements for a university with the electoral requirements for an African parliament. African parliaments have on the whole insisted on competence in either English or French before an African could become a member. As we indicated, a candidate could speak ten African languages and still be ineligible for parliament if he did not speak the imported metropolitan language. Conversely, a candidate could speak only English or French and no African language, not even the language of his immediate constituents, and still be eligible for parliament. Okot p'Bitek saw the linguistic and formal requirements of university appointments in terms similar to the formal requirements for a parliamentary career in Africa: "You cannot become a member of *their* parliament unless you can speak English or French. . . . You may be the greatest oral historian but they will never allow you anywhere near *their* University. . . . Our Universities and schools are nests in which black exploiters are hatched and bred, at the expense of the taxpayers, or perhaps heartpayers."[5] The question that arises is whether there are specialists of oral history in African societies who can be appointed to university faculties without having a formal degree. Presumably this might be difficult if these oral historians are unable to read or write. A compromise situation would be one in which only those oral historians who can in addition read and write might be regarded as eligible. Admittedly, literary skills are still a departure from ancestral ways in many African societies, but even readiness to acknowledge competence regardless of formal Western-type degrees would be revolutionary in African universities.

A related area is that of African languages. There are specialists in African languages who know not only how to use an African language but also how the language behaves. Some of them are superb teachers at the university level. I know of at least one who spent many years in an American university, teaching Kiswahili with a sophistication unmatched by many of those who have actual degrees in the subject and in Bantu linguistics. Yet in the United States he could never hope to have a proper tenure appointment or even formal rank, since he did not possess a degree. Yet the same university would be quite prepared to appoint a distinguished British Swahilist from the London School of Oriental and African Studies who had a less intimate knowledge of certain African languages than the Kenyan had already demonstrated over several decades.

There is a case for broadening the criteria for recruiting academic staff to include both formal degrees and, where appropriate, indigenous traditional skills adequately demonstrated and capable of being effectively utilized on both teaching and research at the university level. Clearly a hybrid of cultures is at play here, and staff recruitment could reflect this dualism.

Departments of sociology could have indigenous specialists in oral traditions; departments and faculties of medicine and preventive medicine could include specialists in indigenous herbs and might even examine the medical implications of sorcery and witchcraft as part of the general training of a rural doctor in Africa. Departments of history, literature, musicology, philosophy, and religious studies could all allow for the possibility of recruiting skills on a different set of criteria from that which has been honored in Western institutions.

But in addition to reforms encompassing student admission requirements, curricula, and faculty recruitment, there must be a broader structural transformation that relates general social needs to the educational system and that reduces the tendency toward a pyramid educational structure with the university at the top and everything below that being no more than a step toward the pinnacle. What is needed is a major change involving a diversification of the content of the curricula of each institution.

At the university level, should studies continue to be organized according to conventional Western disciplinary categories? Or is there a case for having, on the one hand, a School of Rural Studies, encompassing agriculture, anthropology, preventive medicine in rural conditions, and the like and, on the other, a School of Urban Studies, examining the rural-urban continuum, labor migration, ethnic associations, criminology, and relevant preventive medicine? Other possible schools could include Oral Tradition and Historiography, Languages and Oral Literature, and Religion and Witchcraft.

Informing all these reforms would be a concept of relevance domestically defined and related to both the economic and cultural needs of the society as a whole.

Dependency: The Therapy of Diversification

The second strategy of development is that of diversifying the cultural content of modernity. This approach rests partly on the assumption that just as economically it is a greater risk to be dependent on one country than on many, so in culture one foreign benefactor is more constraining than many. To be owned by one person is outright slavery; but to be owned by many masters, who can be played against each other, may be the beginning of freedom. The self is better protected in a multicultural world.

The African university has to move from being a multinational corporation to being a multicultural corporation. From what we have discussed, it is clear that in spite of the fact that African university systems have grown up with structural or other links with metropolitan universities in Europe and North America, the African university has continued to be heavily unicultural: it has been more a manifestation of Western culture in an African situation than an outgrowth of African culture itself.

For as long as the African university remained a multinational corporation in this sense, it has denied itself the wealth of its own society. But in order to become a multicultural corporation, it is not enough to combine African traditions with the Western heritage. It becomes more important than ever that African universities should take seriously the cultures and experiments of other civilizations. The educational system should not talk simply about European history, combined increasingly with African history, but should in addition pay attention to Indian civilizations, Chinese civilizations, and, most immediate of all, Islamic civilizations. Although Arabic is the most widely spoken language in the African continent, the language has received very little acknowledgment in the educational syllabuses of Africa south of the Sahara. It has not even received recognition from countries that border Arabic-speaking areas or include large numbers of Muslims among their own citizens. The Muslim community in Nigeria runs into millions, and the bordering countries contain millions more, yet Nigeria's universities once favored Latin and Greek rather than Arabic studies. As for Chinese studies, there is at most some interest in Mao Tse-tung in political science departments these days, but still no interest in Confucius. Mao's China is relevant not only to ideology and economic organization but also to intermediate technology, medicine, and new methods of agriculture. A conscious effort to learn more about what has been done in China since Mao, and an attempt to see how much of it is relevant for African needs, could help to add technical richness to cultural pluralism.

A multicultural corporation requires not only a revival of interest in African indigenous traditions but also a cultural diversification of the foreign component in African curricula. A twin process is then underway: increased Africanization, as the society is permitted to reciprocate the impact of the university, and increased internationalization as the foreign component ceases to be Eurocentric and attention is paid to other parts of the total human heritage. Multiculturalism may help the recovery of authenticity.

An important subject that should be introduced into African secondary schools is the history of science. It is possible that the dependency complex among young African school children arises partly out of their being overwhelmed by Western science. The prestige of the Western world, in a continent that is very conscious of the power of prestige, derives disproportionately from Western leadership in science and technology. So great has that leadership been in the last three hundred years that Westernism and science are sometimes regarded as interchangeable.

In reaction to this Western scientific preeminence, some Africans have sought refuge in *negritude* as glorification of a nonscientific civilization. The leader of negritude as a romantic movement in Africa, Léopold Senghor, former president of Senegal, has defined negritude as "the sum of African cultural values" informed by their "emotive attitude toward the world."[6] Other Africans have sought answers in Marxism—partly because it seems to offer Africans the chance of rebelling against the West without ceasing to be scientific. After all, was not the Marxist heritage a scientific critique of the West? These two responses symbolize wider forces at work in Africa. The negritudist rebels against the scientific West by idealizing his own heritage; the African Marxist rebels against the West by embracing an alternative scientism.

Léopold Senghor, a cultural nationalist, has been denounced by some African radicals as an intellectual primitivist who has tried to reduce African modes of knowledge to pure emotion and has turned the history of Africa into the story of the Noble Savage. But Senghor denies that he has deprived the African of the capacity to reason and innovate technologically. "It is a fact that there is a white European civilization and a black African civilization. The question is to explain their differences and the reasons for these differences, which my opponents have not yet done. I can refer them back to their authorities. 'Reason has always existed,' wrote Marx to Arnold Ruge, 'but not always under the rational form.'"[7] Senghor then proceeds to quote Engels, whom he regards as even more explicit on this question in his work "preparatory to the *Anti-Duhring*": "Two kinds of experience . . . one exterior, material; the other, interior; laws of thought and forms of thinking. Forms of thinking also partly transmitted by heredity. A mathematical axiom is self-evident to a European, but not to a Bushman or an Australian aboriginal."[8] This debate between African cultural nationalists and African scientific socialists is likely to continue even in the era after the cold war. What the two groups have in common is a rebellion against the West and the inferiority complex that has been created by Western scientific preeminence.

The curriculum in African schools should at some stage reflect these disagreements. But at least as fundamental as the question of whether African culture was traditionally scientific or whether Marxism is a science is the issue of how much Western science owes to other civilizations. From the Indus Valley to ancient Egypt, from imperial China to medieval Islam, the West has found intellectual and scientific benefactors over the centuries. Yet very little of this is communicated to young children in schools in Africa. The cultural pluralism that lies behind the scientific heritage is lost to these young minds, as they continue to be dazzled at a formative period by Western civilization alone. Secondary school curricula in Africa must therefore put science in its proper historical context, reveal the diversity of the human heritage, and break the dangerous myth of Western scientific preeminence.

Another major change that would need to be introduced into primary and secondary schools concerns the teaching of languages. Each African child should learn a minimum of three languages—one European, one Asian, and one African. The era of learning multiple European languages—some ancient and some modern—while other linguistic heritages of the world are ignored should come rapidly to an end.

Because of the colonial legacy, some African students in former British Africa will need to learn French and some francophone Africans will continue to learn English. Pan-Africanism will need the teaching of an additional European language for a minority of students. But any additional European language has to be a fourth language—chosen instead of, say, geography or fine art, but certainly not at the expense of either an African language or an Asian one. These linguistic requirements are partly based on the assumption that access to a culture is considerably facilitated by knowledge of its language. At the university level, language requirements should continue in a modified form. Each undergraduate—regardless of the field—should take either an African or an Asian language at an advanced level. In addition he should take a course on a non-Western civilization, preferably, but not necessarily, linked to the language of his choice.

But perhaps the most fundamental of all reforms must be a change in attitude in all departments in African universities away from excessive Eurocentrism and toward a paradoxical combination of increased Africanization and increased internationalization of the content of each department program. It is only in this way that the African university can evolve into a truly multicultural corporation, at once univeralist and loyal to the authenticity of the African self.

Dependency: The Therapy of Counterpenetration

But domestication of modernity and the diversification of its cultural content will not achieve final fulfillment without reversing the flow of influence back into Western civilization itself: There are reformers in Africa who urge only domestication—and some of them would go to the extent of espousing cultural autarky. But this is a strategy of withdrawal from world culture, the outcome of which would be the continuing marginality of Africa in global affairs. In a world that has shrunk so much in a single century, there will be many decisions made by others that are bound to affect the world as a whole.

For Africa to attempt a strategy of withdrawal or total disengagement would be a counsel not only of despair but also of dangerous futility. Modernity is here to stay; the task is to decolonize it. World culture is evolving fast; the task is to save it from excessive Eurocentrism. The question that arises is how this task is to be achieved.[9] This is where the strategy of counterpenetration is relevant. If African cultures have been penetrated so deeply by the West, how is Western culture to be reciprocally penetrated by Africa?

The West has not, of course, completely escaped Africa's cultural influence. It has been estimated that the first piece of carving made by an African to reach modern Europe arrived on a Portuguese trading ship in 1504. African workmanship in leather and probably gold had a much older presence in Europe.

> However, African art burst upon the awareness of the Western world only in the turn of the nineteenth century. Army men like Pitt-Rivers and Torday brought back large collections with good ethnographic description. . . . No one should jump to the idea that Picasso's women who look two ways at once, or anything else about his work, is a copy of something he discovered in African art. There was little direct, stylistic influence, although some can be discovered by latter-day critics. Rather, what happened was that with the discovery of African and other exotic art, the way was discovered for breaking out of the confines that had been imposed on European art by tradition—perspective, measured naturalism, and anti-intellectual sentimentality.[10]

At least as important as this artistic counterpenetration has been Africa's indirect influence through its sons and daughters exported to the New World as slaves. Africa's impact on jazz and related forms of music has already been documented. So has the influence of African tales on the literatures of other lands, particularly of the southern United States and the Caribbean area.

Africa's cultural influence on the West has been far more modest than the West's influence on Africa. This asymmetry will continue for at least the rest of this century, but the gap in reciprocity can be narrowed. To achieve this Africa will need allies. The continent's most natural allies consist of the Black Diaspora and the Arab World. The Arabs share a continent with Black people. Indeed, the majority of the Arabs are within Africa; so is the bulk of Arab land. Black and African states share the Organization of African Unity. This organization and the Arab League have overlapping membership. There are possibilities of exploiting this relationship to the mutual advantage of both peoples.

The Arab oil producers have already started the strategy of economic counterpenetration into the West. This ranges from buying real estate in England to controlling a bank in the United States, from acquiring a considerable share in the Benz complex in West Germany to the possibility of extending a loan to Italy. The whole strategy of recycling petrodollars is full of possibilities of economic counterpenetration. As a result, the West is at once eager for the petrodollars and anxious about their long-term consequences for Western economic independence.[11]

But alongside this risk is an opportunity for a new Third World alliance to counterpenetrate the West. Once again economic power and cultural influence might be linked. The Organization of Petroleum Exporting Countries is heavily Muslim in composition and includes the largest Muslim country in the world, Indonesia. The largest oil-exporting country is Saudi Arabia, where the spiritual capital of Islam, Mecca, is to be found. Other large oil producers are Iran and Iraq when at peace, both of them potentially influential Muslim countries in world affairs. Two-thirds of the membership of OPEC is Muslim—but this membership represents more than two-thirds of OPEC's oil reserves. Nigeria, another OPEC member, contains all three parts of the soul of modern Africa—the Euro-Christian, the Islamic, and the indigenous religious traditions. All three are vigorous—and Islam is already the strongest single rival to Westernism there.

The rise of OPEC in world affairs—however transient—has heralded the political resurrection of Islam. By the end of this century African Muslims will probably outnumber the Arabs and will be making a strong bid for shared leadership of Islam. It would not be surprising, if, within the next decade, Black Muslims direct from Africa were establishing schools and hospitals in Harlem and preaching Islam to Black Americans. The funding for this Islamic counterpenetration would probably come from the oil producers of the Arab world. But since African Islam is distinct from Arab Islam, and carries considerable indigenous culture within it, Islamic counterpenetration into the United States would also be, in part, a process of transmitting African indigenous perspectives as well.

But at least as important as Arab money for African cultural entry into the West is the African-American population. The second largest Anglophone Black nation in the world (second only to Nigeria), Black America is situated in the middle of the richest and mightiest country in the twentieth century. At the moment, African-American influence on America's cultural and intellectual life is much more modest than, say, the influence of Jewish America. But as the poverty of Black America lessens, as its social and political horizons widen and its intellectual and creative core expands, African-American influence on American culture is bound to increase. A central task for African universities will therefore be to reach Black America, and, by influencing the most powerful country of the Western world, to reach the rest of the West as well.

African universities would do well to encourage more African-Americans to gain part of their education in Africa. Here again, Arab money could find a new use in scholarships available to African-Americans to study in the African continent, north or south of the Sahara. Later, Brazilian as well as Caribbean Blacks might be encouraged to follow suit.

However, counterpenetration as a third strategy required for effective decolonization of African modernity is a longer term endeavor than either domestication or diversification, requiring conditions that make it possible for Africans to innovate sufficiently to teach others a thing or two. This counterpenetration by the whole African continent into the mainstreams of cultural and intellectual skills elsewhere might begin with influence from outside into the African rural area, followed by a balancing influence from the rural areas on educational systems in Africa, stimulated by foreign cultural, intellectual, and technical skills.

But the full maturity of African educational experience will come when Africa develops a capability to innovate and invent independently. Full reciprocal international penetration is a precondition for a genuinely symmetrical world culture. As Africa first permits its own recovery of the cultural self to help balance the weight of Western cultural influence, then permits other non-Western external civilizations to reveal their secrets to African researchers and teachers, and then proceeds to transform its educational and intellectual world in a manner that makes genuine creativity possible, the continent will be on its way toward not only decolonizing modernity but also helping to recreate modernity anew for future generations. Africa may do more than recover its own authenticity; it may at last begin to recognize the ultimate boundary between the African self and the Alien other in the cultural domain.

Notes

1. L. Pyle, "Engineering in the Universities and Development" (paper presented at the conference "The Future Relationships between Universities in Britain and Developing Countries," Institute of Development Studies, University of Sussex, England, March 17–20, 1978), 2–3.

2. John Plamenatz, *On Alien Rule and Self-government* (London: Longmans, 1960), 111.

3. Okot p'Bitek, *Song of Lawino* (Nairobi: East African Literature Bureau, 1966), pt. 4.

4. Ibid., pt. 7.

5. Okot p'Bitek, "Indigenous Ills," *Transition* 32 (August–September 1967): 47.

6. See *Senghor: Prose and Poetry*, ed. and trans. John Reed and Clive Wake (London: Oxford University Press, 1965), 34. The emphasis is original.

7. Ibid.

8. Engels as cited by ibid., 33.

9. Aspects of the Eurocentrism of world culture are also discussed with passion and insight by Chinweizu, *The West and the Rest of Us: White Predators, Black Slavers and the African Elite* (New York: Random House, 1975). Chapters 14 to 16 are particularly relevant from the point of view of this article. Consult also Ali Mazrui, *World Culture and the Black Experience* (Seattle: University of Washington Press, 1974).

10. Paul Bohannan and Philip Curtin, *Africa and Africans: American Museum of Natural History* (New York: Natural History Press, 1971), 97–98.

11. This is argued more fully in Ali Mazrui, "The New Interdependence: From Hierarchy to Symmetry," in *The United States and the Developing World: Agenda for Action*, 1975, ed. James Howe (Washington, D.C.: Overseas Development Council, 1975). See also Ali Mazrui, *Cultural Forces in World Politics* (London: James Currey, 1990; Portsmouth, N.H.: Heinemann Educational Books, 1990).

Contributors

Angelika Bammer is Associate Professor of German Studies and Comparative Literature and codirector of the Program in Culture, History and Theory in The Graduate Institute of Liberal Arts at Emory University. She is the author of *Partial Visions: Feminism and Utopianism in the 1970s* (1991) and the editor of *Displacements: Cultural Identities in Question* (1994). Her current work is on issues of ethnic and gender identity in relation to national culture.

Robert F. Barsky is a researcher, working on issues concerning refugee studies and discourse theory, in the Department of Ethnic Studies and Immigration of the Institut québécois de recherche sur la culture (IQRC). He is also an Associate Member of the Inter-University Centre for Discourse Analysis and Text Sociocriticism, and the managing editor of its publication including the journal *Discours social/Social Discourse*, which he cofounded in 1988. He received his Ph.D. in Comparative Literature at McGill University in 1992 and is author of *Constructing a Productive Other: Discourse Theory and the Convention Refugee Hearing* (John Benjamins, 1994). He is presently beginning work on a film, with George Szanto, dramatizing the Convention Refugee Hearing process. In 1995 he took up a position at the Philosophy Institute, Free University of Brussels to research legal discourse in the novel.

Christina von Braun is Professor of Cultural Studies at the Humboldt University Berlin and a film director. She has directed more than forty documentary and fiction films and previously taught gender studies and philosophy at the Universities of Vienna and Frankfurt am Main. She is the author of *Nicht ich: Logik Lüge Libido* (1985); *Der Einbruch der Wohnstube in die Fremde* (1987); *Die schamlose Schönheit des Vergangenen: Zum Verhältnis von Geschlecht und Geschichte* (1989); and

363

Der ewige Judenhaß: Christlicher Antijudaismus, deutschnationale Judenfeindlichkeit, rassistischer Antisemitismus (1990).

Gisela Brinker-Gabler is Professor of Comparative Literature and Director of Graduate Studies at Binghamton University. She previously taught at the University of Florida in Gainesville, and the Universities of Cologne and Essen (Germany). She started and edited from 1978 to 1986 the series *Die Frau in der Gesellschaft—Frühe Texte und Lebensgeschichten* (Frankfurt am Main: Fischer Taschenbuch Verlag). Her published books include *Deutsche Dichterinnen vom 16. Jahrhundert bis zur Gegenwart* (1978; 4th ed. 1991); *Poetische-Wissenschaftliche Mittelalter-Rezeption* (1981); *Lexikon deutschsprachiger Schriftstellerinnen: 1800–1945* (1986, together with K. Ludwig and A. Wöffen). She is editor of two volumes of critical studies, *Deutsche Literatur von Frauen: Vom Mittelalter bis zum 18. Jahrhundert* (1988) and *Deutsche Literatur von Frauen: Vom 18. Jahrhundert bis zur Gegenwart* (1988). She has also published several women's autobiographies and anthologies of women's theoretical and political writings: *Zur Psychologie der Frau* (1978); *Frauenarbeit und Beruf* (1979); *Fanny Lewald: Meine Lebensgeschichte* (1980); *Frauen gegen den Krieg* (1980); *Tony Sender: Autobiographie einer deutschen Rebellin* (1981); and *Kämpferin für den Frieden: Bertha von Suttner* (1983). She is currently completing a book entitled *Modernity, Woman, Modernism* and is coeditor with Sidonie Smith of the forthcoming *(Re)Writing Identities: Gender, Nation and Immigration in New European Subjects* (University of Minnesota Press).

Abena Busia is an Associate Professor in the English Department at Rutgers State University, New Jersey, where she has taught since 1981. She was previously an external tutor at Rushkin College, the Labor Relations College affiliated with the University of Oxford, and a visiting lecturer in the Program of African and Afro-American Studies at Yale University. She has published numerous articles on criticism, theory, and leterature by Black women and is currently working on two book manuscripts, *Song in a Strange Land: Narrative and Rituals of Remembrance in the Novels of Black Women of Africa and the African Diaspora* (for Indiana University Press, and The Women's Press, London) and *When Memory Yields: Cultural Elision, Erasure, and Anmesia in Repre-senting "Africa": Patterns of Experience in British Novels 1948–1980).* In addition to being a teacher, Abena Busia is a poet and short story writer. She was born in Accra, Ghana, and it is the central experience of exile across three continents that informs both her writing and teaching. Her poetry has been published in various magazines in West Africa, North America, and Europe and she has given numerous readings and interviews. Her first volume of poems, *Testimonies of Exile,* was published in Africa World Press, Trenton, NJ, in 1990.

Frederick Garber is Distinguished Professor of Comparative Literature at Binghamton University. His published books include *Thoreau's Redemptive Imagination* (1977); *Wordsworth and the Poetry of Encounter* (1971); *The Autonomy of the Self from Richardson to Huysman* (1982); *Self, Text and Romantic Irony: the Example of Byron* (1988); and *Thoreau's Fable of Inscribing* (1991); and *Repositionings*, a study on contemporary poetry and photography is forthcoming. He has edited several of Ann Radcliffe's novels as well as *Microcosm: an Anthology of the Short Story* (1969), and *Romantic Irony* (1988). He served as president of the American Comparative Literature Association and cosecretary of the International Comparative Literature Association.

Sander L. Gilman is a Professor of German, History of Science, Psychiatry and Jewish Studies at the University of Chicago. He was a long-time faculty member at Cornell University where he was Goldwin Smith Professor of Human Studies. He also taught History of Psychiatry at the Cornell Medical College. Gilman is author or editor of more than thirty books, the most recent in English being *Freud, Race, and Gender* (1993). He is the author of the basic study of the visual stereotyping of the mentally ill, *Seeing the Insane* (1982), as well as the standard study of *Jewish Self-Hatred* (1986). During 1990–91 he served as the Visiting Historical Scholar at the National Library of Medicine, Bethesda, Maryland. He has been the Northrop Frye Visiting Professor of Literary Theory at the University of Toronto, the Old Dominion Fellow in the Department of English at Princeton University, and the Visiting B. G. Rudolph Professor of Jewish Studies at Syracuse University. He also served as a visiting professor at Colgate University, Tulane University, the University of Paderborn, and the Free University of Berlin (Germany) and has been a Guggenheim Fellow. He is the president-elect of the Modern Language Association.

Ali A. Mazrui is Albert Schweitzer Professor in the Humanities and Director of the Institute of Global Cultural Studies, Binghamton

University, and Albert Luthuli Professor-at-Large, University of Jos, Jos, Nigeria. He is also author of the BBC/PBS television series, *The Africans: A Triple Heritage* (1986). He has written more than twenty books, including a novel *The Trial of Christopher Okigbo* (1971) which is still in print. He is also the author of *Cultural Forces in World Politics* (1990). Ali A. Mazrui is also Senior Scholar at the Africana Studies and Research Center and Andrew D. White Professor-At-Large Emeritus, Cornell University.

Aaron Perkus is Assistant Professor at Paul Smith's College. He received his doctorate in Comparative Literature, Binghamton University. His dissertation is on the androgenic creation of monsters: the Minotaur, the Golem, and Mr. Hyde. He has presented papers on Hesiod, Borges, Cortázar, the Minotaur, *Romeo and Juliet,* and graduate student teaching pedagogy.

Ineke Phaf is Associate Professor in the Department of Spanish and Portuguese at the University of Maryland, College Park. She previously taught at the Latin American Institute, Free University of Berlin. She is author of *Drie helden en andere verhalen van Jose Marti* (1979), *El Caribe y America Latina/The Caribbean and Latin America* (with Ulrich Fleischmann, 1987), *Drei mal drei Lektüren von* Terra Nostra (with Hanns-Albert Steger, 1990); *Novelando la Habana* (1990); *Narrando la nacion. Una modernidad criolla en Curacao, Suriname, Puerto Rico, Cuba y Mexico* (1994).

Velma Pollard is a Senior Lecturer in Language Education in the Faculty of Education of the University of the West Indies, Mona, Jamaica. Her major research interests are Creole Caribbean Literature and Caribbean Women's Writing. She is also involved in Creative Writing and has published poems and short stories in regional and international journals. She has on the market two volumes of poetry, *Crown Point and Other Poems* (1988) and *Shame Trees Don't Grow Here* (1992), and a volume of short fiction, *Considering Woman* (1989). Her novella *Karl,* which won the Casa de las Americas literary award (1992), has been published by Casa as a bilingual text in Spanish and English. Her most recent publication is the novel *Homestretch* and a collection of short stories (1994).

Eliana S. Rivero is Professor of Spanish at the University of Arizona in Tucson. Her most recent publications include *Infinite Divisions: An*

Anthology of Chicana Literature, coedited with Tey Diana Rebolledo (1993), and "Cuban American Writing," in *The Oxford Companion to Women's Writing in the United States* (1993). Critic and poet, she is also the author of *El gran amor de Pablo Neruda: estudio critico de su poesia* (1971), *De cal y arena* (1975), *Cuerpos breves* (1977), and she is coeditor of *Siete poetas* (1978). Between 1975 and 1993, she published numerous articles on contemporary Latin American literature and U.S. Hispanic literatures, especially on women authors, as well as poems in collections, magazines, and anthologies.

Stephen David Ross is Professor of Philosophy and Comparative Literature at Binghamton University. He is the author of *Transition to an Ordinal Metaphysics* (1980); *Philosophical Mysteries* (1981); *Perspective in Whitehead's Metaphysics* (1983); *A Theory of Art: Inexhaustibility by Contrast* (1982); and, more recently, *Metaphysical Aporia and Philosophical Heresy* (1989); *The Ring of Representation* (1992); and *Injustice and Restitution: The Ordinance of Time* (1993). He is also the author of *Inexhaustibility and Human Being: An Essay on Locality* (1989); *The Limits of Language* (1993); and *Locality and Practical Judgment: Charity and Sacrifice*, as well as several other books and many articles. His most recent book, *Plenishment in the Earth: An Ethic of Inclusion*, is forthcoming from SUNY Press.

Leo Spitzer is Professor of History at Dartmouth College. His most recent book, *Lives in Betweeen* (1989), is a comparative historical study of assimilation and marginality, focusing on the life histories of several generations of Austro-Jewish, Afro-Brazilian, and West African Creole families. He is currently writing *Surviving Memory*, a book about the representation of Central European Jewish refugee emigration to South America in the era of World War II.

Konstanze Streese was Assistant Professor in the Department of German at New York University before she moved to Germany. She is presently teaching at the University of Frankfurt am Main. Her contribution to this volume is part of her ongoing work on identities and identifications against the grain. She is the author of *"Cric? - Crac!" Vier literarische Versuche, mit dem Kolonialismus umzugehen* (1991) and of various articles on (neo-)colonial discourse. Currently, she is editing an anthology of significant texts on culture and politics from journals published in West Germany during the 1970s (in English translation).

Michael Strysick is Assistant Professor of English at Kent State University Tuscaraws. He received his doctorate in Comparative Literature at Binghamton University in the Program in Philosophy, Literature, and the Theory of Criticism. He previously taught at the School of Literature, Communication, and Culture at the Georgia Institute of Technology as a Brittain Fellow in Writing. He has coedited an interview with Jean-Francois Lyotard.

Sidonie Smith is Professor of English and Comparative Literature at Binghamton University. She is the author of *Where I'm Bound: Patterns of Slavery and Freedom in Black American Autobiography* (1974); *A Poetics of Women's Autobiography: Marginality and the Fictions of Self-Representation* (1987); *Subjectivity, Identity, and the Body: Women's Autobiographical Practices in the Twentieth Century* (1993); she is coeditor with Julia Watson of *De/Colonizing the Subject: The Politics of Gender in Women's Autobiography* (1992); and coeditor with Julia Watson of the forthcoming *Getting a Life: The Everyday Uses of Autobiography* (University of Minnesota Press). She is currently completing *Gender in Motion: Women Narrating Travel in the Twentieth Century* a book on women's travel narratives, and is coeditor with Gisela Brinker-Gabler of the forthcoming *(Re)Writing Identities: Gender, Nation and Immigration in New European Subjects* (University of Minnesota Press).

Bernhard Waldenfels is Professor of Philosophy at the Ruhr-University, Bochum (Germany). Among his published books are: *Das Zwischenreich des Dialogs: Sozialphilosophische Untersuchungen im Anschluß an E. Husserl* (1971); *Der Spielraum des Verhaltens* (1980); *In den Netzen der Lebenswelt* (1985); *Phänomenologie in Frankreich* (1983 and 1987); *Ordnung im Zwielicht* (1987); *Der Stachel des Fremden* (1990); he is coeditor with J. M. Broekman and A. Pazanin of *Phänomenologie und Marxismus*, 4 vols. (1977–79), with R. Grauthoff of *Sozialität und Intersubjektivität. Phänomenologische Perspektiven der Sozialwissenschaften im Umkreis von Aron Gurwitsch und Alfred Schütz* (1983), and with A. Métraux of *Leibhaftige Vernunft: Spuren von Merleau-Pontys Denken* (1986).

Jason M. Wirth teaches philosophy at Oglethorpe University. He graduated with a Ph.D. in Philosophy from the Philosophy, Interpretation, and Culture program at Binghamton University. His dissertation is on the late philosophy of Friedrich Wilhelm von Schelling. He was recently a Fulbright student at the University of Tübingen, Germany. He has published on Aristotle, translated Heidegger letters on politics, and presented talks on Nietzsche, Benjamin, and Schelling. He is currently translating Schelling's *Weltalter* (1815).

Susanne Zantop teaches German, Comparative Literature, and Women's Studies at Dartmouth College. She has written a book on literature and history, *Zeitbilder: Geschichtsschreibung und Literatur bei Heinrich Heine und Mariano José de Larra* (1988) and edited two anthologies, one on literature and painting, *Paintings on the Move: Heinrich Heine and the Visual Arts* (1989) and one—in collaboration with Jeannine Blackwell—on German women writers, *Bitter Healing: German Women Writers from 1700 to 1830* (1990). Her current project focuses on colonial fantasies in eighteenth- and nineteenth-century Germany.

Index